Studies in Eighteenth-Century Culture

Volume 48

Studies in Eighteenth-Century Culture

Volume 48

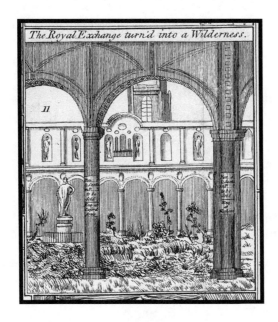

Published by Johns Hopkins University Press for the
American Society for Eighteenth-Century Studies

Johns Hopkins University Press
Baltimore and London
2019

Johns Hopkins University Press
2715 North Charles Street
Baltimore, Maryland 21218-4363
www.press.jhu.edu

ISBN 978-1-4214-2866-6
ISSN 0360-2370

Articles appearing in this annual series are abstracted and
indexed in *Historical Abstracts* and *America: History and Life*.

Contents

ARTS AND MANUFACTURES

Clifford Lecture

DEVOTION AND OTHER PASSIONS

Devotion in the Enlightenment

ASECS Affiliate Societies

American Antiquarian Society
Aphra Behn Society
Bibliographical Society of America
Burney Society
Daniel Defoe Society
Early Caribbean Society
East-Central ASECS
Eighteenth-Century Scottish Studies Society
Goethe Society of North America
Historians of Eighteenth-Century Art and Architecture
Ibero-American SECS
The International Herder Society
Johnson Society of the Central Region
Lessing Society
Midwestern ASECS
Mozart Society
North American British Music Studies Association
Northeast ASECS
North American Kant Society
Northwest SECS
Samuel Johnson Society of the West
Samuel Richardson Society
Rousseau Association
International Adam Smith Society
Society of Early Americanists
Society for Eighteenth-Century French Studies
Society for Eighteenth-Century Music
Society for the History of Authorship, Reading and Publishing
South Central SECS
Southeastern ASECS
Germaine de Staël Society for Revolutionary and Romantic Studies
Voltaire Society of America
Western SECS
Atlantic SECS
Canadian SECS

Editors' Introduction

We are happy to announce that with David Shields's Clifford Lecture, Dena Goodman's Presidential Address, and its combination of panels, forums (roundtables), and individual essays, *SECC* has finally attained the new format that we envisioned. *SECC*'s previous editor, Michelle Burnham, had noticed that the journal unaccountably had ceased to publish the Presidential Address and Clifford Lecture, and she took the first steps to restore them. Our aim in reintroducing these lectures, and in including a selection of panels and forums, has been to fulfill the journal's mission of reflecting the work done at the ASECS's annual conference by more closely approximating the intellectual experience of the meeting and capturing some of its highlights, as well as by continuing to make some of our members' most thought-provoking individual interventions widely accessible to the ASECS's community and beyond.

Nevertheless, all of our goals have not yet been met. We have, during the past three or four years, published a broad variety of fields—Literature, Art History, National and Transnational History, the History of Science, Music, Philosophy, Sociology, Political Economy, and more. We have also published on a broad variety of cultures—English, French, Scottish, Italian, Portuguese, Irish, Spanish, American, Austro-Hungarian, South American, African, and Caribbean—and on relations between them. Organizing the journal into a few topic units has given coherence to this variety and made it possible to compare almost simultaneous treatment of the same or similar issues in different cultural and disciplinary environments, which we have found very intellectually exciting. We are grateful to everyone who has contributed. So far, however, we have failed to achieve our goal of persuading ASECS's regional and affiliate societies to take *SECC* seriously as an outlet for their own revised conference materials: most of the submissions to *SECC still* come from ASECS's annual meeting.

Let us therefore take this opportunity to call on members of regional and affiliate societies to help us in celebrating 50 years of ASECS in 2020 by joining the conversation in the 50th edition of *SECC,* which will appear that year. Submissions for this anniversary edition are due to us no later than 1 August 2019. The list of eligible societies is printed before the Editors' Introduction.

Editorial Readers for Volume 48

MANUSCRIPT COMMUNICATIONS

Presidential Address

A Secret History of Learned Societies

DENA GOODMAN

On 14 November 1979, Ron Rosbottom, Executive Secretary of the American Society for Eighteenth-Century Studies, wrote a long letter to the ASECS Steering Committee. "The Society is at a transitional point in its history," he wrote. "Despite Don Greene's repeated reminders that he handled everything with a few boxes of files and a mimeograph machine, ASECS has grown considerably in the past few years. . . . We cannot continue to fly by the seat of our pants." Ten years after a constitution was drafted, the first officers were elected, and the first annual meeting was held, ASECS required more administration than a single secretary could handle. "We are no longer a small group of devotees to the eighteenth century," Rosbottom continued, "but a major learned Society with all the complexity and diversity of responsibilities that implies." Correspondence alone took up much of his time. "We receive around 150 pieces of mail per week," he reported, and until he purchased a cassette recorder, he was typing "about 40 drafts of letters per week."[1]

Rosbottom proposed that a second person be brought in to assist him, "not simply another clerk," he explained, "but someone with major responsibilities." In fact, he had already recruited one of his colleagues, John Sena, to act as Associate Executive Secretary and proposed that the Society both confirm Sena's appointment and make the position official. Rosbottom stressed that in addition to helping with the newsletter and the program for the annual meeting, Sena acted "as a companion and colleague to whom I can turn for immediate responses and reactions about numerous matters."

The beleaguered secretary noted that with Sena's help his phone calls to members of the Board had decreased significantly.

In December, the Board approved Sena's appointment as Associate Executive Secretary, but the constitution was never amended to make this ad hoc solution permanent; he was the first and last person to hold this position. When the Society sought someone to succeed Rosbottom as secretary in 1981, Sena was the obvious candidate.[2] But, Sena withdrew his name from consideration. "The responsibilities of the Executive Secretary are awesome," he explained. "To assume them would be to terminate virtually all other areas of academic life."[3] Fortunately, others stepped forward, and R. G. Peterson was selected to succeed Rosbottom as executive secretary.

The work, of course, only increased as ASECS and its operations continued to grow. By 1991, the Board was seriously considering the idea of a "paid, full-time, 'permanent' Executive Secretary," in light of what President Jane Perry-Camp called "the enormous burden of the Executive Secretaryship in directing ASECS's complex, varied, and ever-increasing activities."[4] The Modern Languages Association and the American Historical Association were now run by paid professional staffs in New York and Washington, but ASECS did not have the resources to take this step. Its administration remained in the hands of a dedicated member rather than a paid professional. Peterson was succeeded by Ed Harris, Harris by Jeffrey Smitten, and Smitten by Byron Wells—all members of the Society who served part-time while continuing to hold academic positions.

And so, as we thank Byron for an extraordinary twenty years of voluntary service to the Society and thank Lisa Berglund for her willingness to pick up where Byron leaves off, I thought we might honor them by reflecting on the contribution of secretaries of learned societies to the intellectual life of the long eighteenth century, to which we, as a society, remain devoted.

Secretaries and Learned Societies: Long-Eighteenth-Century Origins

Let me begin with the word *secretary*. It comes from the word "secret" and referred originally to a subordinate entrusted with his master's secrets. Secrets eventually came to be associated with letters: the materialization of the master's thoughts in writing. The secretary was the person to whom the master entrusted those thoughts in order to be able to transmit them to a distant other and to produce a record of that communication. If a secretary at one end of a correspondence created the letter, a secretary at the other end filed, archived, and penned the response to it. The *Oxford English Dictionary* thus gives as a second definition, "One whose office it is to write for another; *spec.* one who is employed to conduct or assist with correspondence, to keep records, and (usually) to transact various other business, for another person or for a society, corporation, or public body."[5]

Because correspondence was essential to the Republic of Letters from which academies emerged in the seventeenth century, secretaries became their key administrative officers. That is, as institutions of the Republic of Letters, academies became nodes in the correspondence networks by means of which knowledge and information were transmitted and exchanged, intellectual debates were powered, and the citizens of the Republic of Letters were bound to one another.[6] The secretary's role was to maintain the lines of communication between the academy and its distant members as well as between the academy and the world. Because he maintained the correspondence files, the secretary was thus often the academy's archivist as well.

When Henry Oldenburg was elected to what would become the Royal Society in December 1660, less than two months after it was founded, the practice of rotating the presidency every month was already established. The president's role was simply to preside at the weekly meetings. The decision had also already been made to hire two servants – one to assist with experiments and the other an "amanuensis to assist the Register," who kept the minutes.[7] When the society became incorporated by royal charter in 1662, the terms of officers—president, treasurer, and two secretaries—were set at one year. The secretaries, who took over from the register, were particularly important, because on behalf of the Royal Society they now exercised one of its most important privileges: to engage in correspondence, including with foreigners, "without any molestation, interruption, or disturbance whatsoever . . . in matters philosophical, mathematical, or mechanical." Oldenburg was one of the two secretaries elected in 1662; he was re-elected to that position for the next fifteen years and handled most of the duties. As his biographer notes, he achieved fame through this position, but not fortune. Like the other officers, but unlike the amanuensis or clerk, the secretary was unpaid. It was years before Oldenburg managed even to have the postage paid on all the mail he received on behalf of the Society.[8]

As secretary of the Royal Society, Oldenburg was responsible for taking and reading the minutes at the weekly meetings. At the meetings he also read aloud letters and papers sent to him by provincial fellows and (increasingly) foreign colleagues and correspondents. He was the recipient of those letters and papers because his major responsibility was to "draw up all letters to be written to any persons in the name of the Society." And although the paid amanuensis was responsible for the clerical work of copying and filing minutes, letters, and papers, the secretary had to supervise him and fill in for him when necessary.[9]

Five years into the job, Oldenburg was feeling the strain, especially since, despite being a gentleman, he also needed to make his living. On 27 April 1668, he presented to the Council of the Royal Society a lengthy description of his duties that ended with the question: "Whether such a person ought to be left unassisted?"[10] What he meant was not, however, that an assistant secretary should be appointed, but that he should be paid for the work he did. Apparently the Council did not agree. It has been suggested that they thought he was already making enough money off the *Philosophical Transactions*, which he edited for the Society. In any case they asserted as principle that the Royal Society's secretaries should collect no salaries—and then agreed to a one-time payment to Oldenburg of fifty pounds. The following year they relented further, granting Oldenburg a salary of forty pounds a year—about what he was making from the *Transactions*.[11]

The salary he began to receive in 1669 no doubt helped ease Oldenburg's concerns about putting food on the table, but his workload did not diminish. Indeed, the success of the Royal Society and his own increasing importance through his role in it meant the growth of his correspondence. In 1676 he was forced to apologize to one correspondent: "The multiplicity of letters, I am obliged to write making me sometimes forget, whether I have written such and such letters or not."[12]

In his 1667 *History of the Royal Society*, Thomas Sprat made clear that his intention was not to "usurp" the role of the secretary, upon whose minutes his account was based. The first official historian of the Royal Society distinguished his role from that of the secretary by writing always about the association, rather than for it, even though, like Oldenburg, he was a member of the Society. As J. Ereck Jarvis has noted, from Sprat's authorial perspective, the Society was always "they" and never "we."[13] This shift in perspective could be effected over time: upon his retirement as ASECS's first secretary, Donald Greene was named its historian.[14] No longer holding the responsibility of representing the Society, he could now write about it.

In France, as the relationship between the Republic of Letters and the public changed in the eighteenth century, so too did the role of the secretary of a learned society.[15] As men of letters and savants began to justify their work in terms of public utility and to orient themselves toward a reading public, the secretary took on the responsibility of representing them and their work to the public. Thanks to Bernard Le Bovier de Fontenelle, who became permanent secretary of the French Academy of Sciences in 1697, in the eighteenth century, writing eulogies of colleagues upon their death became the most notable public responsibility of secretaries of French learned societies. In the *Encyclopédie*, Jean le Rond d'Alembert, who served as permanent secretary of the Académie Française in the 1770s, argued that the main purpose of academic eulogies was to produce an *histoire des lettres*, or intellectual history.[16] For d'Alembert, the value of eulogies lay in the collective impact of the history traced through them rather than in the moral example of each one individually. His protégé, Marie Jean Antoine Nicolas de Caritat, Marquis de Condorcet, gave the academic eulogy a political purpose when he became permanent secretary of the Academy of Sciences by calling particular attention to the ways in which his colleagues applied their scientific expertise to industry, agriculture, and economic policy. In so doing, as Tim Reeve has argued, he merged d'Alembert's history of scientific progress with a modernizing history of France whose aim was to support and encourage the mobilization of science in the service of the state.[17]

As Friedrich-Melchior Grimm wrote in a critical review of Condorcet's first efforts as a eulogist, "The job of a secretary of the Academy of Sciences is to make accessible to everyone the most complicated systems, the most profound ideas, the most abstract matters."[18] To this end, the secretary also wrote and delivered a report on the activities of the Academy at its annual public meeting, which was attended by the elite public, including fashionable women and dignitaries from the highest levels of the court. The secretary was now the academy's public face; his job was as much to communicate to the public as to facilitate communication within his society and between it and other individuals and institutions within the Republic of Letters. For Condorcet, this meant that as secretary of the Academy of Sciences, his role was to coordinate all scientific activity and publication in France.[19]

I have been thinking (and learning) about the work of a secretary of a learned society recently not only in my capacity as a member of the ASECS Board, but also through my research on Augustin-François Silvestre, whose major contributions to the history of science took the form of secretarial work. From 1791 to 1803, Silvestre was secretary of the Société philomatique, and, from 1799 to 1841, he was permanent secretary of the French Society of Agriculture. Here I would like to bring his experience into the history that begins with Henry Oldenburg and lives on today in learned societies such as ASECS.

François Silvestre and the Société Philomatique

In December 1788, six young men, including twenty-six year old François Silvestre, librarian of the king's brother, formed a club whose modest purpose was to keep themselves up to date on the latest scientific research. They met weekly until the spring of 1789, around the time the Estates General opened in Versailles. They reconvened in the fall, after the National Assembly was formed, the Bastille had fallen, the Great Fear had subsided in the countryside, the privileges of the Old Regime had been abolished, and the Declaration of the Rights of Man and Citizen had been adopted.[20]

As the deputies in Versailles got to work on a constitution, the six young scientists who gathered in Silvestre's apartment in the Louvre dubbed themselves the Société philomatique and took as their motto "Etude et Amitié," Study and Friendship.[21] They then elected officers and three new members. Silvestre was elected both president and treasurer, the naturalist Gaspard Riche was elected secretary, and Alexandre Brongniart, a recent graduate of the Ecole des Mines, was elected vice-secretary. Silvestre and Riche were both 27 years old, Brongniart was 19. Eighteen months later, when Riche joined the Entrecastaux Expedition to the South Seas, Silvestre replaced him as secretary. As presidents came and went, each serving a three-month term, Silvestre and Brongniart steered the Society through the Revolution. Silvestre served as secretary until 1803, and Brongniart, who had been elected treasurer in April 1791, continued to be re-elected to that office for the next forty years.

Over the course of the twelve years that Silvestre served as secretary of the Société philomatique, not only did the French Revolution take its course but the Society grew to fifty resident members, sixty-five correspondents, and two emeritus members. By the turn of the century, the Société philomatique was widely recognized as second in importance in the French Republic of Science only to the Institut de France, which had been established to replace the old royal academies in 1795.

Like Oldenburg before him, Silvestre saw his correspondence increase as the Society grew. Correspondence was particularly important for connecting the corresponding members to the Society. The first four corresponding members were elected in 1789, two days after the founders elected the first three new resident members.[22] Friendship bound them to the society, but their distance from Paris meant that letters were their only means of expressing and renewing those ties. Silvestre's exchanges with the corresponding members show that he saw his role as more than simply administrative; he was also responsible for renewing the intellectual and affective ties of "study and friendship" that made a Philomath a Philomath.

On 31 May 1791, the minutes record that the decision was made to establish "une correspondance suivie et sans interruption avec ses correspondants." To formalize this correspondence, the secretary was charged to send out a newsletter to which the corresponding members were subscribed.[23] The next day Silvestre wrote to the foreign minister to ask that he support the Society and its work on behalf of the sciences by allowing his secretarial correspondence with foreign members to be sent under diplomatic cover. The minister granted the Society this valuable privilege which was renewed by his successors.[24]

One of the first corresponding members was Charles-Louis Dumas, a young physician who had come to Paris in 1787 to continue his medical studies but had returned to Montpellier the following year to take up a chair at the medical school.[25] In 1790, he dedicated his doctoral thesis to the Société philomatique; seven years later he sought the Society's approval for a plan he had devised for improving medical education.[26] Silvestre responded with a long letter. He spoke first for the Society, which had recognized the utility of Dumas's plan. He then noted that the Society's newsletter, to which the corresponding members were expected to contribute, was particularly weak on medical topics. He urged Dumas to send in any news items that might be appropriate, reminding him that these should be based on "des observations bien constatées" of rare phenomena that led to "des résultats vraiment utiles." The Society would be particularly interested in receiving extracts of papers delivered at Montpellier's Société des sciences, of which Dumas was a member. "Nous ne recevons que pour donner comme vous savez," Silvestre continued, "et ce centre d'instruction que nous voulons toujours perfectionner acquerrait un grand signe d'intérêt si toutes les sociétés savantes de la république l'enrichissaient du résultat de leurs travaux."[27]

After sharing with Dumas the sad news that their friend and colleague, Gaspard Riche, had died, Silvestre wrote in closing as a friend to a friend whom he had not seen in many years:

> J'ai quelquefois mon cher ami l'occasion de rencontrer votre aimable frère et je lui me rappelle toujours avec grand plaisir notre ancienne liaison. Je ne désespère pas de nous voir unis quelque jour au moins momentanément. Il faut croire que vous voudriez revoir Paris et que vos anciens amis pourront entrer pour quelque chose dans vos projets. Adieu, mon cher Dumas. Quel que soit l'incertitude de mon sort je ne puis pas désespérer pas de voir encore quelques instants de bonheur et je devrai toujours les plus chers à l'amitié. Ecrivez moi, et donnez-moi des détails sur tout ce qui vous touche et qui par cours y viens de m'intéresser si vivement.[28]

In this letter to a corresponding member, friendship weighed more heavily than study, but the balance often fell the other way. One particularly rich exchange began in 1796.[29] That March, corresponding member Justin Girod-Chantrans sent in the latest in a series of papers based on research he had been conducting for several years on a type of algae called *conferva*.[30] A self-taught naturalist who had retired to Besançon after a career in the army, Girod-Chantrans was pursuing a line of research on polyps that went back to the mid-eighteenth century.[31] In June, Silvestre read to the Society the first part of Girod-Chantrans's paper, in which he made the bold argument that, like coral, conferva were not plants but animals. A committee was then appointed to repeat his experiments and validate his controversial conclusions. The importance the Society attached to this research is evidenced by the further decision to have one of the members present Girod-Chantrans's work to the newly-formed Institut de France, should the results be validated.[32] Girod-Chantrans responded with more papers on the same subject enclosed in a letter to Silvestre expressing his gratitude for the support of the Society and especially its secretary. "Personne n'est plus sensible que moi au pouvoir de l'amitié," he wrote, "elle est la bonne comme le tourment de ma vie et l'union donc vous me faites le tableau, jointe à l'estime réciproque qui règne parmi les membres de votre société."[33]

Fifteen months later, in October 1797, Silvestre wrote again to Girod-Chantrans to thank him for two more papers he had sent in. They too would be sent to the Institut where, Silvestre wrote encouragingly, the earlier ones had received a warm reception. However, in order to repeat his new experiments and thus validate the results, the Society needed samples of the specimens that Girod-Chantrans had examined under the microscope. Silvestre also asked Girod-Chantrans to clarify the terminology that he had used in one of the experiments. Admitting that the existing literature was unclear on the subject, several members of the Society who had done relevant research believed nevertheless that more precision was possible. Mentoring his colleague, Silvestre explained the importance of including a good description of the phenomenon under discussion so that readers would be able to recognize it, even if their opinions about it differed. He closed the letter with an expression of friendship for a member whom he had never met: "Je vous renouvelle l'expression du désir que nous avons de vous voir au milieu de nous à Paris, vous trouverez dans les membres de la société autant d'amis qui se feront un plaisir de vous voir, et de vous communiquer les travaux dont ils sont occupés."[34]

As secretary of the Société philomatique, Silvestre not only actively encouraged correspondents like Dumas and Girod-Chantrans to send in their papers and reports, he also mediated intellectual exchange between them and their colleagues in Paris, softening the criticism and helping them to respond to it. In addition, he facilitated the circulation of their findings beyond Paris through the reports he delivered at the Society's annual public meeting and then published.[35] In 1798, he closed the botany section of his first *Rapport général des travaux de la Société Philomatique de Paris* with a long discussion of Girod-Chantrans's research, pointing out both the originality of his conclusions and the extent of his microscopic observations. After describing these observations and findings in detail, Silvestre addressed his colleagues directly, reminding them of the special actions they had taken to make this important research known. "Sur le rapport des commissaires que vous aviez chargés d'examiner cet immense travail," he wrote, "vous avez cru devoir le communiquer à l'institut national; tant pour donner la publicité néessaire à ces observations curieuses, que pour faire jouir le citoyen Chantrans de la portion de gloire qu'il lui a méritée, en le soumettant à l'appréciation de juges aussi éclairés."[36] When Girod-Chantrans published his *Recherches chimiques et microscopiques sur les conferves, bisses, tremelles, etc.* in 1802, he acknowledged the support and encouragement of his colleagues in the Société philomatique, citing Silvestre's report in a footnote.[37]

Girod-Chantrans represented what Silvestre thought the Société philomatique was all about: original research carried out meticulously through observation and experiment by a novice with the encouragement and support of the Society. The critical back and forth between members, both in the discussions that took place at the weekly meetings and through the correspondence that he facilitated as secretary, was an essential part of the process of scientific research as he and the Philomaths conceived it. Through Silvestre's efforts as secretary, the results of the labors of an obscure retired military officer became part of the collective and growing body of scientific knowledge.

Silvestre's correspondence on behalf of the Société philomatique extended beyond individual members to the learned societies that were springing up across France in the late 1790s. In November 1797, he wrote to the Société d'agriculture et arts of Boulogne-sur-Mer that the Société philomatique "a accepté avec joie la correspondance que vous lui proposez." In exchange for copies of the Société philomatique's newsletter, Silvestre requested materials to contribute to it in the future and suggested that his counterpart send accounts of the work presented at their meetings. Such an exchange would contribute to the Society's larger goals, as Silvestre explained, using the same language that he had used a month earlier when he asked Dumas, the Society's correspondent in Montpellier, for material for the newsletter: "Nous pensons que le centre d'instruction que nous voulons toujours perfectionner acquerrait un grand degré d'intérêt si toutes les sociétés savantes de la République l'enrichissaient du résultat de leurs travaux."[38]

At the meeting of 23 germinal year 6 [12 April 1798], Silvestre read aloud a letter from the secretary of the Société d'émulation of Abbeville. He had included a report on his society's activities since its inception three months earlier, and the Société philomatique charged its secretary to request copies of several papers discussed in it.[39] In August, the secretary of Bordeaux's Société des sciences, belles-lettres et arts thanked Silvestre for the copy he had just received of the *Rapport general* published that year and expressed his colleagues' desire "d'augmenter de plus en plus ses rapports avec une société aussi distinguée qu'est la société philomatique de Paris."[40]

The Société philomatique's network of institutional correspondence often built on the individual relationships established with its correspondents. In November 1796, the secretary of the Société d'émulation of Rouen wrote fraternally that as one of their mutual colleagues had shared with them the report on the Paris society's work, the Rouen society was returning the favor with a report on their activities. In doing so, Secretary Auber made sure to acknowledge the nature of the relationship between the two societies: "Si Paris est le centre principal des lumières, les grandes communes des Départements doivent les répandre les propager & même les seconder."[41] Seven months later, Silvestre acknowledged receipt of reports that Auber had sent of the subsequent work of the Rouen society, along with its by-laws and a list of its members. In return, the Rouen society would receive several back issues of the newsletter and be subscribed to it for the future.[42]

The following year, it was Auber's turn to thank Silvestre for the report he had sent of the Société philomatique's work. "La Société en lisant votre éloquente introduction a partagé votre tristesse et vos regrets lorsque vous avez rappelé à son souvenir les Pelletier, les Vicq d'Azyr et les Lavoisier," Auber wrote to his counterpart. "L'Éloge du Citoyen Riche n'a la pas moins émue. Il lui a fait aussi verser des larmes avec le Citoyen Cuvier son panégyriste." Auber then reflected optimistically on the larger picture that Silvestre had painted in his report. "En voyant ces grandes pertes faites par votre Société et par la République des Lettres," he wrote, "on tremblerait pour le sort des Sciences et des Arts, si le sang des généreux martyrs de la Philosophie n'était pas une semonce féconde de Philosophes et de Savants, si la liste de vos membres et de vos correspondants, ne nous offrait pas un grand nombre d'hommes de génie et de défenseurs courageux de la vérité bien propre à affermir son empire et à relever nos espérances."[43]

Letters such as this one were the reward Silvestre reaped for the many hours he spent on the Society's affairs. Like Oldenburg, however, Silvestre also had to earn a living. In January 1795, he was hired to run the educational programs at the state Mining Agency, including its engineering school, the Ecole des Mines. He also served as secretary of the Conférence des Mines, the weekly meeting of the Agency's savants, engineers, and professors.[44] By 1801, Silvestre's responsibilities for the Société philomatique had become so time-consuming and the Society's correspondence so substantial that a proposal was put forward to establish a new position of corresponding secretary to ease the burden on the secretary.[45] It is unclear if Silvestre put forward the proposal himself, or if his friends did so in order to keep him from resigning his office. In any event, in early June, a committee composed of Silvestre, Brongniart, and Georges Cuvier was charged with evaluating the proposal and creating a job description.

In their report the committee pointed to an increased volume of correspondence, both with corresponding members and with other learned societies, due to the visibility the Society had achieved through its publications. In order for the Society and its members to benefit from its success, someone had to maintain this correspondence, and the current secretary was simply too busy to do so. The committee also noted the importance of including in the Society's newsletter reports and results of research being conducted beyond Paris and the laxity of the corresponding members in providing it. They needed to be reminded that in exchange for receiving the newsletter they were expected to send in news for it. This could only be done by means of personal correspondence, not form letters. Finally, the committee also noted the necessity of conveying to the correspondents the substance of the discussion of the papers they submitted for review by their Parisian colleagues. In short, correspondence on a vast scale was crucial for the exchange and dissemination of scientific information and ideas that were central to the Society's purpose and vision.[46]

The committee thus proposed that the Society's constitution (*règlements*) be amended to include among the officers a corresponding secretary whose duties would be as follows: to maintain a regular correspondence with savants and learned societies; to respond in the name of the Society to all letters addressed to it that deal with the sciences; to remind the corresponding members of the Society as often as possible of the commitment they have made to it; to communicate to those who sent papers to the Society the discussions that these papers raised.

The corresponding secretary would also serve on the editorial board of the newsletter. In other words, the corresponding secretary would take over all the secretary's duties except taking minutes and handling routine administrative correspondence. The committee had effectively described the job of the secretary himself.[47]

The committee presented its report on 2 July 1801, just two days after Silvestre had accepted a new position as head of the Bureau of Agriculture in the Interior Ministry. In fact, the idea of creating a corresponding secretary had been raised just around the time that Silvestre's nomination for this post had been put forward.[48] It was thus no doubt in anticipation of this hoped-for result that Silvestre and his friends sought to scale down his responsibilities as secretary of the Société philomatique without, however, losing him entirely. His experience and the continuity he provided were just too valuable. Happily, the committee's recommendation was accepted by the membership, since Silvestre had anticipated correctly the demands of his new job. In August, he wrote to his nephew: "Ne sois ni inquiet ni fâché mon cher ami, si depuis quelque temps tu reçois moins fréquemment des lettres de moi, mais j'emploie tant de temps à écrire pour les autres qu'il ne me reste pas souvent le courage de prendre la plume pour moi."[49]

The astronomer Jean-Baptiste Biot was elected corresponding secretary, but, less than two years later, Silvestre stepped down as secretary anyway. Biot was elected to replace him, and the position of corresponding secretary was never filled or brought up again. But the archives suggest that no subsequent secretary threw himself into the role as Silvestre had. Their letters tend to be businesslike, whereas his reflect a belief in the importance of correspondence to forging and maintaining the bonds of friendship through which individual study entered into the dynamic of active collaboration and science progressed.

Conclusion

Secretaries of learned societies are much rarer today than they were when ASECS was founded in the 1960s. ASECS, in fact, no longer has an executive secretary but an executive director. This makes me sad because the title reminds us of the roots of societies such as ours in the long eighteenth century and its tradition of gentlemanly voluntarism. Following Steven Shapin's lead, historians of science have shed welcome light on the invisible labor of the laboratory, especially that of family members subsumed under patriarchal authority; they have also begun to look at invisible labor in the field: those who wielded picks and hunted specimens for others to collect, dissect, and classify.[50] The invisible labor of the secretary, however, has by and large escaped serious attention precisely because secretaries of this sort were not clerical workers but gentlemen members of the societies to which they belonged: their labor was not labor. When secretaries of learned societies are studied, it is generally from the other side of the power dynamic, as power brokers and wielders of power who achieved high status and honor through holding this position.[51]

Why then abandon such an honorable title? The answer lies, I think, in the gendered connotations that came to adhere to the word secretary in the late twentieth century.[52] By 1988, the Conference of Secretaries of the American Council of Learned Societies raised the question: "Who are we, anyway? Or at least, what do we call ourselves?" While acknowledging that learned societies had always been run by secretaries, Dorothy Atkinson from the American Association for the Advancement of Slavic Studies noted that no one seemed to know "what the *secretary* of a learned society does. Rather than performing purely secretarial functions," she complained, "we are the people who make the organization work. Newspaper advertisements for *secretaries* identify a different occupation." Margaret King of the Renaissance Society of America echoed Atkinson's frustration. Her own society was "so confused by the title *secretary*," she recounted, "that they one time sent the office secretary to the Conference of Secretaries." Joe Hickerson from the Society of Ethnomusicology had already complained to his colleagues that his title was "archaic;" in his opinion, the ethnomusicologists should have a "business office with an *executive director*." Irene Tichenor of the Bibliographical Society of America agreed: "I think *secretary* is a loaded and confusing word," she declared.[53]

Secretary had become a dirty word. I find it significant that most of the secretaries who raised the issue and were most adamant about it were female. As such, they were more likely to be confused with clerical workers than their male colleagues were, and less likely to have the honor of holding their important offices in the Republic of Letters recognized by their chairs and deans in Academia. The hours of work they put in were seen as merely clerical. For men like Joe Hickerson, of course, masculinity itself might have been at stake.

In any case, a motion was introduced to change the name to "Conference of *Executive Officers*," but when various members objected that they were not CEOs of their organizations, the motion was amended to "Conference of *Administrative Officers*." When the further objection was raised that no one actually had that title, R. G. Peterson of ASECS informed his colleagues that in fact he did. When the motion was put to a vote, it carried overwhelmingly. "The name change will take effect at the April meeting," wrote Nina Kressner Cobb of the ACLS. "I dare say it will take some getting used to."[54]

Peterson was only half right when he said that he was ASECS's administrative officer. He, was in fact, its executive secretary. However, the ASECS constitution defined the secretary as "the chief administrative officer of the Society."[55] Sometime between 1992 and 2011, when the constitution was last revised, the title was finally changed to "Executive Director."[56] Byron Wells is the first person officially to hold that title. But I hope that he and Lisa Berglund and their successors will be proud to see themselves as following in the honorable eighteenth-century tradition of the secretary of the learned society—and especially of Henry Oldenburg and François Silvestre—who dedicated themselves selflessly to the societies they served and the larger goals of the Republic of Letters advanced through them.

NOTES

The research for this article was conducted in the idyllic precincts of the Henry E. Huntington Library with the support of a Dibner Distinguished Fellowship in the History of Science and Technology. I am grateful to the Huntington and its director of research Steve Hindle for an exceptionally pleasant and productive year there. I am also grateful to Peter Reill, former director of UCLA's Center for Seventeenth- and Eighteenth-Century Studies for facilitating my consultation of the ASECS archives in the William Andrews Clark Memorial Library, which was closed that year for earthquake retrofitting. Rebecca Marschall, the Library's curator of manuscripts, and her staff were extremely gracious and welcoming in cramped circumstances. Howard Weinbrot, who has been an active and enthusiastic member of ASECS since its founding and who is now happily resident at the Huntington, was kind enough to read a draft of this paper and provide very useful suggestions for its improvement. I thank him too.

1.   Ron Rosbottom to Members of the Steering Committee and Philip Harth, 14 November 1979. ASECS archives, William Andrews Clark Library, UCLA, Box 2, folder 19. On the founding of ASECS, see "Report of the Provisional Executive Board, 1969–1970," ASECS archives, Box 7, folder 4; and Donald Greene, "The ASECS's Early Years: A Personal Memoir," in Carla H. Hay and Syndy M. Conger, eds., *The Past as Prologue: Essays to Celebrate the Twenty-fifth Anniversary of ASECS* (New York: AMS Press, 1995), 3–17.

2.   Madeleine B. Therrien, President, ASECS, to [members of the ASECS Board], 6 December 1979, ASECS archives, Box 2, folder 19. Shirley Bill, chair of the Society's Constitution Committee, had offered her opinion that such an appointment would be possible without amending the Constitution, especially if the title were Editor of the News Circular and Associate Executive Secretary, since the Constitution allowed for the appointment of unspecified editors of the Society's publications. Shirley [Bill] to Ron [Rosbottom], 12 September 1979, ASECS archives, Box 2, folder 19.

3.   John F. Sena to Jean Perkins, 1 May 1981. ASECS archives, Box 35, folder 3.

4.   Jane [Perry-Camp] to Barbara Brandon Schnorrenberg, 1 September 1991, ASECS archives, Box 34, folder 3; [Perry-Camp] to E. P. Harris, ASECS Executive Secretary, 11 August 1991. In her letter to Harris, Perry-Camp laid out a four-year plan, from appointing a committee to do a feasibility study to searching for and hiring a permanent secretary.

5.   "One who is entrusted with private or secret matters; a confidant; one privy *to* a secret." Secretary, n.1 and adj." *OED Online*, accessed 25 May 2016, March 2016. Oxford Univ. Press. *http://www.oed.com.proxy.lib.umich.edu/view/Entry/174 549?rskey=WfTHKP&result=1&isAdvanced=false.* Having a secretary was a form of power and a privilege primarily of princes. The *OED* notes that the history of the usage of the term shows that for a long time *secretary* referred quite narrowly to "the officer who conducted the correspondence of a king.". Here is the first definition in

the *Dictionnaire* of the Académie Française in 1694: "Celui dont l'emploi est d'écrire pour son maître, de faire des lettres, des dépêches pour son maître, pour celui dont il dépend." ["Someone whose job is making and writing letters, dispatches for his master, for the person on whom he is dependent."] (I have modernized French spelling here and in subsequent quotations; all translations are my own.) Virtually the same wording is found in other French dictionaries throughout the eighteenth century. See *Dictionnaires d'autrefois,* accessed 7 April 2016, *http://artflsrv02.uchicago.edu/philologic4/publicdicos/query?report=bibliography&head=secretaire*. Examples show that secretaries could range from ordinary clerks to the venal officeholders known as *secrétaires du roi*.

    6. See, e.g., Hans Bots and Françoise Waquet, eds., *Commercium Litterarium, 1600–1750: La Communication dans la République des Lettres/Forms of Communication in the Republic of Letters* (Amsterdam: APA-Holland Univ. Press, 1994); Ann Goldgar, *Impolite Learning: Conduct and Community in the Republic of Letters, 1680–1750* (New Haven, CT: Yale Univ. Press, 1995).

    7. Marie Boas Hall, *Henry Oldenburg: Shaping the Royal Society* (Oxford: Oxford Univ. Press, 2002), 57–58.

    8. Hall, *Henry Oldenburg*, 70, 74.

    9. Hall, 71, 74, 78–79.

   10. Hall, 276.

   11. Hall, 276–77.

   12. *Correspondence*, 12: 364, 6 July 1676; quoted in Hall, 293.

   13. J. Ereck Jarvis, "Thomas Sprat's 'Mixt Assembly:' Association and Authority in the History of the Royal Society," *Restoration* 37 (Fall 2013): 63–64.

   14. Greene, "ASECS's Early Years," 3.

   15. On the eighteenth-century Republic of Letters, see Dena Goodman, *The Republic of Letters: A Cultural History of the French Enlightenment* (Ithaca, NY: Cornell Univ. Press, 1994).

   16. Jean le Rond d'Alembert, "Academic Eulogies," trans. Dena Goodman, in *The Encyclopedia of Diderot & d'Alembert Collaborative Translation Project* (Ann Arbor: Michigan Publishing, Univ. of Michigan Library, 2013), accessed 12 October 2013, *http://hdl.handle.net/2027/spo.did2222.0002.991*. Originally published as «Eloges academiques,» *Encyclopédie ou Dictionnaire raisonné des sciences, des arts et des métiers* (Paris, 1755), 5: 527–28. Similarly, the anatomist Félix Vicq d'Azyr, who delivered more than fifty eulogies as secretary of the Academy of Medicine in the 1770s and 1780s, called the eulogies of scientists "des matériaux pour l'histoire de l'esprit humain" [materials for the history of the human spirit]. He also noted that whereas Fontenelle had to be concerned about boring his listeners and readers with too much scientific detail, in his own day, "les circonstances sont changées: le goût des sciences est universellement répandu, et les lecteurs demandent une histoire de leurs progrès" [circumstances have changed: the taste for the sciences is universal, and readers demand a history of their progress]. Vicq-d'Azyr, "Eloges historiques: considérations générales," in *Œuvres complètes*, ed. Jacques Louis Moreau (de la Sarthe) (Paris: Duprat-Duverger, 1805), 1: 1–6. On Vicq-d'Azyr's eulogies, see Daniel Roche, "Médecins et Lumières au XVIIIe siècle : talents, raison et sacrifice,"

in *Les républicains des lettres: Gens de culture et Lumières au XVIIIe siècle* (Paris: Fayard, 1988), 309–14.

17. Tim Reeve, "Science in the Service of the State: Condorcet's *Eloges des académiciens de l'Académie royale des sciences*," *British Journal for Eighteenth-Century Studies* 28 (2005): 229–38; see also Charles Paul, *Science and Immortality: The "Eloges" of the Paris Academy of Sciences (1699–1791)* (Berkeley, CA: Univ. of California Press, 1980), 62.

18. *Correspondance littéraire, philosophique et critique*, ed. Maurice Tourneux (Paris: Garnier frères, 1879), 10: 198 (February 1773).

19. Keith Michael Baker, "Les débuts de Condorcet au secrétariat de l'Académie royale des Sciences (1773–1776)," *Revue d'histoire des sciences et de leurs applications* 20 (July–September 1967): 256–58.

20. The definitive study of the Société philomatique is Jonathan Renato Mandelbaum, "La Société Philomathique de Paris de 1788 à 1835: essai d'histoire institutionnelle et de biographie collective d'une société savante parisienne," (Ph.D. dissertation, École des Hautes Études en Sciences Sociales, 1983). On Silvestre, see Dena Goodman and Emily Talbot, "Documenting Art, Writing Biography: Construction of the Silvestre Family History, 1660–1868," *Journal of Family History* 40 (July 2015): 277–304.

21. On the meanings and functions of friendship during this period, see Kenneth Loiselle, *Brotherly Love: Freemasonry and Male Friendship in Enlightenment France* (Ithaca: Cornell Univ. Press, 2014); and Sarah Horowitz, *Friendship and Politics in Post-Revolutionary France* (University Park, PA: Pennsylvania State Univ. Press, 2013).

22. Mandelbaum, "Société Philomathique de Paris," 462. The other three correspondents were a physician named Guichard (about whom nothing else is known); Antoine de Lasalle, a world traveler and self-made philosopher who became a disciple of Lazarro Spallanzani in Rome, invented the pantographe, came to Paris to study in 1780, published his first major work there in 1788: *La Balance naturelle, ou essai sur une loi universelle appliquée aux sciences, arts et métiers et aux moindres details de la vie commune*, and then retired to Semur in Burgundy; and, Friedrich-Ludwig Schurer, who received his medical degree in Strasbourg in 1789 and went on to become a professor of chemistry at the artillery school there. For biographical details on La Salle, see Ferdinand Hoefer, *Nouvelle biographie universelle* (Paris: Firmin Didot, 1842–1877), 29: 730–31.

23. ". . . a regular uninterrupted correspondence with the corresponding members." Unsigned document in Brongniart's hand, extracted from minutes of 31 May 1791, Bibliothèque de la Sorbonne (hereafter BS), Box 129.

24. Silvestre to M. de Montmorin, ministre des affaires étrangers, 1 June 1791, BS Box 128; Silvestre to secrétaire du département des affaires étrangers sur la réponse de M. Dumouriez en date du 18 avril 1792, BS Box 128.

25. Prunelle, *Eloge funèbre de Charles-Louis Dumas, prononcé dans l'Assemblée publique de la Faculté de Montpellier, le 14 Décembre 1813* (Montpellier: Jean Martel aîné, 1814), 26–27.

26. Claude-Louis Dumas, *Q. F. F. F. F. Q. S. Quaestiones medicae duodecim* (Montpellier: Joseph-François Tournel, 1790) ; C. L. Dumas to Société philomatique, 14 fructidor an 5 (31 August 1797), BS Box 133.

27. "... the most well-documented observations possible and which lead to truly useful results;" "We only receive in order to give, as you know, and this center of education that we are always trying to improve would attract great interest if all the learned societies of the republic enriched it with the results of their labors." Draft of Silvestre to Dumas, 30 vendémiaire an 6 (21 October 1797), BS Box 128.

28. "I have sometimes had occasion to run into your nice brother and I am reminded always with great pleasure of our long relationship. I do not despair of seeing us together again one day, at least briefly. I have to believe that you would like to see Paris again and your old friends would enter into your plans. Goodbye my dear Dumas. Whatever the uncertainty of my future, I cannot despair of seeing again a few moments of happiness and I will always owe the dearest ones to friendship. Write to me, and share with me everything that touches you and which will, of course, interest me deeply." Draft of Silvestre to Dumas, 30 vendémiaire an 6 (21 October 1797), BS Box 128.

29. See Mandelbaum, "Société philomathique de Paris," 90–97, for a detailed discussion of this case.

30. Girod-Chantrans to Société Philomatique, 13 ventôse an 4 (3 March 1796), BS Box 133.

31. See Mary Terrall, *Catching Nature in the Act: Réamur and the Practice of Natural History in the Eighteenth Century* (Chicago: Univ. of Chicago Press, 2014), 119–31; Marc J. Ratcliff, *The Quest for the Invisible: Microscopy in the Enlightenment* (Farnham, Surrey, England: Ashgate, 2009), 103–23 and 237–39.

32. Minutes of meeting of 3 messidor [an 4] (21 June 1796), BS Box 123. Georges Cuvier, who was a member of both the Société philomatique and the Institut, was to present the work.

33. "No one is more sensitive than I to the power of friendship; it is both the good and the torment of my life, and you thus bring them together for me, joined to the mutual esteem that reigns among the members of your society." Girod-Chantrans to [Silvestre], 7 thermidor an 4 (25 July 1796), BS Box 133. Silvestre read these new papers to the assembled Philomaths at the next meeting. Minutes of meeting of 13 thermidor [an 4] (31 July 1796), based on multiple partial drafts in BS Box 123.

34. "Let me express once again our desire to see you among us in Paris. You will find in the members of the Society so many friends who would be pleased to see you, and to share with you the work that they are doing." Draft of Silvestre to Girod-Chantrans, 1 brumaire an 6 (22 October 1797), BS Box 128.

35. Although the bylaws of 1791 specified that a public meeting was to be held once a year on the anniversary of the founding of the Society, none was held for several years after the first one, in December 1791, when Riche was still secretary.

36. "Based on the report of the committee you had charged with examining this immense body of work you believed that it must be communicated to the Institut national, both to give the necessary publicity to these curious observations and so that citizen Chantrans could enjoy the portion of glory he had earned, by submitting it to

the appreciation of such enlightened judges." Augustin-François Silvestre, *Rapport général des travaux de la Société Philomatique* (1798), 99–102. Although public meetings and reports were supposed to be annual, this report covered the period from January 1792 through 23 frimaire an 6 (13 December 1797)—the date of the Society's first public meeting since Silvestre became secretary.

37. [Justin] Girod-Chantrans, *Recherches chimiques et microscropiques sur les conferves, bisses, tremelles, etc.* (Paris: Bernard, an 10 [1802]), vi.

38. ". . . accepted with joy the correspondence that you propose;" "We believe that the center of education that we are always trying to improve would attract great interest if all the learned societies of the Republic enriched it with the results of their labors." Copy of Silvestre to Société d'agriculture et arts de Boulogne sur Mer, 15 brumaire an 6 (5 November 1797), BS Box 128.

39. Minutes of meeting of 23 germinal [an 6] (12 April 1798), BS Box 123.

40. ". . . to strengthen more and more their connections with a society as distinguished as the Société philomatique of Paris." Leupold, Secretary of the first class of the Société des sciences, belles-lettres et arts of Bordeaux, 23 thermidor an 6 (10 August 1798), BS Box 133.

41. "If Paris is the main center of Enlightenment, the great communes of the Departments must spread, propagate, and indeed support it." Auber, Secretary of Société d'émulation of Rouen to Société philomatique, 28 brumaire an 5 (18 November 1796), BS Box 133.

42. Copy of Silvestre to Auber, Secretary of Société d'émulation of Rouen, 4 messidor an 5 (22 June 1797), BS Box 128.

43. "In reading your eloquent introduction, the Society shared your sadness and your regrets when you recalled to its memory Pelletier, Vicq d'Azyr, and Lavoisier. The eulogy of citizen Riche was no less moving. It caused tears to be shed with Citizen Cuvier, his panegyrist. In seeing these great losses suffered by your Society and by the Republic of Letters one would tremble for the fate of the Sciences and the Arts, if the blood of the generous martyrs of Philosophy had not been the fertile seed of Philosophes and Savants, if the list of your members and your correspondents did not offer us a great number of men of genius and brave defenders of the truth well suited to strengthen its empire and raise our hopes." Auber, Secretary of Société d'émulation of Rouen to Silvestre, Secretary General of the Société philomatique, 30 thermidor an 6 (17 August 1798), BS Box 133. The minutes record that Silvestre read this letter aloud at the meeting of 3 fructidor an 6 (20 August 1798), BS Box 123. At the same meeting he read a letter acknowledging receipt of the *Rapport general* from the Société des sciences, belles-lettres et arts (Bordeaux), as well as one from the secretary of a society in Boulogne-sur-Mer reporting on an unusual childbirth.

44. On the Agence des Mines, see Isabelle Laboulais, *La Maison des mines : la genèse révolutionnaire d'un corps d'ingénieurs civils (1794–1814)* (Rennes: Presses Univ. de Rennes, 2012). Silvestre's start date is unclear. In a document prepared in 1819, Silvestre dates his hire as 16 nivôse an 2 (5 January 1794), which is before the agency was established. Archives Nationales de France (hereafter AN) F/1Bi/279/3. Laboulais does not give a precise date, but says he started at the beginning of the

year 3, which would be October 1794. Laboulais, *Maison des mines*, 59, 99. I am suggesting that they got the dates mixed up— Silvestre got the year wrong, and Laboulais might have meant the beginning of 1795, not the year 3.

45. Report in Brongniart's hand, [13 messidor an 9 (2 July 1801)], BS Box 129, item no. 439. The initial proposal was recorded in the minutes of 23 prairial an 9 (12 June 1801), BS Box 123.

46. Report in Brongniart's hand, [13 messidor an 9 (2 July 1801)], BS Box 129.

47. ASECS executive secretary Paul Korshin proposed dividing up the administrative duties similarly when the decision was made in 1977 to hire a business manager. Paul Korshin to Phillip Harth, 28 February 1977. ASECS archives, Box 4, folder 25.

48. Silvestre to Augustin-Henry Bonnard, 12 prairial, an 9 (1 June 1801), 18 messidor an 9 (7 July 1801), AN 352 AP 43; Silvestre to Interior Minister Jean-Antoine Chaptal, 11 messidor an 9 (30 June 1801), AN F/10/1483.

49. "Don't be either worried or angry at me, my dear friend, if for a while you have been receiving letters from me less frequently, but I am spending so much time writing for other people that often I don't have enough courage left to take up the pen for myself." Silvestre to Bonnard, 20 thermidor an 9 (8 August 1801), AN 352 AP 43.

50. Steven Shapin, "The Invisible Technician," *American Scientist* 77 (November–December 1989): 554–63; a later version appears as chapter 9 of Shapin, *A Social History of Truth: Civility and Science in Seventeenth-Century England* (Chicago: Univ. of Chicago Press, 1994).

For an overview of the scholarship on invisible labor in the household, see Alix Cooper, "Homes and Households," in *The Cambridge History of Science*, ed. Katharine Park and Lorraine Daston [Online]. The Cambridge History of Science (Cambridge: Cambridge Univ. Press, 2006). Available from Cambridge Histories Online <*http://dx.doi.org.proxy.lib.umich.edu/10.1017/CHOL9780521572446*> [Accessed 07 April 2016], 224–38. Particular studies include Monika Mommertz, "The Invisible Economy of Science: A New Approach to the History of Gender and Astronomy at the Eighteenth-Century Berlin Academy of Sciences," trans. Julia Baker, in *Men, Women, and the Birthing of Modern Science*, ed. Judith Zinsser (DeKalb: Northern Illinois Univ. Press, 2005), 159–78; and, Terrall, *Catching Nature in the Act*. Lydia Barnett is currently embarked on a study of invisible labor in natural history fieldwork.

51. Keith Baker frames this episode in Condorcet's career in relation to the philosophes' struggle for control of the academies; with his appointment as secretary of the Academy of Sciences, he writes, "Condorcet was set on the road to power in the most powerful scientific body in Europe." Keith Michael Baker, *Condorcet: From Natural Philosophy to Social Mathematics* (Chicago: Univ. of Chicago Press, 1975), 40. Although she shows how hard Oldenberg worked as secretary of the Royal Society, Hall emphasizes that his election gave him "a post of responsibility and a distinguished position in the world of learning both at home . . . and abroad." Hall, 52.

52. I examine this issue from another perspective in "The Secretaire and the Integration of the Eighteenth-Century Self," in Dena Goodman and Kathryn Norberg, eds., *Furnishing the Eighteenth Century: What Furniture Can Tell Us about the European and American Past* (New York: Routledge, 2006), 183–203.

53. Minutes of 11–13 November 1988 meeting, Conference of [heretofore] Secretaries, American Council of Learned Societies. ASECS archives, Box 18, folder 23.

54. Nina Kressner Cobb, Executive Associate, ACLS, to ACLS Conference of Administrative Officers, 14 March 1989. ASECS archives, Box 18, folder 23.

55. ASECS constitution (1980), ASECS archives, Box 19, folder 21. The same language was used in the job descriptions written for searches to fill the position of executive secretary in 1987 and 1992. Box 2, folder 18; Box 34, folder 3.

56. ASECS Constitution (2011), accessed 24 May 2016, available at *https://asecs.press.jhu.edu/*.

Richard Whitworth,
Benjamin Franklin, and
Political Electricity

CARLA J. MULFORD

In their multivolume *Catalogue of Prints and Drawings in the British Museum* (1883), Frederic George Stephens and Edward Hawkins characterized Richard Whitworth's 1770 broadside satire, *Political Electricity*, as (with just one exception) "the most complex and difficult of all the satirical prints yet catalogued in these volumes." This "extraordinary" sheet "advisedly styled a 'Prophetical Print,'" created, they wrote, "a very remarkable reference to the then recent researches of Benjamin Franklin in electrical science."[1] Given their knowledge of the collections of prints in the British Museum, the comparative analysis offered by Stephens and Hawkins is striking. As they introduce their discussion of the broadside, they call it "[t]he most elaborate, if not the most recondite of all the sequential satires in the entire National Collection."[2] In more recent years, this broadsheet has been brought to our attention by the insightful scholarship of historian of science James Delbourgo, who uses the satire as visual evidence of scientific imagery in the Opposition's "conspiracy narrative on the eve of revolution."[3]

Richard Whitworth's singular broadside offers us an opportunity to examine significant issues of political allegiance, alliance, and interest in Britain during the second half of the eighteenth century. Richard Whitworth (the primary concern of this essay) was, like Benjamin Franklin, working on the critical question, "what is liberty," at a crucial moment during Britain's evolution toward global empire. Whitworth's intriguing broadside, *Political Electricity*, aligned him with the Opposition against the Administration and its central leaders, John Stuart, third Earl of Bute, and Augustus FitzRoy, third Duke of Grafton. Yet, as we shall see, Whitworth's politics, across his lifetime, were far more complicated and volatile than his early career and publications—the best known part of his life—would suggest. We can best attend to the complications of Whitworth's broadside and his life if we have a passing recollection of the political circumstances of the late 1760s and early 1770s and the concerns of Opposition propagandists, some of whom were, it seems, genuinely alarmed by the imperial war machine that seemed to deny Britons their ancient liberties. After a brief summary of relevant events of the day, I will turn to a discussion of the broadside itself and then to its intriguing creator whose life and writings have remained obscure before now.

The Political Scene, 1769–1770

The British political scene was in turmoil during the late 1760s and early 1770s, the air definitely replete with political electricity, as Whitworth (Veridicus) framed it. Parliament and ministry were embroiled in power disputes within and across party lines.[4] Britons in North America were pressuring for equal legal status with Britons in England, and they resisted Grenville's Stamp Act and then the Townshend Acts, which imposed duties on necessities used daily, including glass, paint, lead, paper, and tea. When a Board of Customs was established to enforce Townshend's duties, protests developed throughout the northern colonies and erupted in Massachusetts in 1768 and 1769, ending in the Boston "massacre" in early March 1770.[5] Britain's expansion into India, a brutal and costly effort, was being contested in Parliament and the ministry, while those like Robert Clive, who had been directly involved in India, were reaping financial benefits.[6] In Ireland, absentee landlords and the plantation system left laborers in poor working conditions while pockets of British leaders were being lined with silver. Irish trades were circumvented by several longstanding acts that constrained the economy of Ireland while enriching England's laboring and manufacturing sector and thus its overall economy.[7] Britain's global imperial project was being challenged by France (in North America and India and at sea) and Spain (especially in the Falkland Islands crisis) at the time that its strong relationship with the Netherlands was weakening.[8]

In the eyes of Opposition members, or those opposed to the government's controlling measures, Britain's leaders were sacrificing the liberties of the people while enhancing their own coffers; rather than watching out for the state, leaders were watching out for their own wellbeing. The turmoil centered on constitutional questions in the view of Edmund Burke and others. Burke's 1770 pamphlet, *Thoughts on the Cause of the Present Discontents*, clarified the ideal relationship that ought to obtain among the different parts of government and through the vehicles of the party system. Burke's was an impassioned but clear statement based in constitutional principle.[9] About this situation, John Brewer once wrote that "the question at issue was not *whether* it [i.e., the constitution] was threatened, but by whom, and why." Brewer frames the situation as a struggle over "pathology and cure." The problem for each side of the debate, Opposition and Administration, "was to accommodate the events of the 1760s to a standard pathology in such a way as to justify their own position and place their opponents beyond the constitutional pale."[10]

At the center of much of the Opposition's critique were key people in leadership roles: Bute; Grafton; George Grenville; Charles Townshend; Frederick North, second Earl of Guilford, known as Lord North; Robert Clive; and eventually John Russell, fourth Duke of Bedford. Protests frequently occurred in the streets, and some ended in bloodshed, as, for instance, when people gathered together in St. George's Fields to protest the imprisonment of John Wilkes, incarcerated in the King's Bench Prison. Wilkes, then a Member of Parliament, had in the early 1760s published in his newspaper, *The North Briton*, a series of articles criticizing King George III and the ministry. In 1764, when found guilty of seditious libel, Wilkes fled to France. After he returned to England in 1768, Wilkes stood for election first in London, where he lost, but then in Middlesex, where he won. The question became one of whether Wilkes could be seated in Parliament. The sentence against him was overturned, but nonetheless he was not permitted to take his seat in Parliament. Worse, he was formally expelled and imprisoned. Wilkes and others speaking in his favor cast the set of events as the government's preventing the people from employing their right of election. Taken together with other political problems, Wilkes's effort reveals what John Brewer has called a "frontal assault on the politics of oligarchy."[11] His success was based in his ability to arouse in the general population a concern about their own rights. After his imprisonment, in early May, people started gathering at St. George's Fields, near the King's Bench Prison, where he was being kept. Local justices of the peace called for military assistance, because they grew alarmed at the great number of people gathered (some estimate 15,000) there. When they arrived, soldiers were challenged by the people, who organized against them and threw stones in an effort to confuse and warn the soldiers off. But the soldiers ended up firing into the crowd in an effort to disperse it. Several people were killed, including a young farm hand named William Allen, who was working the fields. The events quickly became known as the "Massacre at St. George's Fields."[12] For many people, the situation evidenced the clear disregard by the government for the well-being of its people.

Opposition protests occurred within different levels in government, as well. Members of the House of Lords began to embrace their ancient privilege of speaking their dissent. Lords' protests were "destined," William Lowe has said, "to become part of the House's public record in the *Journals of the House of Lords*." For this reason, Lords considered that their "protests were . . . public statements, unlike debates and individual votes," and thus protests were not to be taken lightly. The protests of Lords commonly appeared in the public press.[13] In this same era, proscription against publishing of parliamentary debates was beginning to be tested. Newspapers began, with John Almon taking the lead, publishing debates of "clubs" and other "society" materials, using clubs and societies as euphemisms for Parliament.[14] Other printers, including Henry Sampson Woodfall, began publishing parliamentary materials in addition to Opposition writings.

Woodfall's most famous Opposition writer in the *Public Advertiser* was Junius, an anonymous writer whom many now believe to have been Sir Philip Francis.[15] Another of Woodfall's well-known writers from 1769 to 1770 was Veridicus (Richard Whitworth, at the time MP for Stafford), the creative mind behind the broadside, *Political Electricity*, among several other articles that appeared in Woodfall's *Public Advertiser*.[16] In considering the letters of Junius alongside those of Veridicus, we can see that both worked through common Opposition positions: the desire to see Bute ousted and to bring down the Grafton and then North ministries; the civic celebration of ancient liberties expressed primarily in anxious condemnation of ministerial intrigue and political oppression; the incarceration of Wilkes; and, the demeaning of William Pitt, first Earl of Chatham, and Charles Pratt, first Earl Camden. When Camden resigned (was dismissed) in January 1770, it signaled to the Opposition that change was afoot. Both Junius and Veridicus attacked the ministry's handling of foreign matters, particularly the loss of Corsica to France. They likewise criticized the Bedford Whigs for their coercive policies against Britons in North America. The Bedford Whigs were so called because they entered the ministry as part of the Opposition, but after shifting leadership roles left Bedford out of power, he joined Bute's cabinet in the service of Administration and fought against Pitt. The key figures were Granville Leveson-Gower, second Earl Gower; Richard Rigby; Thomas Thynne, third Viscount Weymouth; Edward Thurlow; and George Spencer, fourth Duke of Marlborough.

Early on, Whitworth did not identify himself to Woodfall. Junius is the one who informed Woodfall—by letter on 6 August 1769—that Veridicus was Richard Whitworth.[17] Junius and Whitworth were, evidently, acquaintances. Themes that interested Junius and Whitworth/Veridicus also preoccupied Benjamin Franklin. With James Burgh, Franklin contributed to Woodfall's paper a series called "The Colonist's Advocate," published in the *Public Advertiser* between January and early March, 1770.[18] This series was being run at the same time that Whitworth/Veridicus's letters and his broadside, *Political Electricity*, were being published. The similarity of goals of all of these writers might make us believe Franklin was known to Junius and to Whitworth, but no evidence exists to support the idea. Their similarity arises from their common goal of undermining the Grafton ministry and the Bedford Whigs. It is possible that the three commonly associated in one of the six London clubs Franklin attended. In fact, Franklin met many of his most important collaborators in the club culture of London—his friendship with James Burgh a good case in point.

Political Electricity

Leaving open the question about whether Franklin and Whitworth were known to one another, we can more conclusively recognize the impact of Franklin's scientific endeavors in Whitworth's work. Indeed, Whitworth himself made explicit the reference to Franklin's recent scientific work. Stephens and Hawkins considered the scientific allusion significant enough to underscore. "The intention of this elaborate satire," they wrote,

> is to declare that the French Court evoked electricity from the body of Lord Bute, which was conveyed through various media, including the King and his mother, and culminated in the shooting of William Allen the younger, and others, who thus became popular martyrs, and in whose persons, as well as in that of the incarcerated Wilkes, the liberties of the nation were alleged to have been wronged.[19]

A chain, electrified by Bute's body, "terminates in that blood-shedding which occurred May 10, 1768, during the suppression of a popular commotion in St. George's Fields."[20]

Calling his broadside *Political Electricity; or, An Historical & Prophetical Print in the Year 1770*, Whitworth elaborated, in thirty-one separate designs, key propaganda issues and devices used by the Opposition. Under the byline, "Bute & Wilkes invent. Veridicus & Junius fect." the broadside announced that it was "Published according to Act of Parliament," all sheer mockery.

Political Electricity attacks all sorts of ministerial intrigue, borrowing from much of the anti-government propaganda of the era.[21] It presents a complicated picture of political shenanigans, the whole scene electrified by Bute as if in a political machine of corruption.

Many experiments in electricity during this era employed the method of chain reaction, so it would be easy to assume that the simple use of an electrical chain was Whitworth's effort to make his broadside express very contemporary knowledge. But it was more than this. Whitworth clarified for his readers that the electrical chain was made possible through the scientific achievement of none other than Benjamin Franklin. The broadside glosses its designs with "References." The opening design is glossed: "No. 1. Represents Ld B--e on ye Coast of France in ye Character of Doctor Franklin his Body ye Electrical Machine shaking Hands with ye Principal Nobles in France ye Chain is convey'd from ye Electrical Tube to ye P--ss of W--s, & from his Hand to ye Advice Frigate on ye Water between Dover & Calais, & from thence to ye D--e of G—n." This was not just any electrical machine. Whitworth identified it as a machine designed by Franklin. Bute, electrified by Franklin's machine, is shaking hands with French nobles, and the electrified chain connects him to the Princess of Wales, on one side, and the *Advice*, a frigate, on the other, extending beyond to the Duke of Grafton (fig. 1).[22] Clearly, Whitworth sought to include Franklin in the mix of characters cast actively in his broadside.

As his broadside entered circulation, Whitworth/Veridicus offered a companion piece providing background on the targets of his satire. In a letter published by Woodfall in the *Public Advertiser* on 24 February 1770, Whitworth/Veridicus addressed the Duke of Grafton, "the great Mover of the great Wheel of that Political Machine," castigating him for tearing down the Constitution and "mangl[ing] the shattered Remains of the Liberties of a Free People." Just as Burgh and Franklin were claiming in their "Colonist's Advocate" essays, Veridicus pointed out that all British dominions were in shambles, beginning with America. Whitworth/Veridicus wrote,

> Look to America, and behold, your unsettled, puny Authority alienating not only the Affections of the whole People of the Colonies, but divorcing that mutual Correspondence in the Trade which had subsisted between us, and for want of which the Manufactories of this Kingdom, if the Colonies persist in refusing to receive and take them off our Hands, must hang like a Mill-stone round the Neck of this Island; your Ignorance and Obstinacy has driven them to Industry, and their Industry will drive you to Poverty and Destruction.[23]

Figure 1. The first numbered design on the engraved broadside, *Political Electricity*, glossed as Lord Bute on the coast of France "in ye Character of Doctor Franklin his Body ye Electrical Machine." Veridicus [Richard Whitworth], *Political Electricity; or, An Historical & Prophetical Print in the Year 1770* (London, 1770). Engraving. Courtesy, Library Company of Philadelphia.

The position illustrated the unintended consequences of bad policy in North America: economic distress in England, especially in the manufacturing sector, and potential poverty for the population.

Whitworth/Veridicus then shifted to India, using a medicinal metaphor to elucidate the soporific effect of money spent on a confused social and political situation that would, in the end, conclude in disease. "Turn your Eyes to India," he wrote,

> and look back upon the unsettled State of those Possessions, still made a greater Heep of Confusion, by the patch'd up Compensation of last Year, in the sleepy Draught of £400,000 administered by the India Company. The Effect of such a Medicine will soon cease, and the Disorder of the Patient will break out into a Putrid Fever.[24]

Whitworth here referred to what has been called the Bengal Bubble or Great East Indian Crash of 1769, resulting from the overvaluation of East India Company stock at a time when British forces began to face retaliatory and hostile battles over areas already subjugated. The Crown bailed out the East

India Company, which was proving to be a drain on the treasury. Robert Clive and others associated with the original military expeditions in India grew wealthy from the speculation and profiteering taking place before 1769, and they thus continued to benefit, once the Crown stepped in to support the endeavor despite the failing economic market.

After identifying failed policy in North America and India, Whitworth pointed out the waste of Ireland, an unproductive possession because its Parliament had been filled with "the necessitous Pensioners of England." The situation of Ireland was brought up by Burgh and Franklin in the second of their Colonist's Advocate essays published in the *Public Advertiser* on 8 January 1770. The various Navigation Acts imposed on the American colonies worked like those imposed on Ireland—trade and production in the colonies were stifled in an effort to support manufacturing and trade in England. Absentee landlords drew off significant possibilities for Irish people by reducing hard currency there. Whitworth/Veridicus's use of scientific discourse—the language of medicine here and the electrical machinery in the broadside—suggest he had some interest in reading about scientific phenomena, even as it shows his cognizance of the language of pathology available in the Opposition press.

Whitworth/Veridicus's letter also spent a good deal of time on the dismissal of Camden, who almost alone in the cabinet at that time held firmly to a position of conciliation with the American colonies and in support of John Wilkes. Grafton had asked Camden about whether there was legal precedent to remove Wilkes from his elected seat and expel him from Parliament. Camden ended up fighting against the expulsion. On 9 January 1770, Chatham made a motion to oppose the government's policies, and Camden spoke in favor of the motion. George III, outraged, formally removed Camden, much to the relief of Grafton, on 17 January. Whitworth/Veridicus used these events as evidence of the heartless villainy of the government. "You had taken Care cruelly to discard L[or]d C[amde]n," he wrote, "the most faithful of his Majesty's Servants, for daring to be of an Opinion consistent with the known Laws of our Constitution, because he differed from that Doctrine you had all along professed." He concluded that the "legal Representatives of the People" have "become, under the Influence of your Administration, mere Cyphers." Throughout the attack, Whitworth/Veridicus pointed to the unrest of Britons in England, to their poverty, lack of food, and engineered elections. The whole country was in shambles, he insisted. He concluded by saying, "while the Nation is at War with itself," Britons should consider "whether our Enemies abroad are not taking Advantage of our Disturbances." The published letter is a penetrating example of the Opposition's attack on Grafton and the Bedford Whigs, to whom Grafton had shifted his alliances.

The themes Whitworth/Veridicus used in the letter are employed in his broadside, *Political Electricity*. In the broadside, he shifted the key blame for the problems in the political machine to Bute, but Grafton is likewise satirized, indicated by the electrical chain directly connecting the two. Bute was a common butt of political satire earlier in the decade. He was unpopular in America, but he was very unpopular in Britain because many conceived that he gave up too much when making the peace treaty with France at the conclusion of the Seven Years War. In the earlier 1760s, he acquiesced to the imposition of unpopular taxes such as the Cider Tax to cover the costs of the war, and many in Britain disliked his close relationship with George III.[25] Wilkes assaulted Bute in his *North Briton*, and, as George Goodwin notes, the "mob repeatedly targeted Bute's carriage in the street, pelting it with filth and smashing its windows."[26] Britons also might have believed the Opposition propaganda that suggested Bute was, behind the scenes, engaging in continued negotiations and accepting bribes from French ministers.[27] Whitworth/Veridicus made use of stories circulating around London that Bute and several others were in secret communication with French nobility. Indeed, conveniently, Bute was in France at the time the broadside appeared.[28]

But the broadside targets Grafton as well. Grafton's personal life was well-known, and Grafton became a popular target of ridicule in the Opposition press. In the broadside's design 4 (not pictured here), Grafton appeared "in ye Character of a Newmarket Jockey" and was betting on the political race, crying, "The odds are 219 to 137." The gloss offered among the "References" indicated much more than the design, however. According to the gloss, Grafton "has turn'd his Riding Filly Loose." This refers to Grafton's having dismissed his much-publicized lover, Ann "Nancy" Parsons, because he was marrying again. (He married Elizabeth Wrottesley in June 1769.) Grafton had just successfully sought and gained custody of the third of their three children with his first wife, Anne Liddell. He and the Duchess divorced in March 1769. She had had a prolonged affair with John FitzPatrick, second Earl of Upper Ossory. She was bearing his child, and she married him in 1769. In order to get Nancy Parsons out of the way of his second marriage, Grafton made her a financial settlement on condition that she should live abroad. Whitworth/Veridicus's broadside is thus one of many that make reference to Nancy Parsons, as a quick glance through Stephens and Hawkins's *Catalogue* series would attest. Junius published several letters belitting Grafton for his scandalous behavior with Parsons, first in taking her out to public events and then in dismissing her.[29]

Whitworth criticized the imbalance of political power in a central image at the top of the broadside, which extended across designs numbered 5, 6, and 7 (fig. 2). This complicated image features a scale on the top bar of which Grenville is shown lying on his belly (design 7), manipulating the scale

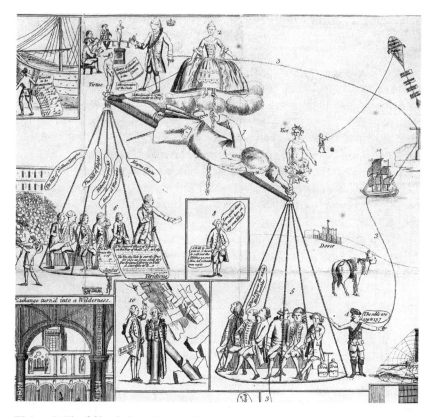

Figure 2. The fifth, sixth, and seventh numbered designs, the scale of "Virtue" and "Vice." Veridicus [Richard Whitworth], *Political Electricity; or, An Historical & Prophetical Print in the Year 1770* (London, 1770). Engraving. Courtesy, Library Company of Philadelphia.

with his hands. On one side is "Virtue" (design 6), which is outweighed by nearly twice the weight of itself, by "Vice" (design 5). "Virtue" (a nearly naked female figure) has on her side of the scale a group of men representing the Opposition. Whitworth used this set of designs to castigate the ministry ("Vice") by giving specific reference to British laws supported by the Opposition.

On the "Virtue" (design 6) side of the scale, the chains supporting the scale are labelled by the several bills and acts featured in Opposition propaganda (fig. 2). The supports are thus labeled "The Bill of Nullum Tempus," "The Bill of Rights," "Habeas Corpus Act," "General Warrants," and "Magna Charta."[30] According to Whitworth's key to "Virtue," this side of the scale includes key speakers in behalf of Opposition: "6 The Opposition Scale which has also Six Orators in it, Ed--- B---e Speaking 1, Wm D---ll 2, Coll. B--e 3, C. C---ll 4, Ld J. C---h 5, R. W---h 6. Ye Acts of Magna Charta against General Warrants, Habeas Corpus, ye Bill of Rights & ye Nullum Tempus Bill &c. are hung upon ye Scale Ropes to make Weight." The speakers thus referenced are Edmund Burke; William Dowdeswell (Chancellor of Exchequer under Chatham); Colonel Barré (Isaac Barré, a supporter of Chatham, sometimes taken to be Junius); Charles Cornwall (a highly reputed lawyer who, at this time, was in the Opposition); and Lord John Cavendish (a liberal MP for York). The sixth figure there, R- W—h, stood for Whitworth himself, MP for Stafford. Burke is delivering a speech, and in front him is a scroll, titled "The Injur'd Ghost of Liberty at the Bar of the H-- of C-- in 1769" and inscribed by Veridicus:

> Yes Yes, the Tale is surely True
> Or else no force cou'd do't
> For Britons Liberty to Fall
> A Sacrifice to B--e
> Veridicus

The poetic lines conform to the metrical system Whitworth employed in a "prophetical poem" included in another letter to the Duke of Grafton he published in the *Public Advertiser* on 12 June 1769. There, Whitworth/Veridicus offered a thirty-six stanza poem under the title used in the broadside. He introduced the poem by declaiming against "Laws . . . relaxed for vitiated Purposes" or "cruelly stretched beyond their Strength" and against a "whole System of Government . . . not consistent with the Genius of the People." Under such circumstances, "Law and Liberty . . . will for ever haunt the Place of it's Nativity in some Ghost-like Form or other," and thus liberty spoke at the bar of the House of Commons in 1769.[31] Whitworth was likely referencing a series of speeches by Edmund Burke in 1769 and early 1770, where Burke spoke for constitutional limits to the power and authority of the monarch and administration.

By intertwining his *Public Advertiser* letters with his broadside, Whitworth drew attention to his position as a key Opposition challenger of the administration. Indeed, Whitworth is recorded as having intervened in debates in Commons over one hundred times, most between 1768 and 1771.[32] My point about Whitworth's self-consciousness about his intervention in debates becomes more interesting in light of his life story, as we will see.

In the broadside, the scale's side of "Virtue" is outweighed nearly two to one by "Vice," design "5," a nearly naked man or Fury, surrounded by howling dogs (fig. 2). Notably, no laws or acts of Parliament are attached to the scales of vice. Instead, the dead weight of state (the Administration) is signified by moneybags of the treasury. Whitworth's gloss read,

> 5 The Great St--e Scales in which ye Ad--n are Weighing against ye Opposition in ye Right Hand Scale, ye Ballance of Power falls on ye Ad--n Side, in this Scale is Ld N--h 1, Sr Fl--r N---- 2, Mr Att—G--l De G--y 3, J--h D--n or Mungo 4, G—On--w 5 or Mulah Ishmael (alluding to an Indian Tale well known to some) Ld Cl--e 6, being some of ye Leaders in Ad--n. The Money from ye T---y in bags being put into ye Scale by way of Weights, ye Chain is convey'd through them.

Called out here are Lord North (First Lord of the Treasury and head of Administration in February 1770); Sir Fletcher Norton (Speaker of the House of Commons); Attorney General William De Grey (Lord Chief Justice of the Common Pleas); Jeremiah Dyson (a Lord of the Treasury); George Onslow (also a Lord of the Treasury, charged with having made fraudulent use of his position); and Lord Clive. The imbalance, featuring key administrators outweighing the side of virtue, features the cultural anxieties of the era. With the addition of colonies, the administration was growing, and with that growth came an enormous ability of the government to sway interests. Members of the different trading sectors (financiers, merchant contractors, and stock-jobbers) were, like placemen (treasury officials and those associated with colonial service), dependent on the goodwill and authority of the Crown for some of their livelihood.[33] The weight of "Vice" in the scale represents the Opposition's common critique of an Administration bloated with factotums who benefited from being paid to serve a corrupt government.

Another design worth investigating in light of Whitworth's critique of political corruption is number 11, "The Royal Exchange turn'd into a Wilderness" (fig. 3). This design reveals the inner courtyard of the Royal Exchange, London, now destitute of people and goods. Grass and other herbage have taken over. The design is described as "The Royal Exchange turn'd into a Wilderness & Notices for B---s & Seats in P---t to be Sold pasted up where Ships Voyages used to be Notified." The point is that boroughs and parliamentary seats were being marketed rather than goods. Stringent trade policies meant no ships were coming to port; instead, the overburdened administrative posts went out to the highest bidders. In the design, two of the pillars have notices that read: "Bor---s & Seats in P---t to be Sold Enq. at (the) Oxford Arms" and "Bor---s & Seats in P---t to be Sold Enq. at Blenheim." According to information offered by Stephens and Hawkins, "It was understood that Oxford and Oxfordshire were, in respect to parliamentary elections, dependent on influences centred at Blenheim,"

Figure 3. Design 11, "The Royal Exchange turn'd into a Wilderness," with "Notices for B---s & Seats in P---t to be Sold pasted up where Ships Voyages used to be Notified." Veridicus [Richard Whitworth], *Political Electricity; or, An Historical & Prophetical Print in the Year 1770* (London, 1770). Engraving. Courtesy, Library Company of Philadelphia.

which would help us understand better the particular placards Whitworth used.[34] As we will see, Stafford's elections were also engineered, and they went to the highest paying bidder in 1768.

Many other designs are worth exploring. The most important of the designs, in the context of this discussion, is the one relating to Britons in North America (fig. 4). In design 24, a design labeled "Boston," people are hewing trees, making cloth and clothes, tilling, grinding wheat or corn, and generally at labor, not standing still, talking. The lengthy gloss for this image relates to the industriousness of the colonists:

> The Coasts of America where ye Inhabitants are Industrious
> in every Art to provide themselves with ye Manufactures that
> Great Britain used to furnish them, being constrain'd & drove

Figure 4. Design 24 showing industrious Americans in Boston. Veridicus [Richard Whitworth], *Political Electricity; or, An Historical & Prophetical Print in the Year 1770* (London, 1770). Engraving. Courtesy, Library Company of Philadelphia.

> as it were to Industry, by ye late M[inisteria]l harsh Proceedings, in forcing ye Stamp & other Acts of Internal Taxes upon them contrary to ye true Spirit of British Policy, & which sooner or later this Kingdom will rue ye Imprudence of. The City of London transferr'd to Boston.

The gloss makes clear the point of the image, a point Whitworth/Veridicus made in his 24 February 1770 *Public Advertiser* letter to Grafton, as we have seen. It also calls up the representation of British American industriousness that Franklin often used, whether speaking with members of the Administration or before Privy Council or Commons, when writing his many letters to the press, and when writing to his American friends to offer advice as to the stances he wished they would pursue. Indeed, the whole scene reminds one of the representation Franklin gave of British Americans in his Examination before the Committee of the Whole of the House of Commons, 13 February 1766, which is given the largest credit in Parliament's vote to repeal the Stamp Act of 1765.

Richard Whitworth, MP

In their catalogue, Stephens and Hawkins pointed out that Whitworth was in the Opposition and an MP for Stafford, but they did not explore Whitworth's life any further. Likewise, Delbourgo, following Stephens and Hawkins, reported that Whitworth was an MP for Stafford who wrote for the Opposition. Neither source offered any further information about Whitworth's life and other writings. I find the life well worth investigating, partly to help elucidate Whitworth's print presence and partly to show the workings of the interest politics he critiqued prior to joining, under pay, the side of the Administration. Sources on Whitworth's life are quite scattered, but when pulled together, they present an intriguing picture of the political electricity of eighteenth-century England, a surprising but not-so-surprising image of interest politics of the era.[35] Whitworth's story is so much more than the tidy report that he was an Opposition MP for Stafford.

In c. 1734, Richard Whitworth was born in the parish of Adbaston, in Bathacre Grange (near Stafford), in Staffordshire, England.[36] The family had ancestral ties to Ireland, and, in the seventeenth century, an ancestor bought land there. Whitworth's education indicates he came from a family of some means, given that he attended Newport Grammar School, then Eton, then Trinity College, Cambridge, graduating in 1753. Whitworth's father died in 1748, while Richard was still at school. The trustees of the homestead, preparing it for young Whitworth's residence as a landed country gentleman, transformed the family's nondescript farmhouse to a rambling country estate. Whitworth came home, around 1756, to manage the large estate at Bathacre Grange, where he became landlord to several tenants in the area. The area was quite rural, without any major roadways leading to towns. To the north, in fact, it was cut off by Bishops Woods, which deprived Adbaston from access to any industrial towns to the north. To the south, a "new" road would be built around 1760 over an old Roman road. The region had been the seat of Augustinian monks, and the Bathacre Grange, along with the Ellerton, Flashbrooke, and Knighton granges, had been a large commons for running sheep for the monastery.

The relative isolation of the locale seems to have been an incentive to Whitworth to seek renovation in his community. He was interested in modernizing the region and making it more accessible for the purposes of trade and rural industries.[37] During the great move throughout England to build turnpikes, roadways, and canals, Whitworth endeavored to get his own roads and his neighbors' roads to a point where they would be more easily passable. In addition, he developed a strong fascination with inland navigation, and he caused a series of private canals to be constructed on his property. His efforts to show leadership in the community brought him, despite his youth or because of it, the post of High Sheriff of Stafford, 1758–59. He set up house at Stafford, then, and stayed there for about ten years.[38]

Among the improvements Whitworth sought in the 1760s was a new infirmary for the region.[39] New hospitals had been built in Manchester and Chester, and hospitals were underway, about this time, in Birmingham, Leicester, and Worcester. With others in Stafford, including Granville Leveson-Gower, second Earl Gower, Whitworth took part in the initial meetings for a hospital in Staffordshire in October 1765. To have been an initial subscriber means that Whitworth would have advanced a significant amount of money. Self-conscious governing, in Paul Langford's words, formed "the duties and pleasures" of becoming a subscriber to an infirmary. Further, such social amelioration was a very high priority for noblemen—thus explaining the presence of Earl Gower among the infirmary's leaders. "The patriarchal role ideally required of a magnate in his own neighborhood," Langford has said, "could be usefully exploited" by leaders to achieve respect and prestige in their locales.[40]

The group chose a board of trustees and officially set about establishing the Staffordshire General Infirmary. Among the hospital's first physicians was Dr. William Withering, a renowned physician drawn away from Birmingham to Staffordshire in 1765. In 1766, the hospital purchased an "electrical machine" for Dr. Withering, who used it for peripheral nerve stimulation. Withering would become known to Benjamin Franklin in succeeding years because he was consulted by Franklin and his friends in an effort to seek a cure for Franklin's bladder stones. Franklin consulted him in the 1780s.[41] Franklin knew many people from Staffordshire, including Josiah Wedgwood, so it is likely that he did come across Whitworth somewhere along the way, though no evidence exists in correspondence. The decision by the hospital trustees to purchase an electrical machine suggests that Whitworth's fascination with electricity, as exemplified by the broadside, was grounded in his experience.

As the hospital was getting established, Whitworth continued working on his canal project at the Bathacre Grange. Whitworth's interior location meant that goods, even just produce, had difficulty reaching markets. Improvements to waterways and canals could alleviate communication difficulties and increase the market share of inland towns. He conceived a huge project to link inland towns with port cities. Whitworth's scheme for inland navigation seems to have been ridiculed by local people like Wedgwood. But he nonetheless pursued his ideas and published in London a tract addressed to Gower, Chatham, and John Murray, third Duke of Atholl ("Lord Strange"), *The Advantages of Inland Navigation; Or, Some Observations offered to the Public to Shew That an Inland Navigation may be easily effected between the three great Ports of Bristol, Liverpool, and Hull; Together with a PLAN for executing the same.*[42] This ambitious scheme was never completed, though portions of it were plotted and completed.[43] Whitworth argues that his subject, canals, "ought to be the leading and principal system of all science" because "it is the very existence of society that creates trade and commerce, and the easier the communication, the greater the increase" in trade, communication, and population. The pamphlet fits squarely into the genre of writing that identifies improvements in the manners and culture of people with improvements in access to markets.[44] Whitworth eventually managed to manipulate the canals on his Bathacre lands, but he ran into legal tangles with his neighbors about issues of encroachment, egress, and water loss.[45]

Perhaps the combination of his growing authority as Sheriff of Stafford, his affinity for litigiousness, and his grand plans for canals and commerce contributed to Whitworth's decision to enter the public arena. But it seems that he began to view serving as an MP as a potentially lucrative opportunity as well. According to John Brooke, "Stafford was an expensive and difficult constituency, with an electorate composed mostly of tradesmen."[46] There were about 400 resident freemen who could vote. The fact that it was "expensive" meant that votes could be purchased but not cheaply. Whitworth was determined to win against the longtime favorite, William Richard Chetwynd, Viscount Chetwynd, who came from a powerful family, and Hugo Meynell, the man supported by Gower. In advance of the election, Whitworth seems to have been assured of winning. He wrote to an associate,

> My men continue very steady and I increase very greatly, everyone says I am sure to be first upon the poll, notwithstanding the high price my opponents give I have greatly the majority. . . . Many people wonder how I dare attack two such powerful men. I did at first wonder at it myself but my success has made me forget those thoughts. . . . I have carried the whole on at my own expense and paid my way, and I think about £900 or £1,000 will settle me there for life.[47]

As it turned out, Whitworth won by a margin of 15 over Chetwynd and 31 over Meynell. Thus, Whitworth bought his seat in the House of Commons in 1768. Early on, Whitworth voted with the Opposition, attended their collaborative dinners, and generally supported Opposition views. During this "political electricity" period in 1770, he was clearly in the Opposition.

But Whitworth began to show signs of wobbling. Horace Walpole wrote in his journal on 16 March 1772 of the debate in committee over the royal marriage bill that "Richard Whitworth, a necessitous member of the

Opposition, who had spoken against the bill, had now been bought off and spoke for it."[48] By February 1773, he was classed in the King's list (kept by North) as a friend.[49] During debates in Commons between 1774 and 1780, Whitworth regularly supported Administration causes. By 1779, he was receiving a secret service pension from North. According to John Brooke's entry on him in *The History of Parliament*, Whitworth seemed anxious about an invasion in England by France. In 1779,

> He recommended erecting beacons immediately round the coast, and teaching people to prepare for an invasion. He also advised every gentleman to direct each of his tenants to provide one man, and arm him, in order to have an immediate local defence throughout the country.[50]

Whitworth followed his own advice and made costly renovations to his home, renovations that fortified the residence and surrounding grounds. Records at court indicate that he was paid by the Administration £700 for "expenses," but he failed badly during the 1780 election. Whitworth was on North's list of pensions as taking £600 per year. He was in 1784 given a bond of £400.[51]

Today, Whitworth might have been called an Independent in Commons, given the range of measures he voted for and against. Yet it seems as if his whole project of joining the Opposition so vociferously might have been a self-conscious design to gain the financial backing and political support of the Crown. In his 1770 broadside, he complained that seats in Parliament were bought and sold at will. But he had bought his own seat—by buying votes in Stafford—in 1768. Within two years of the broadside's publication, Whitworth allowed his voice in Commons, along with his vote, to be bought. By then, he had developed a hankering after lands in North America. Whitworth was evidently one of the many different political leaders whom Robert Rogers met with when he came to London in 1769. After the Seven Years War, Rogers had gained, perhaps with Franklin's assistance, the direction of the fort at Michilimackinac. He surveyed the area and reported in 1767 that Michilimackinac ought to become a separate state. Rogers was accused of treason in 1768, because he was attempting dealings, for his own part, with the French in Canada. He was bombarded by creditors wherever he went, so he returned to London in 1769 with a handful of petitions and memorials for support for different endeavors.

Rogers must have met with Whitworth, and Whitworth developed land fever. By 1774, Whitworth had full support of the Administration and was attempting to use his position in Parliament to learn more about North America and to fund and find support for his own efforts to gain a series of royal grants for lands, mining, and perhaps even a distillery, in North

America. Whitworth was working toward a grand scheme, devised and established with Jonathan Carver and with Rogers, to persuade Parliament to fund an expedition to find a Northwest Passage in North America. From Carver's and Rogers's surviving letters, we learn that Whitworth himself had planned to take part in the expedition until he perceived that colonial agitation would interfere with such a plan. If his plans to seek a royal grant of lands for the areas now called the upper Mississippi riverine region and western Great Lakes, he would have come up against a competing plan from 1769 fostered by Franklin's friend, Samuel Wharton, initially called the Indiana Company, then the Vandalia Company, and then the Walpole Company, after Thomas Walpole, a leading political figure and one of its sponsors.[52] Several different groups in North America were competing for the lands in the upper Midwest, starting with the Virginians (in the late 1740s) forming the Ohio Company in the same area that had interested Franklin. Few considered the lands beyond Ohio as having any reliable potential.[53]

Working behind the scenes, Whitworth, Rogers, and later Carver hoped to bypass the competing and politicized claims and run their own expedition under royal charter, for Great Britain. I surmise that in an effort to sponsor his own land schemes between the years 1770 and 1773, Whitworth shifted his alliances to the government. It is possible that as early as 1770, Whitworth was pensioned by Lord North to become part of the same spy network that worked against Franklin and included Edward Bancroft.[54] Whitworth's name does not come up in Franklin's papers, but Bancroft's does, of course. Did Franklin learn about the scheme of Robert Rogers, Jonathan Carver, and Richard Whitworth? The answer to that question remains unresolved. We do know that Robert Rogers arrived in London in September 1769, to discuss his existing grant of lands to the south of present-day Lake Superior. Rogers's active pursuit of support from individuals coincided with Whitworth's decision to pursue land acquisition, and the two teamed up, adding in Jonathan Carver in 1773, to seek a royal grant.[55] Whitworth's efforts came to nothing. He had no money. He was not returned to Parliament in 1780, and, in leaving Parliament, he lost his Crown pension. He was always reported to have been mercurial and a bit odd, but after he returned to Bathacre, he became cantankerous. He created a series of legal disputes with his neighbors, which made him decide he needed to continue to fortify his home, this time making an arsenal and Martello tower. Locals thought he was very odd; they called his home Castle Whitworth. Whitworth died a lonely man in 1811.[56]

What is Liberty?

What can we make of a significant Opposition supporter turning to the side of the Administration? The Opposition rhetoric of ancient rights as Britons, constitutional rights after the Glorious Revolution, and individual rights against an encroaching monarchy—all of these matters and more entered the political stream and became factors in Americans' self-conscious setting up of their new government. They are featured in key documents associated with the American system. Likewise, these ideals inform the ideology of Britons, then and now.

Whitworth had been a superior spokesperson for these ideals and against political corruption. It is possible that once Whitworth got to London, he could see the way the Crown was operating and wanted to have the opportunity to gain a lucrative income, as well, because his plans for improvements at Bathacre had become too costly. It is also possible that, from this distance in time, it is difficult to understand the shifting political scene, a scene electrified by opportunities in many quarters. Just as Richard Whitworth sought a piece of a land deal in the Michilimackinac, so Benjamin Franklin sought a way to profit from opportunities made possible by his position in government and the friendships he had established with men in high station. Franklin's project—part of which included the ouster of Wills Hill, Lord Hillsborough, Secretary of State for the Colonies—had a much higher chance of success than Whitworth's. But both men were seeking to gain from speculation in American lands.

It is difficult to reconcile Franklin's and Whitworth's very vocal support of liberties and constitutional rights in light of their efforts to establish for themselves significant power and personal property in western lands. Clarence Alvord long ago observed that "[b]old speculation was one of the characteristics of the eighteenth century;" yet even this statement makes it difficult to reconcile, for instance, Benjamin Franklin's willingness to consort with leading members of the Administration in making the effort to secure a share in the Walpole Company.[57] Perhaps this is an instance of Mandevillean "private vices, public benefits" thinking.

Finally, it is worth acknowledging that both Richard Whitworth and Benjamin Franklin were deeply concerned about civic matters, technological and environmental improvements, and scientific inquiry. Both men showed, early on, very clear goals of supporting projects that would assist other people. They helped develop and invest in roads projects, canals, and communication systems. They developed plans for and sat on boards for hospitals in their districts. They were committed to seeing what medical benefits might arise from the use of electrical current to damaged limbs. At this crucial moment in Britain's history, both men pursued a set of conflicting projects, some that would benefit many others and one that could benefit themselves. Perhaps, in the longest run, each conceived that personal political liberty was best represented by the freedom to take advantage of whatever opportunities presented themselves along the way. If this is so, then the satire effected in Whitworth's broadside importantly shows the extent to which political action, even in behalf of liberty, can be empty of moral justice. Such a conclusion might say as much about politics then as now.

NOTES

1. Frederic George Stephens and Edward Hawkins, *Catalogue of Prints and Drawings in the British Museum*, Division I: Political and Personal Satires, 11 vols. (London: By Order of the Trustees, 1870–1954), 4: xxiv, xxv.

2. Stephens and Hawkins, *Catalogue*, xlviii.

3. James Delbourgo, *A Most Amazing Scene of Wonders: Electricity and Enlightenment in Early America* (Cambridge and London: Harvard Univ. Press, 2006), 160–63, 160.

4. For background on the political turmoil, see John Brewer, *Party Ideology and Popular Politics at the Accession of George III* (Cambridge: Cambridge Univ. Press, 1976).

5. For a more complete discussion of these matters, see Carla J. Mulford, *Benjamin Franklin and the Ends of Empire* (New York: Oxford Univ. Press, 2015), 183–273. See for additional background, Alison Gilbert Olson, *Making the Empire Work: London and American Interest Groups, 1690–1790* (Cambridge, MA, and London: Harvard Univ. Press, 1992).

6. For background on the situation in India, see Mulford, *Benjamin Franklin*, 239–60. See also P.J. Marshall, *The Making and Unmaking of Empire: Britain, India, and America, c. 1750–1783* (Oxford: Oxford Univ. Press, 2005) and David Washbrook, "The Indian Economy and the British Empire," in *India and the British Empire*, ed. Douglas Peers and Nandini Gooptu (Oxford: Oxford Univ. Press, 2012), 44–74.

7. See Mulford, *Benjamin Franklin*, 234–54. See also Thomas Bartlett, "Opposition in Late Eighteenth-Century Ireland: The Case of the Townshend Viceroyalty," *Irish Historical Studies* 22, no. 88 (1981), 313–30.

8. On the political situation as it relates to the Falklands and Corsica, see Jeremy Black, *Parliament and Foreign Policy in the Eighteenth Century* (Cambridge: Cambridge Univ. Press, 2004), 99–136, especially 103–104. See Geoffrey W. Rice for a useful examination of the Falklands situation: "British Foreign Policy and the Falkland Islands Crisis, 1770–1," *International History Review* 32 (2010), 273–305.

9. Edmund Burke, *Thoughts on the Cause of the Present Discontents* (London: J. Dodsley, 1770). The best recent discussion of Burke is Richard Bourke, *Empire and Revolution: The Political Life of Edmund Burke* (Princeton, NJ and Oxford: Princeton Univ. Press, 2015); see especially 257–67.

10. Brewer, *Party Ideology*, 245–57, quotations at 245, 246.

11. Brewer, 163–200, quotation at 164.

12. A useful background study of popular protests is Charles Tilly, *Popular Contention in Great Britain, 1758–1834* (1995; New York: Routledge, 2005). For the St. George's Fields discussion, see 154–57. It is worth noting here that, for his part, Benjamin Franklin—even though he was deeply concerned about the political issues Wilkes represented—felt dubious about the "Wilkes and Liberty" movement. He was not a Wilkesite and did not favor popular protests like that at St. George's Fields.

13. See William C. Lowe, "The House of Lords, Party, and Public Opinion: Opposition Use of the Protest, 1760–1782," *Albion* 11 (1979), 143–56, 144.

14. See Peter D. G. Thomas, "The Beginning of Parliamentary Reporting in Newspapers, 1768–1774," *English Historical Review* 74 (1959), 623–36, and Hannah Barker, *Newspapers, Politics, and Public Opinion in Late Eighteenth-Century England* (Oxford: Clarendon Press, 1998).

15. See John Cannon, ed., *The Letters of Junius* (Oxford: Clarendon Press, 1978), 539–72.

16. Richard Whitworth's "Veridicus" letters in the *Public Advertiser* appeared on the following dates: 6 September 1764; 24 April 1769; 12 June 1769; 9 February 1770; 24 February 1770; 21 December 1778; 21 October 1785. In 1769, "Veridicus" grew so popular that his letters drew rebuttals and ridicule in several pieces also printed in the *Public Advertiser* in May and then in September.

17. "Junius" wrote to Woodfall, "Your Veridicus is Mr. Whitworth. I assure you I have not confided in him." See *The Letters of Junius*, ed. John Cannon (Oxford: Oxford Univ. Press, 1978), 353.

18. The series of eleven essays were published on the following dates: January 4, 8, 11, 15, 25, 29; February 1, 5, 12, 19; March 2, 1770. See Mulford, 233–5. See also Carla H. Hay, "Benjamin Franklin, James Burgh, and the Authorship of 'The Colonist's Advocate' Letters," *William and Mary Quarterly*, 3d ser., 32 (1975), 111–24.

19. Stephens and Hawkins, xxv.

20. Stephens and Hawkins, xxv.

21. The cross references offered by Stephens and Hawkins throughout their entry on this broadside show the extent to which Whitworth was employing key Opposition complaints in his work.

22. HMS *Advice* was a fifty-gun, fourth-rate ship launched in 1745 but broken up (taken out of service and dismantled) in 1756. For background on the *Advice*, see Brian Lavery, *The Ship of the Line, vol. 1, The Development of the Battlefleet, 1650–1850* (London: Conway Maritime Press, 2003), 172. Given that HMS *Advice* was broken up in 1756, it would not have been in existence at the time the broadside appeared. For background on the Georgian fleet, see N.A.M. Rodger, *The Wooden*

World: An Anatomy of the Georgian Navy (Annapolis, MD: Naval Institute Press, 1986). My thanks to Dennis Baird, Jon Bryant, Alexandre Dubé, Jack Fryar, Sally Hadden, David Rawson, and Tom Southall, for answering my online "Eighteenth-Century Questions" query about shipping matters on 10 May 2018.

23. *Public Advertiser*, 24 February 1770, 1–2, 1. See Stephens and Hawkins, 652.

24. *Public Advertiser*, 24 February 1770, 1–2, 1.

25. George Goodwin provides an interesting analysis of Bute's relationship with George III in *Benjamin Franklin in London: The British Life of America's Founding Father* (New Haven: Yale Univ. Press, 2016), 133–65.

26. George Goodwin, 156.

27. See Stephens and Hawkins, 649.

28. For the information that Bute was in France, see Stephens and Hawkins, 649.

29. See the *Public Advertiser* for 30 May, 12 June, and 22 June 1769. Junius made additional references to Grafton's treatment of Parsons in 1771 and later. The letters are available in *The Letters of Junius*.

30. "The Bill of Nullum Tempus" refers to the Crown Suits Act of 1769, which in effect allowed individuals to evict longstanding tenants who formerly, by using the land for over sixty years, would have been able to claim ownership according to use. "The Bill of Rights," "Habeas Corpus Act," and "Magna Charta" relate to laws dating to the accession of William and Mary in 1689. The Bill of Rights allowed for basic civil rights to be granted to all Britons. It laid out limitations on the power of the monarch, among other things. The passage of the Bill of Rights of 1689 was accompanied by other bills, the Habeas Corpus Act, Magna Carta, and the Petition of Right, all of which supported the personal liberties enshrined in British common practice. "General Warrants" refers to the writs of assistance that were being used to evict people from land that they had been occupying. Writs of assistance for general search warrants were being used in North America in the 1760s to enable the examination and taking of personal property by British officials.

31. Letter to the *Public Advertiser*, 12 June 1769, 1–2, 2.

32. John Brooke, "Richard Whitworth," in *The History of Parliament: the House of Commons 1754–1790*, 3 vols., ed. Lewis Namier and John Brooke (London: Secker and Warburg for the History of Parliament Trust, 1964), 3: 634–5. The entry is available online at <*http://www.historyofparliamentonline.org/volume/1754–1790/member/whitworth-richard-1734–1811*>; accessed 11 May 2018.

33. Brewer, 250.

34. Stephens and Hawkins, 653.

35. Richard Whitworth's story has been told in different pieces in a number of different venues. A good but very spotty biography based on local and family papers appeared in S.A.H. Burne, "Presidential Address," *Transactions of the North Staffordshire Field Club*, vol. 62 (1928), 15–59. Whitworth begins at page 20. Burne did not treat Whitworth's hospital support, his parliamentary career, or his effort to secure a land grant and fund an expedition in North America. No one before now has compiled the several different sources into one narrative.

36. For the refinement on the point of Adbaston and not Stafford, reported in other sources, see Burne, 20. Information in this paragraph is drawn from Burne, 20–36, especially 22, 25.

37. For background on the economic impact of the modernizing of roadways during this era, see Dan Bogart, "Turnpike Trusts and Property Income: New Evidence on the Effects of Transport Improvements and Legislation in Eighteenth-Century England," *Economic History Review*, n.s. 62 (2009), 128–52.

38. Burne, 26–27.

39. For background on Whitworth's role with the hospital, see J. MacD. Holmes, "Bicentenary of the Staffordshire General Infirmary," *British Medical Journal* 2, no. 5521 (29 October 1966), 1064–65.

40. Paul Langford, *Public Life and the Propertied Englishman, 1689–1798* (Oxford: Clarendon Press, 1991), 490–500 and 558–69, 496, 561.

41. When Franklin fell ill from bladder stones, William Vaughan reached out to William Withering sometime in 1782, and Withering returned to him an essay, "On Calculus Complaints." Franklin's problem continued. On 1 March 1784, he sent Withering a case history of his ailments; a brief correspondence ensued. See *The Papers of Benjamin Franklin*, 42 vols. thus far, ed. Leonard W. Labaree, et al. (New Haven: Yale Univ. Press, 1959–), 38: 39–41, and 42: 5–6, 148–50.

42. R. Whitworth, *The Advantages of Inland Navigation; Or, Some Observations offered to the Public to Shew That an Inland Navigation may be easily effected between the three great Ports of Bristol, Liverpool, and Hull; Together with a PLAN for executing the same.* (London: Baldwin, 1766). Here we must not confuse Richard Whitworth with his much more famous distant relative, Robert Whitworth, an esteemed canal designer and builder. This particular pamphlet is known to have been Richard Whitworth's work.

43. Burne discusses Whitworth's plans and even his boat-building, 31–35.

44. For background on the idea of cultural benefits of commerce, see Paul Langford, *A Polite and Commercial People, 1727–1783* (NY: Oxford Univ. Press, 1994). But see also a more recent analysis based in economic history by Sophus A. Reinert, *Translating Empire: Emulation and the Origins of Political Economy* (Cambridge and London: Harvard Univ. Press, 2011), especially 72–128.

45. Burne, 34–36.

46. John Brooke, "Stafford," in *The History of Parliament: the House of Commons 1754–1790*, 3 vols., ed. Lewis Namier and John Brooke (London: Secker and Warburg for the History of Parliament Trust, 1964), 1: 375. Available online at <http://www.historyofparliamentonline.org/volume/1754–1790/constituencies/stafford>; accessed 11 May 2018.

47. Quoted in John Brooke's entry for Richard Whitworth in *The History of Parliament*, 3: 634. Available online at <http://www.historyofparliamentonline.org/volume/1754–1790/member/whitworth-richard-1734–1811>; accessed May 11, 2018.

48. Horace Walpole, *The Last Journals of Horace Walpole during the Reign of George III*, 2 vols., ed. A. Francis Steuart (London and New York: John Lane, 1910), 1: 54.

49. For details, see Brooke, "Whitworth" in *The History of Parliament*, 3: 635.

50. See Brooke's entry for Whitworth in *The History of Parliament*, 3: 634.

51. The accounts are part of the discussion by Brooke, *The History of Parliament*, 3: 635.

52. A detailed discussion of this project in light of the situation in the Ministry appears in Jack M. Sosin, *Whitehall and the Wilderness: The Middle West in British Colonial Policy, 1760–1775* (Lincoln: Univ. of Nebraska Press, 1961), 181–210.

53. The view at court probably derived from communications from Thomas Gage, who believed that forts and settlements in Indian country were, as Clarence Alvord phrased it long ago, "of little value either as centers of commerce or as protection against Indian attacks." See Alvord, *The Mississippi Valley in British Politics*, 2 vols. (New York: Russell and Russell, 1959), 2: 47–51, 48.

54. Information in this paragraph is derived from several pieces in an occasional publication of the Clements Library at the Univ. of Michigan, including the following: John Parker, "New Light on Jonathan Carver" (4–18); John C. Dann, "Northwest Passage Revisited, a Collection of New Documents on Robert Rogers' Northwest Passage Expedition" (19–35); Daniel E. Moerman, "'Herbs, Plants, and Shrubs that Possess Uncommon Virtues': Remarkable Letter of Robert Rogers on the Dyes and Medicines of the American Indian" (36–44); and David Bosse, "The Maps of Robert Rogers and Jonathan Carver: Analysis, and Annotated, Selective Bibliography" (45–61). These articles form the *American Magazine and Historical Chronicle, Published for the Edification and Amusement of Book Collectors, Historians, Bibliographers and the Discriminating General Public* 2, no. 1 (Spring/Summer 1986). This reliable, ephemeral publication is available here: <*http://clements.umich. edu/AmericanMagazine/AmericanMagazine_v2no1_SpringSummer,%201986.pdf*>. My thanks to Jayne Ptolemy, Clements Library, University of Michigan, for assisting me with my inquiries about the Whitworth archive.

55. For background on Whitworth's plans in North America, see John C. Dann, "Northwest Passages Revisited."

56. See Burne, 38–44.

57. Alvord, *The Mississippi Valley in British Politics*, 1: 86.

MANUSCRIPT COMMUNICATIONS

Learned and Sociable Manuscript Circulation

Panel Introduction: Learned and Sociable Manuscript Circulation

COLIN T. RAMSEY

Early in his *Autobiography*, Benjamin Franklin remarks that "prose writing has been of great Use to me in the Course of my Life, and was a principal Means of my Advancement."[1] Consistent with this claim, the modern literary study of Franklin overwhelmingly focuses on his prose, beginning with the teenaged satirical essays he published in the *New England Courant* under the pseudonym "Silence Dogood" and continuing all the way to the above referenced *Autobiography*, a text that was only printed posthumously but which is now Franklin's most widely anthologized work.[2]

Notably, the earliest writing by Franklin for which we have any record is poetry, not prose. In the *Autobiography*, Franklin describes writing some doggerel "in the Grub Street style" as a teenager—work that his brother James apparently printed as broadsides so that Franklin could sell them in the streets of Boston—but, we know that Franklin was writing poetry as early as age seven.[3] Franklin's father Josiah was so impressed by his young son's verse that he mailed some of the poems to Franklin's namesake uncle—the family's most committed poet—who was then still living in England. Franklin's uncle Benjamin was likewise impressed, as is evident from his poem in reply to his nephew that includes verses full of praise and encouragement: "Go on, My Name, and be progressive still/Till Thou Excell Great Cocker with Thy

51

Quill."[4] As is suggested by this particular exchange of verse, there was a tradition in the Franklin family of writing poetry, though most of this poetry circulated only in manuscript copies, a fairly common way of sharing verse among Puritan poets around the British Atlantic. That is, the bulk of the poetry produced by members of the Franklin family, a body of work that included playful and sometimes visually striking anagrams and acrostics, as well as serious poems of religious devotion, moral advice, and offerings of consolation and remembrance upon sad occasions, were almost never written with any plan for the works to see print.

Nevertheless, it is a mistake to think of the Franklins's manuscript poetry as always and completely unpublished: instead, such poems were read, copied, and exchanged within a concentrically expansive coterie of family, friends, and acquaintances, a practice that very much resembles the more well-known mode of scribal publication used by some of the most highly regarded poets of early modern Britain, writers such as Philip Sidney, John Donne, and George Herbert.[5] Indeed, manuscript circulation continued to be an important medium through which writers all around the British Atlantic could and often did choose for a wide variety of written communications even through the eighteenth century.[6]

Franklin's most famous poetic work now is likely his "Epitaph," a text that he seems to have composed while a relatively young man, circa 1728, but that he continued to rewrite often during the course of his life. In the poem, Franklin adapts what was then a reasonably well-known metaphoric conceit comparing the body after death to an old book, refocusing the conceit so as to explore authorship, the complex relations between text and book, and, of course, body and soul:

> The Body of B. Franklin,
> Printer,
> Like the Cover of an old Book,
> Its Contents torn out,
> And Stript of its Lettering and Gilding,
> Lies here, Food for Worms.
> But the Work shall not be wholly lost,
> For it will, as he believes, appear once more,
> In a new and more perfect Edition,
> Corrected and amended,
> By the Author.
> He was born Jan 6. 1706.
> Died 17_[7]

Visitors to Franklin's grave in Philadelphia, however, may be surprised to discover that no such epitaph appears on his tombstone: the marker instead simply records Franklin's name and that of his wife, Deborah, and the year of Franklin's death, 1790. But, the absence of the above "Epitaph" from Franklin's actual grave is less surprising if we bear in mind the uses to which Franklin put his poetic epitaph during his life. His practice was to write out copies from memory at social gatherings—making small changes here and there as his mood and memory might dictate—and then to give those manuscript copies to the guests in attendance as keepsakes; some recipients even went on to write out additional copies to give to others, with Franklin's blessing.[8]

If Franklin's behavior seems in strange taste, perhaps even a little macabre, that is partly because we are insensitive to the literary and social traditions both his poem and his circulation practices were comically refracting: as I note above, a tradition of circulating poetry in manuscript was common all around the early modern British Atlantic; additionally, the poem's form, an "Epitaph," recalls the special zeal for elegiac and funereal verse that developed in Puritan New England over the course of the seventeenth century. At funeral services, for instance, family and friends of the deceased would often attach poems of sad remembrance directly to the caskets as the cortege passed—poems they had composed specifically for the purpose—and additional elegies were often composed and sent by friends from further afield, some of which were printed as broadsides for even wider circulation around the community.[9]

Indeed, the composition of elegies had become so popular by the beginning of the eighteenth century that they were sometimes written for individuals who were still alive, and those individuals would, on occasion, receive copies, which they seem to have read with pleasure.[10] Franklin undoubtedly saw many such elegies growing up in Boston, and he was familiar enough with the form by the time he was a teenager that he was able to satirize it in one of the comic letters he submitted surreptitiously to the *New-England Courant*, the newspaper produced by his older brother James Franklin. This series of essays is now commonly known as the "Silence Dogood Letters," after the punning pseudonym Franklin used to disguise his authorship, and in "Dogood Number 7," which appeared the *Courant* for the week of 25 June 1722, Franklin wickedly mocked the popularity of elegies in New England, deeming such poems almost always "wretchedly Dull and Ridiculous."[11] Others of James Franklin's stable of satiric writers—a group known as "Couranteers"—similarly lampooned Puritan funereal verse. For instance, in a letter signed by a "Hypercriticus" that appeared in the issue of the *Courant* for the week beginning 5 November of that same year, the pseudonymous author derides the genre as highly silly and embarrassing: "I find the *Funeral Elegy* to be the most universally admir'd and used in

New England. There is scarce a Plow-Jogger or a Country Cobler that has read our Psalms, and can make two Lines jingle, who has not once in his Life, at least, exercised his Talent this way. Nor is there one Country House in Fifty which has not its Walls garnished with half a Score of these Sort of Poems (if they may be so call'd)."[12]

The content and circulation of Franklin's "Epitaph" marks a combination of material ephemerality and personal intimacy that was common to Puritan elegies, while it also comically refracts their public nature and social function, displayed as they were for all to see and read as part of communal rituals of death and mourning. Similarly striking combinations of ephemerality and public significance are likewise central concerns of all of the essays included below. Each essay was developed from a paper presented during one of two sessions entitled "Publicity and Publics: Manuscript and Print Circulation for Instruction and Pleasure" that were sponsored by the Society for the History of Authorship, Reading, and Publishing at the 2017 ASECS annual conference.

The first essay, "Exhibitions of Manuscript Verse in the Salon du Louvre," by Ryan Whyte, analyzes some manuscript poetry of eighteenth-century France that was no less public and yet was even more ephemeral than the Puritan funeral elegies. Whyte's essay focuses on the brief manuscript poems that were frequently pinned up alongside works of painting and sculpture in the great art salons at the Louvre palace in eighteenth-century Paris. Such poems now only survive in printed texts that commented on the art on display at the Salons after they were concluded—early bodies of written art criticism. Whyte convincingly argues that in their uniformly laudatory content such poems invoked an older form of aristocratic patronage that had traditionally supported the production of art. Salon poems were performative and participatory, and, Whyte argues, they ultimately demonstrate the complexity of the interrelations between artistic and written media and the cultural and social tensions that typified the Salon during the period.

The second essay, "Scribal Publication of Elizabeth Graeme Fergusson's Commonplace Books," by Chiara Cillerai, uncovers the expansive patterns of discourse found in Fergusson's manuscript commonplace books. Cillerai argues that Fergusson fashioned a highly unusual form of common-placing that helped her to realize a kaleidoscopic array of often self-interrogating objectives. Much of her commonplace writing was, "deeply interior and intimate," while, simultaneously, it allowed her imaginatively to recreate and re-experience the quasi-public physical spaces and social interactions of the literary salons that she had enjoyed earlier in her life. And, finally, Fergusson seems to have used common-placing for a kind of literary self-critique, to generate a kind of continuous dialogue with herself about the poetry she was inscribing within those same commonplace books, poetry that she also sometimes shared with other readers.

The final essay, "Correspondence between Benjamin Franklin and Johann Karl Philipp Spener on the American Revolution," by Jürgen Overhoff, returns us to Benjamin Franklin. Overhoff carefully analyzes the interplay of manuscript and print media as they formed a series of recursive stages that led to the popularization of Franklin's thought in Germany and France, and that positioned Franklin's philosophical and political writing within a Kantian conception of Enlightenment. Overhoff details the web of connections that brought Franklin to the attention of the printer and publisher Johann Karl Philipp Spener, who had earlier printed Kant's essay "What is Enlightenment?" Spener and his friend the French printer Jean-Georges Treuttel eventually began to petition Franklin by letter to provide them with his thoughts on a variety of subjects related to the American Revolution: this, they felt certain, would offer the best, most direct understanding of Franklin's views possible. As Overhoff argues, were it not for these letters and Franklin's willingness to provide replies, also in quickly written letters, that revealed his latest views on American political philosophy, the subsequent printed books in German based on those views would likely never have existed, and, thus, readers in Germany would have failed to understand both Franklin's thought, and, more broadly, the ideas that drove the American Revolution. Overhoff thus concludes that the exchange of letters which he outlines constitutes an important example of the transnational Republic of Letters, and that the exchange fundamentally shaped the way that the American Revolution was understood in Germany for much of the following century.

NOTES

1. Benjamin Franklin, *Benjamin Franklin's Autobiography*, ed. J. A. Leo Lemay and P. M. Zall (New York: Norton, 1986), 10.

2. James Green and Peter Stallybrass, *Benjamin Franklin: Writer and Printer* (New York: Oak Knoll Press, 2006) 3–4. Green and Stallybrass note that Franklin's own criticism of his skills as a poet tends to obscure the fact his first writing to appear in print was ballad poetry commissioned by his brother James.

3. Franklin, *Autobiography*, 10.

4. *The Papers of Benjamin Franklin*, ed. Leonard W. Labaree, vol. 1, 6 January 1706 through 31 December 1734 (New Haven: Yale Univ. Press, 1960), 5.

5. Harold Love, *Scribal Publication in Seventeenth-Century England* (Oxford: Clarendon Press of Oxford Univ. Press, 1993). See also Arthur Marotti, *Manuscript,*

Print, and the English Renaissance Lyric (Ithaca and London: Cornell Univ. Press, 1995).

6. David S. Shields, "The Manuscript in the British American World of Print," *Proceedings of the American Antiquarian Society* 102 (1993): 403–16.

7. Labaree, *Papers*, 111.

8. Labree, 110. At least three copies in Franklin's autograph have survived to the present day, and numerous additional copies in the hands of others are likewise extant.

9. David E. Stannard, *The Puritan Way of Death: A Study in Religion, Culture, and Social Change* (New York: Oxford Univ. Press, 1977). Ola Elizabeth Winslow, *American Broadside Verse: From Imprints of the 17th & 18th Centuries* (New Haven: Yale Univ. Press, 1930), xix.

10. David S. Shields, *Civil Tongues and Polite Letters in British America* (Chapel Hill: Univ. of North Carolina Press, 1997), xxvi, 219–21. Shields interrogates what he calls the "hidebound dichotomies" between, among other binaries, "public and private," especially when seen as equivalent to texts-in-print and texts-in-manuscript. The portion of Shields's analysis most relevant to the above discussion concerns the poetic elegies that became popular at Harvard in the late seventeenth century, and all surviving examples of such poems were printed. As Shields notes, a good deal more such verse was likely written and circulated both in manuscript and print.

11. Benjamin Franklin [Silence Dogood, pseud.], *"To the Author of the* New-England Courant [No. VII]," *New-England Courant*, 25 June 1722. All of Franklin's so-called "Silence Dogood Letters" have been reprinted widely; for especially well edited versions, consult *The Papers of Benjamin Franklin*, vol. 1.

12. Hypercriticus [pseud.], *"To the Author of the* New-England Courant," *New-England Courant*, 5 November 1722. The author of this letter has not been identified definitively, though Leo Lemay argues that Nathaniel Gardner used the pseudonym in another letter to the *Courant* on a different subject. See J. A. Leo Lemay, *The Life of Benjamin Franklin*, Volume 1 Journalist, 1706–1730 (Philadelphia: Univ. of Pennsylvania Press, 2006), 463.

Exhibitions of Manuscript Verse in the Salon du Louvre

RYAN WHYTE

In the eighteenth century, spectators placed hand-written poems on or beside artworks in the Paris Salon du Louvre. Overlooked in the history of exhibition practice, this unofficial spectatorial response to art physically intruded on a space where only members of the Académie royale de peinture et de sculpture were allowed to exhibit their work. The jurisdiction of the Académie over every aspect of the Salon, including the policing of its space by the Bourbon monarch's Swiss guards, is a precedent for the top-down model of curatorial control, channeling of spectatorial movement, and regulation of spectatorial behavior that characterizes modern exhibition practice. Yet, manuscript verse reveals how art exhibitions in the ancien régime were in certain respects more participatory, and, from a modern perspective, more strange than their modern inheritors.

This essay situates manuscript verse within the complex media ecosystem of the Salon. Like the information society that Robert Darnton describes in his famous article on eighteenth-century Parisian news media, in which news circulated simultaneously in oral, manuscript, and print forms, the Salon encompassed different artistic and communications media associated with overlapping social practices and cultural spheres.[1] Combinations of media, including manuscript, served different social groups there in distinct and sometimes contradictory ways. To understand the operation of media in the Salon is to grasp their interrelations.

This essay argues that interactions between artistic and communications media corresponded to social and cultural tensions in the Salon. First, this essay contextualizes manuscript verse with respect to the range of poetry about art in the Salon, including encomiastic verse and print verse. Second, this essay traces the genealogy of manuscript verse in period poetic genres and practices, notably verse for portraits and impromptu verse. Third, this essay locates manuscript verse at the intersection of competing interests in the Salon, where absolutist, aristocratic, and popular rhetorics entwined; manuscript verse represented a courtly and aristocratic response to printed art criticism.

The Writing on the Wall: Verse in the Salon

The phenomenon of manuscript verse in the Salon is unexplored in modern scholarship perhaps because the history of art criticism has been written as a history of prose. It is easy to forget that art criticism was never far from poetry in this period. Manuscript verse resembled in form and purpose other kinds of poetry associated with the Salon. Like manuscript verse, these genres of poetry in response to art testify to the continuity of poetic and exhibition cultures in this period.

Manuscript verse displayed in the Salon only survives where art criticism has preserved traces of this no doubt common but largely unrecorded practice. For example, in his review of the Salon of 1747, Jean-Bernard Le Blanc documents one such manuscript poem for a portrait bust by Jean-Baptiste Lemoyne of Prince Charles Edward Stuart (fig. 1).[2] Le Blanc notes that below the bust were written these lines:

> By his virtues, by his deeds
> Sovereigns, learn how to be worthy
> Warriors, instruct yourself, and Englishmen blush
> To have underestimated your master.[3]

The verse reflects the status of Bonnie Prince Charlie, pretender to the thrones of England, Scotland, France, and Ireland, as a romantic hero following the unsuccessful Jacobite uprising of 1745 and his subsequent flight to France where he was in exile.

Manuscript verse was always laudatory. For example, in the Salon of 1747, the pastel portrait of the Maréchal de Saxe by Maurice Quentin de La Tour inspired two manuscript poems glorifying the marshal general of France and hero of the War of Austrian Succession (fig. 2).[4] Le Blanc reports that "this verse has been placed below the portrait:"

> Hero without vanity, courtier without baseness,
> Never has he felt the blow of any reversal of fortune;
> Condé[5] would have envied his valour;
> Turenne[6] would have praised his wisdom.[7]

Figure 1. After Jean Baptiste II Lemoyne, *Prince Charles Edward Stuart*, 1746. Gilt Plaster, h. 48.3 cm. Sizergh Castle, Cumbria, UK © National Trust / Barbara Pointon / Bridgeman Images.

Figure 2. Maurice-Quentin de La Tour, *Maurice de Saxe*, 1747. Pastel, 58 x 48 cm. Paris, Musée du Louvre / Bridgeman Images.

Le Blanc further records "other verse that has been written under the portrait of this prince:"

> LOUIS, aided worthily by this hero,
> Renders the alliance of the German [i.e. the Habsburg Monarchy]
> and the English vain:
> MAURICE is another TURENNE,
> CLERMONT[8] is a second CONDÉ.[9]

These poems echo the nationalistic pride expressed in the manuscript verse in this same Salon honoring Prince Charles Edward Stuart, on whose father's behalf the Maréchal de Saxe had been chosen to command the abortive French Invasion of Britain in 1744.

Other manuscript verse in the Salon intersected with art critical discourse by lauding the artist. In the Salon of 1767, La Tour's portrait of the royal eye doctor Pierre Demours—of which Denis Diderot wrote, "hideous face, fine piece of painting"—prompted a manuscript poem (fig. 3).[10] In this Salon, La Tour exhibited his portraits without having had them recorded in the *livret*, the numbered hand list of works exhibited that allowed the public to identify individual works by numbers hung beside them. The *Mercure de France* observes that the public was able to discern its author even without the assistance of the *livret*:

> The public is more insightful than one thinks. . . . [La Tour's] talents spoke for him. The truth revealed his secret, and we dare to claim that one hundred people recognized him through the veil of his modesty. On the back of his portrait of M. Demours, eye doctor to the king, these lines were found:
>
> Dibutade, long ago led by love,
> Traced a striking image of her lover.
> Today friendship, taking its turn to triumph,
> To depict the truthful image of a friend,
> Has guided the pastel of the famous *la Tour*.[11]

To the back of la Tour's portrait of Demours, displayed on a stand on one of the tables reserved for small pictures and sculptures, someone attached manuscript verse that identified the artist. This unofficial manuscript verse identifying La Tour filled a lacuna in the official printed documentation of the *livret*. It was a public performance of poetic wit and connoisseurship.

Manuscript verse replicated the functions of other kinds of poetry for art in the Salon. For example, encomiastic poems extended courtly discourse into the realm of printed art criticism. A typical example is the *Epitre au Roy* published on the occasion of the Concours, or state-sponsored competition for history painting, whose eleven paintings were exhibited as an extension of the Salon of 1747.[12] The *Epitre* extolled the enlightened patronage of Louis XV together with the qualities of the exhibited paintings, for example as in the stanza on François Boucher's *Rape of Europa* (1747), which lauds its palette, composition, brushwork, and expression.[13] In another case, an anonymous review of the Salon of 1741 included a laudatory poem on Charles-Antoine Coypel's painting of a scene from Jean Racine's *Athalie* (1691).[14]

Figure 3. Maurice-Quentin de La Tour, *Pierre Demours*, 1764. Pastel, 45 x 38 cm. Paris, private collection.

If encomiastic poetry was typically published after the Salon had closed, another kind of verse was actually displayed in the Salon, physically incorporated into the artworks exhibited there. Versified prints exhibited in the Salon included poetry in what is called the print letter, that is, a textual component located in the margin beneath the image, which typically included a title, artists' names, and often a dedication and coat of arms.[15] Print verse, as Antony Griffiths shows, descended from Latin verse that Netherlandish humanists composed for prints.[16] Print verse related to an established culture of versification in response to artworks that was already commonplace in the seventeenth century when the visit of Rubens to France inspired a flurry of poems.[17] In eighteenth-century France, this humanist tradition intersected with the practice of versification in the literary salons and thus represented a cross-fertilization of visual and literary cultures.

Versified prints—very often portraits—were not abundant in the Salon, yet they appeared there frequently enough to suggest an association between print verse and certain subjects of portraiture, namely actors and actresses, composers, artists, and what were called *savants,* such as doctors and mathematicians. A typical example is a print by Bernard-François Lépicié after Joseph Aved exhibited in the Salon of 1740, depicting the actress Catherine-Marie-Jeanne Dupré Deseine (sometimes referred to by her married name Quinault-Dufresne) in the role of Dido (fig. 4).[18] Its verse reads:

> Art does not lend you its frivolous imposture,
> Dufrêne, your appealing qualities, your enchanting talents,
>   Have never owed but to nature
> The gift of pleasing the eye and moving the heart.[19]

The quatrain combines the compact ingenuity of the epigram and the *bon mot* while alluding to classical inscription—considered in the period to be the origin of the epigram—a reference supported by the illusionistic representation of the verse as if carved into the sculptural base supporting the portrait.[20]

The only two genres of poetry to be physically displayed in the Salon, print verse and manuscript verse resemble one another. Both tend to take the form of the quatrain, often but not always of classical twelve-syllable alexandrines. Both are laudatory and directed toward the subjects of portraiture and to artists themselves. Both qualify as what was called *poésie fugitive*, poetry that, whether manuscript or print, "by the smallness of its volume is easily lost."[21]

Pour mettre au bas de son Portrait: Poetry for Art

Verse for portraiture was a subgenre of poetry that cut across social levels. In 1766, the poet and dramatist Claude-Joseph Dorat published one such poem in the literary anthology the *Almanach des muses*, most issues of which included several poems intended to adorn artworks. "A Mlle Doligni, Pour mettre au bas de son Portrait," dedicated to the promising 20-year-

Figure 4. Bernard-François Lépicié after Joseph Aved, *Catherine Quinault-Dufresne, called Mademoiselle de Seine*, 1735. Engraving, 43 x 30.4 cm. © Victoria and Albert Museum, London.

old actress, Louis-Adélaïde Berton-Maisonneuve, called Mademoiselle d'Oligny, in its subject, form, and laudatory quality resembled print verse and manuscript verse in the Salon.[22] Some poems published in the *Almanach des muses* were even intended to adorn artworks shown in the Salon. For example, Joseph-Siffred Duplessis's portrait of the poet Antoine-Léonard Thomas, exhibited in the Salon of 1781, inspired a quatrain published in the *Almanach des muses* of 1782.[23] The practice was not unique to the Salon. In 1779, Jean-Antoine Houdon exhibited a bust of Christoph Willibald Gluck in the Salon de la Correspondance, the exhibition space and literary/scientific circle of the writer Pahin de La Blancherie, at the base of which a spectator placed a poem in praise of its subject.[24]

In spite of its typically low status as *poésie fugitive*, reflected in its usual anonymity, poetry for portraits was sometimes associated with celebrated authors, suggesting the genre's penetration into multiple levels of poetic culture.[25] Not all portraits were created equal: unlike print verse and in contrast to *poésie fugitive* more generally, inscriptions for major public monuments were sometimes produced competitively and reported in the press, as for example when Paul-Henri Marron, chaplain to the Dutch ambassador to Paris, composed a Latin poem for Houdon's statue of George Washington, published in the *Journal général de France* in 1787.[26] Marron offered this as an alternative to the inscription of James Madison that the Virginia General Assembly selected in 1784. Later, in a letter to Madison, Thomas Jefferson noted that Houdon had criticized Madison's inscription for its length, and Jefferson recorded other proposed texts, including that of Marron and a quotation from Horace offered by Jean-François Marmontel.[27]

Though inscriptions for monuments such as the *Washington* of Houdon merited international public debate, the subgenre of poetry for portraiture encompassed humbler material that nevertheless engaged famous authors. Voltaire provided verse for Jean Daullé's print reproducing the portrait of the mathematician Pierre-Louis de Maupertuis, exhibited in the Salon of 1743.[28] Its patron, Maupertuis's friend Jean-Marie-François du Parc, marquis de Locmaria, solicited this verse from Voltaire:

> The poorly known globe that he was able to measure,
> Becomes a monument on which his glory is founded:
> His fate is to please, enlighten, and fix the image
>   of the world.[29]

In a letter to Locmaria, Voltaire modestly dismissed his own verse as a "feeble quatrain."[30] The problem, he said, was the French language itself:

> A Latin inscription displeases me, because I am a good
> Frenchman. I find it ridiculous that our jetons, our medals, and
> our *Louis* are in Latin. In Germany, in England, most mottos are
> in French; it is only we who do not dare to speak our language on
> the occasions when foreigners speak it. I know full well that every
> inscription should be made in French, but also that that is too
> difficult. The flow of our language is too constricted; our rhyme
> spins out into four lines what Latin could easily express in one.[31]

Voltaire links print verse, and the subgenre of verse for portraiture more
generally, with traditions rooted in the classical inscription. He reveals that
one of the poet's tasks was to provide text for artworks, be it verse for prints,
mottos for medals, or inscriptions for monuments, so that what defines such
poetry is not that it is *fugitive*—a genre light, often frivolous, ironic and
satirical in tone—but applied.[32]

Subject as well as mood and medium organized the hierarchy of the
various forms of poetry. For example, impromptu verse was fashioned in
response to artworks shown in the Salon. Impromptu verse was a genre
recognized in the period by that name as a type of poetry close in form
to manuscript verse in the Salon: Louis de Jaucourt, in the *Encyclopédie*,
defined the *impromtu* as short verse, related to the epigram or to the brief,
ingenious, gallant poem called the *madrigal*, but made without preparation
on a subject that presents itself.[33] The *Mémoires secrets* documents one such
impromtu composed—though not displayed as manuscript—in response to
the *Sainte Thérèse* of Jean-Joseph Taillasson, exhibited in the Salon of 1785
(illustrated here by Gilles-Antoine Demarteau's print after it, fig. 5): "It is
said that a wit addressed the following *impromtu* on this piece to the artist."[34]

> Taillasson, remove from this place
> Your too adorable Theresa!
> Whereas she gives herself to God,
> She makes us give ourselves to the devil.[35]

The poet's argument that Theresa is so beautiful that she prompts impure
thoughts is both praise and critique, and it aligns with what Jaucourt described
as a defining property of the impromtu: "an ingenious mockery."[36] The
impromtu, such as this one directed to Taillasson, could praise an artist, but
with a satirical or critical edge.

Like the lesser genres of the epigram and madrigal with which it was
associated, the impromtu was *léger*, light.[37] It arrived as an unpremeditated
flash of wit that illuminated a specific social context; it was performative,
an expression of oral culture.[38] Its instantaneity and ephemerality can be
contrasted with the ponderous temporality of the inscription that is written

Figure 5. Gilles-Antoine Demarteau after Jean-Joseph Thaillasson, *Sainte Thérèse*, 1786. Crayon manner engraving, 55 x 41.5 cm. Private collection.

"on copper, on marble, on public buildings, on triumphal arches, etc., to preserve the memory of some important person or event" (*Dictionnaire* of the Académie).[39] The medium of copper and marble was not that of poésie fugitive, a genre named for its ephemerality.

Word of Mouth: Dialectical Tensions of Communications Media in the Salon

In the Salon, poems on art proffered a laudatory or ceremonial discourse as an alternative to prose criticism, an opposition between encomiastic and critical texts that reflected a contradiction in purposes in the exhibition of the Académie. One function of the Salon was to celebrate the enlightened patronage of the king and the state. Another was to encourage competition between artists. Manuscript poems in the Salon highlighted the ceremonial as opposed to the competitive function, exemplified in the verse offered to Lemoyne's portrait of Louis XV in the Salon of 1747.[40] "Someone inspired by a truth-loving Muse," Le Blanc reports, "has attached the following verse to the base of this bust:"

> The model of kings, the love of his subjects,
> If he fills the earth with the sound of his name LOUIS,
> His great soul does not have ambitious projects;
> He presents the olive branch armed with his thunder,
>   And this hero makes war
>   Only to guarantee us peace.[41]

Within the public arena of the Salon, manuscript verse was a survival of an older, courtly system of patronage and display in which praise was a public matter and criticism was a private matter.

By claiming territory in the official space of the exhibition, manuscript verse declared its primacy over printed art criticism, which was always elsewhere. Unlike printed art criticism, manuscript verse was an index of the encounter between poet and artwork. Printed art criticism circulated in numerous more or less identical copies and was often issued after the exhibition ended; its multiplicity and belatedness separated it from the time and space of spectatorship. The manuscript poem, tacked to the wall or to the back of an artwork during the exhibition, memorialized its locus of inspiration.

Like impromptu verse, manuscript verse was performative. Its very physical nature emphasized its impromptu aspect. Le Blanc observes that the verse for Lemoyne's bust of Prince Charles Edward Stuart in the Salon of 1747 was written "*au crayon*,"—a term encompassing graphite and pastel—a humble medium that lacked the cachet and permanence of ink.[42] *Crayon,* more portable than ink that is used at a desk, afforded improvisatory, on-the-spot writing; one pictures the poet standing before the bust, jostled by the crowd, scribbling verse on a scrap of paper. In the display space of the Salon, the medium represented a compromise between the ephemerality of oral performance and the durability of the inscription.

Manuscript poems in the Salon, produced in a context of orality, were an outgrowth of the aristocratic ethos that abjured publication and for which the worldly distractions of polite society provided a framework for versification.[43] Manuscript poems in the Salon related to the poems composed to amuse and entertain literary salons that society hostesses such as Julie de Lespinasse and Madame du Deffand preserved in manuscript form. Such verse was so intimately connected to the sociability in which it was created that its publication in print drained its essence. As Jaucourt observes in his *Encyclopédie* article on the *bon mot*, another social, epigrammatic, poetic form, "not all bons mots are capable of surviving in print. Most lose their grace when they are removed from the circumstances that gave birth to them, circumstances that are not easy to make perceptible to those who were not witness to them."[44]

If manuscript verse in the Salon du Louvre related to practices of versification in the literary salons, its physical presence in the Salon on the occasion of an exhibition intended to glorify the king's patronage tied it to the rhetoric of courtly display. Absolutist rhetoric depended on the presence (actual or represented) of the monarch before an audience. This rhetoric was both implicit and explicit in the Salon, which took place in the King's house, whose centerpiece was a representation of the king, usually in the form of a portrait displayed on a dais.[45] Manuscript poems in the Salon related to poems in literary salons and at court because the literary salons were in certain respects an extension of court society.[46]

In the face of the emerging public sphere of art criticism, manuscript verse, by insisting on the site of encounter with art, affirms both the social logic of the aristocratic ethos and the indexical logic of absolutism. That different media of communication corresponded to different social spheres and logics is evident in the hierarchical relationship between manuscript verse in the Salon that addressed reigning monarchs and representatives of the state, and print verse whose subjects were bourgeois heroes. Print—reproductive prints, art criticism, printed poetry—transcended space. In contrast, voice and manuscript insisted on their unique site of encounter in the representational grandeur of absolutism where the monarch's power is visualized in personal display, and the aristocratic ethos of the literary salon defined by orality.[47]

Manuscript poems co-existed with both the oral practices of the Salon and the literary salons and the print practices of journalism. Rather than representing distinct spheres, these logics of engagement and communication were entwined. Such was the network of rumor that manuscript verse passed into print when it was reported in the press, just as the poems of the literary salons passed into manuscript and eventually into print. The dialectical tensions of media of communication comprised the contradictory discursive environment of the Salon.

NOTES

1. Robert Darnton, "An Early Information Society: News and the Media in Eighteenth-Century Paris," *The American Historical Review* 105, no. 1 (February 2000): 1–35.

2. Salon 1747/52; a gilded plaster after the lost original is in Sizergh Castle, Cumbria, North, National Trust inv. NT 998576.

3. "Par ses vertus, par ses exploits / Souverains, apprenez à mériter de l'être, / Guerriers instruisez-vous, & rougissez Anglois/ D'avoir méconnu votre Maître." *Lettre sur l'exposition des ouvrages de peinture, sculpture, etc. de l'Anné 1747 . . .* (1747), 101.

4. Salon 1747/111; Musée du Louvre INV. 27611-recto.

5. Louis de Bourbon, Prince de Condé.

6. Henri de La Tour d'Auvergne, Vicomte de Turenne.

7. "on a mis ces Vers-ci au bas de ce Portrait: Héros sans vanité, Courtisan sans bassesse, / Jamais d'aucun revers il n'éprouve les coups; / Condé de sa valeur auroit été jaloux; / Turenne eut vanté sa sagesse." Le Blanc, *Lettre*, 84.

8. Louis de Bourbon, comte de Clermont.

9. "Voici d'autres Vers qui ont été écrits au-dessous de Portrait de ce Prince. LOUIS, par ces Héros dignement secondé, / Du Germain, de l'Anglois rend l'alliance vaine: / MAURICE est un autre TURENNE, / CLERMONT est un second CONDÉ." Le Blanc, 84.

10. Paris, private collection; Albert Besnard and Georges Wildenstein, *La Tour. La vie et l'oeuvre de l'artiste* (Paris: Les Beaux-Arts, 1928), no. 95; "figure hideuse, beau morceau de peinture," *Oeuvres complètes de Diderot*, 20 vols. (Paris: Garnier frères, 1876), 11: 151, see also 24 (*Salon de 1767*).

11. "Le public est plus clairvoyant qu'on ne pense. . . . Ses talens ont parlé pour lui. La vérité a trahi son secret, & nous osons assurer que cent personnes l'ont reconnu à travers le voile de sa modestie. Au revers du portrait de M. Demours, Médecin Oculiste du Roi, on a trouvé ces vers : Dibutade, autrefois conduite par l'Amour, / Traça de son amant une image frappante. / Aujourd'hui l'Amitié, triomphant à son tour, / Pour rendre d'un ami l'image ressemblante, / A conduit le crayon du célèbre la Tour." *Mercure de France* (October 1767): 179.

12. Antoine Bret, *Épitre au roy, Sur quelques Tableaux exposés au Louvre pour le Concours proposé par Mr. de Tournehem, Directeur Général des Bâtimens* (1747). On the Concours of 1747, see Christophe Henry, "La peinture en question: Genèse conflictuelle d'une fonction sociale de la peinture d'histoire en France au milieu du XVIIIe siècle," in Thomas W. Gaehtgens, *L'art et les normes sociales au 18e siècle* (Paris: Éditions de la Maison des sciences de l'homme, 2001), 459–76.

13. Bret, *Épitre*, 3. Musée du Louvre INV. 2714.

14. Salon 1741/2; *Athalie interroge Joas*, Musée des beaux-arts de Brest, inv. 967.3.1. One could add the subgenre of the epistle to painting, for example *Epitre sur la Peinture, à monsieur de S . . .*, Georges Duplessis, *Catalogue de la collection des pièces sur les beaux-arts imprimées et manuscrites, recueillie par Pierre-Jean Mariette, Charles-Nicolas Cochin et M. Deloynes, Auditeur des Comptes, et acquise récemment par le Département des Estampes de la Bibliothèque Nationale* (Paris, 1881), hereafter Deloynes 2056; *Epitre à madame de S . . . sur la Peinture* (1714), Deloynes 2055, and the epistle to the artist, e.g. Gabriel Bouquier, *Epitre à monsieur Vernet peintre du roi membre de l'académie royale de peinture et sculpture par m. bouquier* (1773), Deloynes 155.

15. For an overview of the phenomenon, see W. McAllister Johnson, *Versified Prints: A Literary and Cultural Phenomenon in Eighteenth-Century France* (Toronto: Univ. of Toronto Press, 2012). However, this book does not contextualize print verse in relation to period literary culture, practice, or institutions.

16. Antony Griffiths, *The Print Before Photography: An Introduction to European Printmaking 1550–1820* (London: The British Museum Press, 2016), 87.

17. Griffiths, *Print*, 88–89.

18. Salon 1740, 24; Roger Portalis and Henri Béraldi, *Les Graveurs du dix-huitième siècle*, 6 vols. (Paris: Damascène Morgand et Charles Fatout, 1881), 2: 661.

19. "L'art ne vous prête point sa frivole imposture, / Dufrêne, vos attraits, vos talens enchanteurs / N'ont jamais dû qu'à la nature / Le don de plaire aux yeux et d'attendrir les coeurs."

20. Edme-François Mallet, "Epigramme," *Encyclopédie, ou dictionnaire raisonné des sciences, des arts et des métiers*, ed. Denis Diderot and Jean le Rond d'Alembert, 28 vols. (Paris: Briasson, David l'aîné, Le Breton, Durand, 1751–72), 5: 793 (1755); Louis de Jaucourt, "Mot bon," *Enc.*, 10: 763 (1765).

21. "Un ouvrage soit manuscrit, soit imprimé, qui par la petitesse de son volume est sujet à se perdre aisément," 2 vols. *Dictionnaire de l'Académie françoise* (Paris: Jean-Baptiste Coignard, 1740), 1: 733, s.v. "Fugitif."

22. "Par les talens unis à la décence, / tu te fais respecter & chérir tour à tour ; / si tu souris comme l'Amour, / tu parles comme l'innocence," *Almanach des muses* (Paris: Delalain, 1766), 13.

23. Salon 1781/74; Clermont-Ferrand, Musée d'art Roger-Quilliot inv. 2329; 861.154.1; 56.271.1. Égide de Lespinasse Langeac, "Pour le Portrait de M. Thomas," "On ne sait en l'aimant ce qu'on chérit le plus, / de son ame, ou de son génie ; / par ses vastes talens, il irrite l'envie, / & la soumet par ses vertus." *Almanach des muses* (Paris: Delalain, 1782), 60.

24. "Plus avant dans les coeurs, par des traits plus profonds, / Sa lyre souveraine a su porter les sons. / Ses chants font respirer les tragiques alarmes : / Il vit par leur pouvoir le zoïle enchaîné, / Trahi par des sanglots, s'abandonner aux larmes, / Et n'opposa jamais à l'effort de ses armes / Qu'un art victorieux et qu'un front couronné," Émile Bellier de La Chavignerie, *Les Artistes français du XVIII siècle oubliés ou dédaignés* (Paris: Veuve Jules Renouard, 1865), 100. For an introduction to the Salon de La Correspondance, see Laura Auricchio, "Pahin de la Blancherie's Commercial Cabinet of Curiosity (1779–87)," *Eighteenth-Century Studies* 36, no. 1 (2002): 47–61.

25. Both print verse and poems for portraits published in the *Almanach des muses* were sometimes anonymous, sometimes attributed.

26. "A l'auteur du Journal, Paris, 8 Janvier 1787," *Journal général de France* 11 (25 Janvier 1787): 43.

27. "From Thomas Jefferson to James Madison, 8 February 1786," *The Papers of Thomas Jefferson*, 33 vols., *1 November 1785–22 June 1786*, ed. Julian P. Boyd (Princeton: Princeton Univ. Press, 1954), 9: 264–71.

28. Salon 1743, 43; Marcel Roux, *Inventaire du fonds français. Graveurs du XVIIIe siècle* (Paris: Bibliothèque nationale, 1949), vol. 6, no 47, 81.

29. "Le Globe mal connu qu'il a sçu mesurer, / Devient un monument où sa gloire se fonde; / Son sort est de fixer la figure du Monde, / De lui plaire, et de l'éclairer."

30. "chétif quatrain," "A M. Loc-Maria, Bruxelles, 17 de juillet 1741," *Oeuvres complètes de Voltaire*, 56 vols. (Paris: Perronneau, 1821), 46: 132.

31. "Une inscription latine me déplaît, parce que je suis bon Français. Je trouve ridicule que nos jetons, nos médailles et nos louis soient latins. En Allemagne, en Angleterre, la plupart des devises sont françaises; il n'y a que nous qui n'osions pas parler notre langue dans les occasions où les étrangers la parlent. Je sens très bien qu'il faudrait faire toutes les inscriptions en français, mais aussi cela est trop difficile. La marche de notre langue est trop gênée, notre rime délaie en quatre vers ce qu'un vers latin pourrait facilement exprimer," *Oeuvres de Voltaire*, 46: 132.

32. Nicole Masson, *La poésie fugitive au XVIIIe siècle* (Paris: Honoré Champion, 2002).

33. "Impromtu," *Enc.*, 8: 630 (1765).

34. Private collection. The original painting is Salon 1785/112; Limoges, private collection.

35. "On veut qu'un plaisant ait à ce sujet adressé l'impromptu suivant à l'artiste: Taillasson, ôte de ce lieu / Ta Thérèse trop adorable! / Tandis qu'elle se donne à Dieu, / Elle nous fait donner au diable." *Mémoires historiques, littéraires et critiques de Bachaumont . . .* , 3 vols. (Paris: Léopold Collin, 1808), 2: 220 (10 Septembre 1785).

36. "une raillerie ingénieuse," Jaucourt, "Impromtu."

37. Noël Étienne Sanadon, *Les poësies d'Horace, traduites en françois . . .* (Amsterdam: Arkstée et Merkus, 1756), 2: 232.

38. *Dictionnaire*, 1: 869, s.v. "In-promptu."

39. "Ce qu'on écrit sur du cuivre, sur du marbre, aux édifices publics, aux Arcs de triomphe, &c. pour conserver la mémoire de quelque personne, de quelque événement considérable," *Dictionnaire*, 1: 870, s.v. "Inscription."

40. Untraced; a marble likely after this work is at Versailles, inv. MV 9045.

41. "Quelqu'un inspiré par une Muse ami du vrai, a attaché les Vers suivants au bas de ce Buste. Le modelle des Rois, l'amour de ses Sujets, / Si du bruit de son nom LOUIS remplit la Terre, / Sa grande ame n'a pas d'ambitieux projets ; / Il présente l'Olive armé de son Tonnerre, / Et ce Héros ne fait la guerre / Que pour nous assurer la paix," Le Blanc, 100.

42. Le Blanc, 101. See *Enc.* (1754), 4:429, s.v. "Craion."

43. On the aristocratic ethos in the Salons and attitudes toward publication, see Antoine Lilti, *The World of the Salons: Sociability and Worldliness in Eighteenth-Century Paris* (Oxford: Oxford Univ. Press, 2015), 158 and passim.

44. "tous les bons mots ne sont pas capables de soutenir la presse. La plûpart perdent leur grace, dès qu'on les rapporte détachés des circonstances qui les ont fait naître; circonstances qu' il n' est pas aisé de faire sentir à ceux qui n' en ont pas été les témoins," Jaucourt, "Mot bon," 763.

45. For example, the portrait of Louis XIV by Hyacinthe Rigaud (1659–1743), Salon 1704, 4; Louvre INV 7492.

46. On the literary Salons, see Dena Goodman, *The Republic of Letters: A Cultural History of the French Enlightenment* (Ithaca: Cornell Univ. Press, 1994); Joan B. Landes, *Women and the Public Sphere in the Age of the French Revolution* (Ithaca: Cornell Univ. Press, 1988); Norbert Elias, *The Civilising Process: The History of Manners,* vol. 1, trans. Edmund Jephcott (Oxford: Basil Blackwell, 1978).

47. On the visual semiotics of absolutism, see Louis Marin, *Le Portrait du roi* (Paris: Les Éditions du minuit, 1981).

Scribal Publication of Elizabeth Graeme Fergusson's Commonplace Books

CHIARA CILLERAI

According to scholars of book history, print did not replace the production of manuscript writing during the early modern period. On the contrary, it encouraged an increase in writing by hand.[1] The manuscript books of Philadelphia poet Elizabeth Graeme Fergusson contain ample evidence of how print inspired the continuous production of handwritten material. The remaining six manuscript copy books that Fergusson composed from the early 1770s to the late 1790s have a miscellaneous content. They include Fergusson's poetic compositions, those of other poets, personal letters, as well as newspaper articles and extracts from printed books.[2] The volumes that Fergusson designed and revised during the last three decades of her life provide evidence of her perception of her audience, her purpose in writing and selecting materials, and her idea of publicity. Fergusson's books reveal her active engagement with eighteenth-century cultural and intellectual life among Philadelphia's literary and social elites. Although poetry constitutes the bulk of her work, her letters and other writings reveal the span of her interests. Her correspondence with the Philadelphia physician Benjamin Rush, for example, shows her interest in and knowledge of philosophy, education, and medicine. Her poetic correspondence with Francis Hopkinson lasted many years and culminated in the production of a long mock-epic poem that Fergusson dedicated to him. One of her copy books is addressed to Annis Boudinot Stockton, Fergusson's lifelong friend and fellow poet. For many years, she also corresponded with the English Juliana Penn and John Fothergill and dedicated poems to both. Each of her connections was a member of intersecting networks of readers that formed the literary culture of eighteenth-century Anglo-America. Her books are hybrid compositions that cross over from the commonplace book to the miscellany to the copy book.[3] Each manuscript book was designed and revised according to the specific recipient, and if a poem was reproduced, one notices adjustments reflecting shifts in audience, place, time, and culture. In this essay, my analysis of some materials in two of Fergusson's extant manuscript books shows how her selections and marginalia are evidence of how her writing, and especially re-writing, reflect and reproduce various aspects of the salon manuscript literary culture that had formed her as a writer. Fergusson's authorial identity emerges in the conversations that the writing in the page of the book establishes with the past, other authors and their work, and her prospective audiences.

Beginnings

Elizabeth Graeme Fergusson belonged to a prominent Philadelphia family. Her mother was the stepdaughter of Pennsylvania governor William Keith, and her father an influential figure in Philadelphia social and political life. In her late teens, Elizabeth met William Franklin and began a long engagement that ended when Franklin left her for another woman.[4] During the years before the war of independence began, Fergusson and her family ran a well-known salon that, in a commemorative essay, Benjamin Rush described as being "for the entertainment not only of strangers, but of such of her friends of both sexes as were considered the most suitable company for them. These evenings were, properly speaking, of the Attic type."[5] When the war began, however, Fergusson's life collapsed. Her loyalist husband, Henry Fergusson, whom she had secretly married a few months before the death of her father in 1771, almost caused Elizabeth to lose the ownership of Graeme Park, the family ancestral residence. As he was trying to leave for England in order to escape prosecution, Fergusson was caught and detained. And when he was eventually released and able to leave Pennsylvania, his wife refused to join him. She never saw him again. Instead, she spent many years fending off the government's attempts to confiscate the family property and the accusations of treason. Elizabeth Fergusson never recovered from the loss of her reputation among her friends and acquaintances and spent the rest of her life in a self-imposed exile from public life.[6]

Despite this retirement from the public life she had led before the war, Fergusson continued to write poetry, transcribe it in her books with other writings, and circulate them among members of her social circles. A largely self-educated poet and scholar, Fergusson had been reading, writing, and translating poetry since her teens. In the mid 1760s, she produced a manuscript two-volume didactic translation of François Fénelon's *The Adventures of Telemachus, Son of Ulysses* and a two-volume adaptation of the Psalms. She also submitted and published a substantial number of poems in local periodicals such as *The Pennsylvania Magazine*. But her preferred form of publication remained the manuscript copy book that consisted of three or four separate smaller handwritten notebooks tied together and professionally bound.

As I suggested earlier, after the loss of her public social standing and her inner circle of friends composed of both loyalists and patriots was disrupted, Fergusson's reproduction of poetry in the books becomes the replacement for the social and literary exchanges of her earlier life.[7] Many of the notes that appear in the margins of the books are visibly directed to the addressee, but they also establish conversations between time periods and between different cultural environments that relate to their contents. These books reflect the participatory structure that Margaret Ezell has identified as the principal feature of manuscript literary culture.[8] This culture depended on a dynamic network of writer and reader who participated in the making and remaking of the books they exchanged. The material form of Fergusson's manuscript books is an essential component of her work. Fergusson's methods of producing the books, including her composition, revision, copying, arrangement, and presentation to specific audiences reveal the multiple technical operations that are involved in the production of her work. Fergusson's books show how the materiality of the text and the textuality of the material form are bound together.[9] Her notations and commentaries to the various versions of her poems and to her responses to printed material are functions of the manuscript nature of the book and the culture it represents and fosters. In this respect, Fergusson's authorial interventions produce a paratext that also exemplifies the fluid relationship that manuscript book publication of this kind had with traditional notions of "private" and "public." The social function of Fergusson's books, in fact, is written on and in the pages bound together according to her choice of theme and audience, and it is this particular medium that allows the author to re-establish the connection with the world of letters and the sociability from which she had been separated.[10] Her commonplace books, as texts that circulated, reveal public moments of readership and reflect that public back into the private realm when they are copied back again into a new book.

Fergusson's own authorial interventions also reveal those of her readers, both in a direct or indirect form.

The public voice which the salon had given Fergusson and the social interactions it permitted are reproduced in the pages of the books that she composes. In a letter in which Fergusson writes about a plan to compose a book for the young daughters of her friend Ann Ridgeley, Fergusson's words reveal her ideas about what her writing is for and what she expects in an audience:

> You are very obliging in pointing out a Method to get the manuscripts, which at least my share of them I fear would not repay you for the pains of developing a bad Hand: But I Will not act the Hypocrite: I declare when by peculiar Circumstances I am as it were a Link Cut off from the Chain of that Society both by Birth and Education which I once was taught to expect, and devote my Hours to Retirement and my Pen, I feel a Latent Wish that those whose tasks are congenial to my own, might with the Eye of not *Candor* But *Partiality* see my turn of thought and mode of Life. But you told me "that your Children are fond of Poetry," of Consequence they have read a great deal and under such a monitress as their mother have read the Best, and as they must be devested of that partiality which perhaps you might have, I fear it will be dull work, But my promise is made, and what is still more cogent my Will is on the side of performing it: Tho It may be a considerable time before I put it in Execution, for among the Portions of time I find most tedious where I live, is the *long long* Winter Evenings Once the Joy of my heart when surrounded by a Groupe of Dear Conextions all gone to the Silent abodes of Death. Those Winter evenings I mean in part to devote to sorting; or Copying out such of my little Things; that I think may have a Chance of meeting your and the young Ladies approbation; Therefore rest assured if I live, have my Eyes, Limbs, and faculties between this and the month of May a volume shall make its appearance.[11]

Fergusson's awareness of the obstacle that the "peculiar Circumstances" of her economic and social decline create is evident in the opening words of this letter. These impediments and the death of close family members and relations are making literary production and distribution difficult. Yet, Fergusson's words also show her eagerness to overcome those obstacles by composing new books and sending her work out. Ridgeley's children, who are educated by a mother whose cultural and social rules Fergusson shares, will become her new audience. By means of the literary activity that her "Pen" engages with, the world that has been lost can be turned back into life during the "Hours of Retirement" when she will complete the new manuscript book. This activity produces the space for her work to re-emerge from its forced exile and to acquire the power to counteract the circumstances behind Fergusson's life away from the society she used to be part of.

Although Fergusson is clearly mourning in the passage just quoted, it is impossible not to notice her eagerness to discuss her own literary abilities and the possibilities that a new and young audience might afford her. Fergusson's words about presenting her work to her prospective readers is also worth noticing. While Ann Ridgeley is characterized as partial, her daughters are "devested" of any bias. Their impartiality to the book's author might make for a "dull" reading experience, but the young women become Fergusson's chosen audience: "But my promise is made, and what is still more cogent my Will is on the side of performing it." Fergusson's wording stresses the power that the idea of a larger public and publicity have for the book's writer. And, by the end of her letter, she promises a volume that she thinks "might have the Chance of meeting your and the young Ladies approbation." What Fergusson says about the production of a new manuscript for the young women reflects an exchange that involves both parties. In the offer to prepare the book for mother and daughters is also implicit the possibility that the expanding audience may alter its contents. The reading experience might produce new material to write about and exchanging the book might produce a new network of readers and possible writers. The culture that emerges from Fergusson's allusions to her readership's responsive reading is based on a social network that exchanged verse and books in the context of literary gatherings such as the salons that Fergusson used to host. The cut off link from the chain of such a society that Fergusson describes in the letter is then tied back when the manuscript book is circulated again.[12]

Textual Reflections

The writing on the inside of the cover and the first page of the earliest of Fergusson's books, *Poemata Juvenilia*, is an example of how the book's author engages in a conversation with her audience that transcends space and time and that invites readers to participate in the composition and interpretation of her art. As the Latin title suggests, the volume contains many poems composed during Fergusson's adolescence and early adulthood. A note written above the bookplate marks the composition of the majority of the poems and broadly describes the book's contents: "The Greatest part of the Poems written between the year 1752 and 1772 before my Mariage [sic]. Not above two or three since. Short little things" (fig. 1). The nice leather binding of the volume attests to Fergusson's pre-revolutionary wealth.

Figure 1. *Poemata Juvenilia* book plate with the author's notes about dates of composition. Courtesy of The Library Company of Philadelphia.

Marginal comments and additional poems tell us the story of the book during the years that followed its original manuscript publication up to the early 1790s. Below the bookplate on the same page, a note dated 1793 addresses potential criticism: "The *Critick* must not glance an Eye/Upon these Artless Lays!/For Wit a thousand Faults will Spy/And Blast my vernal Rays." And on the opposite page, two poems dated 1789 and entitled "The Interrogation" and "A Reply to the Same" complete the additional textual material.

The two poems are written as a series meant to be read together, and, as the titles suggest, the first poem asks a set of questions that the second poem answers. Their formal structure produces a model of reading and responding to poetry that invites the audience to actively participate as both readers and writers. The poems represent the past and the present facing each other. Rhetorical questions asked in the first poem, such as "Oh why does man forever Mourn/ The absent Good, the present Woe?/ From Instant Comfort always torn:/ And Best in Prospect Bliss to know?" are answered in the second: "Tis *Heaven* the Answer this Returns,/ This Shame from Latent Sources flow,/ Tis to point out our Pilgrim State;/ That no abiding place is here:/ That Short and Fleeting is the Date,/ Of Days and Hours alloted Here." From the distance created by time and experience, the voice speaking in the second poem placates the fears the first poem raises and addresses the futility of her worries in the face of our transient state on earth. The various notes and the two formulaic poems are a reflection of how the poetic collection that they introduce is organized and how it works. The poems, structured as a dialogue, mimic for the audience the reading experience that they present in the rest of the book. The dialogue between the two poems reflects the dialogue between book and readers and reproduces the poetic exchanges and the conversations that characterized the salon evenings with which Fergusson was familiar.[13]

Fergusson's retrospective notes precede the book's table of contents and its opening pages and form a new introduction. The additional text that now introduces the book provides a frame that highlights the writer's engagement with the processes of thinking about and responding to texts. It also signals the author's intention to re-publish the book with a new public in mind. Throughout the pages of the book, we find erasures, additions, and rewritings that perform the same task. The epistolary form that Fergusson also often employs for writing her poems participates in the exchange among author and reader or author and author that the book encourages. Epistolary poems or poems written in response to other texts similarly contribute to strengthening the interdependence between the volume's contents and its material form as a book designed to be circulated and reproduce the dynamics of conversation and social interactions. The two poems in the volume that immediately follow the table of contents further exemplify this mechanism. "A Dream," the first of the two poems opening the collection, is dated 1752 and recounts Elizabeth's entrance in society and her first experience of love. "A Dream" begins with the poet falling asleep and seeing "a Nymph arise;/ Friendship her Name of Social Virtues Queen!" Friendship takes her hand and leads her to a secluded bower in which she introduces the girl to her "favorite Strephon." The nymph tells Strephon that Elizabeth's name is Truth and leaves her with him without explaining what she should do. Despite her lack of experience and fear of the unknown, the poet tells us that she "found it hard my Strephon to forsake:/I feared some danger if I made delay,/Tho' my Heart Pleaded for a longer Stay." The arrival of the day saves her from making the feared decision and as the "Eastern Light" advances, Strephon leaves her with the shades of the night. In this poem, the fifteen-year-old Graeme conflates the discovery of sociability and friendship with her first sentimental involvement. Friendship leads the young woman to the bower and introduces her to love. The features of this process are rewritten in the response composed almost fifty years after the composition of the first poem.

What immediately follows "A Dream" is an additional short poem dated 1789, the same year of composition as the set of poems that introduces the collection. The poem is again a visible companion to the earlier one. The correlation between the two poems as well as the thematic revision that Fergusson made are evident in the title of the second one "On the Preference of Friendship to Love:"

> Let Girlish Nymphs and Boyish Swains
> Their Amorous Ditties Chant!
> Make vocal Echoing Hills and Plains;
> And Loves frail Passion paint,
> But Friendship's Shady Flame as far;
> Out shines that transient Blaze
> As Midday Sun is a glimmering Star
> Which faintest Beam display.

The thematic units of the earlier poem—friendship, sociability, and love—reappear in the later one in a new order and with new connotations. The "Shady Flame" of friendship is given the brilliant power of a "Midday Sun" and made to outshine the "transient Blaze of Love." If love and its voices exist within the "Echoing Hills and Plains" and are made larger by refraction, friendship has acquired a new overarching strength as well. It now allows Fergusson, the poet, and her readers to see where each item in the grouping she had done when she was fifteen could be displaced. Now friendship is not a nymph anymore. Her power and importance are pitted against those of the girlish nymphs who are lost in their chanting and their "Amorous Ditties." Now friendship observes and assesses the poet's and love's doings. When Fergusson returns to the book years after its first composition, the manuscript additions reshape the laws of sociability in order to invert the relationship between love and friendship. Friendship becomes the leading force that determines how the parties involved in the exchange communicate and relate to each other, and the old can learn from the new and vice versa.

We do not know if Fergusson shared *Poemata Juvenilia* and who saw it in between the time of its first composition and that of the additions. The notes at the beginning of the volume and "The Preference of Friendship to Love," among other inclusions, tell us that Fergusson returned to it at least two times, in 1789 and in 1793. We also know that some of the poems from this book were copied by members of her writing circles in their own books. "The Invitation," for example, a poem that in *Poemata Juvenilia* is dated 1753 appears in Milcah Martha Moore's copy book, which the latter composed towards the end of the 1770s. Moore's book also contains extracts from a journal that Fergusson kept while visiting England in 1764. As the editors of Moore's book notice, both authors belonged to the circle of middle-Atlantic women writers that formed the center of the active literary culture of this period.[14] As I have already observed, writers like Fergusson and her peers formed this culture by exchanging manuscript prose and poetry. The poems and the notes inserted at the beginning of the book and those in its pages attest to Fergusson's engagement with that world and her employment of its mechanisms of expression and communication. The acts of writing, re-writing, and circulating the manuscript work both in book form and as single texts to show the persistence of this culture in Fergusson's practice. They recreate the patterns in which ideas were formed, circulated, and changed throughout time.

The last of the textual examples that I analyze here is one in which the author engages in a dialogue among several texts that evolves in the pages of one of Fergusson's later books. The poem reflects the dynamics of the manuscript culture in which it originated. This volume was prepared in 1789 for Fergusson's long-time friend Annis Boudinot Stockton. In contrast to *Poemata Juvenilia*, the book for Stockton is filled with writings that date from the 1770s to the time of its composition. Poetry is central to the book, which is introduced by a long quotation from Addison and Steele's *The Tatler* about the power of the imagination to create poetry and foster virtue: "I have always been of opinion that virtue sinks deepest into the heart of man when it comes recommended by the powerful charms of poetry. The most active principle in our mind is the imagination: to it a good poet makes his court perpetually, and by this faculty takes care to gain it first."[15] Poetry and poetic conversations in the form of occasional poems and poems inspired by other texts form the bulk of the book's contents. And, as the quote from *The Tatler* placed as an epigraph to the book suggests, writing and reading poetry are leading themes in the works copied in the manuscript book.[16]

Fergusson's occasional poem is inspired by another one extracted from an English magazine. With its structure as a response to the words of another author, Fergusson's composition also incorporates the publicity of a printed and well known text, Johann Wolfgang von Goethe's 1774 epistolary novel *The Sorrows of Young Werther*. The combination of these sources becomes the occasion for furthering the larger conversation the book develops with its addressee Annis Stockton. In the book, the poem copied from the magazine is numbered 42. Number 43 is Fergusson's composition. The following note introduces the English poem: "Lines Spoken Extempore by a young Lady on Seeing a Drawing of Charlotte over the Tomb of Werter. The Lady speaks in the Character of Werter. Taken from an English Magazine."[17] The poem from the British magazine begins the dialogue. It is spoken in the voice of Werther, the main character in Goethe's novel. At the end of the novel, Werther, who has fallen in love with Charlotte, a young woman already engaged to another man named Albert, commits suicide. The novel ends with the implication that Werther's death has broken Charlotte's heart and that she too may commit suicide. Werther's words in the poem aim at consoling the grieving Charlotte, yet, by the last line, he also reminds her that no other man could ever love her as he did. The two poems are both paraphrases and literary commentaries on the implicit writers' experiences of reading *The Sorrows of Young Werther* and seeing a representation of the final scenes of the story when Werther's sorrow is now Charlotte's own. The four-line poem from the magazine reads as follows:

> Why does my *Charlotte* mourn our Werters Grave
> Pleased Should she be that Death has found her slave
> Be Blest in *Albert*, as hes [sic] blest in Thou!
> But Surely He Can never Love like Me.
> Juliana

In her response poem, Fergusson speaks to both the story that the poem tells and to its author, who signed it as Juliana. Fergusson simultaneously establishes a dialogue with the poem she has read about the novel and with the Werther speaking in the poem:

> Mistaken Youth, thy love to Frenzy wrought
> Spurnd Calm Reflection and each Sober thought
> A Little time had Showd that Charlots Charms
> Would [have] Died and Faded in A Werter's arms
> For Guilt and Meanness ne'er Could Dwell with Thee
> And Virtuous Friendship would have Set Thou Free.

Various acts of reading lay behind the process of writing the two poems. An anonymous reader, inspired by Goethe's story, has drawn a picture; the picture has then inspired Juliana to write the lines published in the magazine. With her answer, Fergusson performs a meta-reading of both texts, and her poem becomes the space that houses comments on friendship as well. If Werther had chosen friendship over love, his and Charlotte's fate would have been quite different. Fergusson's words to Werther/Juliana, who is addressed as "thee," but also de-personified as the subject of an illicit embrace, become the occasion for Fergusson to write about passion and friendship at the end of her poem, which is one of the leading themes in the entire book dedicated to Stockton.

Fergusson's poetic voice is part of a network that involves the magazine where the poem is first found, its author, Goethe's novel, and the addressee of the book, Annis Stockton. The structure and content of Fergusson's compositions reproduce the model that defines the culture of manuscript production and circulation that I have argued characterized Fergusson literary work. The features of the manuscript book as an object that circulates, but which is in continual transformation, are reflected in the poetics that Fergusson's compositions develop. In responding to the magazine's representation of the final scene of the novel, Fergusson is actively engaging with other readers at the same time that she is preparing the book for her own friend. Fergusson's ultimate achievement is that the manner in which her manuscripts were constantly evolving allowed her to continually modify and renew the content and style of her poetry and thus to contribute to the transformative and participatory manuscript literary culture of her time.

NOTES

1. Peter Stallybrass, "Printing and the Manuscript Revolution," in *Explorations in Communication and History*, ed. Barbie Zelizer (New York: Routledge, 2008), 111–18.

2. While Fergusson's letters refer to a large number of books addressed to different groups of readers, only a small number of them remain. The leather binding and original content of the earliest of these books show that it was probably prepared for publication in the early 1770s, while additions and annotations have dates that span from the 1780s through 1790s. The title, *Poemata Juvenilia*, is printed in gold letters on the book's spine. The Library Company of Philadelphia has this volume and a later manuscript entitled *Laura to a Friend*. The latter book seems to have been composed in the mid-1780s. A third manuscript entitled *A Willing Sisters Book* is kept at Graeme Park, the family estate, now a museum, in Horsham, Pennsylvania. The Historical Society of Pennsylvania houses two shorter books, probably composed in the early 1790s. One other book, dedicated to Fergusson's lifelong friend Annis Boudinot Stockton, is at Dickinson College. Works extant in manuscript include a didactic translation from the French of Fenelon's *The Adventures of Telemachus, Son of Ulysses* (two volumes), a verse adaptation of the Psalms (two volumes), and decades of letters and poems exchanged with Benjamin Rush and other correspondents fill volume 40 of The Rush Family Papers of The Historical Society of Pennsylvania.

3. Useful sources for understanding differences and similarities among forms of manuscript collections of writings are David Allan, *Commonplace Books and Reading in Georgian England* (Cambridge: Cambridge Univ. Press, 2010); George L. Justice and Nathan Tinker, eds. *Women's Writing and the Circulation of Ideas: Manuscript Publication in England, 1550–1800* (Cambridge: Cambridge Univ. Press, 2002); Arthur F. Marotti, *Manuscript, Print, and the English Renaissance* (Ithaca: Cornell Univ. Press, 1995); and, David S. Shields, "British-American Belle Lettres," in Sacvan Bercovitch, ed., *The Cambridge History of American Literature* (New York: Cambridge Univ. Press, 1994), 307–43.

4. Anne M. Ousterhout, *The Most Learned Woman in America: A Life of Elizabeth Graeme Fergusson*, intro. Susan M. Stabile (University Park, PA: The Pennsylvania State Univ. Press, 2003), 33–35.

5. The evening gatherings to which Rush refers were held at Graeme Fergusson's house in Philadelphia and at her country estate in Horsham, PA, nineteen miles west of the city. These gatherings began after she returned from an extended period spent in England during the winter of 1765 and continued until 1775, when she found her property in danger of being confiscated due to the loyalism of her English husband, Henry Hugh Fergusson (Ousterhout, *The Most Learned Woman*, 122–24). Benjamin Rush, "An Account of the Life and Character of Mrs. Elizabeth Ferguson," *Portfolio* n.s. 1 (June 1809): 520–27, 522.

6. Ousterhout, 163–213.

7. If, as Susan Stabile has argued, Fergusson's commonplace books are a textual analogue of the literary salon, a place in which private and public coexist and embody the mixed social sphere of early America, then the commonplace book is also a site where individuals develop memories to be shared, divided, and continually transformed; see Stabile, "Introduction," in Ousterhout, *The Most Learned Woman in America*, 4–5.

8. Margaret J. M. Ezell, *Social Authorship and the Advent of Print* (Baltimore, MD: The Johns Hopkins Univ. Press, 1999), 21–44.

9. Roger Chartier, and Peter Stallybrass, "What is a Book?" in Neil Fraistat and Julia Flanders, eds., *The Cambridge Companion to Textual Scholarship* (London: Cambridge Univ. Press, 2010). Margreta De Grazia and Peter Stallybrass, "The Materiality of the Shakespearian Text," *Shakespeare Quarterly* 44, no. 3 (1993): 255–83.

10. Ezell, *Social Authorship,* 38.

11. From a letter to Ann Ridgeley (neé Moore), 14 September 1797. Simon Gratz, "Some Materials for a Biography of Mrs. Elizabeth Fergusson, neé Graeme," *Pennsylvania Magazine of History and Biography* 39 (1915): 406.

12. Margaret Ezell's analysis of the dynamics of seventeenth- and eighteenth-century manuscript culture in England provides a useful description of how these networks worked and the role they had in fostering writing, in particular for women. See Ezell, 21–44. Susan Stabile also discusses the ways that social and literary networks developed in eighteenth-century Anglo-America with a focus on the book as both keepsake and literary product; see Susan M. Stabile, *Memory Daughters: The Material Culture of Remembrance in Eighteenth-Century America* (Ithaca: Cornell Univ. Press, 2004), 1–16.

13. See David S. Shields, *Civil Tongues and Polite Letters in British America* (Chapel Hill, NC: North Carolina Univ. Press, 1997).

14. For the connection between Milcah Martha Moore and Fergusson, see Karin A. Wulf and Catherine La Courreye Blecki's introductory essays in *Milcah Martha Moore's Book: A Commonplace Book from Revolutionary America* (University Park: The Pennsylvania State Univ. Press, 1997).

15. George A. Aitken ed., *The Tatler,* no. 98 (24 Nov 1709), vol. 2 (New York: Hadley & Mathews 1899) (The Gutenberg Project Kindle Locations 4900–4902).

16. In a dedicatory note to Stockton, Fergusson wrote about the book as a gift to remember her poetry and the significance it had for her and her friend: "Remember my dear Friend, that you often ask'd me for my little pieces; And I Have comply'd with your Request. It is time you Said, that if I Surviv'd you you wishd to have them. But I know that you have a Sensibility of Friendship which would make you Sigh at Reading them when this writer of them was no More, But alas when I copy them I find it makes past Ideas very feverishly in my mind: And do what I will the Sigh and the tear obtrudes its Self But I show Patience more than my Genius in these Works of your Obligd Friend, Laura."

17. *The Sorrows of Young Werther* was first published in 1774. A French translation was published in 1777, and the first English translation was 1779. In 1787, Goethe reissued the novel with significant changes to the original version. Fergusson was probably familiar with the novel and might have read either the French or English translation; see Orie W. Long, "English Translations of Goethe's Werther," *The Journal of German Philology* 14 (1915): 169–203.

Correspondence between Benjamin Franklin and Johann Karl Philipp Spener on the American Revolution

JÜRGEN OVERHOFF

B enjamin Franklin was, as his biographer Carl van Doren once famously put it, "a harmonious human multitude:" he was a public-minded citizen, a self-taught scientist, inventor of the lightning rod, a gifted educator, and prominent founder of the University of Pennsylvania.[1] Yet, until the end of his long life, Franklin was particularly proud to call himself a printer.[2] The printing business was his profession since he was a twelve-year old boy. Printing usually meant publishing news and exciting innovative ideas as quickly as possible. Sometimes, however, Franklin decided to take his time before setting something into print. He then circulated his ideas—spelled out in letters and manuscripts—among trustworthy readers, soliciting the thoughts of friends or colleagues for many weeks or even months. Sometimes it was highly advisable to refrain from immediate publication and to collect, assemble, and weigh the relevant material—to obtain the best, the most mature result.

Obviously, in the eighteenth-century Republic of Letters, Franklin was not the only printer who had grown used to circulating certain ideas—or even illustrations, engravings, and copper plates—among friends and acquaintances. The best and most prominent printers of North America and Europe regularly tested their thoughts by sharing their ideas. As Carla

Mulford has pointed out in her magisterial study of Franklin's political thought and his understanding of the ends of empire, circulating handwritten materials to reliable friends and colleagues offered an opportunity for information-sharing, critique, and mutual improvement. Circulating one's thoughts by way of manuscript was a method—a form of coterie publication —that Franklin and other printers used when they were still thinking about their data and positions on various topics.[3]

One of the leading European printers with whom Franklin shared his views on the history of the American Revolution was the renowned German publisher and bookseller Johann Karl Philipp Spener. Both men's interests strongly coincided in the spring and early summer of 1783, when the American War of Independence had come to an end and the United States emerged on the scene as a new political body of federated free states. Spener wanted to gather reliable and accurate information about the inspiring new American nation and the American people's republican constitution to feed his German readership with the most up-to-date information.[4] Franklin wanted to propagate the gospel of liberty and republicanism in Europe, hoping to pass on the torch of freedom to as many countries as possible.

Spener was one of Germany's leading publishers of his day. He was also the great-grandson of the Lutheran theologian Philipp Jacob Spener—the author of the famous 1675 tract "Pia desideria"—who was later dubbed the Father of Pietism.[5] Born in 1749 and based in his hometown and birthplace Berlin, the striving capital of the Kingdom of Prussia, Johann Karl Philipp Spener was by privilege of the Prussian King Frederick the Great director of the Berlin publishing firm Haude & Spener, a firm he had inherited from his father Johann Karl Spener and his uncle Ambrosius Haude in 1772. His father and uncle started their business partnership as early as 1740, when they published the first issue of the politically influential and commercially successful newspaper *Berlinische Nachrichten von Staats- und gelehrten Sachen*. Their publishing house was then formally and officially founded in 1748.

When Johann Karl Philipp became his late father's successor as the publishing house's sole director, he quickly made extensive use of his excellent contacts with the leading philosophers of the enlightenment in London and Paris. Between 1769 and 1772, Spener had travelled widely in Germany, Italy, France, England, Switzerland, and the Netherlands, and had become one of the closest friends of the botanist Sir Joseph Banks and of the famous naturalists Johann Reinhold and Georg Forster, who accompanied James Cook on his second voyage around the world.[6] During that formative and inspiring period of his youth, he also established firm relationships with some of the most important European publishers and printers. Despite

Spener's huge impact on the development of Germany's enlightenment culture—an impact that cannot be overestimated—it is a perplexing fact that no comprehensive, critical, modern biography of the man and his astonishing achievements exists to this day.[7]

Spener continued publishing the *Berlinische Nachrichten*, and he began editing a geographical weekly *Wöchentliche Nachrichten von neuen Landcharten*; yet, his most popular and highly influential publication was a monthly magazine called *Berlinische Monatsschrift*.[8] It appeared for the first time in January 1783 and soon became the preferred journal of the German philosophers of the enlightenment and of the Königsberg university professor Immanuel Kant, mainly due to the magazine's numerous contributions to the heated debate on the true concept of enlightenment. Kant's own article "Answering the Question: What is Enlightenment?" with its world-famous definition "Enlightenment is man's emergence from his self-incurred immaturity," was published in the fourth volume of Spener's *Berlinische Monatsschrift* as a reply to a similar question posed in the first volume of the Berlin monthly.

When Spener prepared the very first volume of the *Berlinische Monatsschrift*, he intended to dedicate it to Benjamin Franklin. The Berlin publisher wanted to pay homage to the United States of America, and, accordingly, he wanted to portray both the new democratic Federation and the man whom he described as the personification of the American Revolution. Moreover, Spener also intended to publish an American Almanac depicting the most important events of the American Revolution and of the War of Independence. Since Spener knew that his friend Georg Forster had regularly met and lunched with Franklin in Paris in 1777, he expected him to provide the relevant information, but Forster had to confess that his knowledge about Franklin's biography and the political reality of the United States was too meagre. Nevertheless, Forster explicitly encouraged Spener to collect and publish new and reliable information about Franklin and America. The cosmopolitan Forster agreed that Germans needed to know more about the U.S., the model state of the age of enlightenment.[9]

Therefore, in the spring of 1783, Spener turned to French acquaintances whom he rightly considered to be friends of Franklin, the historian and lawyer Michel-René Hilliard d'Auberteuil and the printer Jean-Georges Treuttel of Strasbourg, asking them to get in touch with the American ambassador to France and tell him about the interesting Berlin publishing project. And this is precisely what they did. In a letter from 12 April 1783, Hilliard d'Auberteuil pointed out to Franklin that "Charles Spener, Libraire du Roi de prusse" intended to publish an important "commemoration de la revolution glorieuse" in Germany, a commemoration of the sensational American Revolution that had come to an extremely satisfactory end in late 1782 and early 1783.[10] By way of this letter, he paved the ground for Spener, who now felt encouraged to approach Franklin himself with a letter of his own.

In a letter to Franklin from 26 May 1783, Spener greeted the American kindly and explained to him his exciting plan of publishing "un Almanac américain en allemande."[11] Spener stressed that the material included in this Almanac ought not to stem from the close reading of printed books. Instead, he sought to acquire written and firsthand information from Benjamin Franklin because he was an eyewitness and a famous protagonist of the American Revolution. And Spener signaled that he was prepared, if necessary, to postpone his publication project for a while because it was of the utmost importance for him to discuss the early history of the United States in his correspondence with Franklin in some detail. Certainly, his personal curiosity determined his exchange of letters with Franklin to a considerable extent—or at least as much as did the promises and expectations of the German book market.[12]

Spener first wanted to find out whether Franklin agreed with the "plan de cet Almanac," which he accordingly described in some detail.[13] Then, the Berlin printer and publisher wished to obtain accurate information not only about his correspondent Franklin but also about John Adams, another important political leader of the Americans and staunch defender of the principle of republicanism whom Spener held in equal esteem. Could Franklin provide him with a "Portrait de John Adams," possibly an engraving depicting the remarkable lawyer, orator, and political philosopher from Massachusetts?[14] Furthermore, Spener asked Franklin to provide him with colored sketches of the uniforms of the heroic General George Washington's regiment.[15] And, finally, he pointed out that he certainly wanted to find out from Franklin what would count as "les événemens les plus remarquables de cette guerre," the most memorable or important events of the American War of Independence.[16] Spener wished to pass on all of this written information to Matthias Christian Sprengel, "Professeur d'histoire" at the leading Prussian university at Halle, who was supposed to write "La partie historique de cet Almanac," designed as a full scale account of the American Revolution.[17]

Just a few days later, on 1 June 1783, Spener's French friend, the printer Jean-Georges Treuttel, gave him very strong support by sending another letter petitioning Franklin from Strasbourg. Treuttel had established himself in that large town—located close to the French border with Germany in the historic region of Alsace near Baden and Switzerland—around 1770 in association with the publisher Jean-Geoffrey Bauer.[18] The German printer Spener—"mon ami à Berlin," as Treuttel emphasized—certainly needed Franklin's indispensable advice in the attempt to understand and portray properly the dramatic course of the American Revolution in all of its most important facets.[19] So, it was really up to Franklin to choose the proper selection of material for the German publisher—"tout ce qu'il plairoit à Votre Excellence d'envoyer à M. Spener"—entirely as it would please His Excellency Franklin, as he himself considered it right, useful, decent, and appropriate.[20]

Unfortunately, Franklin's written response to Treuttel or Spener did not survive, it is obviously lost—but, luckily, not lost without a trace. For, on 15 January 1784, the French printer Treuttel expressly thanked Franklin on behalf of his Berlin friend Spener, "au nom du libraire entrepreneur le Sr. Spener," for having sent the much-desired material as a valuable contribution to a German-American enterprise of a very special kind.[21] Only because Franklin had been willing to share his special insights—in the form of some carefully assembled letters and manuscripts—with his European colleagues, outstanding printers from France and Germany, would the people of Germany obtain the opportunity, to experience—as it were, as first-hand witnesses—the American Revolution and its most important steps since its first beginnings in the 1760s.

The American Almanac, published in Berlin at the end of 1783, had already pleased many German readers. It consisted of three parts, separately paginated: an almanac, a genealogy of the principal courts of Europe, and a beautifully illustrated history of the American Revolution by Sprengel, the professor of history at the University of Halle whom Spener had recommended to Franklin in his letter of 26 May 1783. Treuttel exuberantly praised the extraordinary care Spener had taken with this "petit ouvrage."[22] Since this aesthetically pleasing American Almanac had come into existence only by way of Franklin's active assistance—or, as it were, under his Excellency's protection, "sous Sa Protection"—Treuttel felt obliged to present the American statesman with his own copy.[23] Thus, Franklin could see for himself whether the contents and illustrations of Spener's Almanac complied and corresponded with his own views on the American Revolution —and with the contents of the letters and manuscripts he had sent to Berlin.

The artist responsible for the thirteen spectacular engravings that adorned the third part of Spener's American Almanac, Sprengel's history of the American Revolution, was the Berlin painter, printmaker, and etcher Daniel Nikolaus Chodowiecki, one of the leading German artists of the late eighteenth century, who also acted as the vice-director of the Berlin Academy of Art. Chodowiecki, born in the Free City of Danzig and a Protestant with Huguenot ancestry, was best known during his lifetime for his rather small drawings and for his sophisticated book illustrations—all carried out in masterly detail—some of which are still considered today as the most famous icons of eighteenth-century German graphic art.[24]

This American Almanac, entitled by its publisher, Spener, *Allgemeines Historisches Taschenbuch oder Abriß der merkwürdigsten neuen Welt-Begebenheiten* (or, in English translation: *Historic Genealogical Calendar or Yearbook of the Most Remarkable New World Occurrences*) gives the reader more than just an idea of what Franklin might have suggested to Spener when pointing to the most memorable or important events of the American War of Independence.[25] Spener's American Almanac, a rare pictorial broadsheet of the American Revolution, depicts and describes the burning of the Stamp Act of 1764 by outraged colonists in Boston; the Boston Tea Party of 1773; the Battles of Lexington and Concord on 19 April 1775; Congress declaring America's Independence from Britain on 4 July 1776; George Washington's Capture of the Hessians at Trenton at Christmas 1776; the Battle of Saratoga in the fall of 1777; Benjamin Franklin's first audience before King Louis XVI of France at the palace of Versailles, 20 March 1778; the landing of a French auxiliary army under the command of the Comte de Rochambeau in Newport, Rhode Island, 11 July 1780; the Capture of the British Major John André on 23 September 1780 near Tarrytown; the Battle of Yorktown, 19 October 1781; and, as the most recent event, the last British soldiers leaving New York on 25 November 1783 (figs. 1 and 2).

Finally, Spener's American Almanac also portrayed George Washington as well as his regiment in a scene depicting the arrival of the General's troops with Hessian prisoners of war in Philadelphia at the end of December 1776. Chodowiecki's set of twelve engravings was published in black-and-white; in addition, there were also three colored plates included at the end of the Almanac: the American flag and a pennant, the uniforms of regular infantry troops from Pennsylvania, and the uniforms of Washington's troops, which is exactly what Spener had asked for in his letter of 26 May 1783, when explaining his publishing project in detail and requesting Franklin's assistance in providing colored illustrations.

All of the marvelous black-and-white engravings as well as the skillfully produced colored plates illustrated an exciting story masterfully told by the historian Sprengel.[26] Born in the northern German Hanseatic town of Rostock in 1745, Sprengel matriculated at the Hanoverian University of Göttingen, one of the leading institutions of higher education in Germany with a focus on North American Studies. The leading scholars of Europe held Göttingen in the highest esteem, and even Franklin had visited that university's excellent library in 1766 on his extended trip through Germany.[27] Sprengel had taken up his studies in the early 1770s, just a few years after Franklin had toured the German Empire. In 1776, shortly after the Declaration of Independence, the young scholar Sprengel published a short treatise on the rebelling colonies—the newly founded United States of America—which

*Die Americaner wiedersetzen sich der
. Stempel-Acte, und verbrennen das aus
England nach America gesandte Stempel-
Papier zu Boston im August 1764 .*

Figure 1. Anti-Stamp Act, Boston, 1765. Bostonians protesting the Stamp Act by burning the stamps in a bonfire. Johann Karl Philipp Spener, *American Almanac* (1783). Engraving by Daniel Nikolaus Chodowiecki. Courtesy of the University Library of the Martin-Luther-Universität Halle-Wittenberg.

went into several editions, and a collection of letters on the present state of North America.[28] His sudden success as a public authority on North America quickly earned him an associate professorship of history at Göttingen in 1778, and his inaugural lecture dealt with the topic of "the history and present situation of the British colonies in America."[29]

Figure 2. Benjamin Franklin at the Court of King Louis XVI of France, 1778. Johann Karl Philipp Spener, *American Almanac* (1783). Engraving by Daniel Nikolaus Chodowiecki. Courtesy of the University Library of the Martin-Luther-Universität Halle-Wittenberg.

In 1779, Sprengel accepted the post of full professor of history at the University of Halle, where he dedicated his first lecture to the origins of the slave trade in North America. At Halle, he soon became acquainted with the professor of natural history and mineralogy Johann Reinhold Forster, later his father-in-law, who had accompanied James Cook on his second Pacific voyage. Forster shared Sprengel's genuine interest in the Western hemisphere and all things American, and he encouraged him to continue writing on that subject. At the University of Halle, Sprengel gave two very popular and well-attended lectures on the War of Independence, and he published two more books on the United States in the fall of 1782.[30]

Obviously, Sprengel had already acquired a unique reputation in Germany as an expert on North America, when Spener, quite understandably, asked him to write an up to date history of the now free and sovereign Union of the thirteen American free states for his American Almanac. When Spener's Almanac was published immediately after the Treaty of Paris of September 1783, Sprengel's account of the early U.S. was the first comprehensive study of the subject available on the German book market. It gained popularity almost overnight. A year after its first appearance in the bookshops of Germany, the historian Johann Friedrich Poppe expressed his great astonishment that the Almanac was by then "in everybody's hands."[31]

The third part of Spener's American Almanac, Sprengel's historical account of the American Revolution, went through five editions between 1783 and 1788. As part of the first reprint of the Almanac, it was published again in Berlin in 1784, but all of the other editions of Sprengel's text appeared in the form of individual, freestanding publications at Speyer in 1785 and at Frankenthal in 1785 and 1788, running to some 180 pages and bearing the new title *Geschichte der Revolution von Nord-Amerika*—making it the most popular German account on North America in the late eighteenth century. Although Sprengel's history of the American Revolution showed some similarities with Guillaume Thomas François Raynal's *Revolution de l'Amerique* of 1781, emphasizing the beneficial effects resulting from the revolutionary character of the recent political upheavals and changes in North America, the author failed to list Raynal's book in his bibliography.[32]

Instead, he pointed to different sources. He acknowledged that, when "the publisher Mr. Spener had spread out his well-thought-out plan" of editing an American Almanac, he had provided Sprengel—the man whom he hired as the best and most competent author on that subject matter—with fresh and relevant material directly "from America."[33] Sprengel, for his part, obviously did not feel the need to highlight or even to mention, that it was Franklin himself, one of the leading revolutionaries, who had assisted and contributed to this German project. Yet, in a biographical sketch of Franklin, which was attached to his lengthy account of the American Revolution in the concluding part of the Almanac, where he sang paeans to Franklin as a man to whom "America will dedicate altars" and "whose name Europe will hold in the highest regards for years to come," the Prussian historian from Halle reported a rumor of particular interest.[34] Sprengel proudly boasted that he had "credibly" heard from a reliable informant that Franklin would soon be writing an autobiographical account of his early life and intellectual development.[35] Apparently, the historian wanted to indicate that he and his publisher Spener had special access to privileged knowledge which ultimately stemmed from Franklin. Thus, it does not come as a surprise that when Sprengel referred to the best of the "existing printed sources," he strongly recommended a recent collection of Franklin's political writings— and he highly prized the political essays of Hillard d'Auberteuil, the French historian who had served as an intermediary in the exchange of letters between Spener and Franklin.[36]

Franklin's visible influence on the particular makeup of Spener's Almanac may also count for the fact that the person who does not play a prominent role in it is John Adams. Chodowiecki's illustration that highlights Franklin's first audience before King Louis XVI at the palace of Versailles on 20 March 1778 depicts a servile Adams in the corner of the picture, while all the magic and splendor of this remarkable situation is bestowed upon Franklin. Whereas Franklin's name is proudly mentioned by Chodowiecki in the engraving's subtitle, Adams goes entirely unnoticed. Even in Sprengel's account of the American Revolution, Adams's name is likewise lacking and his contribution to the course of events entirely ignored by the author. Perhaps Franklin did not even refer to Adams in his lost letter to Spener and Treuttel—maybe he wanted to downplay the role Adams played in the American Revolution. This is at least exactly what Adams later complained about when he insinuated that Franklin always wished to blacken his reputation.[37]

Spener's American Almanac, one can safely conclude, was the result of a close transnational cooperation among American, French, and German printers and publishers, who discussed the right kind of portrayal of the newly founded United States of America in 1783 in letters—before this portrayal of America actually went into print. One could argue that these letters— praising and describing the exciting democratic and republican structures established on the North American continent during the time of the War of Independence—can count as some discernable and interesting instances of a particular paradigm of manuscript literature which has been aptly called "republican literature."[38] Later, in the 1790s, it became fashionable to publish the newest reports about America in the form of printed letters.[39] A decade earlier, however, Spener's American Almanac was the first illustrated history of the American Revolution to be published in Germany—and the way it was described and depicted shaped the understanding of the early history of the United States in Germany for a long time.[40]

NOTES

1. Carl Van Doren, *Benjamin Franklin* (New York: Viking Press, 1938), 782; on the civic minded Franklin, see Walter Isaacson, *Benjamin Franklin: An American Life* (New York: Simon and Schuster, 2003); on Franklin as scientist and inventor of the lightning rod, see the insightful and elegantly written monograph by James Delbourgo, *A Most Amazing Scene of Wonders: Electricity and Enlightenment in Early America* (Cambridge MA: Harvard Univ. Press, 2006); on Franklin's pedagogical efforts, see Jürgen Overhoff, "Franklin's Philadelphia Academy and Basedow's Dessau Philanthropine. Two Models of Non-Denominational Schooling in Eighteenth-Century America and Germany," *Paedagogica Historica: International Journal of the History of Education* 43 (2007): 801–18.

2. Franklin always identified himself the way he would do in the opening words of his last will and testament: "I, Benjamin Franklin of Philadelphia, Printer," Last Will and Codicil, 23 June 1789, ed. David W. Packard, *The Papers of Benjamin Franklin*, Packard Humanities Institute (CD-ROM-Version), 46 (1988): 20.

3. Carla J. Mulford, *Benjamin Franklin and the Ends of Empire* (Oxford: Oxford Univ. Press, 2015), 164–65.

4. On the general reception of the American Revolution in late eighteenth-century Germany, see Horst Dippel, *Germany and the American Revolution. 1770–1800,* trans. Bernhard A. Uhlendorf (Chapel Hill: Univ. of North Carolina Press, 1978).

5. Philipp Jacob Spener, *Pia desideria oder herzliches Verlangen nach gottgefälliger Besserung der wahren evangelischen Kirche* (Frankfurt am Main, 1675). Many of Spener's early followers migrated in 1683 from Frankfurt am Main and Krefeld to Philadelphia, where they founded Germantown and became close allies of the colony's founder William Penn, who had visited Frankfurt am Main in 1677.

6. Spener's close relationship with Georg Forster has been aptly described by Klaus Harpprecht, *Georg Forster oder die Liebe zur Welt* (Reinbek bei Hamburg: Rowohlt, 1987).

7. A brief biographical sketch of Spener is offered by Klaus Bender, "Johann Karl Philipp Spener," ed. Heinz-Dietrich Fischer, *Deutsche Presseverleger des 18. bis 20. Jahrhunderts.* (Pullach bei München: Verlag Dokumentation, 1975).

8. The *Wöchentliche Nachrichten von neuen Landcharten, geographischen, statistischen und historischen Büchern und Sachen* was edited by the Hamburg geographer Anton Friedrich Büsching and published by Haude & Spener in Berlin from 1773 to 1788.

9. Jürgen Overhoff, "Benjamin Franklin und die Berliner Aufklärung," eds. Ursula Goldenbaum and Alexander Kosenina, *Berliner Aufklärung. Kulturwissenschaftliche Studien,* 4 vols. (Hannover: Wehrhahn, 2007), 3: 64–86, 74.

10. Michel-René Hilliard d'Auberteuil to Benjamin Franklin, 12 April 1783, ed. Ellen R. Cohn, *The Papers of Benjamin Franklin,* 39 vols. (21 January through

15 May 1783), (New Haven and London: Yale Univ. Press, 2008), 39: 458; for background on this planned publication, see Eugene E. Doll, "American History as Interpreted by German Historians from 1770–1815," *Transactions of the American Philosophical Society*, new series 38 vols. (1948–49): 461–64.

11. Johann Karl Philipp Spener to Benjamin Franklin, Berlin, 26 May 1783, in *The Papers of Benjamin Franklin*, 40 vols. (16 May through 15 September 1783), (New Haven and London: Yale Univ. Press, 2011), 40: 68.

12. With regard to the history of the book and manuscripts in the eighteenth century, David S. Shields rightly emphasizes the importance of "the arenas of manuscript publication, where an economy of gift rather than a market determines the circulation of most texts" in *Civil Tongues and Polite Letters in British America* (Chapel Hill: The Univ. of North Carolina Press, 1997), xxx-xxxi.

13. Johann Karl Philipp Spener to Benjamin Franklin, Berlin, 26 May 1783, in *The Papers of Benjamin Franklin*, 40: 68.

14. Johann Karl Philipp Spener to Benjamin Franklin, Berlin, 26 May 1783, 40: 69.

15. Johann Karl Philipp Spener to Benjamin Franklin, Berlin, 26 May 1783, 40: 69–70: "Uniforme des Troupes américaines, nommément des Regiments de Washington."

16. Johann Karl Philipp Spener to Benjamin Franklin, Berlin, 26 May 1783, 40: 68.

17. Johann Karl Philipp Spener to Benjamin Franklin, Berlin, 26 May 1783, 40: 70.

18. Jean-Dominique Mellot and Elisabeth Queval, comps., *Répertoire d'imprimeurs/libraires* (Paris, 1997), 63–4, 578.

19. Jean-Georges Treuttel to Benjamin Franklin, 1 June 1783, 40: 108.

20. Jean-Georges Treuttel to Benjamin Franklin, 1 June 1783, 40: 108.

21. Jean-Georges Treuttel to Benjamin Franklin, 15 January 1784, in *The Papers of Benjamin Franklin*, 41 vols. (16 September 1783 through 29 February 1784), (New Haven and London: Yale Univ. Press, 2014), 41: 474.

22. Jean-Georges Treuttel to Benjamin Franklin, 15 January 1784, 41: 474.

23. Jean-Georges Treuttel to Benjamin Franklin, 15 January 1784, 41: 475.

24. On Chodowiecki, see Ernst Hinrichs and Klaus Zernack, eds. *Daniel Chodowiecki (1726–1801): Kupferstecher, Illustrator, Kaufmann* (Tübingen: Niemeyer Verlag, 1997); Helmut Bernt, *Eine Berliner Künstlerkarriere im 18. Jahrhundert: Daniel Nikolaus Chodowiecki; vom Kaufmannslehrling zum Medienstar* (Graz: Leykam, 2013). Chodowiecki's engravings are published and described in Wilhelm Engelmann, *Daniel Chodowieckis sämmtliche Kupferstiche. Nachträge und Berichtigungen von Robert Hirsch*. Reprint of the Leipzig editions of 1857 and 1906 (Hildesheim: Olms Verlag); Jens-Heiner Bauer, *Daniel Nikolaus Chodowiecki (Danzig 1726–1801 Berlin). Das druckgraphische Werk. Die Sammlung Wilhelm Burggraf zu Dohna Schlobitten* (Hannover: J. H. Bauer, 1982).

25. Matthias Christian Sprengel, *Allgemeines Historisches Taschenbuch oder Abriß der merkwürdigsten neuen Welt-Begebenheiten enthaltend für 1784 die Geschichte der Revolution von Nord-America* (Berlin: Haude und Spener, 1783).

26. A modern biography of Sprengel is a significant desideratum in scholarly research. The most reliable information on the Prussian historian is provided by Bruno Felix Hänsch, *Matthias Christian Sprengel, ein geographischer Publizist am Ausgange des 18. Jahrhunderts* (publ. Ph.D. diss., Univ. of Leipzig, 1902).

27. On Franklin's trip to Germany and his stay at Göttingen, see Jürgen Overhoff, "Benjamin Franklin, Student of the Holy Roman Empire: His Summer Journey to Germany in 1766 and His Interest in the Empire's Federal Constitution," *German Studies Review* 34, no. 2 (2011): 277–86.

28. Matthias Christian Sprengel, *Kurze Schilderung der Grosbritannischen Kolonien* (Göttingen, 1776); Matthias Christian Sprengel, *Briefe den gegenwärtigen Zustand von Nord Amerika betreffend* (Göttingen: Dieterich, 1777).

29. Hänsch, *Sprengel*, 15.

30. Hänsch, 17; Matthias Christian Sprengel, *Geschichte der Europäer in Nordamerika* (Leipzig, 1782); Matthias Christian Sprengel, *Über den jetzigen Nord-Amerikanischen Krieg und dessen Folgen für England und Frankreich* (Leipzig, 1782).

31. "in jedermanns Händen:" Johann Friedrich Poppe, *Geschichte der Europäischen Staaten,* 2 vols. (Halle: Gebauer, 1784), 360.

32. Matthias Christian Sprengel, *Geschichte der Revolution von Nord America* (Frankenthal, 1785). The two-page bibliography is attached to the preface to the reader.

33. Sprengel, *Geschichte der Revolution*, Preface: "Als mir daher der Verleger Herr Carl Spener, diesen von ihm wohl ausgesonnenen Plan eröffnete;" Sprengel, 180: "aus America."

34. Sprengel, 266: "America wird ihm . . . Altäre bauen" and "Europa wird noch spät den Namen des Mannes mit Achtung nennen."

35. Sprengel, 171: "wie wir glaubwürdig wissen."

36. Sprengel, Preface: "gedruckten vorhandenen Quellen;" Sprengel referred to the following writings: Benjamin Franklin, *Political, Miscellaneous and Philosophical Pieces* (London: J. Johnson, 1779). This collection of political and philosophical essays had been translated in 1780 by Gottfried Traugott Wenzel, *Des Herrn D. Benjamin Franklin's Sämmtliche Werke: Abhandlungen über Gegenstände der allgemeinen Staatskunst*, 3 vols. (Dresden, 1780), and Michel-René Hilliard d'Auberteuil, *Essai sur les Anglo-Americains*, 3 vols. (Paris, 1782).

37. On reproachful Adams, see David McCullough, *John Adams* (New York, 2001), 276–77.

38. Michael Warner, *The Letters of the Republic: Publication and the Public Sphere in Eighteenth-Century America* (Cambridge, MA: Harvard Univ. Press, 1982), 132–37.

39. See, for example, [George Logan], *Letters Addressed to the Yeomanry of the United States* (Philadelphia, 1791); J. Hector St. John [M. G. St. J. de Crèvecoeur], *Letters from an American Farmer* (Philadelphia, 1793).

40. Overhoff, "Benjamin Franklin und die Berliner Aufklärung," 83.

ARTS AND MANUFACTURES

Clifford Lecture

What Remains of the Flavors of the Eighteenth Century?

DAVID S. SHIELDS

Mine is a culinary and an agricultural inquiry. I approach the question avoiding the narrowest way of construing what remains of the flavors of the eighteenth century? I can imagine a foodie magazine (*Lucky Peach* before its demise) commissioning an epicurean writer to secure fruit from the oldest bearing fruit trees in the world—from the Zenji-Muro Persimmon Tree at Ozengi Temple in Japan; the Pizzaro Fig planted at the Governor's Palace in Lima in 1540; the Breadfruit Tree at Galle, Sri Lanka; the Muso di Bui Apple growing in a seventeenth-century homestead outside of Foligno, Italy; the John Endicott Pear Tree in Danvers, Massachusetts planted in the 1640s; the Olive Tree of Vouves in Chania, Greece, reckoned to be well over two millennia old; or, one of the dozen James I Mulberries still living in Britain (planted to promote the silk trade though it was later discovered silk worms did not savor the leaves of the Persian Black mulberries that the king promoted).[1] But I am aware this approach only invites precisionist objections: "Oh, the water of the 1640s contained less cadmium and so would have tasted different than that of 2016," or "Because accidentals of weather produce different epigenetic responses season by season, giving rise to greatly different tastes each year in crops, it is nonsense to speak of an enduring same flavor in even the same plant in the same place." I wish humans could taste cadmium, since it is toxic, and they, therefore, could detect and avoid it.

105

There is, however, a set of questions about tasting and taste explored by Denise Gigante in her *Taste: A Literary History* that I think has traction in the inquiry we're about to make.[2] Our reception, our basic understanding of what we are tasting, depends on expectations that are learned, indeed schooled. Of the ancient fruit listed above, I have only tasted one: the Endicott Pear.[3] (Another person in the tasting party, upon biting into a ripe fruit, exclaimed "Oh—sour—terrible!" He had never tasted out of hand a fruit intended for making Perry before. Half of the first pear trees shipped to America were intended to generate fruit for cider-making. These varieties tend to have a pronounced sharpness to their flavor that becomes bright when processed into alcohol.)

In 2017, fifteen apple varieties accounted for 90 percent of production in the United States. They monopolize groceries' produce bins: McIntosh, Fuji, Red Delicious, Gala, Crispin (or Mutsu), Braeburn, Honey Crisp, Jonagold, Granny Smith, Empire, Golden Delicious, Cameo, Jazz, Macoun, Ambrosia, Paula Red, Cortland, and Pink Lady.[4] The oldest is McIntosh, which was introduced in 1811.[5] Ten of the fifteen date from the last half of the twentieth century. All of these fruits were designed for versatility: they are so-called all arounders. We have little experience of the old apples bred and finely attuned to specific purposes—for drying, making apple sauce, baking, eating out of hand. Not knowing ahead of time the particular use of the apple, an eater risks misapprehending its taste.

I suppose the most 2017 thing about the experience that I have described above is that my audience is envisioned exclusively in the position of a consumer. None of you did the breeding that shaped the flavor of an apple, vegetable, or grain. We all operate at a moment when the creation of plants is for the most part conducted by a scientific priesthood of geneticists and commercial plant breeders. This is a recent development in history: 1887 in the United States marks a demarcation point in plant creation, for, in that year, the U. S. government established the system of agricultural experimental stations. Prior to this time, most grains, vegetables, and fruits were farmer improved, shaped by seed selection, natural mutation, and cross pollination.[6] The oldest and most enduring varieties of vegetables so created are called *landraces*.

Since 2003, I have been closely involved in the preservation and restoration into cultivation of the landrace grains associated with southern food. In addition to my academic appointment, I head a non-profit organization, The Carolina Gold Rice Foundation, that has repatriated approximately thirty cultivars to American fields and tables.[7] Our efforts have been chronicled in *The New Yorker*, *The New York Times*, *The Wall Street Journal*, NPR, the BBC, "The Mind of a Chef" TV show, *Modern Farmer*, and *National*

Geographic. Why the attention? Because invariably each restoration has been viewed as a recuperation of a splendid flavor in the face of an industrial food system that inveterately prioritizes the productivity, disease resistance, appearance, transportability, processability, and shelf life over the intrinsic taste of ingredients.[8]

When communities of farmers bred the grains that they consumed, they invariably bred for good flavor. The quality they sought was wholesomeness—an unsensational, satisfying, agreeableness that communicated rightness, healthfulness, and desirability. These judgments were rendered usually on the simplest of preparations—a whole grain porridge for instance. We should in no way regard flavor in this effort as an ornamental quality, an aesthetic supplement. For human beings, as with all biological entities, from paramecia to birds, taste was the means by which living beings determined what was edible and nourishing in their environment.[9] We are chemically hard-wired to respond to certain flavors that clue us about their benefit to us. Landraces were edible plants tweaked by seed selection over hundreds, sometimes thousands of plant generations to be maximally wholesome.[10] Sometimes, certain plants constitute a prehistoric culture's wisdom about human sustenance. The plants themselves are the books that contain the knowledge of physic, cultivation, and climate. The fifty-nine surviving maize landraces preserved in Mexico are strains that have come down to us from before the arrival of Cortez.[11]

Globally, the eclipse of the landraces began in the late 1960s when Norman Borlaug inaugurated the Green Revolution. It was the high point of twentieth-century salvific science, when farmers' traditional landraces were supplanted by new, high-yielding varieties (HYVs) of cereals, especially dwarf wheats and rices, in association with chemical fertilizers and agro-chemicals, with controlled water supply (usually involving irrigation), and new methods of cultivation, including mechanization. All of these together were seen as a package of practices to supersede traditional technology and to be adopted as a whole. Cereals planted for centuries were no longer cultivated, and the seed was no longer selected and preserved. Instead, a global rice or corn bred without concern for how it suited cultural foodways was disseminated by international agencies and large corporations. It promoted food self-sufficiency while putting the farmers in the developing world in a dependency relation with multinational seed and chemical companies. Cultivators who signed onto the global initiative surrendered control over seed. Seed saving and the farmer improvement of grains and vegetables ceased.[12]

There are four multinational corporations that control most of the crop seed in the world—over 75 percent: Bayer, Corteva (Dow & Dupont), Chemchina, and Limagrain-Vilmorin-Mikado.[13] The companies have several goals: the yearly purchase of seed from the company (no farmers saving seed); the yearly purchase of a package of soil supplementations, herbicide, fungicide, and insecticide; and, the elimination of competition from other companies. The genetic engineering of seed so that crop plants cannot be replicated, the creation of plants designed to convert the chemical mixtures in fertility packages into organic matter, and the buying up of all conventional and traditional seed companies to eliminate redundancy in the offerings of plants have led to a situation in which genetic bottlenecking is the norm. Because landraces are public domain—there is no proprietary claim to them—because their seeds *can* be saved—and because they were bred to interact with living soil rather than sterilized fields into which a chemical supplement package has been injected, the landraces have been everything industrial agriculture regards as recherché. But because these old plant strains have root systems much more intricate than modern cultivars designed to suck up fertilizer, the landraces have a greater capacity to interact with the fungal agents, microbes, and minerals in the soil to extract and produce nutriment.[14]

Landraces taste better and are more nutritious. So how did the industrial farming system direct its genius to breeding less tasty and less nutritious ingredients? A capsule history of a famous watermelon will suggest why.[15] In the antebellum United States, Nathaniel Napoleon Bradford crossed the Lawson watermelon, a West Indian landrace, with the Carolina Long to produce the Bradford melon. Everyone concurred that it was the finest melon ever produced. The Civil War takes place. There is one intact rail line from the South heading northward, and it goes through Augusta, GA. In the spring and summer of 1865, the farmers of the South scrambled to produce anything that would generate revenue. They shipped boxcars of Rattlesnake and Bradford watermelons to Washington Market, New York City. New Yorkers had never tasted anything so heavenly and demanded more. So, southern truck farming for northern markets was born. But there was a problem—that fork tender, one-inch rind of the Bradford might make the perfect rind pickle, but it could not support the weight of a stack of melons on top of it. Farmers could not make a profit if 40 percent of the melons that they shipped north were destroyed. What to do? Well, why not cross the Bradford or the Rattlesnake with another melon with a skin as tough as a rhino hide? The Scaly Bark. This was done: the Kolb's Gem watermelon could be stacked four deep in a boxcar with no compression. It didn't taste as good as a Bradford—but, hey, it was New Yorkers who were eating it. (We grow Bradfords in our back patch.) But the truth of the matter is that farmers put their heart where the money was, and hundreds of square miles of Georgia and South Carolina were planted with Kolb's Gem.

Entire counties were converted to watermelon fields. And when farmers create hundreds of square miles of just one thing, sooner or later that pest or pathogen will show up and find the promised land. This happened in 1893 when fusarium wilt appeared in southern Georgia and began wiping out hundreds of square miles of fields. The cultivators began pleading for a disease resistant melon. So the Kolb Gem was crossed with a Congo. The Bradford, best tasting melon in the U.S., had its last commercial crop in 1920 until we rediscovered it in 2011.

We see how flavor is marginalized by other matters, called by breeders, "harvestibles." But you know, someone kept the Bradford alive. There was something about its taste. And that is a truth manifested in many places around the world: if a fruit, grain, or vegetable is truly the most flavorsome or wholesome of its category, there will be some true believer somewhere who defies the international agencies, the American USDA, and the seed companies who keeps the strain alive. Sometimes, the agencies themselves do—because the qualities of some ancient things have been so superlative that they were used to breed novelties. This is what happened with the landrace rice Carolina Gold that was the staple of the southern Lowcountry from 1786 to 1918. It was a funny thing—in the 1990s, old people who had tasted the classic recipes from Charleston, SC and Savannah, GA—rice pudding, hopping john, perloo, chicken bog—found that they just didn't taste right. Not as good. They had the recipes right. The bag of rice at the grocery store had Carolina Rice printed on it. But it was a charade. It was a brand name for Cocodrie, a long grain HYV crop rice. It doesn't matter how accurate a family recipe is if the ingredients are all wrong; the taste just won't come right.

Charleston's chefs demanded that something be done. They wanted real Carolina Gold Rice. This demand was in the wake of chef Alice Waters's campaign to focus on the quality of the vegetable in cookery. Those in the culinary-know knew something was wrong—something had vanished. What had been lost? What needed to be returned? Unfortunately, these are questions that have never mattered much in agricultural history. Glenn Roberts, a miller of heirloom grains, took the initiative, founding Anson Mills and searching for survivals. Oddly enough, he found me in 2003.[16] He had determined that the only way out of the quagmire was to delve into old agricultural journals and seed catalogues, to learn the growing systems that gave rise to Lowcountry cuisine. Archival research required the investigation of multitudes of sub-literary texts: grist for a book historian, not a miller or a chef. I descended into the microfilm bunker of the University of South Carolina library—three years later, I emerged with a list of what we had lost. Then, we went searching for germ plasm, trying to see if and where something survived. While this story purportedly has a local focus (we were recuperating southern cooking and Lowcountry cuisine after all), the searches necessarily involved us in webs of commerce that spanned the Atlantic and the hemisphere.

Perhaps the story of our most recent recuperation will suggest something of the nature of this quest. Thomas Jefferson thought that one of his greatest accomplishments was introducing dry cultivation upland rice to the United States.[17] Growing rice like a garden plant, not in a water impoundment, avoided the scourge of malaria and made rice growing affordable to farmers lacking the huge capital resources of coastal rice planters. It could be grown in the Piedmont South and not just the tidal zone of coastal rivers. It could be cultivated by any farmer with access to seed of a rice strain bred to thrive in upland settings. In the third world today, dry cultivation garden style rice (also called System of Rice Intensification or SRI cultivation) is the cutting edge of rice growing systems. Jefferson had been inspired to search out upland dry culture rice from reports on its existence in Cochin China (Vietnam) published in the 1770s. Despite diplomatic overtures, he could not secure the rice from Asia, but he learned of an upland rice growing on another continent.

In 1789, Jefferson secured upland rice from West Africa through Captain Nathaniel Cutting. This bearded rice with a red bran sheath around the grain subsequently would be distributed throughout the South. Abraham Baldwin, founder of University of Georgia, shipped seed throughout Alabama, Mississippi, and Georgia. Eventually, it spread to Tennessee and Kentucky.[18] Sometime in the early twentieth century, it disappeared, driven from the landscape by cheap white rice grown in Texas and Arkansas. Though historians often speak of enslaved West Africans bringing their native glaberrima rices to the New World, all of the great crop rices (Carolina Gold, Carolina White, and their offspring) were sub-tropical Japonicas whose genetic lineage led back to South Asia—except, perhaps, for this one upland rice grown widely in the non-coastal South.

In the twenty-first century, upland bearded rice was no longer found anywhere in North America. In late 2016, The Carolina Gold Rice Foundation went looking for it as part of an effort to document and restore the African rice heritage of the South. Gullah chef B. J. Dennis and I encountered it in December in Trinidad, where it is called Merikin Hill Rice. Ethnobotanist Francis Morean had invited us to Arima, Trinidad, to participate in the Inaugural Trinidad and Tobago International Hill Rice Symposium and Festival. I went because I suspected the Hill Rice that Dr. Morean had been studying might be the lost bearded upland rice from West Africa.

How did the bearded upland rice get to Trinidad? Apparently, it was taken there from coastal Georgia in 1816. During the War of 1812, the British recruited enslaved Africans to fight against their masters with the promise of liberation and settlement somewhere in the empire. These Georgia coastal recruits made up the 4th British Marine Company. In 1816, the British fulfilled their promise and settled the ex-soldiers in southern Trinidad. Since that time, they have called themselves the Merikins (i.e,. Americans) and they have grown the crops that their ancestors grew in lowcountry Georgia: benne, okra, tanya, and rice—including the bearded dry patch rice now lost in the South.

Figure 1 depicts John Eliot, a sixth generation descendent of one of the 4th regiment soldiers, working his rice field.[19] How do we know that what John Elliott holds aloft in his hands is the same as the product brought to North America in 1789? Well, it is not the same, just as any sexually propagated creature introduces variability with each generation. But landraces are shaped by a traditional sense of what is pertinent in a plant. It becomes more of what made the plant originally valuable. And since Moruga Hill Rice has been bred and propagated by farmer seed selection since 1816 in Trinidad (there are no commercial suppliers of seed), there has been a communal endeavor to keep its qualities.

For an integral, traditional community of long standing to maintain a landrace is not so unusual. There are places all over the world where a favorite cereal has been kept by a district of farmers, sometimes a family. When Portugal made the island of Madeira its bread basket at the end of the fifteenth century, it secured durum wheat from Sicily. Approximately sixty landraces have survived to the present day. Some were imported in later centuries from the other parts of the Iberian empire, particularly during the era when the thrones of Portugal and Spain were combined, and numbers of landraces arose from crosses of the earliest varieties that were seed selected for qualities. These landraces became of interest for me because of the report of the early naturalist Mark Catesby, who, in the 1720s, observed the wheat being grown in the Carolina Lowcountry: "That which is propagated in Carolina, came first from the Madera Island, none being found so agreeable to this Country, it lying in a parallel Latitude. The Grain has a thinner Coat, and yields more Flour than that of England."[20] The wheat of England here referenced was White May wheat, which did not thrive in the hot climates of the deep South. Durum wheat is a hard wheat, ideal for breads and pastas; White May was a soft white wheat, suited for cake, confections, and, after the invention of chemical leavening in the late eighteenth century, biscuits.

The kind of latitudinal thinking we find among the early Lowcountry planters is found in others. The Salzburgers, the group of Austrian dissenters who settled in Georgia in the 1740s, knew that the wheat of their old

Figure 1. John Eliot at his field of Moruga Hill Rice, outside Princes Town, Trinidad. Photo David S. Shields, Carolina Gold Rice Foundation.

home would not serve in their settlement at Ebenezer. So they used their connections to secure a landrace durum from Sicily, Timilia.[21] They were the finest millers and bakers in the British American southern colonies, and their three mills produced wheat until the dissolution of their group during the American Revolution.

What happens when cultivators do not take climatic difference into consideration? Well—what happened in Virginia with the White May wheat that the colonists brought from Lincoln in England: it became prone to diseases, such as rust, and insects, such as the joint worm, and, finally, it crashed entirely in the 1820s—a genetic collapse. Disgruntled farmers in the eighteenth century, tired of the declining vitality of their wheat, secured another seed stock—one with an extremely short time to maturity. They planted it in the winter, harvesting it before it was warm enough for bugs to thrive or disease to flourish. It took on a number of names: purple straw, blue stem being the commonest, and it survived in the southern landscape from the 1770s to the 1970s, supplanted only because hybrid wheat varieties were more productive per acre. The Amish in southern Ohio still grow it. This was the original biscuit, cake, and whiskey wheat of the South.[22]

And, White May wheat? What happened to it? Some was brought into the American Southwest by Spanish missionaries for communion bread. It was adopted by native Americans and survived in plots in Arizona and New Mexico as Sonora White wheat. Early in the nineteenth century, Australian colonists grew the English strain, improving it, and, in the mid-nineteenth century, shipped it to California, where it was known as blue stem wheat (not to be confused with blue stem purple straw wheat). And a third trajectory: in the 1810s, some of the Virginia germ plasm was sent out to plant the fields around Fort Vancouver, the British fort and trading post in the Pacific Northwest. White May wheat was planted as Washington's major variety into the twentieth century. A USDA plant hunter secured germ plasm in 1909. Ten years ago, Richard Scheurman and the Palouse Heritage project secured seed from the USDA and restored White May in Washington state, the botanical people at Monticello in Virginia secured seed from him, and we did as well.[23] But if it crashed 200 years ago, then I'm in no way sanguine about how it will prosper now.

I have told this story because three landraces of White May wheat crossed the globe and the continent to survive into the twenty-first century. Since it was one of England's staples and extensively grown for centuries, we can look at the genetic deviation of these three strains from material secured by thatch archaeologists in Great Britain. And what do we find? As with all landraces, the populations possess some genetic diversity. This is what allows the plants to adapt to conditions more readily than modern hybridized varieties. But the family resemblance remains pronounced. Furmity—wheat porridge (cream of wheat) made from the three different populations—tastes exactly the same. Can the flavors of the eighteenth century still be tasted? Yes.

NOTES

1. Widget Finn, "The turbulent history of the mulberry," *The Telegraph* (10 September 2015); Lifestyle, 1. This newspaper story sparked a major increase in tourist visitation of the various mulberry sites in England.

2. Denise Gigante, *Taste: A Literary History* (New Haven: Yale Univ. Press, 2005), 140–41, 166–72.

3. Katharine Stanley Nicholson surveyed all of the important old stone fruits standing from the colonial period in *Historical American Trees* (New York: Frye Publishing, 1922), 96. Of the pear trees discussed—The Stuyvesant Pear Tree (1644) on 18th Street in Manhattan, the Old French Pear Trees in Water Works Park in Detroit (1722), the Petre Pear Tree in Bartram's Garden in Philadelphia (1760), the original Seckel Pear south of Philadelphia (1819)—only the Endicott Pear in Danvers, Massachusetts now stands. S. P. Flower supplied the background of the tree in "Gov. Endicott as Horticulturist," *The New England Farmer* 4, no. 9 (September 1852), 429–30.

4. The U.S. Apple Association keeps an annual count of commercial preference on its web homepage: *http://usapple.org/the-industry/apple-varieties/*. Assessed 1 January 2019.

5. Rowan Jacobson, *Apples of Uncommon Character: 123 Heirlooms, Modern Classics, & Little-Known Wonders* (New York: Bloomsbury, 2014), 137.

6. Noel Kingsbury, *Hybrid, the History and Science of Plant Breeding* (Chicago: Univ. of Chicago Press, 2014), 55–76.

7. Mission: The Carolina Gold Rice Foundation is committed to rebuilding the fundamentals of local culinary heritage through scholarship, research, farming, exploration, pro bono rare seed distribution, and good wholesome food: *http://www.thecarolinagoldricefoundation.org/*.

8. I documented the historical reasons for the marginalization of flavor in plant breeding for commercial scale food production in *Southern Provisions: the Creation and Revival of a Cuisine* (Chicago: Univ. of Chicago Press, 2015).

9. John McQuaid, *Tasty, the Art and Science of What We Eat* (New York: Scribner, 2016), 17–23.

10. A term in use in biology since 1908, landrace is summarized in Francesc Casañas, Joan Simó, Joan Casals, and Jaime Prohens, "Toward an Evolved Concept of Landrace," *Frontiers of Plant Science* 8, no. 145 (6 February 2017): *https://www.ncbi.nlm.nih.gov/pmc/articles/PMC5296298/*.

11. Mexico's maize legacy is overseen by the International Maize and Wheat Improvement Center (CIMMYT). Forty-five of the landraces appear on the organization's homepage: *https://www.cimmyt.org/maize-from-mexico-to-the-world/*.

12. This critique of the cost of green revolution being the loss of biodiversity was first fully formulated in Vandana Shiva, *Monocultures of the Mind: Perspectives on Biodiversity and Biotechnology* (London & New York: Zed Books Ltd., 1993).

13. Phil Howard of Michigan State has mapped the commercial ecology of the world seed industry: *https://philhoward.net/2018/12/31/global-seed-industry-changes-since-2013/*.

14. Alexander Shaposhnikov, A. I. Morgounov, Beyhan Akin, I. A. Tikhonovich, "Comparative Characteristics of Root Systems and Root Exudation of Synthetic, Landrace, and Modern Wheat Varieties," *Agricultural Biology* (January 2016), 68–78.

15. Jill Neimark, "Saving the Sweetest Watermelon the South Has Ever Known," *The Salt* (National Public Radio, 19 May 2015): *https://www.npr.org/sections/thesalt/2015/05/19/* 407949182/saving-the-sweetest-watermelon-the-south-has-ever-known.

16. Glenn Roberts articulated his vision of the ingredient revival in a series of videos published by Big Think in 2010: *https://bigthink.com/videos/the-miller-who-tilts-at-windmills*. Anson Mills remains the foremost miller of landrace grains in the United States: *http://ansonmills.com/*.

17. Lucia Stanton, "Rice," *Thomas Jefferson Encyclopedia*. Originally published as "Cultivating Missionaries," in *Spring Dinner at Monticello, April 12, 1990, in Memory of Thomas Jefferson* (Charlottesville: Thomas Jefferson Foundation, 1990): *https://www.monticello.org/site/house-and-gardens/rice*.

18. David S. Shields, "The Merikans of Trinidad Preserve Upland Bearded Rice," *News Feed*, The Carolina Gold Rice Foundation (27 December 2016): *http://www.thecarolinagoldricefoundation.org/news/*.

19. Kim Severson, "Finding a Lost Strain of Rice, and Clues to Slave Cooking," *The New York Times* (13 February 2018): *https://www.nytimes.com/2018/02/13/dining/hill-rice-slave-history.html*.

20. Mark Catesby, *Natural History of Carolina, Florida, and the Bahama Islands* (London, 1729–1747), xviii.

21. Samuel Urisperger, George Fenwick Jones, Renate Wilson, *Detailed Reports on the Salzburger Immigrants who Settled in America,* 17 vols. (Athens, GA: Univ. of Georgia Press, 1968), 11: 44.

22. Dan Nosowitz, "University Farmers Bring Heirloom Purple Wheat Back From Brink of Extinction," *Modern Farmer* (22 June 2016): *https://modernfarmer.com/2016/06/purple-straw-wheat/*.

23. "White Lammas Wheat," Palouse Heritage: *https://www.palouseheritage.com/white-lammas/*.

Aerostatic Bodies and the View from Above in Late Eighteenth-Century Britain

JASON PEARL

The first balloonists risked life and limb, sometimes losing both, ascending in machines that were impossible to steer and impotent against the elements.[1] The envelopes above them, buoyed by smoke or hydrogen, caught fire and exploded, often failing to lift, which could incite violent riots.[2] Indeed, many of the earliest aeronauts were doctors studying the still-unknown effects of the thinner air on the human body.[3] Jean François Pilâtre de Rozier, trained as a surgeon, piloted the first manned launch in 1783 with the Marquis d'Arlandes; de Rozier died two years later, with Pierre Romain, in an attempt to cross the English Channel.[4] Taking that honor was John Jeffries, a doctor himself, and Jean-Pierre Blanchard, though they would have failed had they not thrown everything overboard, including the clothes on their backs, and still they descended until both leaned over and relieved themselves of "between five and six pounds of urine," which finally did the trick and allowed the balloon to rise.[5] For all these balloonists, to look down over the basket was to stare death in the face.

Beforehand, the view from above was only an abstraction. This was the perspective of maps and topographic engravings, which pictured the world from the position of a disembodied eye in the sky.[6] It was a vista imagined in fantastic voyages featuring whimsical machines of flight.[7] And, throughout the eighteenth century, poets in various genres, from georgic to lyric, assumed viewpoints above for the sake of gentlemanly impartiality and visionary transcendence.[8] There are exceptions, of course, but typically these fictions allowed the subjectivity in question to leave the body and its circumstances back on solid earth.[9] And, the conceit persists today as an epistemology of authority in geography and urban planning and military reconnaissance.[10] The gaze from above—the bird's-eye view but also the god's-eye view—objectifies but can never itself be objectified, and so is removed from contingency, capable of defining value independently of the world below.

In contrast, narratives of balloon flight posited a view from above that was contingent and precarious, a perspective that entailed not just ocular superiority, if it was superiority at all, but also bodily vulnerability. We still think of it as a triumph of science when the French papermakers Joseph-Michel and Jacques-Étienne Montgolfier invented the hot air balloon, making possible the age-old dream of human flight.[11] But, the fact remained: balloons were dangerous, unsteerable, practically useless. Whatever the advantage of the god's-eye view, human eyes are connected to human bodies, which are heavy and fragile. And, actually, like a lot of inventions, the balloon was mainly a showpiece, its usefulness exhausted by mere demonstration. What mattered was not the view from above so much as the view from below, the view of spectators—some, no doubt, attracted by the possibility of disaster. To ride in a balloon, therefore, was to expose oneself to the public, risking not just life but also reputation. And, that is to say nothing of the experience ontologically, aesthetically. Up in a balloon, we become part of the atmosphere, embedded in the material conditions around us, pushed and pulled as one of many meteorological things, our bodies brought to a level with the elements. As Derek McCormack puts it, "The prospect of infinity was one of the more unsettling aspects of aerostatic flight: free ballooning, in particular, involved coming to terms with a new kind of immersive experience, a sense, potentially overwhelming, of the vastness of atmospheric space."[12] It is a situation dependent on but irreducible to vision alone, though in the eighteenth century, that sense was generally understood as passive and vulnerable, contrary to contemporary theories of the domineering gaze.[13] Thus, balloon narratives give the lie to cartography's myth of the disembodied Apollonian eye, showing how aerial perception was highly variable and how it was shot through with accident and anxiety. Ballooning might conjure ideas of extrication and disengagement, of an un-situated eye unconstrained by contingency, but the first balloonists never took their safety for granted. The upper atmosphere was potentially hostile to life, the ground or water below potentially deadly.

In what follows, I focus on three balloonists in particular and the ways they helped readers imagine not just the view from above but the fully embodied experience of lifting, floating, and descending in a balloon basket. Vincenzo Lunardi, the first to fly in England, faced angry crowds below and erratic weather above. He wrote of strange fits of up-and-down passion, though he never raised himself above others, always deferring, until he finally fell out of favor. The first Englishwoman in a balloon, Letitia Anne Sage, had to walk the line between bravery and impropriety, since aerostatic bodies were judged according to male fears and fantasies. High in the clouds, she escaped such criticism but ultimately felt alienated from familiar places and friends and family below. Thomas Baldwin sought to explain his experience scientifically but instead buzzed with excitement and searched in vain for adequate descriptions. Baldwin was the first to draw the view from above, though what he saw was not the stable and objectified surface of a map but a rolling countryside obscured by clouds and colored by shifting light. All three rode one of Lunardi's balloons, each for different reasons: Lunardi for profit; Sage for pleasure; and, Baldwin for knowledge. And, each reveals a different kind of vulnerability related to the body: for Lunardi, it was immediately physical; for Sage, it was social; for Baldwin, intellectual and psychological. I dwell on these specific figures—all of them firsts—because of the special difficulties of doing anything without predecessors. Yet, I set aside the very first balloonists in France because that nation offered state support, whereas England did not, leaving the enterprise to daredevils and adventurers.[14] At any rate, my argument is not wholly negative: in acknowledging the limits of aerostatic bodies, Lunardi, Sage, and Baldwin make an argument for the positive value of humility, of not raising oneself too high, so to speak, not placing oneself above others.[15] They thus contradict not just the myth of the disembodied eye but also the illusion of superiority aligned with it.

Vincenzo Lunardi, First to Fly in Britain

The first to succeed was not the first to try. That feat had been done in France but never in English weather. Before Lunardi, there was James Tytler, a hapless apothecary from Scotland: on his first attempt, Tytler's balloon caught fire; the second time, it was overset by wind, causing a riot; the third, it made several high leaps and fell clumsily (success, some claimed); the next time, the balloon was blown into a patch of trees, injuring one man, dropping another in the branches; next, it rose 300 feet without Tytler and collapsed; and finally—mercifully—the balloon was wrecked by a storm before liftoff. Soon after, a mysterious Frenchman named Moret, likely a charlatan, tried ascending in a balloon the shape of a Chinese temple: he too failed before an angry mob tore up his equipment, burnt it, and, as Lunardi writes, "spread desolation and terror through the whole district."[16] John Sheldon, an eccentric anatomist, failed twice; the second time, his balloon was destroyed by the fire that fueled it.[17]

Lunardi, for his part, drew an estimated 150,000 people, one of the biggest crowds yet assembled in England.[18] The Prince of Wales and a number of Members of Parliament enjoyed seats up close, but spectators of all ranks thronged the peripheries, many unconvinced by news reports from France about the Montgolfier brothers. Thieves picked pockets. Fights broke out. Someone was ducked in a nearby pond as viewers on the periphery threw rocks at carriages obstructing their view. A pole supporting the balloon snapped, and rumors spread that the envelope itself had burst. According to one observer, "the impatience of the people threatened to overleap the bounds of discretion . . . in every quarter murmurs increased to a height indicating a disposition to riot."[19] And alas, those filling the balloon had gotten drunk and never finished their work, leaving Lunardi to choose either the wrath of the crowd or the uncertainty of the sky. "Delay," he understood, "would have been construed into guilt; and the displeasure impending . . . would have been fatal" (*First Voyage* 38). George Biggin, his friend and patron, had planned to join, but the saggy balloon possessed insufficient lift, so Lunardi forged on alone—or rather with a cat, dog, and pigeon, the better to test the effects of the atmosphere. Luckily, the weather was mild, and the launch was a resounding success. Lunardi rose high into the air without incident and enjoyed a clear prospect for miles in every direction.

Still, whatever his courage, he comes across as emotionally vulnerable, defenseless physically but also psychically against the elements—especially before his second voyage in Liverpool. Bad weather caused several postponements, again raising fears of putting off the audience. "The Sky," we are told, "was drest in Stormy Terrors; Thick black Clouds drove after one another in quick Succession."[20] And then it was "as if a *thousand* DEMONS were hurrying to Destruction on every Blast," prompting Lunardi to lament, "The ceaseless howling of the Storm plays with too great a Force, upon my Heart Strings, to produce a *soothing Harmony*" (14). That attitude was typical of the charismatic Italian, who styled himself a man of feeling, someone who internalized the changeability of the British climate.[21] The newspapers wrote of this "sentimental strain," and remarked on its appeal to women, observing that in the lead-up to the first launch, in an "hour of desponding anxiety," the handsome foreigner "found himself buoyed up by the flattering solicitations of many amiable ladies."[22] Again and again, Lunardi himself linked the ups and downs of the weather, the ups and downs of his emotional state, and the ups and downs of the balloon itself, at one point apostrophizing, "How chequered is the scene of life in which I act! And what vicissitudes of joy and woe do I experience! FORTUNE makes me her sport: one minute she raises me aloft on the airy pinions of hope, the next precipitates me into the fathomless abyss of despair."[23] Notice the double-meaning of "raises" and "precipitates:" vertically but also affectively. So vehement were these fits that on his first voyage Lunardi forgot his instruments, precluding systematic observation.[24]

But he made no pretense to distance or detachment, which today we might expect from someone thousands of feet overhead. Lunardi presented his experiences in-the-moment, promising on the title pages of two of his three narratives that what followed was *Written under the Impression of the Various Events that Affected the Undertaking*. And form incarnates content: as Clare Brant points out, all three accounts are epistolary, a form used in eighteenth-century novels to make thoughts and feelings seem immediate.[25] Indeed, despite the high vista, there is an aspect here of Samuel Richardson's "keyhole view of life."[26] Lunardi "wrote, just as in [his] study," jotting down observations on pieces of paper and tossing them overboard, a kind of fugitive testimony (*First Voyage* 33). Some of these notes he then published in his narratives, including the "CARD from the SKIES" in the *Second Voyage* (23). What he wanted was to capture the affective experience itself of balloon flight, translating it as closely as possible into language and thus making it available to readers vicariously, rather than stilling himself and addressing them from a position of disembodied abstraction.

For Lunardi, therefore, flight was intensely physical. He shivered in the plunging temperatures, collecting icicles on his clothes and gorging himself on meat and glass after glass of wine. He was so busy, especially at first, that he barely looked down, a common predicament: Sage spent much of her voyage tending a broken door in the basket; Baldwin reminds us each time he abandoned the rapturous view to maintain or correct his course. Thus, looking over the edge was only part of the larger experience, in some cases a small part, snatched in rare moments of inactivity. After liftoff, Lunardi plied oars and wings, waved a hat and flag, addressed the crowd with a speaking trumpet; he tended the ropes, adjusted the ballast, managed his animals. It was a lot to do with only two hands, and it was exhausting. High in the air, he experienced "so strong a propensity for sleeping, that it was with the utmost difficulty that he could keep himself awake" (*Grand Aerostatic Voyage* 8). And there was talk that the climb of the balloon was erotic, arousing. The etching *Love in a Balloon* (1784) depicts Lunardi lifting with an admirer and saying, "Ah, Madame, it rises majestically!" She, feeling his body against hers, replies, "I feel it does, Signor," as a peanut gallery below adds, "Damn me, he's no Italian but a man, every inch of him."

Up in the air, the wind took over, making all effort useless. In a sense, Lunardi had only to rest and enjoy the view, as in the imaginary lunar journeys of Francis Godwin and Cyrano de Bergerac. He asserts, "The broom-sticks of the witches, Ariosto's flying-horse, and even Milton's sun-beam . . . have all ideas of effort, difficulty, and restraint, which do not affect a voyage in a Balloon" (33). Yet, effort would have been pointless; the oars and wings did nothing to direct his course—actually he dropped an oar during his first ascension. To fly in a balloon is to give up agency, surrendering to the wind, moving only with, never against, the atmosphere. The senses themselves are disoriented, making detection of movement impossible without visible reference points: "I had not the slightest sense of motion from the Machine. I knew not whether it went swiftly or slowly, whether it ascended or descended, whether it was agitated or tranquil, but by the appearance or disappearance of objects on earth" (33). For this reason, early balloonists carried feathers in order to throw them overboard and mark their distance.

Finally freed from labor, Lunardi looked down without *looking down on* those below. He admits his audience "might suggest to a tyrant . . . a pavement of human heads," but of course he was beholden to them (*First Voyage* 27). From up high, he pays his respects by calling the host nation "an enormous beehive," praising its prosperity and orderliness: "The face of the country has a mild and permanent verdure, to which Italy is a stranger. The variety of cultivation, and the accuracy with which property is divided, give the idea, ever present to a stranger in England, of good civil laws and an equitable administration" (40, 33). Workaday routines, seen from above, acquire a dignity imperceptible on the ground. In one of the letters tossed down, Lunardi declares, "the view before me is heavenly. Happy England! I see reasons to hail thy peculiar felicity!" (50). Thus, the world below, in an odd reversal, becomes heavenly. But, none of the praise accrues to Lunardi: an Italian, he is "a stranger in England." Indeed, he was concerned less with seeing than with being seen, with how he appeared to everyone else; fittingly, the final pages of the *First Voyage* include positive testimonials by spectators. As Caitlín Rósín Doherty explains, "The line of sight between the balloonist and the crowd flowed in two directions"; the balloonist's "main concern was to imagine the ways in which he was or would be perceived by the audience."[27] Lunardi was not a scientist but a performer, a foreign adventurer, who depended on admirers to buy subscription tickets. And, ultimately, he was deserted after a disastrous accident that carried up and dropped an attendant, who fell so forcefully that he was driven knee-deep in a flower bed. The man died shortly after, the first fatality of England's balloon craze. In *Aerostation out at the Elbows* (1785), Thomas Rowlandson portrayed Lunardi down and out, a washed-up celebrity who "roams about from Town to Town / Collecting Pence t'inflate his poor Balloon" (fig. 1).

Figure 1. Thomas Rowlandson, *Aerostation out at the Elbows* (1785). Image courtesy of the Metropolitan Museum of Art.

Soon, he had another invention to show off, a chest-like lifeboat, for saving shipwrecked sailors.[28]

Letitia Ann Sage, First Woman to Fly in Britain

Sage too risked both her life and name. She knew of the "melancholy fate of poor Pilatre de Rozier," and she herself was injured when her foot struck a sharp piece of metal in the basket.[29] But her reputation was yet more vulnerable—as would have been the case for any woman attempting a feat performed only by men. Perhaps the former actress was familiar with the stakes of gossip and slander. She worried about the "illiberal reflections" on Lunardi, who canceled a prior launch and now heard accusations of cowardice (4). Soon, the town talked of Sage, as well. For her voyage, the party was to be five, but they were far too heavy, so Lunardi and two others yielded, leaving Sage and Biggin and prompting jokes about Sage's above-average weight, or, as she put it, her "*en-bon-point*" body (12). Balloons foster dreams of weightlessness, but in fact nothing matters more than the ratio of weight-to-lift—the balloon is a de facto scale. Before all this, as the envelope was inflated, Sage waited offstage, hidden from the 100,000 in attendance to forestall "those remarks which . . . would naturally be made, had the *multitude* got an idea of the woman who was about to make so bold an attempt" (10–11). The remarks were made anyway, many of them, predictably, about her body. The *Public Advertiser* called her "the female Falstaffe;" *The London Magazine* noted she "was found to have more *gravity* than what belonged to a *wise* name."[30] In *A Sage Lady's Second Experiment* (1785), Rowlandson showed her drifting through the air, dress outstretched like an umbrella, buttocks exposed for all below to see (fig. 2). Women were often targets, especially for their balloon-inspired fashions.[31] Sage was attacked for the opposite, for undertaking what had been—at least in England—an exclusively masculine activity. In the decades that followed, women aboard balloons enjoyed acceptance, even adulation. Sophie Blanchard was appointed Aéronaute des Fêtes Officielles by Napoleon Bonaparte.[32] England lagged behind in more ways than one.

Sage, though, sought pleasure, not profit, and in her *Letter, Addressed to a Female Friend* (1785), she called the journey her "favourite experiment," professing, "I feel myself more happy, and infinitely better pleased with my excursion than I ever was at any former event in my life" (3). In the sky, she casts off social constraints and forgets about unfair criticisms, looking back to the ground and remarking, "It is surely a great misfortune to have an expanded heart, when the power to indulge it is so circumscribed" (8). Thus, as Lunardi had done, Sage connects feeling and flying, sensibility and spatial amplitude. With plenty of room above, "floating in the boundless

Figure 2. Thomas Rowlandson, *A Sage Lady's Second Experiment* (1785). Image courtesy of the Metropolitan Museum of Art.

regions of the air," she felt "perfect tranquility of soul," finding herself at once "in the presence of the Deity" but also perfectly at home, as if she had been a "native of the aerial regions" (14, 16, 31).

Still, Sage was never lost in thought. To have one's head in the clouds—literally to be in a balloon among the clouds—is a vivid experience, a physically sensuous thrill that supplants airy speculations. There was little time for that. For much of the journey, Sage toiled with Biggin, assisting in technical duties. To fix the broken door, she ducked under the rim of the basket, which led to rumors that she had fainted, though she assures readers that she "never was more mistress of [her] reason" (13). She and Biggin monitored gradual alterations in altitude—as all balloonists must—and threw over ballast as necessary throughout the flight. Even in a moment of leisure, rather than indulging fanciful reflection, Sage and Biggin feasted on ham, chicken, and wine. She got cold and had trouble breathing. He felt his ears pop, "an unusual sensation . . . he seemed to think proceeded from the rarefaction of the air contained in the cellular organs, which extended the tympanum" (22). Before Biggin, Jacques Charles, who helped invent the hydrogen balloon, also complained of "a most extraordinary pain . . . in the interior of the ears and in the maxillary glands," which he attributed to "the dilation of the air contained in the cellular tissue of the organ as much as to the cold outside."[33]

We cannot escape our bodies, but, in this case, Sage seemed to outstrip the force of gender norms. She confesses to "a little trait of female weakness," yet this weakness is the bold desire to relaunch and continue the journey after the first landing (26). We ought to call it female fortitude. Up in the clouds, far from the crowd, what mattered was only ungendered mass, or "human weight," irrespective of norms below (26). Whereas Lunardi wanted to be seen, Sage wanted to disappear, to look without being the object of observation herself. And, that is what she experiences, reaching a position of independence in the air above, a space where she can define herself however she likes. There, she and Biggin had "withdrawn [them]selves from earthly connection," rising to a position where, in her words, "I seemed to exist but for myself" (16, 20).

But freedom comes with loss, a feeling of alienation from friends and family and familiar objects and places below. Sage's account is epistolary, like Lunardi's, but hers conveys a much stronger bond between writer and reader, the "female friend" of the title. This was Sarah Ward, Sage's then-pregnant sister, called "my dear friend" and told that "your understanding is more elevated, and your conceptions better arranged than most other women" (3). Elevated in understanding, Ward remained on the ground far from the launching site, and Sage feels the pain of separation and her sister's anxiety: "I am sensible of the strength of your attachment to me, and know that, at the distance of more than two hundred miles from the place of action, not being able to learn the event for so many days, you must have been miserable" (3–4). Later, she tells of a moment when she was composing her narrative: she put down her pen and stopped, but then continued, acknowledging Ward was "too affectionately attached . . . to await the arrival of the next post, for a conclusion of a matter in which [Sage was] so much interested" (15). Biggin's heart, too, grows stronger in the absence of "some fair inamorata, who might . . . be sending up her prayers for his safe return" (19). Looking down, Sage picks out beloved places, too: "we hung some time over St. James's Park, and particularized almost every house we knew in Piccadilly." What disturbs her is that "[t]he objects of [her] affection or esteem were at that time . . . so very distant" (20). As the balloon drifts, she states, "I . . . lost sight of some particular objects which I was contemplating with great pleasure" (21). We might equate distance with irony, and Sage jokes about how small things look, but actually this distance reminds her of the tenuousness of earthly connections and the need to maintain them. After landing, she was restored to ground-based society, taken under the protection of a generous family, and carried to their home for dinner, where she was happy to find "a numerous party of friends with sincere marks of joy" (29, 31). She writes at length about this experience, a friendly alternative to the carping crowd at the launch site. None of that prejudice remains among the circle of admirers who await her.

Thomas Baldwin: First to Draw the Balloon Prospect

The same balloon was then borrowed by Baldwin, a clergyman with an interest in natural philosophy. His book, *Airopaidia* (1786), differs from those of Lunardi and Sage in the bulk of its non-narrative content: tables, drawings, descriptions, calculations. Others, too, collected data, though not so plentifully, and Baldwin declares, "Balloon-Voyagers have . . . been particularly defective in their Descriptions of aerial Scenes and Prospects."[34] Reviewers played up the difference. One said, "This Gentleman appears to have made a more successful voyage than any of his predecessors, and his work is by far the most valuable . . . it presents to us a great number of interesting facts and observations."[35] Another called the book "by far the most philosophical . . . of the celestial voyages which hitherto have been published."[36] Unlike predecessors, Baldwin offered not so much a narrative of adventure as a collection of descriptions, buttressed by measurements and after-the-fact theorizations. He carried up a bevy of instruments, and, indeed, he objectifies even himself, using the third person, distancing the retrospective scientist from the in-the-moment balloonist: throughout the text he is simply "Mr. Baldwin" or "the aeronaut" or "he." Thus, the text too functions as an instrument, or, as Brant puts it, "textual order...help[s] keep disorder in check."[37]

But Baldwin was not so different as he and reviewers claimed. He too wrote of strong impressions and passionate feelings—only they are tied more empirically to specific stimuli: strange cloud shapes, unique plays of light. And the neutral register leaves the experiencing subject at the center of the frame, allowing Baldwin the scientist to study Baldwin the balloonist. One of his primary interests was the effect of the atmosphere on the body. He tested his pulse and breathing. He brought along salt, pepper, and ginger, having heard taste was diminished at high altitudes. He wrote of an intensely physical joy elicited by the vista, a declaration of feeling that betrays not just the balloonist's but also the narrator's excitement: "A Tear of pure Delight flashed in his Eye! of pure and exquisite Delight and Rapture" (37). What interested Baldwin was the feeling of flight, the sensation of moving through the air, which, at another point, results in "a Sensation of Levity . . . communicated by the Air to the Lungs" (109). Later, he offers this analogy: "The Ascent of the Balloon is not unlike what is felt, in the *ascending* half of the Swing: and the Descent is attended with that agreeable Sensation known to those who sink throu' the *descending* half," a feeling "*grateful* to the Nerves" and in some cases "so *exquisite*, as to be full as much as the human Frame can support" (124, 125, 126). After landing, Baldwin took up other passengers and noted the various effects, with the tacit acknowledgement that each balloonist is particular, not universal. One volunteer "became *silent*; *pale*; his *countenance* the *Picture of Distress*; looking *down* as if *for help*" (156). Another "was no sooner raised a few Yards above his Companions than the *florid* Colour forsook his Cheeks; he *trembled*; bent himself *double* with Fright" (159).

Baldwin himself was filled with awe, ecstatic and often bewildered by an experience that resisted intelligible description. As Marie Thébaud-Sorger argues, he lacked "both the concepts and—even more so—the words that fit the occasion."[38] To fill the void, or account for it, Baldwin has steady recourse to the inexpressibility topos. He loads the narrative with poetic effusions followed by exclamation points. And, he confesses to a "rational Humiliation," a humility achieved by reason that reflects reason's limitations (3). Spectators of Lunardi, people on the ground, had called the experience "a mixture of anxiety and delight, not unalloyed, however, by a friendly dread for the ultimate effect" (*First Voyage* 45). And, Baldwin insists, as Lunardi had done, "The BEAUTIFUL and SUBLIME were . . . united, in a Manner perfectly novel and engaging" (48). For Edmund Burke, these categories were opposed and inversely relational, and, perhaps, we expect the balloon prospect to align with sublime expansiveness. According to Burke, "Infinity has a tendency to fill the mind with that sort of delightful horror, which is the most genuine effect, and truest test of the sublime."[39] But, in a balloon, the distinction dissolves, or more accurately the feeling alternates. On the one hand, Baldwin felt safe and wrote of "an empyrean Calm! Unknown to Mortals *upon Earth;*" on the other, he was confounded by the emptiness around him and felt like "a mere Atom floating *invariably* in the Center of the empty Space" (46, 50). For Burke, the sublime entailed terror leavened by "certain distances," "certain modifications"—otherwise, it would be truly painful, not enjoyable (40). Here, though, distance was literal: everything really was far away. And the danger was real. Viewed from high up, what is massive becomes tiny, though its massiveness is appreciable only with the distance that reduces it. Existing terms were insufficient. Thus, Baldwin coins his own, claiming to feel "a peaceful SERENITY of *Mind* . . . an ENVIABLE EUROIA . . . An Idea of which it is not in the Power of Language to convey, or to describe" (109). The obscure Greek word, "euroia," associated with Stoicism, means "good flow" or "free passage."[40]

Flowing through the sky, the balloon yielded "*ever varying* Prospects," not a synoptic view but many, all differently situated, none transcending another, none even fixing in place amid the blowing wind and the ever-shifting clouds and light (72).[41] Balloonists, after all, could not control their direction, could not even settle their vision as one does looking at a map on a wall or table. They floated at the mercy of the elements, rising, falling, twisting, turning—apparently at random, propelled by invisible forces. Some prospects were less expansive than constrictive, some more deceptive than informative. Gradually lifting up, Baldwin notices an illusion that made the surface of the Earth seem concave, instead of convex, as of course he knew it was. The surrounding horizon, edged with clouds, appeared to rise up around the center point underneath, which looked like "the central Concave of an unmeasurable Crater Bowl or Bason" (48). At the same time, topographic variety—different heights on the terrain below—seemed to flatten out, so that a "lofty Summit was *apparently* reduced to a common Level with the Valley" (77). The scene was in constant motion because the balloon itself was in motion. The big became small, shrinking as the balloon ascended, but the small, like pointillist dots, added up to ever-bigger patterns. Sharp lines and fine details faded; new contrasts emerged, contrasts imperceptible on a smaller scale. And nothing was self-evident: scale and distance cannot be intuited; they must be learned, or, in Baldwin's words, "It is from *frequent* EXPERIENCE only that the *Diminution of Objects* presuppose their *Distance*" (129). But this was no frequent experience. Long after landing, Baldwin, now the retrospective scientist, continued parsing the view, working out calculations, most of them pushed to the book's more speculative second half.

Of course, all this assumes a clear line of sight. Baldwin wrote at length about the clouds that framed and obscured his view and sometimes entranced him, stealing his attention entirely. At one point, the view from the basket—the supposedly almighty view from above—afforded no sight of land, which was "covered with a WHITE *Veil*" (131). Sage described a similar situation in which she and Biggin "saw the objects on earth . . . as if through gauze" (23). Clouds, though, were not just obstructions. They were, for Baldwin, a focal point, a mobile sky-borne architecture, "moving slowly in all Directions; rising to great Heights, falling, melting away, and again condensing" (71). Transfixed, he describes one cloud mass thus: "The lowest Bed of Vapour . . . was of a *pure white*; in detached Fleeces . . . . They presently coalesced, and were aggrandized into a SEA *of Cotton* . . . tufted here and there by the Play of Air, and gentle Breezes in Every Direction…the whole became an extended Firmament or *white* Floor of thin Cloud, thro' whose Intervals the Sun must shine with fiercer Gleam" (53–54). Pacifically beautiful one moment, ominously sublime the next: "Thro' this *white* Floor uprose in splendid Majesty and awful Grandeur, at great and unequal distances, a vast Assemblage of *Thunder-Clouds*: each Congeries consisting of whole Acres in the densest Form" (54). Indeed, it is easy to see why clouds invite the projection of affective states.[42] The world still awaited Luke Howard's influential *Essay on the Modification of Clouds* (1804), which gave us our enduring typology—cirrus, stratus, nimbus—but even with this system, clouds confuse our sense of depth and proportion, refusing the logic of linear perspective.[43] We can never quite tell where the vapor is closer, where it is farther away, where the mass is bigger, where it is smaller, to say nothing of the hazy boundaries.

In the plate "A View from the Balloon at Its Greatest Elevation," Baldwin, through the engraver James Heath, represents—or tries to—the foregoing sea of cotton with rising thunderclouds (fig. 3). Here, a dense blanket encircles the city of Chester, which, despite its position at the center, becomes an afterthought, secondary to the vaporous world above. The clouds seem to wrap around the horizon, bending downward, with small columns rising up and out, centrifugally. On first glance, it looks like the curvature of the Earth or perhaps a rounded cone formed adventitiously by the elements. In fact, Baldwin wants to show how objects directly below are closer than those at a lateral distance. Indeed, he attempts to show not just the view from above but also the view from the side—that is, the vista around him, represented in the plate, oddly, as an azure border around the clouds. And, the dark space in the corners gives us the view from below, the extent of sight upward, occluded by the balloon overhead. The line of vision, then, bends down, out, and up, three vectors reduced to two dimensions, hinting at the falsity of what we think of as the view from above: turn your head, move your eyes, and see in every direction, never just down.[44]

Even without clouds, the ground below looked nothing like a map. There were no lines or colors denoting borders and territories. Objects that were one color below seem another higher up. The River Dee, a "Silver Stream," became "when seen from an Eminence . . . the unvaried Colour of *red Lead*," its contours "infinitely more serpentine than . . . expressed in Maps" (41). The slate roofs of Chester became "entirely *blue*" (43). "RED, YELLOW, GREEN, and BLUE . . . all . . . seemed to GLOW, tho' in a *less* Degree, like the Colours of a Prism" (117–18). In "A Balloon Prospect from Above the Clouds," another colored engraving, this one above Cheshire and Lancashire, Baldwin again shows us what he saw, what he experienced, further refuting the schematization of a typical map (fig. 4). The plate is a jumble of shapes and colors that were the effect of varied light on varied surfaces. Air and clouds float above hills, valleys, roads, and rivers, each legible only by color and contrast, without the graphic aids we take for granted in maps. The Earth is flattened this time, conveying a boundless expanse below the clouds, a terrain spreading in every direction, checked only artificially by the pictorial frame.[45] For Thébaud-Sorger, "Aerial vision clarifies the structural nature of things and increases the legibility of land usage" (59), but what clarifies in this case is the "EXPLANATORY Print," an adjoining plate that drains the

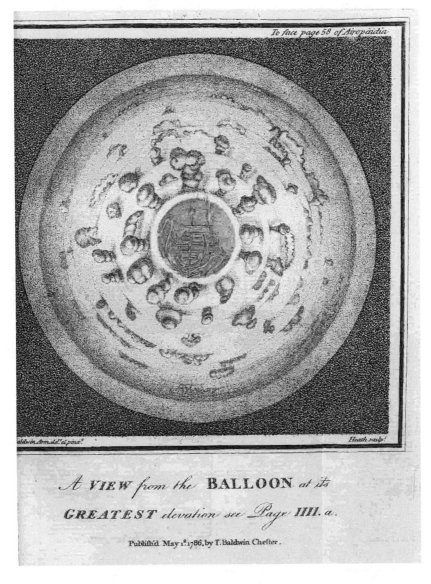

To face page 58 of Airopaidia

aldwin from del.' et pinx.'   Heath sculp.'

A VIEW from the **BALLOON** *at its*

GREATEST *elevation see Page IIII. a.*

Publish'd May 1.ˢ 1786, by T. Baldwin Chefter.

Figure 3. Thomas Baldwin, "A View from the Balloon at Its Greatest Elevation" (1786). Originally published electronically on the University of Maryland's *Romantic Circles* website.

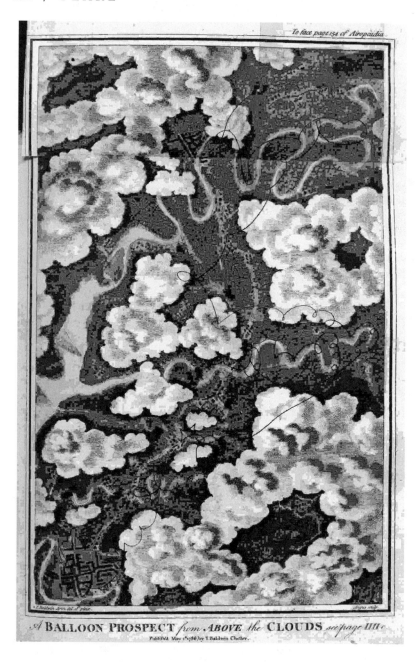

Figure 4. Thomas Baldwin, "A Balloon Prospect from Above the Clouds" (1786). Originally published electronically on the University of Maryland's *Romantic Circles* website.

scene of color and introduces place names. Aerial observation elucidates only through abstraction, only through simplification—what makes it helpful is its very abstractness and simplicity. Indeed, the path of the balloon, marked by the thin black line, implies a field of vision always in motion, always determined by a particular position. Such a path could be pictured only through a higher view, a location of still-greater altitude and stability that had to be imagined, likely with the assistance of maps and books. To see from above, to look down from the basket, was to feel disoriented, to lose one's sense of direction. Thus, it should be no surprise that after landing, Baldwin humbly admits, "The first Question was, "Pray where am I?" (151).

Hard to believe, but the *Airopaidia* failed to make a splash, even with its novel images, and the book was an outlier. As Thébaud-Sorger puts it, "The invention of balloons did not immediately give rise to pictorial representations of the vistas that they enabled" (46). The real breakthrough came in the nineteenth century, when Gaspard-Félix Tournachon, popularly known as Nadar, took the first photographs above Paris.[46] Before that, much more common was the view of the spectator, who looked up at the balloon from the ground, a vantage depicted again and again in prints and paintings from the 1780s on.[47] Baldwin himself gives us this perspective in yet another plate, "The Balloon over Helsbye Hill in Cheshire," which, from a relatively low standpoint, shows him and the balloon as a tiny speck high above tall cliffs and colossal clouds in the distance. The view from above, available to so few, had to be contextualized dialectically with the more accessible view from below. And actually, as Caren Kaplan notes, even the drawings from the balloon basket conflict with one another, each positing a different system of representation that ultimately suggests "not so much a scopic, unifying mastery as a series of varied views."[48]

Conclusion

Throughout the ensuing decades, the technology got better, but only slowly and partially. Ballooning became safer, despite well-publicized tragedies.[49] And balloons were put to use during the French Revolutionary Wars and the American Civil War, though without much capability beyond surveillance—generally, they were tethered to the ground.[50] More advances followed, first with dirigibles, or navigable balloons and blimps, and more importantly with aerodynes, or heavier-than-air aircrafts, which made flight at once safer for some, more deadly for others. But this is a different technology; it would be simplistic to plot eighteenth-century balloons on a straight causal line leading to twentieth-century fighter aircraft. According to Kaplan, aesthetic responses and military intentions "emerge in a jumble in the late eighteenth century and only move fully away from each other as the divide between the purpose and practices of science and art . . . intensifies in the nineteenth century."[51] Baldwin noted, "It seems a favourite Question . . . to ask 'Of what Use can Balloons be made?' and without waiting for an Answer, to say—'they pick the Pockets of the Public, risque the Lives of the Incautious, encourage Mobbing and Sharpers, and terrify all the World'" (259). He and many others thought this was unfair and shortsighted, but the question remained.[52] Indeed, we might ask ourselves: of what use are balloons even today? One answer, true then and now, is balloon flight thrills us with danger and humbles us before the vastness of the natural world.

Epistemologically, the view from above—real or imagined—is immensely fecund. It could satirize human grandiosity, diminishing our achievements from high above, as in anonymous novel *The Devil in an Air Balloon* (1784). It could help us see past borders and understand common features among disparate peoples, as in another novel, *The Aerostatic Spy* (1785). Additionally, it could enable us to take the measure of modern industrialism and the ecological footprint of the human-built world, as when Henry Mayhew, in the next century, looked down on smog-shrouded London.[53] Of course, none of these various uses involves a strict sense of control or domination.

What makes Lunardi, Sage, and Baldwin interesting, I believe, is their struggle to assert an authority we now take for granted. Icarus flew too high, but so did many early balloonists, and today we forget the brute force and engineering required to heave anything aloft and keep it flying. There remains a useful lesson here about the smallness and fragility of the human body, as well as the ungraspable enormity of our world and its unopposable forces. Early balloonists saw more of the Earth in one gaze than anyone before them, and this extended horizon gave a new context and scale to human life, offering a prospect that was humbling before it was empowering.

NOTES

1. See Michael R. Lynn, *The Sublime Invention: Ballooning in Europe, 1783–1820* (New York: Routledge, 2010), 21–26; and Jessika Wichner, "Hot Air and Chilly Welcomes: Accidental Arrivals with Balloons and Airships in the Eighteenth Century and Beyond," *Citizens of the World: Adapting in the Eighteenth Century*, ed. Kevin L. Cope and Samara Anne Cahill (Lewisburg, PA: Bucknell Univ. Press, 2015), 19–39.

2. Lynn, *Sublime Invention*, 110–16.

3. Joseph Black, George Fordyce, James Tytler, John Jeffries, and John Sheldon: all these early balloonists also studied medicine. See William Carleton Gibson, "Medical Pioneers in Aviation," *Journal of the History of Medicine and Allied Sciences* 17 (1962): 83–93. In the eighteenth century, little was known about what we now call hypobaric hypoxia, or altitude sickness, caused by low levels of oxygen in body tissues. See John B. West, *High Life: A History of High-Altitude Physiology and Medicine* (New York: Oxford Univ. Press, 1998), 40–73.

4. See L.T.C. Rolt, *The Aeronauts: A History of Ballooning, 1783–1903* (New York: Walker and Company, 1966), 41–49, 90–93.

5. Jeffries, *A Narrative of the Two Aerial Voyages of Doctor Jeffries with Monsieur Blanchard* (London: Printed for author at J. Robson, 1786), 48. See also Tom Crouch, "Lost Balloons: Depicting the Dangers of Early Ballooning," Smithsonian National Air and Space Museum, 8 May 2017, *https://airandspace. si.edu/stories/editorial/lost-balloons-depicting-dangers-early-ballooning*. Accessed 14 March 2018.

6. See Christian Jacob, *The Sovereign Map: Theoretical Approaches in Cartography throughout History*, trans. Tom Conley (Chicago: Univ. of Chicago Press, 2006), 318–27; and Kimberley Skelton, *The Paradox of Body, Building and Motion in Seventeenth-Century England* (Manchester: Manchester Univ. Press, 2015), 80–113.

7. See Marjorie Hope Nicolson, *Voyages to the Moon* (New York: Macmillan, 1948); and Mary Baine Campbell, *Wonder and Science: Imagining Worlds in Early Modern Europe* (Ithaca: Cornell Univ. Press, 1999), 151–80.

8. See John Barrell, *English Literature in History, 1730–1830: An Equal, Wide Survey* (London: Hutchinson, 1983), 51–109; and David Fairer, *English Poetry of the Eighteenth Century, 1700–1789* (New York: Routledge, 2003), 122–66.

9. Exceptions include the floating island in Jonathan Swift's *Gulliver's Travels* (1726), where head-in-the-clouds idealists cannot get by without food from below. And, in Samuel Johnson's *Rasselas* (1759), a mechanical artist builds a flying machine but almost dies when it fails and crashes into a lake. Moreover, Ivan Ortiz has shown how writers continued to rely on fancy to mediate the new mobility, in "Fancy's Eye: Poetic Vision and the Romantic Air Balloon," *Studies in Romanticism* 56 (2017): 253–84.

10. See Henri Lefebvre's concept of "abstract space" in *The Production of Space*, trans. Donald Nicholson-Smith (Malden, MA: Blackwell Publishing, 1991), 38–39. See also Michel de Certeau, *The Practice of Everyday Life*, trans. Steven Rendall (Berkeley: Univ. of California Press, 1984), 91–114; and Caren Kaplan, *Aerial Aftermaths: Wartime from Above* (Durham: Duke Univ. Press, 2018).

11. On the Montgolfier brothers, see Charles Coulston Gillispie, *The Montgolfier Brothers and the Invention of Aviation* (Princeton: Princeton Univ. Press, 1983). On the romance of invention, see Christine MacLeod, *Heroes of Invention: Technology, Liberalism, and British Identity, 1750–1914* (New York: Cambridge Univ. Press, 2007), 59–90.

12. McCormack, "Aerostatic Spacing: On Things Becoming Lighter than Air," *Transactions of the Institute of British Geographers* 34 (2009): 35. See also McCormack's "Atmospheric Things and Circumstantial Excursions," *cultural geographies* 21 (2014): 605–25. On modern flight and embodiment, see Peter Adey, *Aerial Life: Spaces, Mobilities, Affects* (Malden, MA: Wiley-Blackwell, 2010).

13. See Rivka Swenson, "Optics, Gender, and the Eighteenth-Century Gaze: Looking at Eliza Haywood's *Anti-Pamela*," *The Eighteenth Century: Theory and Interpretation* 51, nos. 1–2 (2010): 27–43; and Swenson, "The Poet as Man of Feeling," *The Oxford Handbook of British Poetry, 1660–1800*, ed. Jack Lynch (New York: Oxford Univ. Press, 2016): 195–209.

14. See Gillispie, "Ballooning in France and Britain, 1783–1786: Aerostation and Adventurism," *Isis* 75 (1984): 248–68. See also Mi Gyung Kim, *The Imagined Empire: Balloon Enlightenment in Revolutionary Europe* (Pittsburgh, PA: Univ. of Pittsburgh Press, 2016), 209–32.

15. Humility, as I see it, is not self-abasement. Rather, it is self-knowledge that makes possible communication with others and, more broadly, justice and harmony. On humility and its virtues, see Jeanine Grenberg, *Kant and the Ethics of Humility: A Story of Dependence, Corruption, and Virtue* (New York: Cambridge Univ. Press, 2005); and Jennifer Clement, *Reading Humility in Early Modern England* (New York: Routledge, 2016).

16. Lunardi, *An Account of the First Aerial Voyage in England* (London: Printed for author at J. Bell, 1784), 15.

17. For more on these figures, see Rolt, *The Aeronauts*, 63–64, 66–67.

18. On the so-called "balloonomania," see Clare Brant, *Balloon Madness: Flights of Imagination in Britain, 1783–1786* (Rochester, NY: Boydell, 2017); and Paul Keen, *Literature, Commerce, and the Spectacle of Modernity, 1750–1800* (New York: Cambridge Univ. Press, 2012), 40–77.

19. *Lunardi's Grand Aerostatic Voyage through the Air* (London: J. Bew, 1784), 4.

20. Lunardi, *Mr. Lunardi's Account of His Second Aerial Voyage* (1785), 9.

21. On weather and sensibility, see Jan Golinski, *British Weather and the Climate of Enlightenment* (Chicago: Univ. of Chicago Press, 2007), 137–202. As a foreigner, Lunardi worked hard to endear himself, Englishing his first name to Vincent, flying a British flag, and decorating his second balloon with the Union Jack.

22. "Account of Aerostatic Experiments," *The Monthly Review* 71 (1784): 383; "*An Account of the First Aerial Voyage in England*," *The Gentleman's Magazine* 54 (1784): 770.

23. Lunardi, *An Account of Five Aerial Voyages in Scotland* (London: Printed for author by J. Bell, 1786), 22.

24. It is worth noting that meteorology then depended on regular measurement, rather than focusing merely on aberrations. On the history of British weather science, see Vladimir Jankovic, *Reading the Skies: A Cultural History of English Weather, 1650–1820* (Chicago, IL: Univ. of Chicago Press, 2000).

25. Brant, "I Will Carry You with Me on the Wings of Imagination," *Eighteenth-Century Life* 35, no. 1 (2011): 168–87.

26. Ian Watt, *The Rise of the Novel: Studies in Defoe, Richardson, and Fielding* (Berkeley, CA: Univ. of California Press, 1957), 200.

27. Doherty, "'Transporting thought:' Cultures of Balloon Flight in Britain, 1784–1785," *British Journal for the History of Science* (2017): 13.

28. See Leslie Gardiner, *Man in the Clouds: The Story of Vincenzo Lunardi* (Edinburgh: W. & R. Chambers, 1963), 158–60.

29. Sage, *A Letter, Addressed to a Female Friend, by Mrs. Sage, the First English Female Aerial Traveller* (London: J. Bell, 1785), 14.

30. "Disappointments," *The Public Advertiser*, 17 May 1785; "Lunardi's Aerial Expedition," *The London Magazine*, May 1785, 373. See also Mark Davis, *King of All Balloons: The Adventurous Life of James Sadler, the First English Aeronaut* (Stroud, UK: Amberley Press, 2015), 265–74.

31. See Keen, *Spectacle of Modernity*, 49–50. More generally, see Cindy McCreery, *The Satirical Gaze: Prints of Women in Late Eighteenth-Century England* (New York: Oxford Univ. Press, 2004).

32. See Richard Holmes, *Falling Upwards: How We Took to the Air* (New York: Vintage, 2014), 40–46.

33. Quoted in Peter Haining, *The Dream Machines: An Eye-Witness History of Ballooning* (New York: World Publishing, 1973), 32.

34. Baldwin, *Airopaidia: Containing the Narrative of a Balloon Excursion from Chester* (Chester: Printed for author by J. Fletcher, 1786), 2.

35. "Baldwin's *Airopaidia*," *The Monthly Review* 75 (1786): 217–18.

36. "Baldwin's *Aeropaidia*," *The English Review* 10 (1787): 433.

37. Brant, "The Progress of Knowledge in the Regions of the Air? Divisions and Disciplines in Early Ballooning," *Eighteenth-Century Studies* 45, no. 1 (2011): 77.

38. Thébaud-Sorger, "Thomas Baldwin's *Airopaidia*, or the Aerial View in Colour," *Seeing from Above: The Aerial View in Visual Culture*, ed. Mark Dorrian and Frédéric Pousin (London: Tauris, 2013), 46.

39. Edmund Burke, *A Philosophical Inquiry into the Origins of Our Ideas of the Sublime and Beautiful*, ed. J.T. Boulton (New York: Columbia Univ. Press, 1958), 73. The word *sublime* derives from a Latin antecedent meaning height or elevation, a high feeling often associated with high mountain altitudes in the period's painting and poetry. See Cyan Duffy, *Landscapes of the Sublime, 1700–1830: Classic Ground* (New York: Palgrave Macmillan, 2013), 28–67.

40. See A.A. Long, *From Epicurus to Epictetus: Studies in Hellenistic and Roman Philosophy* (New York: Oxford Univ. Press, 2006), 18. Usually, the word is part of the phrase "euroia biou," meaning "good flow of life."

41. On the variability of aerial representation, see Martyn Barber and Helen Wickstead, "'One immense black spot': Aerial Views of London, 1784–1918," *The London Journal* 35 (2010): 236–54; and Wickstead and Barber, "A Spectacular History of Survey by Flying Machine!" *Cambridge Archaeological Journal* 22 (2012): 71–88. On contemporaneous interest in variable perspectives, see Cynthia Wall, "The Impress of the Invisible: Lodges and Cottages," *English Literary History* 79 (2012): 989–1012; and Julie Park, "The Poetics of Enclosure in *Sense and Sensibility*," *Studies in Eighteenth-Century Culture* 42 (2013): 237–69.

42. See Mary Jacobus, *Romantic Things: A Tree, a Rock, a Cloud* (Chicago, IL: Univ. of Chicago Press, 2012), 10–35. On the age-old game of watching clouds, John Durham Peters argues, "Random clouds, imaginative viewer: nothing quite divides subject and object like clouds. There are few reading practices that are as rigorously policed to expunge projections as looking at clouds." See *The Marvelous Clouds: Toward a Philosophy of Elemental Media* (Chicago, IL: Univ. of Chicago Press, 2015), 255.

43. On the classification of clouds, see Richard Hamblyn, *The Invention of Clouds: How an Amateur Meteorologist Forged the Language of the Skies* (New York: Picador, 2001). Hubert Damisch examines the ways paintings of clouds frustrate the otherwise-dominant ideal in Western painting of linear perspective in *Theory of a /Cloud/: Toward a History of Painting*, trans. Janet Lloyd (Stanford, CA: Stanford Univ. Press, 2002).

44. See Keen and Melissa Speener, "'Philosophical Playthings': The Spectacle of Air-Balloons," Romantic Circles Gallery, *https://www.rc.umd.edu/gallery/exhibit/ miniaturizing-the-sublime-hot-air-balloon-flight-in-the-romantic-era*. Accessed 14 March 2018.

45. Barbara Marie Stafford discusses this effect in *Voyage into Substance: Art, Science, Nature, and the Illustrated Travel Account, 1760–1840* (Cambridge: Massachusetts Institute of Technology Press, 1984), 149.

46. Sadly, the pictures do not exist today. See Stephen Bann, "Nadar's Aerial View," *Seeing from Above*, 83–94.

47. See Crouch, *The Genesis of Flight: The Aeronautical History Collection of Colonel Richard Gimbel* (Seattle: Univ. of Washington Press, 2000).

48. Kaplan, *Aerial Aftermaths*, 94.

49. For example, the tragedy of Thomas Harris, who inspired tales of chivalry in 1824 when, story has it, he jumped from a fast-descending basket to lighten the load and save his fiancée. See Rolt, *Balloonists*, 115–16.

50. See Rolt, *Balloonists*, 159–82; Crouch, *The Eagle Aloft: Two Centuries of the Balloon in America* (Washington: Smithsonian Institute Press, 1983), 335–415; and F. Stanbury Hayden, *Military Ballooning during the Early Civil War* (Baltimore, MD: Johns Hopkins Univ. Press, 2000).

51. See Kaplan, *Aerial Aftermaths*, 69.

52. After observing a launch in France, Benjamin Franklin asked the rhetorical question, "What is the use of a newborn baby? As no one could predict all that a child might grow into, so no one could foresee the uses to which balloons might be put." See *The Papers of Benjamin Franklin*, ed. Leonard W. Larabee et al., 41 vols. (New Haven: Yale Univ. Press, 1959–2014), 4: 17. And, Tiberius Cavallo wrote at length on the possible utility of balloons in his *History and Practice of Aerostation* (1785).

53. See Holmes, *Falling Upwards*, 80–85.

Administrative Fictions of Domestic Manufacture: Eighteenth-Century Excise Guides

MATTHEW MAUGER

An official publication of the Board of Excise, printed in 1729, offers a series of *Instructions to be Observed by the Officers Employ'd in the duties on Paper*.[1] It begins with a short "Description of the Way and Manner of Making Paper." This explains how the "Rags, Ropes, Cables, &c" are "sorted and wash'd," beaten into "Half-stuff" in large mortars using "four or five Hammers," laid to "mellow" before being beaten again into "fine Stuff," and then soaked in luke-warm water in "a Vessel call'd a Fatt." A sheet of paper is produced by drawing a "Mould" comprising a fine sieve through the mixture. By the "Dexterity and Skill of the Workman," the stuff gathered is laid between two felt sheets. A second layer of stuff is laid on top, with another felt sheet placed above, "and so on 'till they have rais'd a Heap of 7 or 8 Quires, which is call'd a Post . . . which Post being put into a Press, and press'd very hard together, till the Water is squeez'd out." The paper sheets are "hung in Parcels of 3, 4, 5 Sheets, or more in each Parcel upon Lines (usually call'd Trebles) in the Drying-house." When dry, they are "wetted" for precise sizing, before being pressed once again and dried a second time "in Parcels of 3 or 4 Sheets." The broken sheets are separated out, and the sheets "tied up into Reams or Bundles for Sale, *viz.* 18 of the good Quires, and 2 of the broken to each Ream."[2]

The manual containing this account of domestic paper manufacture is an example of the fascinating and little-studied body of texts on which this essay focuses: the instruction booklets issued by the eighteenth-century Board of Excise to its officers in the field, known colloquially as "gaugers." These guides describe the techniques of scrutiny, measurement, and detection to be adopted when measuring (or "gauging") the goods produced in a range of manufacturing contexts across the country. The brief account of paper making detailed above is typical: a text issued to excise districts across the country assumes a single consistent "*way* and *manner*" of manufacture. It asserts a set of production steps and technical terms presented as universal: the "Mould" used to skim the "Stuff;" the pile of "Quires," which "is call'd a Post;" the drying lines, "usually call'd Trebles;" the "Reams" into which the good and broken sheets are packaged for sale according to a ratio of one broken sheet for every nine good. These terms are, in turn, deployed in the record-keeping practices that the gaugers are required to observe. Below the level of these terms, the precise techniques associated with the "Dexterity and Skill" of the artisan are invisible.

In this essay, I argue that the textual abstraction of artisanal practices that we can see at work in the excise manuals establishes an administrative fiction of a consistent national approach to the manufacture of each excised commodity: an inevitable, even sought-after, consequence of the emerging state regulation of manufacture. These descriptions function as an enabling text for the state's collection of a tax. Indeed, the implication of the excise manuals in the state's technologies of surveillance allows us to probe further the relationship between theoretical and practical knowledge, especially where the process of description might best be understood as enacting the state's desire to lay claim to those skills-based technologies. By employing the abstraction of descriptive text to find a level at which a single set of national production processes can be theorized, the guides effectively invoke a field of manufacturing uniformity. Accordingly, they offer a case study of the ascendance of the national over the local, of the universal over the particular, of the movement from observation and description, to surveillance and prescription. Reading the guides affords the opportunity to consider how the state managed a key interface with national manufacture—the excise— through the medium of text. To this end, I argue that the guides exhibit an emergent concern for ensuring product quality, effectively setting out a series of national standards for production across a range of industries.

The National Measurement of Local Production

In recent decades, a renewed interest in the history and imposition of taxation in the seventeenth and eighteenth centuries has focused attention on revenue as a site of encounter between the state, manufacturers, and consumers. John Brewer in *The Sinews of Power* (1989) described the emergence of a "fiscal-military state" in the century following 1688, in which the expansion of British power was connected with its ability to raise taxes.[3] Subsequent studies have widened Brewer's approach, demonstrating how the expansion of taxation is revealing of wider social and cultural renewal in Britain in this period. The excise in particular is one of the historical geographies traced by Miles Ogborn in *Spaces of Modernity* (1998), through which the temporal and spatial transformations that reshaped eighteenth-century London can be located, evidenced, and particularized.[4] In producing a complex administrative system comprising a series of "planned, rationally ordered, hierarchical, routinized and scrutinized roles, practices and spaces," Ogborn argues, the excise reflects the modernity of the eighteenth-century state. Recent work by William Ashworth has furthered our understanding of the relationship between the state and national manufacture when read through the taxation of goods, particularly the increasing tendency for manufacture to be policed and systematized.[5] The excise, Ashworth has shown, was both the government's chief source of manufacturing knowledge and a framework within which domestic production could be regulated, standardized, and controlled.[6] The excise guides themselves—although they feature in Ogborn's and, more significantly, in Ashworth's studies—have received little extended consideration in their own right as a genre of trade writing.

An excise is an "inland duty" laid on goods at the point of production and payable by the manufacturer. It can broadly be contrasted with a customs duty levied on articles of foreign manufacture at a British port, and with a sales tax payable by the purchaser at the point of sale. Excise has its roots in the fiscal reforms of the Commonwealth and Protectorate Governments of the 1650s, though Charles I also experimented with excise at the outbreak of the Civil War, and was confirmed at the Restoration through the Statute of Tenures of 1660.[7] Early excises were raised on alcoholic drinks; such charges, together with tobacco and vehicle fuel, are perhaps the most familiar instances of excise charges for twenty-first century consumers. Under innovations of the 1720s and 1730s, the scaffolding of the excise system was also instrumented to survey the movement through the economy of certain imported goods not technically produced in Britain, such as tea, coffee, and chocolate.[8] Of particular interest for this essay is the rapid extension of excise in Britain across the early-eighteenth century to cover wrought items of local manufacture in contexts such as candle-, glass- and soap-making, hide tanning, the production of paper, the printing of fabrics such as calico, the preparation of starch, and, from 1784, brick manufacture.[9]

Excise was typically levied by a standard charge (reckoned by unit or by weight) set through legislation enacted in the national Parliament, rather than an *ad valorem* rate based on a product's market value (typically the basis of a sales tax). This, together with practices of manufacture that spread across the urban and rural communities of eighteenth-century Britain, meant that the assessment of excise was dependent not only on the precise measurement of production but also on the even application of such standards across the country. Confidence in the equitable application of the system was contingent on the excise measurements being seen to be applied with uniformity, certainty, and regularity, according to a set of commonly-agreed approaches, with broadly fixed severity. The accurate assessment of excise charges depended upon a detailed and ongoing surveillance of the excised industries by a large workforce of gaugers each charged with the oversight of a specified geographical area, the monitoring and recording of the activities of its producers, and the measurement of the goods produced. The excise system thus demanded a consistent national monitoring of manufacturing processes, processes that were themselves inconsistent and subject to significant local variation. Gaugers were distributed across the country within excise regions known as "Collections," fifty-three in total by 1770, each of which was presided over by a "Collector."[10] Each collection was sub-divided into smaller units called "Divisions," the responsibility of a "Supervisor."[11] A supervisor had oversight of a team of excise officers (totaling over 2,700 by 1770), each observing local manufacture across all excised goods in a single "ride" (although occasionally a dedicated ride might be established to cover a single dominant industry in a specified division).[12] In London, the scale of production required a different approach to excise organization; by 1763, 684 officers were regulated by a team of "Surveyors."[13] Urban officers, whose area of responsibility was defined as a "walk," were more likely to specialize in the charging of a particular commodity (or set of commodities).

Such was the extension of the excise that, by the early decades of the eighteenth century, large provinces of British manufacture were under the unrelenting surveillance of a "standing army" of excise officers, each of whom was charged under oath to ensure the fair application of national law.[14] The situation clearly presented the Excise Board with a number of challenges: organizational, logistical, and practical. Among those that must have seemed most insurmountable were those which arose, on the one hand, from the vast scale of the task; and, on the other hand, from the fundamental disconnection between the almost infinite diversity of local and regional practice in relation to both the processes and the products of manufacture. A further challenge was the national legislative framework built on the assumption of consistency. Among these complications, three are pivotal. The first relates to the practicalities of surveillance: outside of London, a single excise officer might be responsible for surveying a number of different industries. It would be a rare individual who would have the diverse range of experiential knowledge to track multiple overlapping manufacturing processes in the detail required. The second practical problem follows from the first: the intimate knowledge of the manufacturing processes was owned primarily by the producers themselves, who thus enjoyed a superiority of knowledge over the officers charged with their surveillance. The third, and perhaps the most intractable, of the problems arose from the fact that techniques of manufacture within the excised industries varied between regions and between individual producers in a way entirely non-commensurate with the even application of a national law. To what extent were excise officers responsible for enforcing some kind of eighteenth-century "British standard" for production that would allow the even and consistent levying of the nationally-defined excise charge?

Establishing a Fiction of National Manufacturing Habits

The Excise Board sought to address these problems by issuing its officers detailed industry-specific instruction booklets. These were effectively handbooks providing detailed guidance on the required approaches for measuring and charging, and on the routines that manufacturers were expected to observe, thus enacting in practical terms the governing text of the excise laws. As a result, a new set of guides was required every time the laws were amended or the contexts of revenue collection changed. I have identified 164 examples covering the period until 1800 in archives across Britain and North America. Next to nothing is known about their authorship: neither the guides themselves nor the detailed minutes of the Excise Board provide any clarity, although there would have been no shortage of expertise available to the Board. In terms of publication, the name Jacob Tonson appears regularly on the title pages of guides issued in the 1720s and 1730s, suggesting that the firm had a government printing contract with the Excise.[15] With two or three exceptions, however, examples from other periods have no named printer.

The excise guides range in length from pamphlets of no more than twelve pages to longer booklets of around forty to sixty, typically in octavo or long duodecimo. In the archives in which they are preserved, these individual booklets—occasionally bearing the annotations of the officers to whom they were issued—have typically been re-bound within hard covers. Given the importance accorded these *Instructions*, conscientious gaugers occasionally may have opted to afford them a similar durability. It seems likely, however, that many would have resembled a single example in the National Archives preserved in its original form, loosely sewed within dog-eared parchment covers (a manuscript note reads "Receiv'd these Orders for Instructions Jan:ʸ 23:ᵈ 1729/30 by me W:ᵐ Woodward").[16] Nearly two-thirds of the publications in the project archive specify that they are to be used in the assessment of manufacture in either "the Country" (sixty examples), or "London" (thirty-five).[17] Just over sixty direct the management of the excise on alcoholic drinks. Eighty-one regulate the production of wrought items that are the particular interest of this essay, dating from across the century (30 percent from before 1750, 70 percent from after); as a result, it is often possible to track the development across the century of the frameworks of surveillance within which particular items of manufacture were enclosed.

The first guide associated with the manufacture of starch, for example, published in 1713 and entitled, according to a semi-regular formula, *Instructions to be Observed by the Officers Employ'd in the Charging the Duty on Starch*, is typical in providing details concerning the frequency of visits to manufacturers and the stages of manufacture at which measurements should be taken (in the vats—or "fats"—during fermentation; when transferred into the "*sower water tubs;*" when strained through the "Lawn Sieve" into the "*Green Starch-tubs;*" when poured into box-frames to harden; when nearly dry).[18] It contains pages of example ledgers and "dimension books" that gaugers are to use as models for their record-keeping and a preface containing a short "Account of the Manner of Making Starch."[19] Subsequent publications (1734, 1769, and 1778) provide increasing levels of detail. They include information about waste products, known as "slimes" and "scrapings," which makers are able to re-use, alternative manufacturing processes such as "weather drying," and a limited acknowledgement of regional variation. Later guides are more prescriptive in terms of the timings of visits: "once at least every Day when there is any Steeping in the Fats," the 1734 guide advises, "but when there are green or white Waters depending, not less than twice or thrice a Day and oftener . . . while they are boxing or setting the Stove, and twice a Day whilst the Stove is drying."[20] The 1778 guide introduces an elaborate system by which makers are required to give notice of their movement through these phases of manufacture. The security of the gauging is ensured by the multiple accounts taken of quantities at the varying stages of manufacture, which, the guides insist, relate mathematically through various rules of thumb. The guides also become more detailed concerning the "sharp practices" designed to fool excise officers: tubs of fermenting starch covered with a layer of worthless slimes; starch-makers quickly "breaking out Boxes, and filling them again between your Surveys, and pretend[ing] that they are the same you took account of before."[21] The 1778 guide recommends a series of techniques by which officers can recognize such frauds. Sudden and unexpected return visits can be an effective way to catch manufacturers in the act of removing and refilling box-frames. The fashioning of a "small spatula of brass, about an inch broad, and an inch and a half long, affixed or screwed on, and a little turned up" can expose good quality starch lurking under a layer of slimes.[22] Unwrapping some of the dried bricks of starch can reveal whether they have been allowed sufficient time to dry thoroughly.[23]

It is the richness of the detail that these guides offer about the terminology, organization, and processes of eighteenth-century manufacture, not to mention the inventiveness of producers in attempting to ameliorate the imposition of the excise, that makes them a remarkable archive of primary materials. For those interested in researching techniques of production in the period, they offer insights into contexts of making where artisanal modes of manufacture were organized in a largely pre-mechanized environment and in which the harbingers of mass production, such as the division of labor, remained the exception rather than the rule.[24] Moreover, their deliberate attitude of non-specialist instruction to the broad contours of production in a given industry makes them, perhaps uniquely, accessible to scholars. But the detail and texture of manufacture preserved in the manuals is also a distortion of real life, advancing a fiction of national manufacturing habits that is a consequence of the role that the guides play as a tool of mediation between the revenue-raising activities of the state and wider civil society.[25] Indeed, we might relate the production of the guides to James Scott's observation, in *Seeing Like a State*, that "state simplifications are always far more static and schematic than the actual social phenomena they presume to typify."[26] The manufacturing processes which excise officers survey have their roots in artisanal traditions of making: a vast body of non-textual knowledge passed down by word-of-mouth and the immediacy of "living" the trade. The excise guides imagine eighteenth-century manufacture as a broadly consistent field by smoothing over the detail of the lived experience of these trades. The guides thus extrapolate across the fields of production the assumption of uniformity upon which the mathematical models underpinning the science of gauging itself depends: techniques which assume the absolute invariability of a cask, a barrel, a container, a frame.[27] In doing so, the state can present a narrative which avers a broad uniformity of production methods across the nation. Such state mapping exercises, of course, inevitably produce the simplified terrain that they claim to observe; as Scott has argued, society has been "thoroughly . . . refashioned by state maps of legibility."[28] Like Ogborn, however, who notes that the guides accordingly play a part in constructing the excise as an "imaginary geography," I find their fictionality compelling.

Through the process of abstraction and rationalization, the guides make the very idea of a national excise imaginable.[29]

The excise manuals mediate between the excise legislation and the everyday reality of manufacture and produce the surveillance mechanisms on which the excise depends. They directed the conduct of gaugers in the field, and equipped them with sufficient information to occupy a role that might best be described as "knowledgeable outsider." In terms of their relationship with the industries they describe, the guides thus lie on the interface between theory and practice, between an ambitious and overarching national policy and the immediate contexts of local production. Whilst they can be understood as a cold abstraction produced by a distant and uncaring eighteenth-century state, they might arguably be regarded more accurately as the attempt of a nascent civil service to make workable the legislation of a national government through the production of an imaginary bureaucratic or administrative space.[30] Moreover, as a means by which the Board of Excise could evidence national consistency and objectivity in the assessment of the inland duties, the guides can be considered alongside the provisions governing the training of the officers themselves, the pains taken in allocating personnel to divisions where they had no private connection, and the regular rotation of officers between collections.[31]

The detailed and time-consuming practices of observation that the printed *Instructions* delineate are directed towards the gaugers' maintenance of manuscript ledgers in which production is tracked through a complex system of numbers and symbols. Each guide typically ends with pages containing examples of these required forms of book-keeping, usually built around the supposed manufacturing businesses of imaginary makers of goods. These fictional creations, reminiscent of the development of "user personas" in contemporary marketing and user-experience design, are particularly striking given the fanciful world of excise symmetry that the guides evoke. The ledgers might include "dimension books" (recording the sizes of the containers in which goods are made at a given production site), and complex tabulations of the manufacturing processes observed. So abstruse can these models be that many excise manuals include additional pages explaining the example data that they contain. In practice, we cannot be certain how strictly excise officers in Collections around the country followed the models offered in the guides, although the minutes of the Excise Board regularly evidence complaints received from Supervisors about the sloppy book-keeping of particular gaugers. An indicative example concerns William Taylor (fourth ride of the Winchester Division, Hampshire Collection), held responsible for a number of "irregularitys and Blunders" in his books, including using non-standard notation; failing to record the cleansing of the apparatus; an instance where "neither the Round nor . . . time is enterd;" and omitting to gauge the capacity of the "utensils."[32] Such records suggest that the specimens of record-keeping found in these appendices accurately reflect the importance placed on systemic, detailed, and schematized forms of record keeping.

The recommendation for a glass ledger contained in the guide for 1778 offers a typical case (fig. 1).[33] It provides a model for recording the production of flint glass (a fine clear glass perfected in England in the late seventeenth century, the forerunner for what is now known as "lead crystal"), and "bottle glass" (a tougher glass from which bottles were made). The entries cover around a week of manufacture at a fictional Liverpool glassmaking business, Samuel Ogden and Co. In general, each row of the table corresponds to a single visit, expressed by a short-hand code used in the first column: "15 m 11" refers to 15 July at eleven in the morning, "18 e 10" to 18 July at ten in the evening (a time notation encountered throughout the excise guides). The second column contains the notices that the glassmaker has given to the excise officer concerning the commencement of a new making of glass through the "charging" of his pots with raw materials. To the right, sets of columns refer to the five numbered glass-making vessels or "pots," and the four annealing ovens (all measured in advance, and corresponding to entries in the gauger's "dimension book"). The physical spaces of the imagined glasshouse, its tools and apparatus, are effectively re-mapped according to the narrative of manufacture, producing in turn a generic schematic arrangement for the recording of glass-making wherever it might be practiced. To re-state this more broadly: the framework of the table visualizes the standardization of space-use relationships in places of manufacture that the excise guides govern (a matter considered in greater depth in the next section of this essay). The data entered in the columns—comprising a strange mixture of symbol, number, and abbreviation that would be anathema to modern computer-based data curation with its insistence on tightly-defined data types—represents the physical activity of those spaces.

What follows is a narration of the fictional glass making that the data represent. The model production record begins with a process of manufacture nearing completion: to this end, we can see on the right-hand side that on 14 July a certain quantity of flint glass and bottle glass is excised. The next row, concerning the inspection of 15 m 6, indicates the start of the next batch, for which the glassmaker had given notice at noon on 14 July; the row of "F"s denotes that pots one, two, and three are to be used to produce flint glass. The gauger finds these vessels "charging" (the raw materials being prepared and placed in the pots), and pots four and five empty (represented by the "O"). Annealing oven one is full (with the last of the earlier batch), whereas ovens two, three, and four stand empty. At 15 m 11, little has changed

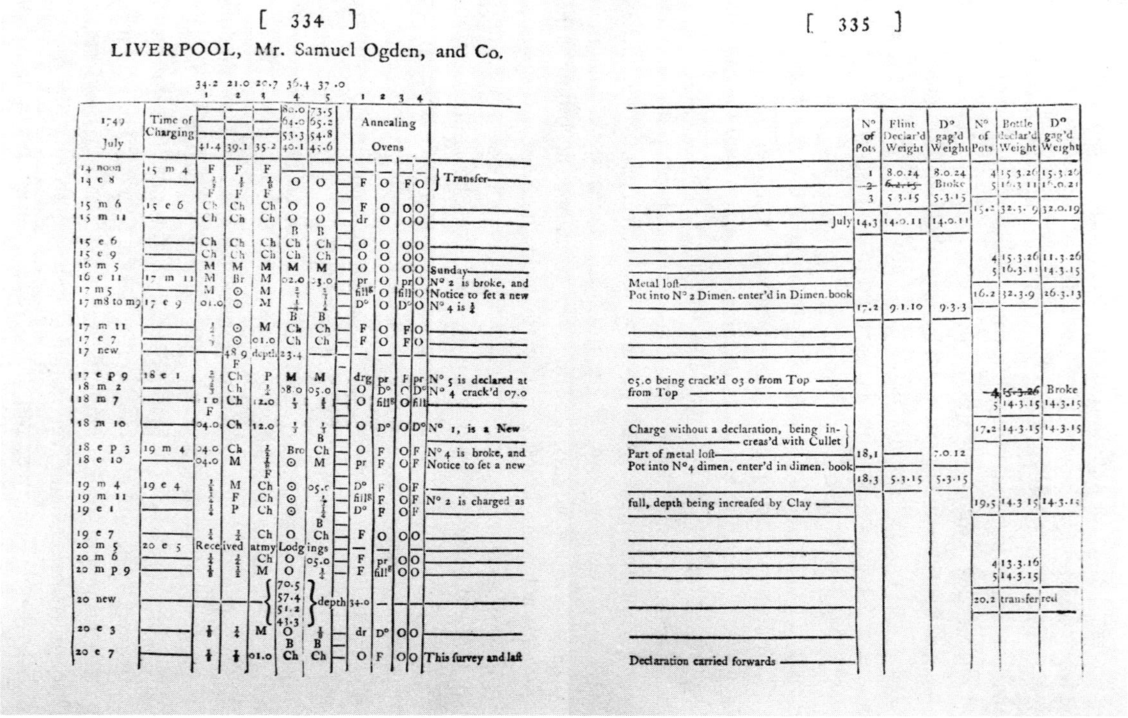

Figure 1. Recommended form for a glass ledger, from *Instructions to be Observed by the Officers concerned in ascertaining the Duties on Glass in the Country* (London, 1762), 34–35 (The National Archives - CUST 142/10).

(although oven one is in the process of being emptied). The "B"s in the next row declare that pots four and five are to be used to produce bottle glass (for which notice was given at 15 m 6). During two evening inspections (15 e 6 and 15 e 9) all five pots are being "charged" with glass materials; and, by the following morning, the gauger notes that all five are now "melting" ("M"). In the evening, however, the entry acknowledges an accident during this early stage of manufacture: pot two has broken in the intense heat ("Br"), the observation in the central column asserting that all the "metal" (the technical term for the molten glass) has been lost. The recognition of this accident accounts for a weight of raw materials which will not materialize in the manufactured glass items, and which might otherwise have been regarded with suspicion by the excise officer or the division supervisor. Pot two is out-of-commission for the rest of the day, although the dimensions of a replacement are noted later that evening. Meanwhile, in a process beginning at 16 e 11, the molten bottle glass in pots four and five is "drawn down" in order to manufacture glass items. Pot four is two-thirds full at 17 m 5, reducing to three-eighths at 17 m 8 (though this is corrected to one quarter in the remarks column). Ovens one and three are filled with wrought products being "annealed," a process by which hot glass items are slowly cooled. As the flint glass in pots one and three is drawn down over the next day or two, we see the commencement of new phases of glass manufacture.

The system that we can see in operation here may be necessarily unique to the particular industry which is being surveyed, but equivalents of this approach are to be found across all forms of excised manufacture: quantities of starch logged at each stage of fermentation and drying; the condition of each vat and press in a paper mill noted; the hides taken out of the "wooze" at the tannery categorized and measured; calico pieces counted at the beginning and end of the fabric printing process, including the "Number of Tables and Machines at Work."[34] The surveillance to which manufacturers are required to submit is not restricted to weighing or counting the wrought goods—the soap, or the glass items, or the candles—but rather to measuring, and thereby validating, each step of the manufacture. As a result, these ledgers represent a gauging not just of product but also of process. If the printed text of the guides establishes a one-size-fits-all framework within which the activities of both the producers and the excise officers are contained, the manuscript ledgers that they describe provide the models by which local businesses along the specific "ride" or "walk" can be accommodated.

Discipline, Process, and the Regulation of Quality

The encounter between state and manufacturer that is staged through the excise manuals is not simply to be understood as a codification of a hitherto unwritten set of production practices; such a systematization is only one of a number of transformations effected through the disciplinary matrix of these texts. The Excise Board's *Instructions* gesture towards—and in places claim to enact—complementary processes of condensing, regularizing, and promoting statutory discipline. These developments point towards national production standards, a nascent form of industry regulation, and, even though glimpsed only fleetingly, what we might now describe as concerns for consumer protection. The final section of this essay concentrates on the way in which the excise manuals acknowledge and, perhaps, produce a system of excise monitoring and collection that manages this interface between the state and civil society. In particular, it considers the way in which guides from across the spectrum of excised goods direct the officers' attention to five core characteristics of production: the use of space; the imposition of time discipline; the recognition of method; the measurement of process; and, the validation of the product.

The control that the excise regulations impose on the use of time and space are familiar aspects of modernity as framed by E. P. Thompson, Michel Foucault, and those who have followed them.[35] This is particularly evident in the urban context, as Ogborn has demonstrated.[36] As the agents—though also the products—of that system, it is unsurprising to find the gaugers' guides both enforcing these processes of methodization (in the aspects of manufacture that officers were required to observe) and generating them (by establishing detailed patterns of spatial and temporal behaviors to which the gaugers themselves were required to conform). Across all excised commodities, producers were required to make statutory declarations concerning the use of spaces within their premises for specific phases of making. Tanners, for example, were obliged to state the places "which shall be made use of for the Tanning, Tawing, or dressing Hides or Skins."[37] The enforcement of these approved space-use relationships was a key responsibility of the excise officer. Gaugers are advised regularly to confirm that the "entered places" are being used for their stated purpose, and that other "undeclared" spaces are not being appropriated. The guides thus direct the process by which a state-sanctioned model for the organization of space in particular manufacturing contexts is imposed. A key feature of the guides is their fondness for the technical terms relating to the sites of manufacture: "the Tan-House, Tan-yard, Work-House, Drying Place;"[38] "Soap-houses" and "soap-boilers;"[39] "the Tallow Chandlers;"[40] "the [Paper] Mill, Sorting-houses, and Ware-houses;"[41] and, "Glass houses."[42] To extend Ogborn's mapping metaphor, the manuals effectively label the architecture of British manufacture, establishing a chart by which excised production becomes legible to those charged with its taxation.

The enforcement of time discipline involved some level of cooperation between officer and producer. The sample glass ledger examined above gives a clear sense of the practical challenge facing a gauger enforcing these regulations: keeping track of overlapping phases of production, recording the receipt of notices from manufacturers, observing these processes across multiple geographical sites. A 1712 guide requires gaugers to visit soap boilers "every six Hours, though silent; when at Work, your Surveys must be more frequent."[43] They must acquaint themselves with the manufacturing rhythms of each producer so that they can be on-hand when newly manufactured soap is poured from the copper vessels in which it is boiled into large casks or frames.[44] This expectation is made manageable through the introduction of a system by which boilers are required to provide notice of their intention to make soap. This is first acknowledged in the 1725 guide for the London area and echoed in the 1732 guide for country collections: "No Maker of Sope is to begin to Make or Work upon any Making of Sope . . . without giving to the Officers of the Division . . . Notice in Writing of the particular Time and Hour when such Making is intended to be begun, 24 Hours before the beginning every such Making."[45] Expressing a desire that officers "may be as little troublesome to the Soap-makers as possible," manuals advise that "where the House is Silent, and the Soap-maker doth agree," the number of surveys may be reduced to "one per day by dropping the visit as would otherwise fall out to be made between one and five the Morning."[46] This represents some degree of recognition of the relationships a gauger might establish among manufacturers. The movement towards surveillance prompted through the provision of notices, whilst assisting officers in making efficient use of their time, also maintains some notion of the makers' freedom to pursue programs of manufacture according to schedules which they (rather than the excise officers) determine. The guides thus facilitate a system which is to some extent based on trust. The temporal rhythms of the soap-house, the chandlery, and the glass-maker—temporal rhythms which in many cases remain closely tied to the time-patterns of domestic life occurring within the same premises—are thus made visible to the state through an awkward compromise.

The tendency of the guides to maneuver manufacturers into state-approved temporal and spatial frameworks extends to a flattening-out of localized distinctions in terms of the processes of production. The guides typically begin with a short "Account" offering gaugers an outline defining the stages of manufacture of the commodity in question. Occasionally, these statements accept that there might be regional variations in practice. Gaugers surveying the production of starch are offered a description of the staged fermentation of the meal (typically the ground, edible part of a grain), and an approach to observation based on that process. There is nevertheless a somewhat grudging acknowledgement from guides in the mid-century onwards that "where they make Starch from Bran [the husk of the grain] you are, according to the best of your Judgement, to compute how many Pounds of Starch a Bushel of such Bran or Meal will produce."[47] Glossaries appended to the guides for the excise levied on hides typically note that "Butts" ("made from the largest Ox-Hide, Bull, Steer, or Cow, and . . . Tann'd whole") and "Backs" (hides cut down the back into two "sides") are "chiefly to be found in *London*, and about 60 Miles round the same," while "Clout-leather" (smaller pieces of hide cured in "Horse-Dung") is found "more particularly in *Taunton, Exeter, Tiverton*, and *Cornwall* Collections."[48] Little practical detail is offered about the implications of these differences on manufacturing processes, however, or on the specific programs of observation that they may require.

Perhaps most striking to a modern reader of the excise manuals are the surveillance frameworks within which the very processes of production are monitored. The regime set in place for observing the printing of fabric cloth is germane here. In their visits to these print-houses, officers were required to be in possession of a frame, the dimensions of which corresponded to the standard fabric size defined in statute. Into this frame was affixed a single "identifying letter," changed periodically (and at random) under the instruction of the district Supervisor. On arrival, officers were enjoined to observe the number of "tables" in use, and the types of fabric being printed upon them. The guide then stipulates that they were to use their frames "fairly to imprint the Length upon each Piece of Callicoe, and also the Breadth, if over or under the Statute, on the End thereof." Whilst it is unclear what "imprinting" means in this context, it would appear that the fabrics were fixed within the frames for the purposes of measurement, and that this process transferred onto the cloth, either through stamping or embossing, the unique combination of "identifying letter" and "progressive [i.e. sequential] number."[49] This allowed the tracking of the onward movement of this piece of fabric through the printing house and formed the basis of the record maintained in the complex ledgers through which gaugers recorded and encoded the business of the fabric printer.[50]

As we have seen, several excises required the keeping of a "Dimension Book," a record of the exact proportions of the apparatus employed at a particular site. A candle manufacturer was required to give notice offering a true account "of the number of rods of which the making is intended to consist . . . or if for moulds, it must specify the exact number, and size of the moulds."[51] Similarly, at the glass-maker's, gaugers measured the empty pots and numbered them; the annealing ovens were also "to be numbered and surveyed in the like Manner."[52] Most extreme is a new regime covering the making of soap, first mentioned in a guide of 1770: "every maker of hard Sope is to provide at his own expence, sufficient wooden covers to every copper, pan, or other utensil, wherein he shall boil, or make any hard Sope, and the locks, keys, and all other necessary fastenings, for securing the coppers, pans, half-boil tubs, or other utensils."[53] The gaugers were the custodians of the keys, thus involving them materially in the manufacturing process.[54] This system is extended even further in the 1797 guide, in which not only are there to be lockable covers on the copper boilers but also "a door securely fixed to every furnace and ash-hole . . . [with] proper locks and fastenings."[55]

The excise guides directed the everyday routines of manufacturers and excise officers, constructing a detailed surveillance regime governing the organization of workplaces, the observance of manufacturing methods, and adherence to a set of production processes. This regime ultimately enabled the one assessment that was critical to the state: the measurement of product quantity necessary in order to levy a tax. What is remarkable about the excise establishment as it is described within the gaugers' manuals, however, is the apparent slippage from a dispassionate assessment of product quantity to a concern for quality.[56] Defects in the standard of goods produced, the *Instructions* suggests, can be the hallmarks of attempts to defraud the excise (or, in the language of the guides, to engage in "sharp practices"). A block of starch which "shall not crackle, on being strongly pressed with your fingers, nor feel crisp" might not have been dried for the expected two days; through its deviation from the expected timelines, this is possibly indicative of an attempt to pass a cycle of making below the radar of the excise officer.[57] Inconsistent grading of the sheets produced at a paper-mill could relate to attempts to pass paper produced for printing (which attracts a higher rate of excise) as paper intended for other uses.[58] On occasion, the attending officer is required to make an apparently drastic intervention: "When you find a Making to weigh off, wherein several of the Candles are crack'd and spoil'd in making, and the Chandler offers to break and deface the same, you are in that Case to weigh the sound, and crack'd Candles separately . . . and to break, and utterly deface such crack'd and spoil'd Candles, that no part of them be left in a Condition to be burn'd."[59]

There is a clear legitimacy for this somewhat brutal treatment in terms of the security of the duty. Candlemakers would want to re-use the tallow or wax in the next making; they would understandably neither wish to pay excise on candles they could not sell nor pay excise twice on the same raw materials. Equally, the excise officer needed to be certain that, having made an allowance for cracked candles, the chandler could not then go ahead and sell them effectively duty free. A similar provision regulated the re-use of sub-standard soap; but from 1732 onwards, gaugers are told more explicitly to be attentive to the quality of soap products, particularly in terms of the critical use of alkali "lyes" in the manufacturing process:[60]

> If sope be weak, it will have a faint Smell . . . and it will either have no Grain, or what is small and pale, and if squeez'd between the Fingers, will feel greasy; it will be soft, because not boil'd to a real Body, and dull and not smooth, because not purify'd with the second Lyes.

> If strong, it will be very thick . . . and have a Grain like a Pease, and if squeez'd as above, will shine and scale if bended, and such Sope being put in to the Frame, and no Lyes put to it afterwards, will sting the Tongue if touch'd with it.[61]

Again, what seems to be particularly at stake here are shortcuts in the process of making which may indicate surreptitious manufacture; yet, concern for the "strength" of the soap, its oiliness, and (most seriously perhaps) its irritancy, seem to have the reasonable expectations of the consumer in mind. One might surmise that these concerns for product quality are borne, at least in part, from anxieties that the incidence of the excise leads manufacturers to seek ways to reduce the basic per-item cost price, either by finding short-cuts in the production process or by reducing the relative quantities of the more expensive constituent materials. As Ashworth observes, such a decline in standards would also have a long-term impact on domestic manufacture and, in turn, the excise by making it difficult to compete with the higher quality products available from abroad.[62] Similar considerations appear to be at play in the provisions concerning printers of fabric. Here, gaugers are required to "discern when they print with false Colours." Again, we might assume that there is both an immediate revenue issue at stake (evidence of production shortcuts which might indicate clandestine production) and a future concern for revenue decline (as a consequence of the availability of higher quality foreign items). "When you find any of the Properties of false Colours," remarkably by employing a taste-test to find if they are "acid" (the hallmark of a cheap pigment) or "smooth and sweetish" (the indicator of "the True"), "you must tell your Surveyor, that the best Measures may be concerted for the Security of the Duty."[63] In terms of a broader concern for quality, then, it seems clear that the Excise Board instrumented the infrastructure of the Excise as a means of enforcing a quasi-national standard. As a consequence, the excise officer became folded into a regime of "quality control," with the gauger standing not only in the role of "measurer" but also "assessor." Through this slippage, the levying of the excise (and the application, for goods such as hides and paper, of the official stamp of excise payment) also became the passing of a basic national quality standard, a sign that the wrought items could now pass from their manufacture into their retail phase with an endorsement that warranted not only their legal propriety but also, in some respects, an affirmation of their conformity to reasonable notions of quality.[64]

Conclusion

The gaugers' guides, together forming a tightly defined genre of trade literature emerging from the executive authority of the state, are most straightforwardly understood as playing a critical role in the hegemony of the eighteenth-century taxation system. They directed the surveillance regime that excise officers were to maintain on their rides and walks whilst they simultaneously defined the relationships between the gaugers and their supervisors by which the excise regulated itself. The Excise Board established in its guides domestic models of manufacture that could be regulated by national policy, creating a fictional world of making in which the contexts, procedures, materials, methods, apparatus and products of national manufacture could be accommodated within a consistent framework. Gaugers in Collections as far afield as Cornwall, Canterbury, and Cumberland were required by their *Instructions* to locate local manufacturing processes within these rational standard models, and—in the requirement to map those practices onto the required schematics of journals, books, and ledgers— became complicit in the creation of that bureaucratic imaginary. The guides are thus strongly suggestive of the way in which manufacture was drawn into disciplinary and regulatory frameworks that foreshadow modern notions of industry regulation and the legislative enforcement of a common set of national production standards. As enabling texts, however, by which public servants attempted to interpret and enact an ambitious state policy, the manuals also may be understood more generously as negotiating a series of contexts for the encounter between local manufacturers and the agents of the state, offering practical advice for the real-world implementation of the excise.

NOTES

1. *Instructions to be Observed by the Officers employ'd in the Duties on Paper* (London, 1729).
2. *Instructions . . . Paper* (1729), 5–8.

3. John Brewer, *The Sinews of Power: War, Money and the English State, 1688–1783* (London: Unwin, 1989), 95–114.

4. Miles Ogborn, *Spaces of Modernity: London's Geographies, 1680–1780* (New York: Guildford, 1998), 163–85.

5. William Ashworth, *Customs and Excise: Trade, Production, and Consumption in England 1640–1845* (Oxford: Oxford Univ. Press, 2003).

6. Ashworth, *The Industrial Revolution: The State, Knowledge and Global Trade* (London: Bloomsbury, 2017), 119–43.

7. For the emergence of excise taxation during the Interregnum, see D'Maris Coffman, *Excise Taxation and the Origins of Public Debt* (Basingstoke: Macmillan, 2013), 1–20; Ashworth, *Customs and Excise*, 15–20; Ogborn, *Spaces of Modernity*, 163–85; Brewer, *Sinews of Power*, 95–114; J. V. Beckett, "Land Tax or Excise: The Levying of Taxation in Seventeenth- and Eighteenth-Century England," *English Historical Review* 100 (1985): 285–308.

8. 1723, 10 Geo. 1, c. 10. These developments were part of Robert Walpole's vision of London as constituting a free-trade zone, customs charges being replaced with inland duties raised when goods passed into British retail; see Paul Langford, *The Excise Crisis: Society and Politics in the Age of Walpole* (Oxford: Clarendon Press, 1975), 31–33; Peter Linebaugh, *The London Hanged: Crime and Civil Society in the Eighteenth Century*, 2nd ed. (London: Verso, 2006), 178; Raymond Turner, "The Excise Scheme of 1733," *The English Historical Review* 42 (1927): 34–57. This system was extended to tobacco through an Act of 1789 (1789, 29 Geo. 3, c. 68); see Kenneth Morgan, *Bristol and the Atlantic Trade in the Eighteenth Century* (Cambridge: Cambridge Univ. Press, 1993), 178–81.

9. See Brewer, "The English State and Fiscal Appropriation, 1688–1789," *Politics & Society* 16 (1988): 335–85, 349–54. The broadening of the excise was part of a more general move from direct to indirect forms of taxation in this period; see Patrick K. O'Brien, "The Political Economy of British Taxation, 1660–1815," *Economic History Review*, 2nd ser., 1 (1988): 1–32. For the introduction of excises in this period, see Linebaugh, *The London Hanged*, 178; Beckett, "Land Tax or Excise?" 303. For the brick excise, see Robin Lucas, "The Tax on Bricks and Tiles, 1784–1850," *Construction History* 13 (1997): 29–55.

10. See Brewer, "The English State," 354–55; *Sinews of Power*, 103.

11. For the relationship between supervisors and gaugers, see Ashworth, *Customs and Excise*, 125–28.

12. See Brewer, "The English State," 355; *Sinews of Power*, 103. Brewer's figures are based on Excise records held at the National Archives. For details concerning the establishment of "spatial administration" of excise in 1683, see Ogborn, 170–72; Ashworth, *Customs and Excise*, 119–20.

13. Brewer, *Sinews of Power*, 105; Ogborn, 194.

14. Quoted in Ogborn, 167.

15. For the role of printers in producing stationery for government revenue collection, see James Raven, *Publishing Business in Eighteenth-Century England* (Woodbridge: Boydell, 2014), 94–96.

16. *Instructions for the Gagers of the Excise in the Country* (London: Jacob Tonson, 1725). Reference here is to the only known copy of this text (CUST 142/3, National Archives, London).

17. In 1778, the guides for the country collections were aggregated and re-published in large volumes, on higher quality paper, with continuous pagination. Guides for the London excise received a similar treatment in 1781. These may essentially have been reference editions produced for Collection offices.

18. *Instructions to be observed by the Officers employ'd in the Charging the Duty on Starch* (London, 1713), 5–9.

19. *Instructions . . . Starch* (1713), 3–4.

20. *Instructions for Officers who survey Starch-makers in the Country* (London: J. Tonson, 1734), 10–11.

21. *Instructions . . . Starch-makers* (1734), 13–14.

22. *Instructions for Officers who survey Starch-makers in the Country* (London, 1778), 263.

23. *Instructions . . . Starch-makers* (1778), 267.

24. For the advent of these new forms of labor organization, see Maxine Berg, "Political economy and the principles of manufacture 1700–1800," in *Manufacture in Town and Country before the Factory*, ed. Maxine Berg, Pat Hudson, and Michael Sonenscher (Cambridge: Cambridge Univ. Press, 1983), 33–58 and (in the same collection) Pat Hudson, "From manor to mill: the West Riding in transition," 124–44.

25. In recent work, Ashworth has argued that the excise was a site of negotiation and brokerage between the British state and national manufacture; see Ashworth, "Quality and the Roots of Manufacturing 'Expertise' in Eighteenth-Century Britain," *Osiris* 25 (2010): 231–54. These are contexts developed more extensively in *The Industrial Revolution*, 119–44.

26. James C. Scott, *Seeing Like a State: How Certain Schemes to Improve the Human Condition have Failed* (New Haven, CT: Yale Univ. Press, 1998), 46.

27. See Ogborn, 173–78, 188–90. Gauging "relied upon conjuring an imaginary calculable space . . . that abstracted the cask and its commodities" (177).

28. Scott, *Seeing Like a State*, 3.

29. Ogborn notes that the guides "offer an idealized vision of excise administration since there would have been a gap between what they contained and what was actually done" (194–95).

30. The establishment in Britain of a modern politically neutral "civil service," based on meritocratic assessment rather than patronage or purchase, is largely a mid-nineteenth-century development. Its emergence was foreshadowed (and increasingly necessitated) by the growth of certain departments of state across the eighteenth century. See John Alexander Armstrong, *The European Administrative Elite* (Princeton, NJ: Princeton Univ. Press, 1973); Ceri Sullivan, *Literature in the Public Service: Sublime Bureaucracy* (London: Palgrave Macmillan, 2013).

31. Ashworth, *The Industrial Revolution*, 122.

32. Excise Board Minutes, 2 April 1761, 91–92, CUST 47/232, National Archives, London.

33. *Instructions to be Observed by the Officers concerned in ascertaining the Duties on Glass in the Country* (London, 1762), 34–35. For the glass excise see Ashworth, *Industrial Revolution*, 130–37.

34. *Instructions for Officers who Survey Printers of Calico &c. in the Country* (London, 1778), 244.

35. Though Thompson developed these ideas in later work, the seminal essay remains "Time, Work-Discipline, and Industrial Capitalism," *Past and Present* 38 (1967): 56–97. The internalization of time and space regulation is central to Foucault's *Discipline and Punish: The Birth of the Prison*, trans. Alan Sheridan (New York: Penguin, 1977), especially 135–69. More recently, scholarship by Michael Kimaid has argued that it is modernity's interest in nationalism that drives changes in the individual's understanding of time and space in *Modernity, Metatheory, and the Temporal-Spatial Divide: From Mythos to Techne* (New York: Routledge, 2015), 49–81.

36. *Spaces of Modernity*, 198.

37. *Instructions for Officers who Survey Tanners, Tawers, &c* (London, 1715), 4.

38. *Instructions . . . Tanners* (1715), 4.

39. *Instructions to be Observ'd by the Officers employ'd in the Duty on Soap* (London, 1712).

40. *Instructions for Officers concern'd in Ascertaining the Duties on Candles in the Country* (London, 1713), 5.

41. *Instructions . . . Paper* (London, 1729), 10.

42. The precise nature of these sites of manufacture was enormously varied. Whilst manufacturing contexts in the eighteenth century were often connected to domestic spaces, other trades required specialist production or storage spaces that might be separate from the manufacturer's home.

43. *Instructions to be Observ'd by the Officers employ'd in the Duty on Soap* (London, 1712), 5.

44. For the soap excise, see Leonard Gittins, "Soapmaking and the Excise Laws, 1711–1853," *Industrial Archaeology Review* 1 (1977): 265–75.

45. *Instructions for Officers Concern'd in Ascertaining the Duties on Sope in the Country* (London, 1732), 12.

46. *Instructions to be Observed by the Officers Employ'd in Charging the Duties on Candles and Soap in London* (London, 1725), 13–14.

47. *Instructions . . . Starch* (1734), 22.

48. *Instructions for Officers of the Duties on Hides, &c* (London: J. and R. Tonson, 1758), 17–18.

49. For a surviving example of such marks, see "Identifying Printed Textiles in Dress 1740–1890," Dress and Textile Specialists Toolkits, accessed 4 August 2017, http://www.dressandtextilespecialists.org.uk/wp-content/uploads/2015/04/Printed-Textiles-Booklet.pdf, 16–17.

50. *Instructions for Officers who Survey Printers of Callicoe, &c* (London, 1748), 7–8.

51. *Instructions for Officers who Survey Makers of Candles in the Country* (London: 1786), 3. See Brewer, "The English State," 364.

52. *Instructions . . . Glass* (1762), 17.

53. *Instructions for Officers Concerned in Ascertaining the Duties on Sope in the Country* (London, 1770), 8.

54. See Brewer, "The English State," 364; Ashworth, *Industrial Revolution*, 128.

55. *Instructions for Officers Concerned in Ascertaining the Duties on Sope, in the Country* (London, 1797), 11. A guide for 1800 suggests that these provisions had extended to candle-makers; indeed, soap and candle manufacture often occurred in a single setting.

56. In London at least, standards of workmanship remained a concern of the livery companies (see Michael Berlin, "'Broken all in pieces:' artisans and the regulation of workmanship in early modern London," in *The Artisan and the European Town, 1500–1900*, ed. Geoffrey Crossick (Aldershot: Scolar, 1997), 75–91). Berlin suggests (following J. R. Kellett, "The Breakdown of Guild and Corporation Control over the Handicraft and Retail Trade in London," *Economic History Review*, 2nd ser., 10 (1957–58): 381–94) that the decline of these powers can be dated from the mid-eighteenth century.

57. *Instructions . . . Starch* (1778), 267.

58. *Instructions for Officers who Survey Paper-Makers and Paper-Stainers in the Country* (London, 1778), 11–12. For the paper excise, see Rupert C. Jarvis, "The Paper-Makers and the Excise in the Eighteenth Century," *The Library*, 5th ser., 14 (1959): 100–116.

59. *Instructions . . . Candles* (1713), 7.

60. Notwithstanding the operation of city guilds, there was little institutional enforcement of national standards of manufacture. Ashworth draws attention to occasional demands in the first half of the eighteenth century to re-institute the excise on cloth as "a means to police quality" ("Quality and Manufacturing Expertise," 235).

61. *Instructions . . . Sope* (1732), 9–10.

62. See Ashworth, "Quality and Manufacturing Expertise," 239–40; and *The Industrial Revolution*, 120–28.

63. *Instructions . . . Callicoe* (1748), 12. See Ashworth, *Industrial Revolution*, 127.

64. In certain areas of retail trade, such as stationery, it was an offence to be in possession of excisable goods that did not bear the excise stamp (see Jarvis, "The Paper Makers," 111).

Scottish Enlightenment Histories of Social Organization

MICHAEL C. AMROZOWICZ

A recent report in the journal *Science* observes that bees "possess complex navigational skills, rudimentary culture, and emotions. They can even use tools: scientists have shown that the insects can learn to pull a string—and so get a sugary reward—by watching another bee perform the task."[1] The bees participating in the study were trained to move a ball to a target by watching previously-trained sister bees or by watching a bee-shaped magnet move the ball, which shows that they adapt their behavior by collectively learning from each other. But scientists still don't understand the communicative mechanisms bees use to coordinate individual actions into the collective behavior of the swarm. This coordination problem is also seen in other natural processes like the synchronized flashing of firefly populations, the harmonization of heart cells, or the phase transitions of water molecules turning to ice, or atoms magnetizing in a bar of iron.[2] One way modern scientists have approached the problem of incommensurability between the actions of atomistic parts and the larger systems into which those actions cohere—a bee and its swarm, for instance—is to analyze swarming, schooling, flocking, and other self-coordinating natural populations for local rules of behavior to which all the parts adhere. The recent coordination of 100 autonomous mechanical drones that emergently self-organize without any direction from remote operators was achieved by using mathematical models that establish local rules of behavior for each individual drone that only take into account the individual's locational relationship to other individuals in close proximity.[3] Their organization, just like natural swarms of bees and starlings, is not coordinated using a top-down model but instead allows for mutual adjustments at the local level.[4] Yet the inherent problem of studying the coordination of natural populations is that populations of bees, birds, fish, and wildebeests are not managed by one individual or small group that directs where the swarm will go next or which task it will collectively undertake.

Coordination problems have been central to the fields of sociology, mathematics, physics, engineering, and the natural sciences for much of the twentieth- and twenty-first centuries, but principles of self-organization and spontaneous order—two twentieth-century terms that conceptualize mechanisms responsible for coordination in complex systems—underwrote theories of natural philosophy, theology, astronomy, and microscopy throughout the seventeenth and eighteenth centuries.[5] From bees to beavers, fish to flocks, polyps to people, natural philosophers were obsessed with self-organization in the natural world. That obsession entailed the application of patterns observed in nature to the analysis of human behavior as individuals in society. Eighteenth-century scientific enquiry did not begin or end with the study of complex dynamic behavior in natural populations, but it extended to the known limits of the physical universe; from atomic motion in fluid dynamics to non-linear planetary ellipses, the European Enlightenment posited a physical world in which matter was always in flux. A significant challenge faced by the scientific Enlightenment was the modeling of dynamic physical processes by finding tangible patterns amongst the messiness and noise of nature's operations.[6] A picture of the natural world as complex, chaotic, and erratic emerged alongside descriptions of the universe as ordered, mechanistic, predictable, and exhibiting equilibrium amongst its systems.

Scottish Enlightenment historiographers were fascinated with human systems of social organization and looked to the workings of the natural world for analogous patterns that would help them describe the social emergences they were seeing in their own times. The empirical method—the observation of mechanisms that lay behind natural processes—allowed them to gather data and separate patterns from the noise. Many saw the human species as a self-organizing system, and the self-organization operated according to unobservable principles that were often likened to hidden springs, the internal workings of clocks and machines, and insensible operations. These analogies are often concerned with the manifestation of social order and the mechanisms by which the natural patterns that indicate order emerge out of the seeming discord and chaos of human social life. And the larger and more complex human social life became, the more disordered it seemed. From Humean skepticism to the invisible hand to the insensible gradualism of social evolution, the Scots saw the natural world in general, and social activity in particular, as a complex of hidden and infinitely complicated forces. Social complexity became a problem for historical representation in the eighteenth century: how does the historian accurately describe an historical event without access to the unperceivable causes responsible for precipitating the event? This question of historical cause and effect pervades Scottish Enlightenment historical discourse and leads historiographers like David Hume, Adam Smith, and John Millar to develop new and innovative methods for observing social patterns in historical data.

The focus of this essay is this moment of generic transition in historical writing—precipitated by Scottish historiographical theories of social organization—from narratives that were limited by neoclassical strictures to narratives that realized the modern need to represent historical events as complex, dynamic, and composed of hidden patterns embedded deep within human social life. The Scottish histories and historiographies that forward this theory, which I call narratives of social organization, assume that there are complex, evolutionary forces shaping and structuring social formations; that these forces are the product of a society's constant adaptation to its environment; that human social behavior naturally develops to account for changes in the material environment; and that there is a dynamic interactive relationship between a system and its component parts in both self-similar and seemingly disordered ways. Thus a type of history writing emerged in the middle of the eighteenth century to account for historical progress previous historiographical forms and modes such as classical/neoclassical, annalistic, and antiquarian histories could not. Many of those earlier histories relied on one-cause, one-effect linearity and obsolete social patterns such as the Great Legislator and Great Man theories of historical explanation whereby a Great Legislator like Solon, Lycurgus, or Alfred the Great hands down a code of laws that organizes society.[7] The Scots, instead, forward a gradualist, anti-teleological theory of history that explains historical development in terms of social complexity, hidden or unperceivable causes, and unintended consequences of individual atomistic social action.

The problem of historical representation in modern commercial society, then, becomes a problem of scale, and problems of scale led to a wholesale problematization of traditional understandings of social organization. Neoclassical, moral exemplar, and annalistic historical narratives were no longer equipped to apprehend the scale, complexity, and organization of modern commercial society. While Scottish history writing appropriated, adapted, and revised many of the generic conventions of traditional neoclassical as well as newly emergent historical narrative forms, it also invented generic conventions that attempted to capture the complex, non-linear social emergences of commercial society and apply the concepts learned from the study of those formations to new descriptions of the past. The Scots are unique in this sense because most of their historiography from midcentury onward posits that history is not planned or organized by any one person or action but instead happens spontaneously through the agglomeration of uncountable social actions. Scottish histories of social organization show up in many forms and guises throughout the second half of the eighteenth and into the nineteenth century, and they inform the practices of objective, fact- and source-based history developed by later historians like Leopold von Ranke, Patrick Tytler, and Thomas Macaulay. Robert Wallace's *Various Prospects of Mankind, Nature, and Providence* (1761), Adam Ferguson's *An Essay on the History of Civil Society* (1767), Sir James Steuart's *An Inquiry into the Principles of Political Oeconomy* (1767) (published nine years before Adam Smith's *Wealth of Nations*), and James Dunbar's *Essays on the History of Mankind in Rude and Cultivated Ages* (1780) can all be classified as histories of social organization because they are concerned with natural human behavior and its interactions with human-created social-behavioral systems. We can read most historical genres of the second half of the eighteenth century in the context of the organizational principles these histories espouse, and, in this essay, we'll examine two national historical narratives from both early and later in this period that attempt to describe human social organization in natural evolutionary terms.

The structure of historical writing was changing rapidly in the eighteenth century, and new genres were emerging to replace those that could no longer provide accurate descriptions of historical movements. The development of a science of modeling emergent social structures signaled an evolutionary as opposed to a static vision of society; and while this evolutionary development was thought to take place gradually, the rapid social changes wrought by an increasingly commercial society forced history writing to specialize in order to represent new complexity in social patterns at the individual atomistic, customs and manners, and institutional levels.[8] David Simpson states in *The Rediscovery of Classical Economics* that "Adam Smith and his contemporaries Hume and Ferguson were among the first to recognise the significance of self-organising systems in human societies," and this essay examines some of the mechanisms Scottish historiographers used to support their theories of social organization and how those innovations contributed to genre change in eighteenth-century historical writing.[9] Concepts of spontaneous order and self-organization have been treated in a number of senses and venues, with one of the most recent being Jonathan Sheehan and

Dror Wahrman's *Invisible Hands*. They survey the "history of the language of self-organization" from the late-seventeenth century through the 1720s in scientific, religious, philosophical, and political writing. Some of the concepts of self-organization on which they focus show up in later eighteenth-century discourses regarding historical, historiographical, and literary writing, but the theological and philosophical problems to which writers were directing their energies at the turn of the eighteenth century become less relevant to history and literary writing later in the eighteenth century, primarily because of the objective scientific turn history writing began to take. Questions of Providence and prime movers, the mind-body problem, and counter-evolutionary science don't necessarily disappear from writing for the masses, but the focus of historical cause-and-effect explanations takes an empirical turn, and histories of social organization focus their methodologies on self-organizing social-evolutionary causes as the real stuff of historical writing. An interesting addition to the current literature of self-organization is Michael Hardt and Antonio Negri's *Assembly*.[10] Hardt and Negri use a model of social organization for their analysis of current socio-political conditions in the West that describes the material level of human action (the self-organization of a society that must organize in order to ensure the material survival of the group) that Marx himself pulled from the writings of the Scottish social-organizational theorists. This link was made especially strong in the late eighteenth and into the nineteenth century by the intertwining nature of historical and political-economic narratives. The two genres often overlapped and used the same descriptive principles and models of social organization to address the same types of problems regarding social organization in the evolutionary world of natural human behavior.

The study of political economy, and later economics, provided a lens through which eighteenth-century historians could observe the natural activities of man that contribute to larger self-organizing social organizations. The twentieth-century economists Michael Polanyi and Friedrich Hayek use the term spontaneous order to describe the self-organization of the marketplace as an evolutionary system and the emergences, or unintended consequences, made possible by social transactions that occur in the marketplace.[11] Ronald Hamowy, Craig Smith, and Christina Petsoulas effectively trace the spontaneous order theories of Polanyi, Hayek, Popper, and the Austrian School back to Scottish Enlightenment theories of social organization and the objective observation of human behavior as a grounding principle of their historiography.[12] David Spadafora and Christopher Berry show how the Scottish Enlightenment concept of the science of human nature informs historiographical theories like that of material and social progress.[13] The onset of modern commercial society vastly increased the distance between one's actions and the social consequences of those actions, while at the same time increasing the impact of those actions across multiple fields of influence.[14] The actors cannot predict how far-reaching or influential the consequences of their actions will be, nor will they ever be able to observe the chains of cause-and effect their actions will set off. Yet, by the eighteenth century, the unintended consequences of social action became a main feature of individual participation in commercial society as well as a main feature of the histories that attempted to capture the complexity of commercial society in narrative form. History writing was just beginning to be able to tell the story of natural social aggregation from the tiers of individual action and choice to the structural formation of customs and manners and the agglomeration of these tiers into the creation of overarching social institutions.

This essay will survey some tenets of eighteenth-century historiography, explain the Scottish Enlightenment's reaction to those tenets that were no longer useful for representing complex social formations, offer the principles of the newly-emergent genre of the history of social organization, and then provide two case studies in David Hume and John Millar's histories. Hume's *History of England* (1754–61) and Millar's *Historical View of the English Government* (1787) rewrote the past using technologies from their present, which then allowed them to explain their present more effectively in terms of cause-and-effect patterns alternative to those forwarded by previous forms of history.[15] Their histories depended on models provided by the natural sciences to construct a picture of human nature that could be used to posit a theory of social organization that operates on a bottom-up basis as opposed to previous top-down models. Both Hume and Millar show that when social formations seem to have emerged out of nowhere, the conditions—or causes—for these emergences are often extant and available, but the historian has to look in the right place and use the right tools to observe them. While on the surface Hume's *HE* may look like a standard neoclassical history with its character profiles and motivations of great men, its focus on political, military, and religious institutions, and its narratives of the actions of the monarchy, nobility, and clergy, Hume can be seen grappling with social complexity as a cause of historical movement. For Millar, even more so than for his teacher Adam Smith, a society's mode of production determines its social organization as observed in the manners and customs and the social institutions of that society. Thus, Millar's histories jettisoned nearly every vestige of neoclassical prescription in favor of an empirical description of history as a series of uncoordinated causes and effects just like one would observe in the growth rate of a plant, the circulation of the blood, or interplanetary motion. Hume and Millar both apply theories of evolutionary dynamism to social systems at different times and places in history in order to ascertain the details of the composition of the mode of production.

Scottish historiographers turned to models provided by the natural sciences in order to construct a picture of human nature that they could then use for modeling historical change, but they quickly ran into a problem: natural systems did not often resemble their individual components and actions. This aggregation problem stymied eighteenth-century thinkers, which is why they often observed bees and other natural, complex populations for insights into the problem of self-organization in human systems. Sheehan and Wahrman point to Denis Diderot's *Dream of D'Alembert* in which if a bee is "minded to pinch in some way the bee to which it is clinging," it will "excite throughout the cluster as many sensations as there are animals; and the whole group will stir itself, rouse itself, and change its location and form."[16] Bernard Mandeville's bees are also self-coordinating: virtue makes friends with vice, which "was the State's Craft, that maintain'd / The Whole of which each Part complain'd: / This, as in Musick Harmony, / Made Jarrings in the main agree."[17] Social harmony emerges out of the seeming discord of atomistic choices—the ancient concept of *concordia discours*—as a force responsible for ensuring the survival of the hive. Mandeville, as Horatio in Part II of *The Fable of the Bees*, explains the same concept using the analogy of fermentation, widespread in the eighteenth century in its application to human social movements:

> Vinosity, so far as it is the Effect of Fermentation, is adventitious; and what none of the Grapes could ever have receiv'd, whilst they remain'd single; and therefore, if you would compare the Sociableness of Man to the Vinosity of Wine, you must shew me, that in Society there is an Equivalent for Fermentation; I mean, something that individual Persons are not actually possess'd of, whilst they remain single, and which, likewise, is palpably adventitious to Multitudes, when joyn'd together; in the same manner as Fermentation is to the Juice of Grapes, and as necessary and essential to the compleating of Society, as that is, that same Fermentation, to procure the Vinosity of Wine.[18]

Mandeville's social theories, alternately adopted and reviled throughout the eighteenth century, would have an incalculable influence on Scottish Enlightenment theories of social organization.[19]

Scottish Enlightenment historiographers often used the concept of self-organization in bees and other natural populations to structure their histories of social organization. James Burnet, Lord Monboddo claims in his *Antient*

Metaphysics that although a bee cannot relate the "rules of Geometry," it "makes its hexagons, and joins them together in such a way, that, with the least expense of materials, it makes its cells contain the greatest quantity of honey possible." And, while the "Bee is no Geometer" according to Monboddo, it still has "Intelligence, as we see many men have, though it be not methodified into Art and Science." Monboddo's bee has no knowledge of the end of its operations, nor does she know the means that bees as individuals use to achieve their collective ends; the individual itself is not intelligent, but the population possesses a collective intelligence "much superior to the human," and "no less Intelligence than the Divine." In Monboddo's schema of human social organization, we also "act by an Intelligence superior to our own, doing what we are directed to do by men wiser than we, without knowing for what purpose we act. And this I say is the case of every well-governed society, where by far the greater part of the subjects act by rules, of which they do not understand the reason."[20] Henry Home, Lord Kames's bees, too, are "qualified for society; which, among quadrupeds, is the case of the beavers; and, among winged animals, of the bees, of the crows, and of some other kinds." These animals are governed by instinct, he claims in his *Principles of Equity*, but it is not the same for man. If we were governed by our instincts alone, he posits, we would not be fit for society because human actions are "generally prompted by the passions;" if man gratified every passion "he would be a ship without a rudder," so Kames subscribes to a version of Frances Hutcheson's "moral sense" which "renders us accountable for our actions, and makes us fit objects of rewards and punishments."[21] The moral sense prevents individuals from gratifying their passions by doing harm to each other; thus it—like the organizing principles of swarming animals—provides a set of local rules by which the individual acts to fulfill the ends of the population, which is the survival of the species. Adam Smith's concept of sympathy, as a revision of Hutcheson's moral sense, also operates according to local rules. The historian and clergyman Adam Ferguson, in refuting the historical idea that human society can be ordered by one man or small groups of men, writes in the *Essay on the History of Civil Society* that "The artifices of the beaver, the ant and the bee, are ascribed to the wisdom of nature. Those of polished nations are ascribed to themselves, and are supposed to indicate a capacity superior to that of rude minds. But, the establishments of men, like those of every animal, are suggested by nature, and are the result of instinct, directed by the variety of situations in which mankind are placed." For Ferguson, those establishments arise through spontaneous order: "Every step and every movement of the multitude, even in what are termed enlightened ages, are made with equal blindness to the future; and nations stumble upon establishments, which are indeed the result of human action, but not the execution of any human design."[22] That humans self-organize and social orders emerge without design or foresight is a primary characteristic of the concept of spontaneous order for Ferguson and many other eighteenth-century historiographers.

The methodologies and vocabularies of empirical science, derived from the works of Francis Bacon, Newton, and Locke, provided eighteenth-century natural philosophers with new models for thinking about how cause and effect works in the natural and social worlds. Scottish Enlightenment historiographers in particular adapted scientific empiricism's method of using interpretations of data gleaned from observation and experience in the physical world to reason towards general principles and models that could be applied—under the condition of *probability*, as Hume is careful to continually warn us in his *An Enquiry Concerning Human Understanding* —to the larger subject being inquired into as a whole. "It is universally acknowledged," Hume writes in the *Enquiry*, "that there is a great uniformity among the actions of men, in all nations and ages, and that human nature remains still the same, in its principles and operations."[23] He continues this passage by explaining that while there appears to be uniformity in human behavior that would allow us to propose general rules regarding the operations of the human system, the mechanisms at work on the local level of the individual may not appear to adhere to the larger patterns. The subtitle of Hume's *A Treatise of Human Nature* also spells out this project explicitly for the reader: "Being An Attempt to Introduce the Experimental Method of Reasoning Into Moral Subjects." Hume opens the *Treatise* with the argument that all of our sciences—*"Mathematics, Natural Philosophy,* and *Natural Religion,"*—and all of our ideas—especially those concerning *"Logic, Morals, Criticism,* and *Politics"*—have as their "only solid foundation" what he terms the "science of man," by which he means the use of "experience and observation" to apprehend the general principles of human behavior in order to understand how the manifestation of that behavior in the world determines our production of knowledge, ideas, and institutions.[24] In Adam Smith's "science of human nature," commonalities exist in human behavior across space and time, and in order to discover these commonalities we can look at human history for evidence.[25] History provides the Scottish historiographers with the raw data they need to make observations concerning the commonalities of human nature. Hume, Smith, and Millar objectively and empirically observe social patterns both in the present and in the past, and those patterns are to be found in their discoveries of the elements of human nature in economics, politics, trade, culture, customs, manners, and even in law, government, and the mental and physical processes governing social interaction.[26] When translated into a model of social, or what the eighteenth-century Scots called "moral," inquiry, the science of human nature becomes a methodology that has profound consequences for conceptions of the ways human beings order themselves into groups and institutions.

The system of social sciences developed by the Scottish Enlightenment took its cues from the natural philosophers of the seventeenth- and early-eighteenth centuries. The environs of the many new geographical, physical, and mental worlds constantly being discovered were explored, dissected, divided, catalogued, and categorized by botanists, biologists, physicists, doctors, political economists, historians, and novelists. The Scottish Enlightenment theories of the science of human nature, or the application of Newtonian scientific principles to human social activity, and of stadial and conjectural history posit the evolutionary self-organizing progress of society through various stages or modes of development and thus offer a dynamic, uncoordinated, and unpredictable movement as well as a movement of emergent patterns through chaos. Human behavioral patterns, the Scottish Enlightenment historiographers argue, can be observed as static, natural human behavior, the expressions and manifestations of which become visible in the coherence of social institutions. Scottish Enlightenment theories of the science of human nature and their expressions in the forms of stadial and conjectural history posit the self-organizing progress of society through various stages or modes of development. These four stages, or stadial history models, were theories of social organization by which, assuming the existence of a particular set of material conditions, and given the society's self-organized systems for procuring a subsistence from those material conditions, the historian could ascertain the individual's role in society and examine the society's customs, manners, and social institutions for data that would establish a picture of how that society organized itself in order to meet its sustenance needs.[27] Society in general would have had to adapt its social institutions to meet its needs, and it is at these three levels of phase transition that Hume and Millar are working in their histories, and that make up, along with the theory of evolutionary gradualism, the organizing principles of Scottish histories of social organization.

The historical process of human development for the Scots is gradual and imperceptible, like the slow grinding of a glacier on the earth's surface, and is just as messy, chaotic, and non-linear as the eskers, moraines, and erratics that a glacier leaves behind. Gradualism as a historical principle is inherent at all three levels of observation in histories of social organization. Millar provides an explanation of these three components of large-scale historical processes, with each component building steam and attaining critical mass, as it were, in pushing forward into the next process. As a society progresses through time and space, these three levels of spontaneous self-organization are at work, each relying on increased orders of complexity: the mode of subsistence, or the simple initial social organization that allows for a society to deal with its original conditions of survival—food, water, shelter, and energy, for example—at the level of atomistic individual interaction; the habits (Millar calls these customs or manners), that originate and solidify particular effective social arrangements concerning the current (or past) mode of subsistence, and that are based on long-term usage and utility; and, the coherence of informal customs and manners into social institutions, the existence of which formalize, communalize, and regulate social behavior. One consequence of society's gradual evolution, according to the Scots, is that as it evolves, it increases in complexity. In the terms of spontaneous order, social customs and manners come about through a gradual accretion of innumerable individual actions that become regular and common behavioral ways because of their utility to the particular group of people who are practicing them, and those customs and manners arrange themselves into social institutions as a society moves into the advanced stages of stadial history. Hume and Millar use all three levels of observation to construct their histories, but here we will examine how customs and manners emerge as patterns of coordination and transform social institutions in the reign of James I in Hume's *HE* and Millar's *HV*. Both historians use this historical moment to show the inefficacy of neoclassical "Great Legislator" models of historical explanation and to forward new models of evolutionary gradualism that depend on theories of spontaneous order and self-organization.

The history of England, according to Hume in 1753, had not yet been written: "You know that there is no post of honour in the English Parnassus more vacant than that of History. Style, judgement, impartiality, care— everything is wanting to our historians; and even Rapin, during this latter period, is extremely deficient. I make my work very concise, after the manner of the Ancients."[28] There was a vacancy on the English Parnassus for a modern Livy, and Hume intended to snatch up the post as soon as possible. Clarendon had been given the title of the English Thucydides, as his was a history written by a "gentleman" who was exiled or retired from public life and in his leisure, and who was close enough to the political action during his career in public life that he could use it as the basis of a "history" of his own times, imitating the physical and social conditions in which Thucydides wrote his own histories.[29] Yet Clarendon's was not a history of England through all the time and space of the country's existence; instead, it was a history of a particular set of events occurring at circumscribed times and places and only including specific individual actors. Clarendon had composed the magisterial *Rebellion* in the seventeenth century, but it was published nearly thirty years after his death when the events and most of the people who had lived them had long passed.[30] The *Rebellion* was greatly admired by Hume and was a valuable source of information for his own *History of England*. Clarendon was called the English Thucydides because of his use of the same internal and external historiographical conventions as his Greek predecessor, and, as his *Rebellion* was almost universally admired, it became the standard for historical writing—and, in the first quarter of the eighteenth century, almost singlehandedly ushered in the precedence of historical neoclassicism.[31]

Yet Clarendon's "noble" *Rebellion* was not the only game in town. Imitators and detractors lined up to get a piece of the early eighteenth-century historical pie. Hume called the eighteenth century the "historical Age," and Britain was the "historical Nation;" and based on the quantity of histories produced, it is easy to see why Hume would give these appellations.[32] By the mid-eighteenth century, British authors were producing a broad spectrum of historical writing in terms of genres, subjects, narrative styles, and political affiliations. Clarendon wrote neoclassical history, while others produced ecclesiastical and clerical history (Gilbert Burnet); antiquarian history (Robert Brady, James Tyrrell); annals and chronicles (Tyrrell again, Laurence Echard); legal, political, and family histories (White Kennett, Abel Boyer, John Oldmixon, Roger North); history as moral exemplar (Bolingbroke); the conjectural histories of the Scots (Adam Smith, James Dunbar, William Robertson, Dugald Stewart); and general histories (James Ralph, William Guthrie, Thomas Carte) or standard, "objective" narratives like Paul Rapin de Thoyras's *Histoire d'Angleterre* (1723–7), translated into English by Nicholas Tindal (1725–31).[33] Nearly all of these writers used some neoclassical historiographical structuring elements in their histories and often took as their models the Greek and Roman historians Herodotus, Thucydides, Tacitus, Livy, and Julius Caesar. They also used other non-classical historiographical traditions like annals and chronicles and new innovations like antiquarian history that made it a point to critically evaluate source materials in order to approach a standard for credibility. The reconfiguring mixture of all of these species of historiography radically destabilized the already unstable neoclassical tradition, already challenged by new forms as it was coming to prominence in the first quarter of the eighteenth century. By the time Hume would write his *HE* at mid-century, "philosophical history" was simply one of a number of genres appearing within the form of historical writing.

Hume's praise of Sir Isaac Newton in what is now Volume VI of *HE* explains his view of mechanistic determinism: "While Newton seemed to draw off the veil from some of the mysteries of nature, he shewed at the same time the imperfections of the mechanical philosophy; and thereby restored her ultimate secrets to that obscurity, in which they ever did and ever will remain."[34] For Hume, while it appears to human sensory perception that the universe is governed by orderly and predictable laws, our observations are limited by our sensory perception; and simply because it is probable that the same effect will follow a cause every time does not mean that it will always be so in the future. While the universe may operate mechanistically, and there may exist general rules to which those operations contribute, in *Enquiry*, Hume shows that we cannot know exactly *how* it works and thus nature's mysteries will remain shrouded in obscurity: "But philosophers observing, that, almost in every part of nature, there is contained a vast variety of springs and principles, which are hid, by reason of their minuteness or remoteness, find, that it is at least possible the contrariety of events may not proceed from any contingency in the cause, but from the secret operation of contrary causes."[35] This argument about the insensibility of the hidden springs and gears of nature blasts previous models of historical contingency that take as given that particular historical effects will always follow from the same causes. While this may be true at the level of general rules most of the time, as we saw Hume aver earlier when discussing his science of man, the minute particulars will always vary and look different than the general principles they combine to support. In his essay "Of the Coalition of Parties," Hume states that "All human institutions, and none more than government, are in continual fluctuation."[36] So, the question for a historian who acknowledges this dynamism must become, how does one represent in narrative form the secret operations and hidden springs that are responsible for this continual fluctuation?

While it is beyond the scope of this study to explore fully the meaning of modernity, one observable difference in Hume's *HE* between his coverage of the medieval period and the reigns of the Stuarts is the problem of complex social coordination.[37] While the medieval English monarchs, their nobility, and their clergy—even as they disputed power amongst themselves— exercised tight political, religious, and economic control over the population, the advent of seventeenth-century mercantilism and early modern forms of capitalism served to diffuse the social and economic power of the monarchy and nobility into the hands of more of the populace, thereby giving subjects more options, choices, and possibilities for action and movement than ever before. The Stuart volumes of Hume's *HE* treat the relationship between its characters and the social institutions they must navigate and struggle to understand: the Stuart monarchs attempt to control the known forces that British monarchs traditionally controlled, yet the forces that wielded power in their world were no longer those over which the monarch had centralized control. Minute revolutions in social life and the individual's relationship with social institutions moved forward and left the monarchs behind, their once-unlimited power and arbitrary authority now circumscribed and besieged by modernity, early-modern capitalism, and globalization.

Hume was no great fan of Elizabeth I and thought her a heavy-handed and arbitrary ruler. His representation of her reign in Volume IV of his *HE* challenged her status as a public hero and instead showed her use of prerogative as a heavy encroachment on the liberty of the people. James I, who held the title of James VI of Scotland for 36 years before his accession to the English throne, was fully cognizant of the rights and privileges the title of King of England granted him, and he was well aware of the use Elizabeth had made of her authority. In Hume's view, James I had done nothing wrong in expecting that his royal prerogative would hold the same power as Elizabeth's and that he would be granted the same power all English kings and queens had traditionally wielded. But the times had changed during Elizabeth's reign, and the world was no longer the same. And while the times were changing, the Stuart monarchy was forever looking backwards and comparing their own lack of power with their predecessors, whom they believed had exercised uncompromising authority over the nobles, the church, the House of Commons, and the population. According to Hume, a new wind was blowing—one that whisked away the possibility of comparison to the past and could no longer be stopped by the will of the sovereign; the interests of the people had begun to coordinate and were manifesting in an "insensible revolution." Hume consistently describes the first two Stuarts as unable to apprehend the dynamic social forces at work in the country at the time: "public transactions depended on a complication of views and intelligence, with which they were entirely unacquainted."[38] One innovation of Hume's historiography is that the Stuart volumes of Hume's *HE* treat the often fraught and frustrated relationship between his characters— often models of traditional neoclassical historiography—and the complex modern social institutions they must navigate and struggle to understand. "About this period," he writes of the accession of James I, "the minds of men, throughout Europe, especially in England, seem to have undergone a general, but insensible revolution."[39] The key word here is "insensible," or, the inability of perceiving a cause-and-effect relationship with the senses, and Hume also applies this same word to the relationship between the King and the commons, where the commons were "insensibly changing, perhaps improving, the spirit and genius, while they preserved the forms of the constitution: And *that* the king was acting altogether without any plan."[40] Uncoordinated and unpredictable forces occurring in every sector of trade, commerce, and culture had brought about these "insensible revolutions."

"Happily" for the nascent cause of English liberty, according to Hume, James I "possessed neither sufficient capacity to perceive the alteration, nor sufficient vigour to check it in its early advances."[41] Instead, James I, and later Charles I, is made by Hume to seem as though he was the unwitting victim of circumstance: a man who, though a capable ruler, could not suit his reign to the changing circumstances surrounding him.[42] Not that he would have known to do so based on prior rulers: until the execution of Charles I, the monarchy remained quite insulated from the public and the people it governed outside of the nobles and highest ranking prelates. One of the powers of Hume's narrative is the way he shows the structure of government, religion, society, and the economy changing around, outside, and independent of both James I and Charles I. These new and unpredictable historical forces challenge the historian, while offering a challenge to neoclassical principles, to describe them because historiographical models had not yet been created to account for these particular forms of social interaction. Classical historiographical prescriptions provided cause-and-effect formulas for describing certain types of human action that occur in specific venues: politics and war. Specific human action always corresponds to a particular range of results in these venues, such as victory or loss in war and good governance or the downfall of the state in politics. Yet seventeenth-century England, as shown by Hume, admits of a far broader range of complexity in human social interaction than classical societies, thus classical historiographical forms cannot account for the much different cause-and-effect relationships—imperceptible even to the actors themselves—at work in seventeenth-, and, by extension, eighteenth-century England.

The historical conditions upon which each of these monarch's public characters relied changed drastically in the final years of James I's and the opening years of Charles I's reigns. It is Hume's inclusion of social, cultural, and economic histories—histories that include a broad range of subjects and peoples, as opposed to the theoretically limited scope of neoclassical history—that allows him to perceive the correlation between social action on a broad, population-level scale and the decisions made by groups in power like the king, parliament, and the clergy. The "Arts, both mechanical and liberal, were every day receiving great improvements. Navigation had extended itself over the whole globe. Travelling was secure and agreeable. And the general system of politics in Europe was becoming more enlarged and comprehensive."[43] While politics makes its appearance in this explanation of the historical forces that would gradually lead to the development of sources of power alternative to and outside of the traditional monarchy not only in England but also all across Europe, Hume's focus here is on letters and literacy, the mechanical and liberal arts, and communication forged by easier and safer methods of travel. "In consequence of this universal fermentation," Hume continues, "the ideas of men enlarged themselves on all sides; and the several constituent parts of the gothic governments, which seem to have lain long unactive, began, every where, to operate and encroach upon each other."[44] The common agent of power and change in Hume's "cultural" explications is, it should be noted, not the king or his ministers, but instead "men" in the plural, general sense of the word.[45] Hume's many moments of willful generalization and lack of particular description when attributing historical change to "men everywhere" are significant and should alert readers to these forces as unconcerted and unplanned spaces of resistance to arbitrary rule and oppressive tradition. "It was not till this age," he writes, "when the spirit of liberty was universally diffused, when the principles of government were nearly reduced to a system, when the tempers of men, more civilized, seemed less to require those violent exertions of prerogative."[46] A problem for historical writing became the increasing complexity of the system, and how to represent complexity in narrative form while still performing some of the traditionally expected functions of historical writing like moral instruction. While Hume's *HE* appropriates a full complement of neoclassical historiographical techniques, Millar's *HV* abandons all pretense of neoclassicism and constructs a completely social history.

In Millar's historiography, human society progresses gradually and oftentimes imperceptibly, and almost all social institutions are the products of slow accretive social change over time. The emergence of customs and manners is based on the surrounding environment and how it changes, and also on how humans change it. Thus, Millar can state in *The Origin and Distinction of Ranks* (1771) that "There is, however, in man a disposition and capacity for improving his condition, by the exertion of which, he is carried on from one degree of advancement to another."[47] But this happens slowly over time, and is contingent upon the social environment within which the changes in the human system are taking place. In the terms of spontaneous order, customs and manners emerge through a gradual accretion of innumerable individual actions that become regular and common behavioral ways because of their utility to the particular group of people who are practicing them. His project in *Ranks* is to show the development of concepts of authority and social rank as they have been practiced in domestic and government life from ancient times up to and including the present state of commercial society in which "The advancement of a people in the arts of life, is attended with various alterations in the state of individuals, and in the whole constitution of their government."[48] Thus, developments in the arts, commerce, and manufacture in a society translate into changes concerning the status of individuals (women, fathers, masters, and servants) within the present mode of subsistence, for which new laws and legislation must be introduced in order to solidify the changes in the social situation, thereby contributing to the progress of society. Millar builds on this theory in *HV* in which he shows the gradual development of British society and its social institutions from the end of the Roman era through the Anglo-Saxons and the Normans and into the reign of William III, in which England became a true commercial society according to Scottish historiography. Millar's point in *HV* is to show how gradual changes in customs and manners contribute far more to the coherence of social institutions such as the military, government, religion, economy, and the arts than the standard set of oversimplified linear historical causes found in neoclassical histories—and, even Hume's *HE*, which Millar expands and critiques at many points throughout *HV*. This is evident from the chapter titles of the expanded 1803 edition of *HV*: "The Gradual Advancement of the Fine Arts—Their Influence upon Government;" "How far the Advancement of Commerce and Manufactures has contributed to the Extension and Diffusion of Knowledge and Literature;" and, "The Advancement of Manufactures, Commerce, and the Arts, since the Reign of William III, and the Tendency of this Advancement to diffuse a Spirit of Liberty and Independence."[49]

While Millar based many of his historiographical principles on Adam Smith's lectures on jurisprudence and Hume's *HE*, he is probably most indebted to Smith for his theory of what Michael Ignatieff calls "materialism," by which he means a radical "challenge to a historiography of kings and queens and to an ethical rationalism which looked down upon 'hunger, thirst and the passion for sex' as aspects of human nature unfit to be placed at the centre of historical process."[50] The first type of historiography that Ignatieff refers to here is the neoclassical variety, while ethical rationalism signifies the privileging of the creation and maintenance of artificial social institutions as historical processes—certain forms of government and policing, religious organizations, restrictions on trade—created by rational planning and foresight that are guided by ethical motivations. Both of these types of historiographies preclude the possibility that large-scale historical movements arise from the intended *and* unintended consequences of a multitude of uncoordinated human social actions, and that those actions are most often quotidian self-interested choices based on physical necessities of food, clothing, shelter, protection, and procreation. This materialist historiographical theory, according to Ignatieff, "made the satisfaction of basic human needs, rather than conscious intention, the motor of historical change" and "interpreted laws, manners and rank systems as dependent upon stages of subsistence."[51] Millar's historiography takes as its root the material conditions of a society as the determinants of its customs and manners, which are systems of behavior that are the product of spontaneous order in that it is essential that humans coordinate in order to meet their physical needs; yet this coordinated self-organization occurs randomly and is not the product of any foresight or design.

While historical debates about the English constitution had been raging since before the English Civil War and was still a hotly contested topic throughout the eighteenth century, Millar's form of historical inquiry had a different object. We can look back to early periods in English history like the Anglo-Saxon period, he argues, in order to consider how "the foundations of our present constitution were laid," but "without examining the principles upon which it is founded, we cannot form a just opinion concerning the nature of the superstructure."[52] Thus, while historical documents like Magna Charta and the Charters are responsible for solidifying British liberty, for Millar it is more important to look at the social formations that generated the conditions in which the Charters could be created and upheld in the first place. Looking at these social "situations," as Millar calls them, can better inform eighteenth-century readers about their own social institutions and how they developed than by looking back through history for ways in which the constitution had been interpreted to justify political action. The forces that created the conditions for the Charters to succeed were not created overnight but developed gradually in Millar's model of social progress: "As the government which we now enjoy at present has not been formed at once, but has grown to maturity in a course of ages, it is necessary, in order to have a full view of the circumstances from which it has proceeded, that we should survey with attention the successive changes through which it has passed."[53] In order to provide an accurate understanding of our current social institutions, we must look back through various historical ages to see how they have progressed and examine the complex forces responsible for this progress.

Millar's historiographical answer to what he calls the myth of the "Great Legislator" is to show the agency of dynamic social forces working on the monarch instead of the traditional other way around. He begins his representation of the reign of James I in the *HV* by stating that it corresponded with "the commencement of what, in a former part of this inquiry, I have called the Commercial Government of England. The progress of commerce and manufactures had now begun to change the manners and political state of the inhabitants. Different arrangements of property had contributed to emancipate the people of inferior condition, and to undermine the authority of the superior ranks. A new order of things was introduced."[54] Social organization for Millar is always based on the material condition of a society

—it was this theory that heavily influenced Marx's base and superstructure, the latter being a term he gets directly from Millar. As in Hume's calculus, Millar's James I is an unwitting pawn of much larger "insensible" forces as the fluctuating social organization of British society self-organized around a different mode of production for the procuration of resources. The social organization of commercial society had rendered the traditional forms of the monarchical system, like the neoclassical historiography that legitimated and codified it, as ill-equipped to manage the emerging dynamics. "From the advancement of society in civilization," Millar shows, "from the greater accumulation of property in the hands of individuals, and from a correspondent extension of the connections and pursuits of mankind, a more complicated set of regulations became necessary for maintaining good order and tranquility."[55] But, just as in Hume, James I—and not necessarily through any fault of his own—cannot observe the system of which he is a part. He doesn't understand his role in the collective emergence of the new mode of production: "He saw that the sovereigns in the principal European kingdoms, exercised an arbitrary and despotical power," and he took the divine right of kings as "the fundamental principle of kingcraft" that he "pretended to fully understand."[56] James I and Charles I were stable but increasingly obsolete equilibriums in a swirling maelstrom of chaos.

Social complexity wasn't just a problem for rulers of state anymore by the eighteenth century. Historical writing was continuously evolving in order to describe a dynamic human system that itself was continuously evolving. The written genres of natural philosophy and political economy were becoming grounded in empirical observation, and thinkers largely focused on describing phenomena in the world as it truly existed instead of conforming their results to current social or cultural expectations. History writing, too, was experiencing this overhaul, and the Scottish brand of history benefitted from a close interplay of the scientific disciplines during the Scottish Enlightenment, which led to a view of historical processes as an aggregation of countless dynamic and spontaneous human actions and events. History's interdisciplinary borrowing of observational and descriptive tools from the natural sciences, political economy, medicine, law, and business drastically changed the nature of the genre of history writing, and Scottish historiographical theories even permeated related genres like novelistic fiction.

The interdisciplinary legacy of eighteenth-century theories of social organization has manifested in many different forms since Hume and Millar's histories. Some direct descendants of the Scottish line of social organization, for good or ill, were Thomas Malthus, John Stuart Mill, and Karl Marx; and their social theories, inflected with early theories of sociology and population biology, were trying to account for the natural evolutionary nature of human society and were responsible for breaching the disciplinary gap between natural philosophy in the eighteenth and nineteenth centuries and what would become the social sciences in the twentieth century. The observed dynamism of the natural world continued to influence historiography's understanding of human history as a natural process, and revolutions in the laws of physics made it apparent to historiographers like Henry Adams that human behavior is also governed by physical forces. Adams called this force social energy, and, with it, he raised the problem of writing history in a world governed by a new and different physics: the Newtonian-ordered mechanical universe was being challenged by pictures of a universal organization of matter that was driven by electromagnetism, thermodynamics, and entropy. The problem of social energy as a physical process "seemed scarcely serious" to the "generation of Lord Macaulay and George Bancroft;" but, in an 1894 letter to the American Historical Association titled "The Tendency of History," Adams, the association's then-president, called for the establishment of what he termed a "science of history."[57] "Any science assumes a necessary sequence of cause and effect," he wrote, "a force resulting in motion which cannot be other than what it is." "Any science of history must be absolute, like other sciences," he continued, "and must fix with mathematical certainty the path which human society has got to follow."[58] This does not mean that history is predetermined but that social energy potentially could be quantified and made into a theoretical law, like observers quantify the energy of the sun's rays that fall on the planet or the dissipation of energy during molecular phase transitions.[59] General laws cannot account for the random behaviors of individual components of a system, but they can be useful for determining the shape and trajectory the system would more than likely take on and therefore allows historical writing to be more precise in both its descriptions of and prescriptions for human social energy.

Albert Einstein, who had already published his now-famous essay "Does the Inertia of a Body Depend Upon its Energy Content?" (1905) by the time Adams was writing "The Rule of Phase Applied to History," covers a wide array of historical, philosophical, political, moral, and scientific topics in his collection of essays titled *Ideas and Opinions* (1960). Hume's skepticism comes in for treatment in an essay about the mathematician and philosopher Bertrand Russell, and the "essential methodological differences between astronomy and economics" are examined in his *Monthly Review* essay titled "Why Socialism?" in order to ascertain how far scientific methods can be applied to "human problems" in the fields of economics and social organization. Echoing the Scottish Enlightenment rejection of the social contract originating in the state of nature, Einstein states that "It is evident, therefore, that the dependence of the individual upon society is a fact of nature which cannot be abolished—just as in the case of ants and bees." Yet, while "the whole life process of ants and bees is fixed down to the smallest detail by rigid, hereditary instincts, the social pattern and interrelationships of human beings are very variable and susceptible to change."[60] Human beings do not conform to strict patterns of social behavior, and their interrelationships—between individuals, between small groups, and between cultures, states, and institutions—often appear disordered in that they don't exhibit ordering mechanisms that would explain the ordering of the larger system of which the elements are a part. Yet somehow humans—necessarily social beings—attain some modicum of equilibrium (albeit for comparatively short periods of time and space) as they order themselves into groups and institutions in order to deal with their material conditions.

The major evolutionary characteristic that explains the success of Homo sapiens as a species is its adaptability to nearly every material condition on the planet. There is no other species on the globe that can live and thrive in—and now create—as many environments as man. Man's evolutionary development was necessarily contingent upon variability and susceptibility to change because man's material conditions—Millar's "situation"—is always also susceptible to change and variability. Neither man nor the life he must consume in order to survive is in an equilibrium state with their environment, so life must necessarily adapt—and, in the story of a species' adaptation, we can locate histories of patterns in its progress on earth. Scottish histories of social organization begin to identify social organization as a physical manifestation of a society's adaptation to its environment in the sense that society is seen as an organism like a bee or fish or starling population. In other words, they identified evolutionary, complex dynamic systems as drivers in the history of human social development. The economist David Simpson describes how Scottish Enlightenment theories of social dynamism were adapted by the natural sciences in the twentieth century when scientists

> noticed that a growing number of empirical studies of both natural and social phenomena contradicted both the static mechanical and thermodynamic dis-ordering notions of process. So far from all structures tending inexorably towards a thermodynamic equilibrium state of maximum disorder, chemical and other processes often seemed to be characterised by increasing organization. They called such systems complex systems, and they began to investigate their properties formally by representing them mathematically as dynamic nonlinear systems.[61]

Scots like Hume, Smith, and Millar were objectively and empirically observing social patterns both in the present and in the past, and those patterns are to be found in their discoveries of particular types of common material relations endemic to economics, politics, trade, culture, customs and manners, law, and government. The Scottish historiographers created technologies for describing the dynamism and complexity of human social systems and their interactions with their material environments. Human-observed systems and environments may appear to be ordered, but those orders are only temporary patterns that always must dynamically change back into chaos and eventually completely disorder. Yet it was unmistakable that emergent orders, both natural and human-created, operate according to systemic laws and patterns that can now in our time be expressed in physics, systems theory, evolutionary and population biology, and chemistry—but were expressed in eighteenth-century Scottish Enlightenment historiography as histories of social organization.

NOTES

1. Olli J. Loukola, Clint J. Perry, Louie Coscos, and Lars Chittka, "Bumblebees Show Cognitive Flexibility by Improving on an Observed Complex Behavior," *Science* 355 (24 February 2017): 833–36. The quoted explanation of the study's findings appears on *Science*'s website: Virginia Morell, "Bumble Bees are Surprisingly Innovative," *Science*, 23 February 2017, accessed 15 August 2017, http://www.sciencemag.org.libproxy.albany.edu/news/2017/02/bumble-bees-are-surprisingly-innovative.

2. For analyses of these and other types of coordination problems, see Steven Strogatz, *Sync: The Emerging Science of Spontaneous Order* (New York: Hyperion, 2003); James Gleick, *Chaos: Making a New Science* (New York: Penguin, 2008); Richard Dawkins, *The Greatest Show on Earth: The Evidence for Evolution* (New York: Free Press, 2009); Stuart Kauffman, *At Home in the Universe: The Search for the Laws of Self-Organization and Complexity* (New York: Oxford Univ. Press, 1995).

3. David Martin, "New Generation of Drones Set to Revolutionize Warfare," CBS *60 Minutes*, accessed 20 August 2017, https://www.cbsnews.com/news/60-minutes-autonomous-drones-set-to-revolutionize-military-technology-2/.

4. Strogatz, *Sync*, 40–69; Dawkins, *Greatest Show on Earth*, 218–20.

5. To my mind, the best recent treatment of the concept of self-organization in social and economic terms is David Simpson, *The Rediscovery of Classical Economics: Adaptation, Complexity and Growth* (Cheltenham, UK: Edward

Elgar, 2013). A survey of the language of self-organization in the seventeenth- and eighteenth centuries appears in Jonathan Sheehan and Dror Wahrman, *Invisible Hands: Self-Organization and the Eighteenth Century* (Chicago: Univ. of Chicago Press, 2015). For explanations of spontaneous order in the eighteenth century, see Ronald Hamowy, *The Scottish Enlightenment and the Theory of Spontaneous Order* (Carbondale, IL: Southern Illinois Univ. Press, 1987); Craig Smith, *Adam Smith's Political Philosophy: The Invisible Hand and Spontaneous Order* (London: Routledge, 2006); Christina Petsoulas, *Hayek's Liberalism and Its Origins: His Idea of Spontaneous Order and the Scottish Enlightenment* (London: Routledge, 2013); Robert C. H. Chia and Robin Holt, *Strategy Without Design: The Silent Efficacy of Indirect Action* (Cambridge, UK: Cambridge Univ. Press, 2009), 31–35. For an enlightening discussion of the use of the word theory as fact, see Dawkins, *Greatest Show on Earth*, 9–18.

    6. See especially David B. Wilson, *Seeking Nature's Logic: Natural Philosophy in the Scottish Enlightenment* (Univ. Park, PA: Pennsylvania State Univ. Press, 2009); Theodore E.D. Braun and John A. McCarthy, eds. *Disrupted Patterns: On Chaos and Order in the Enlightenment* (Amsterdam: Rodopi, 2000); Hans-Walter Lorenz, *Nonlinear Dynamical Economics and Chaotic Motion* (Berlin: Springer-Verlag, 1989), 5–15.

    7. See Philip Hicks, *Neoclassical History and English Culture: From Clarendon to Hume* (London: Macmillan Press, 1996); Irène Simone, *Neo-Classical Criticism 1660–1800* (Columbia, SC: Univ. of South Carolina Press, 1971); Mark Salber Phillips, *Society and Sentiment: Genres of Historical Writing in Britain, 1740–1820* (Princeton, NJ: Princeton Univ. Press, 2000); Victor Wexler, *David Hume and the History of England* (Philadelphia, PA: American Philosophical Society, 1979); Laird Okie, *Augustan Historical Writing: Histories of England in the English Enlightenment* (Lanham, MD: Univ. Press of America, 1991); Everett Zimmerman, *The Boundaries of Fiction: History and the Eighteenth-Century British Novel* (Ithaca and London: Cornell Univ. Press, 1996).

    8. For an evolutionary as opposed to a static society, see Jerry Evensky, *Adam Smith's Moral Philosophy: A Historical and Contemporary Perspective on Markets, Law, Ethics, and Culture* (New York: Cambridge Univ. Press, 2005). On the specialization of history writing, see Phillips, *Society and Sentiment*.

    9. Simpson, *Rediscovery,* 72.

    10. Michael Hardt and Antonio Negri, *Assembly* (New York: Oxford Univ. Press, 2017).

    11. Michael Polanyi, *The Logic of Liberty* (London: Routledge, 1951); Friedrich Hayek, *Law, Legislation and Liberty*, 3 vols. (London: Routledge, 1982).

    12. Hamowy, *Scottish Enlightenment*; Smith, *Adam Smith's Political Philosophy*; Petsoulas, *Hayek's Liberalism*.

    13. Christopher Berry, *The Idea of Commercial Society in the Scottish Enlightenment* (Edinburgh: Edinburgh Univ. Press, 2013) and *Social Theory of the Scottish Enlightenment* (Edinburgh: Edinburgh Univ. Press, 1997); David Spadafora, *The Idea of Progress in Eighteenth-Century Britain* (New Haven and London: Yale Univ. Press, 1990).

14. In his essay "Cognitive Mapping," Fredric Jameson identifies this difficulty in measuring these alienating distances as a problem of "figuration:" "they may be conveyed by way of a growing contradiction between lived experience and structure, or between a phenomenological description of the life of an individual and a more properly structural model of the conditions of existence of that experience. Too rapidly we can say that, while in older societies and perhaps even in the early stages of market capital, the immediate and limited experience of individuals is still able to encompass and coincide with the true economic and social form that governs that experience, in the next moment these two levels drift even further apart and really begin to constitute themselves into that opposition the classical dialectic describes as *Wesen* and *Erscheinung*, essence and appearance, structure and lived experience." Fredric Jameson, "Cognitive Mapping," *Marxism and the Interpretation of Culture*, eds. Cary Nelson and Lawrence Grossberg (Urbana and Chicago, IL: Univ. of Illinois Press, 1988), 349.

15. David Hume, *The History of England From the Invasion of Julius Caesar to The Revolution in 1688*, 6 vols. (Indianapolis: Liberty Fund, 1983), henceforth cited parenthetically in the text as *HE*; John Millar, *An Historical View of the English Government*, eds. Mark Salber Phillips and Dale R. Smith (Indianapolis, IN: Liberty Fund, 2006), henceforth cited parenthetically in the text as *HV*.

16. Sheehan and Wahrman, *Invisible Hands*, 178.

17. Bernard Mandeville, *The Fable of the Bees: Or Private Vices, Publick Benefits,* 2 vols. (1924; repr., Indianapolis: Liberty Fund, 1988), 1: 24.

18. Mandeville, *Fable of the Bees*, 2: 188–89.

19. E. G. Hundert, *The Enlightenment's Fable: Bernard Mandeville and the Discovery of Society* (Cambridge, UK: Cambridge Univ. Press, 1994); Pierre Force, *Self-Interest Before Adam Smith: A Genealogy of Economic Science* (Cambridge, UK: Cambridge Univ. Press, 2003); Hamowy, *The Scottish Enlightenment*, 7–10.

20. James Burnet, Lord Monboddo, *Antient Metaphysics: Or, The Science of Universals* (London: T. Cadell, 1782), 2: 299–300.

21. Henry Home, Lord Kames, *Principles of Equity*, 3rd ed., ed. Michael Lobban (Indianapolis, IN: Liberty Fund, 2014), lvi–lvii.

22. Adam Ferguson, *An Essay on the History of Civil Society*, ed. Fania Oz-Salzberger (Cambridge, UK: Cambridge Univ. Press, 1995), 173,119.

23. David Hume, *An Enquiry Concerning Human Understanding*, ed. Peter Millican (Oxford: Oxford Univ. Press, 2008), 60. Hume's further elaboration on his "science of man" is worth reproducing here: "The same motives always produce the same actions: The same events follow from the same causes. Ambition, avarice, self-love, vanity, friendship, generosity, public spirit; these passions, mixed in various degrees, and distributed through society, have been, from the beginning of the world, and still are, the source of all the actions and enterprizes, which have ever been observed among mankind. . . . Mankind are so much the same, in all times and places, that history informs us of nothing new or strange in this particular. Its chief use is only to discover the constant and universal principles of human nature, by shewing men in all varieties of circumstances and situations, and furnishing us with materials, from which we may form our observations, and become acquainted

with the regular springs of human action and behaviour. These records of wars, intrigues, factions, and revolutions, are so many collections of experiments, by which the politician or moral philosopher fixes the principles of his science; in the same manner as the physician or natural philosopher becomes acquainted with the nature of plants, minerals, and other external objects, by the experiments, which he forms concerning them."

24. David Hume, *A Treatise of Human Nature*, eds. David Fate Norton and Mary J. Norton (Oxford: Clarendon Press, 2011), 1, 4.

25. Adam Smith, *The Theory of Moral Sentiments*, eds. D.D. Raphael and A.L. Macfie (1976; repr., Indianapolis, IN: Liberty Fund, 1982), 319.

26. For the Scottish Enlightenment "science of human nature," see especially Berry, *Commercial Society* and *Social Theory*.

27. The Scots were neither the first nor the only eighteenth-century writers to use stadial history models, nor were all of the Scottish models alike—some only had three stages instead of the customary hunter-gatherer, pastoral, agricultural, and commercial stages, and some used stages that were not included in these four. See Ronald L. Meek, *Social Science and the Ignoble Savage* (1976; repr., Cambridge, UK: Cambridge Univ. Press, 2010); and Berry, *Commercial Society*, 38–50, for a full genealogy of stadial history and a correction of Meek.

28. David Hume to John Clephane, 5 January 1753, in *The Letters of David Hume*, ed. J.Y.T. Greig, 2 vols., 1: 170.

29. It is important to note here that these conditions of production in which "noble" histories were composed, conditions that lie outside of the generic, internal properties of the historical text itself, were conventions that were prescribed by classical, and later neoclassical, criticism. See Hicks, *Neoclassical History*; Wexler, *David Hume*; and J. G. A. Pocock, *Barbarism and Religion, Volume Two: Narratives of Civil Government* (Cambridge, UK: Univ. of Cambridge, 1999).

30. Another of the external neoclassical strictures was that a gentleman doesn't publish a history of his own times in his own lifetime.

31. Okie, *Augustan Historical Writing*; Hicks, *Neoclassical History*.

32. David Hume to William Strahan, August, 1770, in *The Letters of David Hume*, ed. Grieg, 2: 230.

33. Hicks, *Neoclassical History*. Tindal's translation of Rapin is one of Laurence Sterne's major sources in *Tristram Shandy*, both for historical information concerning Toby and Trim's oft-recounted military campaigns and for parody of the generic conventions and styles of early-eighteenth century historical writing.

34. Hume, *HE*, 542.

35. Hume, *Enquiry,* 63.

36. David Hume, *Essays Moral, Political, and Literary*, ed. Eugene F. Miller (Indianapolis, IN: Liberty Fund, 1987), 494–95.

37. For an analysis of dynamic coordination problems in Hume's *History of England*, see Andrew Sabl, *Coordination and Crisis in the History of England* (Princeton: Princeton Univ. Press, 2012).

38. Hume, *HE*, 5: 91.

39. Hume, *HE*, 5: 18.

40. Hume, *HE*, 5: 174.

41. Hume, *HE*, 5: 18–19.

42. Hume states that "In all history, it would be difficult to find a reign less illustrious, yet more unspotted and unblemished than that of James in both kingdoms" (*HE,* 5: 121).

43. Hume, *HE*, 5: 18.

44. Hume, *HE*, 5: 18.

45. These are not solely confined to the end of particular reigns in Hume's narrative as some scholars have claimed in trying to either downplay the *HE*'s attention to socio-cultural matters or claim it as a pure neoclassical history.

46. Hume, *HE*, 5: 179.

47. John Millar, *The Origin and Distinction of Ranks*, ed. Aaron Garrett (Indianapolis, IN: Liberty Fund, 2006), 84, henceforth cited parenthetically in the text as *Ranks*.

48. Millar, *Ranks*, 229.

49. Millar, *HV*.

50. Michael Ignatieff, "John Millar and Individualism," *Wealth and Virtue: The Shaping of Political Economy in the Scottish Enlightenment*, eds. Istvan Hont and Michael Ignatieff (Cambridge, UK: Cambridge Univ. Press, 1983), 318.

51. Ignatieff, "John Millar and Individualism," 318.

52. Millar, *HV*, 12.

53. Millar, *HV*, 11.

54. Millar, *HV*, 437.

55. Millar, *HV*, 490.

56. Millar, *HV*, 512.

57. Henry Adams, "The Tendency of History," *The Degradation of the Democratic Dogma* (New York: Macmillan, 1919; repr., New York: Peter Smith, 1949), 126–28.

58. Adams, "Tendency of History," 129.

59. See Adams's essay "The Rule of Phase Applied to History," *Democratic Dogma*, 267–311.

60. Albert Einstein, "Why Socialism?" *Ideas and Opinions* (New York: Crown Publishers, 1960), 154.

61. Simpson, *Rediscovery*, 76.

Buffon's Language of Heat and the Science of Natural History

HANNA ROMAN

'I will burn it in a golden crucible,' said Guyton de Morveau, in order to be certain that diamonds contain oxides. 'The best crucible is the mind,' replied Buffon.[1]

In a short, unpublished text, *On the Art of Writing*, the French Enlightenment natural historian Buffon described the process of translating observations into language and transmitting them to readers.[2] In these notes for the famous *Discourse on Style*, he wrote that natural phenomena were best depicted through painting, which not only represented their order and structure but also made them flow together in such a way that they resembled and transmitted life itself:

> Painting and description are two very different things. The latter considers only the eyes, the former demands genius. . . . Description coldly and sequentially shows all the parts of an object; the more detailed it is, the less effect it has. Painting, on the other hand, seizes first upon the most salient traits, retaining the imprint of the object and giving it life. In order to write a good description, cold observation suffices; but painting requires the use of all the senses. Seeing, hearing, touching, feeling: these are

all elements which the writer must sense and render in energetic strokes. He must link the finesse of color and the vigor of the paintbrush, nuancing, condensing, or melting these colors, and ultimately shaping a living ensemble of which description could only have presented dead and detached parts.[3]

In contrast to the activity and liveliness of painted language, a purely descriptive work was like a sketch that lacked shading, depth, and thus vitality—as indicated by the recurrence of the expressions cold and coldly. Description sapped the vivacity of nature, producing a lifeless text of "dead and detached parts."

Buffon's contrast between description and painting when characterizing his writing about nature was borrowed from the visual arts; moreover, it referred to a disciplinary convention wherein history only described and enumerated events without attempting to extrapolate more general meaning and relationships between them.[4] In his rethinking of the discipline of natural history, Buffon sought to combine history with physics, or the search for causes, moving from specific, detailed observations of events and phenomena to a narrative of the large-scale activities of nature as it moved through time. The term painting allowed him to articulate what he wanted language to do: reproduce the temporal energy of nature on the page. In the *Discourse on Style,* he wrote of how the natural historian should mirror the continual process of natural creation, with a language like an uninterrupted brushstroke. To write well, Buffon stated that an author must "develop a succession [of thoughts], a continuous chain, of which each link represents an idea; and once one has taken up the pen, it will be necessary to guide it successively from this first line, without letting it stray."[5] The goal was to develop a poetic power that operated in the same manner as the creative power of natural laws except through words and not the events themselves. Buffon believed that this language of natural history would gradually transform into a convincing reproduction of nature, rendering the works of the natural historian and nature seemingly inseparable.

In order to mimic nature's continuous movement through time, the language of painting had to be warm, rich, and animated. In fact, Buffon seemed to think that words could render ideas even more visible than could an actual painting: a talented writer's "sentences and words will have more effect than the paintbrush and the colors of the artist."[6] The painter of words not only could see but also "hear, touch, feel," composing with both passion and intellect. His mind "seizes" upon nature; in *On the Art of Writing*, Buffon used verbs such as "to join," "to bring nuance to," "to condense," "to melt," "to form," and "to render"—"the use of all of the senses"—to illustrate the activity of combining ideas and observations into a new whole, the text. With "energetic strokes" of the pen, Buffon strove to recreate "a living ensemble," ultimately relating all aspects of nature in the reader's mind.[7]

Buffon characterized the transmission of nature's energetic movement through the medium of painted language as having heat:

> The great writer can . . . heat up, set alight, his reader through the representation of several activities that will all have heat, and that, by their union and their rays, will engrave themselves in the reader's memory and will live on independently of the [original] object.[8]

Written nature, more powerful than cold, lifeless description or even direct observation, was designed to set readers' minds ablaze, leaving them with a lasting "heat," which would perpetuate and "engrave" in their memories nature's phenomena, order, laws—its history in a new sense.

Why begin an article about Buffon with his notes on writing, which do not directly address the cosmology, geography, and natural histories of animals, birds, and minerals for which he was so famous in the thirty-six volumes of *Natural History: General and Particular*, published between 1749 and 1788? By introducing the idea of heat, *On the Art of Writing* provides a more complete understanding of the relationship between language and knowledge in this work and in Enlightenment natural science more generally. Buffon sought not only to detail the world around him but also to render its general and systematic laws visible and palpable to the mind through language, a discursive simulacrum of nature that had both poetic and material force. The epistemological value of the *Natural History* derived from the ability of its language to reproduce convincingly and powerfully the structure and activity of nature. For Buffon, language was itself *scientia*: it gave order and demonstrability to knowledge of the world and endowed its author and readers with the ability to investigate, understand, and, ultimately, intervene in the work of nature.

Near the end of his career, heat became part of this intervention, not only a property of language but also an actual physical activity that could raise the temperature of an environment. In *The Epochs of Nature* (1778), Buffon argued that the Earth began as a molten ball of fire (torn off of the Sun by the force of a passing comet) and depicted its slow cooling over historical time. He implied that the depletion of the planet's heat would lead to its inevitable end as a frozen globe of ice; yet, he attempted to convince readers of their ability to slow down the Earth's cooling by transforming the heat of his language into real heat in the world—an idea to which I will return later. The lyrical, dynamic quality of Buffon's language and the physical phenomenon of heat, which directed the course of natural history, coalesced: discourse gave people the ability to change their surrounding environments.

While deeply indebted to foundational studies on Buffon's life, work, and philosophy by authors such as Benoît de Baere, Thierry Hoquet, and Jeff Loveland, I seek to reevaluate his contemporary scientific value through a close reading of his language.[9] These scholars address the importance of language for Buffon; however, they understand it as a manner of expression, an added layer atop his ideas, missing its fundamental connection to knowledge. Using the concept of heat as a tool for examining and asserting the strength of this connection, I demonstrate how written language was not simply a vehicle for conveying knowledge in a lyrical and entertaining manner but also a form and a practice of natural knowledge itself. The idea of heat draws inspiration notably from Joanna Stalnaker's work on the language of natural history and Peter H. Reill's study on vitalism.[10] Combining these, I argue that in Buffon's corpus, heat was both a quality of writing that transmitted natural knowledge and an activity that transformed the temperature and operation of nature itself. Heat enables an understanding of the materiality of language in eighteenth-century natural science: not simply a manner of knowing the world but also a part of this world, shaping its future, blurring literary and real.

In *On The Art of Writing,* the heat that Buffon asserted to be produced by painting sounds like a metaphor for the reproduction of natural knowledge on the page. However, language and physical processes were linked; both were material activities affecting the mind and the world. Early in his career, Buffon had taken an interest in the physical heat of nature, studying the mechanisms of life and vitality and asking what made some things alive while others were not. Such a question was deeply rooted in chemical, mechanical, and medical philosophies of the time. An examination of some of these theories expands heat beyond the discursive, revealing the physicality and materiality of thought. As something that circulated in and between bodies, heat could be understood as a tangible mode of communication, part of the language of nature that Buffon sought to read and impart.

Buffon's *La statique des végétaux et l'analyse de l'air* (1735), a translation of the English physiologist Stephen Hales's *Vegetable Staticks* (1727), allowed him to speculate upon the movement and circulation of nutrients and other organic compounds in living bodies. Hales's work was a foundational essay in the area of plant physiology and an example of the implementation of Newtonian law in the study of living nature. It drew from the work of physiologists of the seventeenth century such as William Harvey, who studied the circulation of blood in animals. Similarly, Hales examined the movement of sap within plants and their material exchange with the surrounding environment.[11] Hales's experiments reflected the application of Newton's physics of the attraction and repulsion of particles to the activity and movement of living things:

> We find by the chymical analysis of vegetables, that their substance is composed of sulpher, volatile salt, water and earth; which principles are all endued with mutually attracting powers, and also of a large portion of air, which has a wonderful property of strongly attracting in a fixt state, or of repelling in an elastick state, with a power which is superior to vast compressing forces; and it is by the infinite combinations, action and re-action of these principles, that all the operations in animal and vegetable bodies are effected.[12]

The fundamental operation of life was an attractive force that held bodies together, giving them form and identifiable, external qualities. Yet this force could not alone explain life's essence: an opposing force, air, resisted the pull of attraction, generating the necessary space and pressure for sap, blood, and water to move through the body, and allowing for a vital economy that nourished and promoted growth. As Violeta Aréchiga has shown, for Hales the idea of air was associated with life; once air entered into a solid body, it lost its elasticity, or expansive power, and "found itself fixed in animal, vegetal, and mineral substances. Indeed, in this fixed state, air made up the ductile and nutritive matter from which the organs of the plant grew."[13] Hales, quoting Newton, described the principle of air as "'this soft and moist nourishment easily changing its texture by gentle heat and motion, which congregates homogeneal bodies, and separates heterogeneal ones.'"[14] Life was characterized by the interaction of homogeneal particles, gravitating to the center of the organism, with heterogeneal ones, tending towards the outside, the ether. (Interestingly, Buffon translated these latter particles as étherogènes and not héterogènes, as Hales originally wrote.) These particles of captured air were also called *fixed fire* and provided the heat necessary for movement and change in living beings.

Hales's dynamic equilibrium between attraction and repulsion returned in Buffon's 1749 second discourse in *Natural History*, about the formation of the solar system. A comet, attracted to the Sun, fell into this star; blazing fragments were pushed outwards, and as they cooled they consolidated to form planets held in orbit.[15] The Earth, its natural phenomena, and the entire universe, could be depicted in terms of the interplay of these perpetually contrasting forces—a model to which Buffon would return later in his experiments on heat and in *The Epochs of Nature*.

This example of heat as a force of life and movement may be contextualized by examining Enlightenment debates about the meaning and mechanics of fire and heat. In his *Encyclopédie* article on fire, D'Alembert began with a definition that raised more questions than it answered:

> The most essential characteristic of fire, the one that everyone recognizes, is to give heat. Thus, fire may be defined generally as the matter, which by its action, immediately produces heat in us. But is fire a specific kind of matter? Or is it but the matter of bodies put into motion? On this subject, philosophers are divided.[16]

Fire produced the physical sensation of heat. Yet this definition did not explain what fire was or how it operated. Was it part of bodies, or was it a substance that moved through bodies, creating flames, heat, or light?[17]

On the one hand, heat could be understood as the product of the element fire, inherent to the substance of matter and present to differing degrees in all bodies. On the other hand, fire was what gave form to, or altered, matter by traversing it. It was thus, according to Bernard Joly, a tool of analysis used to understand the composition of bodies.[18] In this second sense, fire either could be construed as a mechanical process that made the particles of a body move faster, thus changing the state of the matter or it could be explained as a "quintessence," "a celestial fire that embeds itself in the heart of matter" creating life, light, and energy in bodies.[19]

Interpreted mechanically, fire was what Joly calls "an agitation of matter" that caused the vortex-like particles that composed the Cartesian world to move faster and to hit against one another, creating sparks perceived as light and heat.[20] Newtonian theories of fire, particularly interested in the emission of light from bodies, added universal attraction to this mechanical explanation, in order to describe how particles of light entered into bodies and changed their state, rendering them hot and luminous.[21] The terms "subtle fluid" or "spirit" of heat, often employed in chemistry, could also be applied to physical theories of heat to show how living bodies continued to move and grow, using attraction and repulsion to give, in Philip Sloan's terms, "a creative and dynamic agency" to nature.[22]

The theorization of heat as a subtle fluid, part of an "active ether," enabled Buffon to order all natural phenomena, inorganic and organic. Buffon defined life not as distinct from death but as the degree of heat in a body. In 1749, he wrote in the essay, "Comparison of Animals and Plants" that "there is no absolutely essential and general difference between animals and plants, but [rather] that Nature descends by degrees and imperceptible nuances from the animal that to us seems the most perfect [humans] to that which is the least perfect, and from there to the vegetal."[23] Degrees of life and heat continued into the mineral realm which contained, in the form of soil, fossils, and stones, the heated traces of previously organized beings and thus the potential to build new life forms.[24] Heat defined the organization of matter and its degree of life, and flowed in between bodies—physical, celestial, and indeed, as the next section will show, textual—changing them.[25] In Reill's words, as a fluid, heat came to be imagined as liquid and thus "entailed the penetration of the solid by an active, subtle fluid that energized the solid, releasing it from its cold imprisonment."[26] In this sense, heat became a mode of communication, a cause of interaction. It engendered a perception of bodies not by how they differed from one another but as related, receptive, continuous.

Buffon took this inter-relatedness of bodies to its most general limit. As he developed his discipline of natural history, he worked to subsume chemistry and mechanics under the generality of natural law, which he considered universal in both extent and expression. From the perfection of the heavens to the sublunary realm of historical change, the universe could be understood and represented through the same principles and structure (attraction, repulsion, and their associated degrees of heat) and hence the same language of mechanics and heat.[27] Heat, flowing through individual bodies, put them into relationship with one another, endowing them with the potential to be expressed through a continuous narrative. It became one of the underlying organizational and grammatical matrixes of life.

The idea of a simultaneously material and ethereal spirit traversing, ordering, and rendering legible the world to human perception had already been theorized by Montesquieu, an important influence upon Buffon.[28] His arguments, culminating in *The Spirit of the Laws* (1748), are helpful to understanding the multidimensional manner in which Buffon used the term heat. Montesquieu maintained that just as the human body could adapt itself to fit a new climate through the reception of physical spirits (e.g., air, food), so the human mind could modify thought through interaction with the outside world in the form of physical sensations and intellectual spirits such as ideas. The surrounding environment, real or textual, influenced and altered the perceiving mind in a material, tangible process of osmosis: spirits passed through the semi-permeable boundaries of the body, changing the economy, disposition, and quantity of thoughts in the brain and causing the observer to see the world differently.[29]

A description in *The Spirit of the Laws* of an experiment in which Montesquieu examined a bit of tissue from a sheep's tongue under a microscope demonstrates how he thought the movement of spirits worked. When he exposed the tissue to cold air, its cells contracted and shrunk. As the cells defrosted, they became larger, taller, and more spread out.[30] This movement, he reasoned, did not only happen on the microscopic level: like a domino effect, the same activity occurred on increasingly larger scales.

When, for example, cold air touched the fibers of the skin, they contracted and became more spring-like and charged. They then imparted these qualities to the surrounding blood, through the vessels and all the way to the heart: cold air "contracts the extremities of the body's surface fibers; this increases their spring and favors the return of blood from the extremities of the heart. It shortens these same fibers; therefore, it increases their strength in this way too."[31] This chain of cause and effect was provoked by a change in temperature that subsequently affected the way fluids moved and interacted in the individual body. From these physiological observations, Montesquieu explained how temperature influenced not only physical fluids such as blood but also less tangible spirits such as passions, desires, and intellect. The French word *esprit* could thus refer simultaneously to thought, mind, and spirit.

In the *Encyclopédie* article "Chaleur," D'Alembert described heat as the experience of a perceiving, feeling body, echoing both its physical and poetic spirit. He defined it as "a unique perception or modification of the soul."[32] Usually, heat was evenly dispersed everywhere and thus undetectable. It was only perceivable when it escalated, causing an exchange of movement that triggered the experience of heat, light, or color, depending not only upon how fast the particles moved but also upon what state of matter the receiving body was inclined to sense. Heat was "a relative sensation;" it was about the dialogue of movement from one body to another such that the receiving body experienced a change in sensation (23). Experience was as important to the definition of heat as mechanics. Equal parts reality and perception, heat was an event. Both something that happened in the world and part of the human experience of the world, heat was amenable to language.

Like cells in a body, language, too, carried its message from author to reader through an outward movement: *energeia* in Classical rhetoric was the realization and materialization of thought's potential in words. This activity was described in the *Encyclopédie* article "Énergie:"

> ENERGY, FORCE, synonyms. (Grammar) Here we only consider these words in terms of the application to discourse . . . . It seems that energy says even more than force; & that energy is applied primarily to discourses which paint, & to the character of style. One might say of an orator that he joins the force of reasoning with the energy of expressions. One also speaks of an energetic painting, & forceful images.[33]

An energetic and forceful spirit could be emitted by language, transmitting the power and order of the author's original ideas. Similarly, in his article

"Force," Voltaire described how the meaning of this term "has been transported from simple to figurative." From its mechanical definition as "all the parts of a body that are in motion," Voltaire enumerated its metaphorical meanings, related to the expression of ideas through language—not demonstrative, mathematical language, which carried its own fixed degree of evidence, but eloquent, persuasive discourse that addressed "questions of debate."[34] In a language similar to Buffon's in *On The Art of Writing*, Voltaire argued that "the force of eloquence is not only in the succession of just & vigorous reasoning, which could subsist in coldness [or insensitivity]; this force demands embonpoint, striking images, energetic terms."[35]

Buffon's writings about nature combined physical matter and rhetorical force; understood as material, his language acted upon and modified the perception of its interlocutors.[36] The heat of his discourse was designed not only to make readers admire his eloquent style but also to provide the requisite epistemological and conceptual tools to experience the world through the experience of reading the text. The "energetic strokes" described in *On the Art of Writing* combined knowledge and inspiration, merging two terms of Aristotelian rhetoric: *enargeia*, or clear and ordered knowledge, and *energeia*, or action and movement, the realization of potential.[37] The vibrant, evocative discourse of *Natural History* thus communicated a systematic view of nature and nature's movement through time.[38]

As indicated in *On the Art of Writing* and in the *Discourse on Style*, Buffon believed the best way to convey the activity of nature was through the force of a written language that literally moved at the same rate as the world it described. His prose, the consecutive, flowing succession of energetic language on the page, would mirror the temporal, vital transpiring of events in nature.[39] Prose was a language, in Stalnaker's words, "more permeable to the natural world" than a painting or a poem, for it echoed nature's structure as a narrative unfolding over time. What was being rendered in the mind of the reader, through the non-simultaneity of writing, was not a single picture but a chain of words, a carefully linked set of relationships that encapsulated and reproduced the dynamic flow of nature through time.[40]

Buffon's prose allowed him to write not only about the visible, surrounding world but also about nature on a broad scale, depicting the hidden operation of its laws. In the 1764 essay, "On nature, first view," Buffon described the world as it could never be physically observed with the naked eye. Climbing to a nearly divine perspective, he illustrated the work and movement of nature as a whole. Nature, controlled by divine power, was God's pen. It rendered the divine plan real, visible, and legible, expressing the physical manifestations of law in time and space as observable phenomena. Nature was both God's creation and immortal worker:

a perpetually living work, a ceaselessly active worker who knows
how to use everything and who, working according to itself and
always on the same foundation, instead of exhausting it [this
foundation] renders it inexhaustible: time, space, and matter are
its means, the Universe its object, movement and life its goal.[41]

Through the laws of gravitation, nature shaped the vast spatial and temporal
distances of the universe. Nature wrote, and writes "perpetually," its book—a
narrative composed through time—upon "the edifice of the world," beginning
with the formation of "millions of opaque globes, [which] circulating
around the original ones, compose the order and moving architecture [of
the universe]."[42] Buffon made it seem as if he were looking over nature's
shoulder, watching the process of writing the book unfold, and recording it
in prose. He used this practice of observation to envision nature's invisible
workings, rendering its story legible and palpable to readers.

By the mid-1760s, Buffon was interested not only in the written
representation of nature's vitality but also in what he believed to be the
fiery, volcanic origins of this vitality, and how this heat shaped the Earth's
history.[43] He inquired into the sources of the Earth's heat, influenced by the
work of his colleague in the Parisian Royal Academy of Sciences, Dortous
de Mairan, whose *New Studies on the General Cause of Heat in Summer and
Cold in Winter* (1765) argued that the Earth did not receive nearly enough
warmth from the Sun to sustain its current temperature, and that therefore it
must have its own, inner fire.[44] Soon after reading this work, Buffon began
experiments on globes of the minerals of which the Earth was composed and
which could be found at different depths and in different strata relative to the
Earth's surface.[45] He observed how long it took for each type of mineral to
heat up and then to cool and to become tolerable to human touch—in other
words, to achieve the relatively warm, temperate state of the present-day
Earth. These models showed the way that internal heat moved and behaved
within each type of mineral, giving it a specific character, and they allowed
Buffon to provide a narrative of the exact sequence of the substances that
cooled first in the history of the world. In general, these substances could be
found deeper within the layers of the Earth's crust. From here he deduced and
calculated the order and duration of the solidification of each mineral with
respect to the others. The amount of time it took each mineral to cool and its
position in what he called the Earth's "archives" created natural brackets for
each chapter of his deep-time history, the *The Epochs of Nature*. Through
the lively heat of his prose, Buffon reenacted the succession of events that
would have been possible at each moment in time and temperature.

Buffon published the results of his experiments in 1774 and 1775. In
an essay entitled "On Light, Heat, and Fire," he explained the operation

of nature through the movement of matter. Recalling Hales's *Vegetable Staticks*, Buffon wrote of two "primitive forces, that which causes gravity, and that which produces heat." The first of these forces he named *attraction*, or gravitation, and, the second, *impulsion*. While attraction pulled particles of matter towards one another, impulsion worked "like a spring," pushing particles away from one another, an action which produced heat.[46] Buffon described impulsion as "an expansive force" because it drove particles "from the center to the circumference" of a body. The particles of "brute" matter, subject to gravitation alone, moved "from the circumference to the center."[47] These two forces were understood as two sides of the same coin: "they are for Nature two instruments of the same type, or rather they are but the same instrument that she [Nature] manipulates in two different directions."[48]

Heat was here a change in the state of matter in a body provoked through the communication of movement of molecules endowed with impulsive force (*HNS*, 1: 31). The state of matter was modified when the activity of impulsion compelled molecules, pulled together by gravitation, to push off of one another in a spring-like manner, and to enter new bodies, in turn making the particles of these bodies move faster and creating heat within them. Buffon concluded, moreover, that the entire universe might be understood as different forms and degrees of heat, controlled by the law of attraction and impulsion: "light, . . . heat, and fire are nothing but states of communal matter; that there exists, in a word, only one single force and one single matter that is always ready to attract or to repulse."[49]

The apparently simple idea of "one single force and one single matter" did not mean that the world was moving towards an equilibrium of attraction and resistance, hot and cold, life and death. Buffon argued in the *The Epochs of Nature* that the heat so necessary to the mechanics, structure, and history of nature was slowly but surely dissipating and that the world was in danger of ending in ice. However, its heat death could be postponed, as people imitated and appropriated the power of nature and its laws by becoming literate in Buffon's language. In an obscuring of the separation between real events and the narrative of them, this language captured the form of impulsion and its ensuing heat, which wrote the events of nature's history, and transferred this heat to readers. Understanding the physical processes through which the Earth's history had been generated and learning to read and interpret its events, were the first steps to taking over the creation of history from a world that was slowly losing its impulsive force.

Inheriting nature's heat, people could conceive of an open-ended historical narrative whose future was not determined but amenable to change and innovation.[50] In *The Epochs of Nature*, Buffon envisioned the fusion of physical heat, the force by which natural phenomena were imprinted in and upon the Earth, with the heat of language discussed in *On the Art of Writing*, the animated narrative of the formation of these phenomena. With the ability to perceive the heat radiating off of the pages of his work, Buffon thought that people could collect it and return it to the environment. They would have to supersede and surpass the productive power of nature in order to keep the planet at a warm temperature suitable to both physical cultivation and intellectual culture in the centuries to come. (Buffon used the same word culture to speak of both phenomena.) In the final epoch of the book, "When the Power of Man Assisted that of Nature," he gave examples from history to convince readers of their potential. Following a simple, deterministic logic, "the whole Earth should be colder today than it was 2,000 years ago; however, tradition seems to prove the contrary:"

> The Gauls and the Germans fed moose, lynx, bears, and other animals who then retreated to northern countries; the movement is quite different than the one you would expect them to make, from north to south. Furthermore, history tells us that every year the Seine was typically frozen during part of the winter; do not these facts appear in direct opposition to the claimed gradual cooling of the globe? They would be, if modern France and Germany resembled Gaul and Germania; if people had not felled the forests, dried up the swamps, contained streams, redirected rivers, and cleared the lands that were covered and overwhelmed with the debris of their own productions.[51]

Humans and animals were "so many little heated hearths" that "radiate heat." (Plants, however, "produce nothing but cold humidity.") A person was not only capable of making heat but also of making it to the degree "that suits him," becoming the "master of the element of fire, that he can augment and propagate at his will."[52] Cold was not just the absence of heat but the absence of the impulsive activity that made history. Cold was nothing; one "can neither grasp nor communicate" coldness.[53] Heat, however, could be communicated through the outward movement of ideas as through that of molecules, preparing people to do what nature could no longer.

In the final chapter of *The Epochs of Nature*, Buffon evoked how, with a more complete understanding of the way that nature operated on a large scale across time, people learned to change the scope of their perception and activity, making their knowledge into a creative power approaching the immensity of nature's laws:

> [Man] followed the lessons of Nature, profited from its examples, used its means, and selected from within its immensity all the objects that could help or please him. Through his intelligence,

animals were tamed, subjugated, controlled, made to forever obey him; through his works, swamps were dried, rivers contained, their cataracts eliminated, forests cleared, heaths cultivated; ultimately the entire face of the Earth carries today the traces of the power of man.[54]

When people learned to modify the temperature of their world, Buffon imagined that they entered into a state of happiness. The inhabitants of a temperate climate could overcome the vanity and egotism which historically caused war and destruction, and they could reflect in an increasingly altruistic sense upon how to make their region, their continent, and finally the whole globe more peaceful and productive. "Happy are the countries," Buffon wrote, "where all elements of temperature are balanced and well enough combined to bring about nothing but good effects!"[55]

To achieve this state, Buffon suggested that history be read as a process of ever-increasing human control over both their own nature and material nature. Enlightened people were not only capable of reheating the world but also of understanding—in this early form of global warming!—how to make the two extremes of hot and cold work together. By creating what Buffon called "a new Nature," they could postpone the cold death of the world through the learned process of temperance, a process at once poetic, natural, historical, and political.[56] The last sentence of the *The Epochs of Nature* reflected on how, after centuries of violence, ignorance, and wasted heat, "finally [man] has recognized that his true glory is science, and peace his true happiness."[57] Through the dynamism of scientific language, came the ability to moderate and regulate natural and human activity.

The happiness that ensued from living in a nature modified by humans resulted from the creation of a temperate zone; the temperate resulted from balancing the expansive force of impulsion with the attractive force of gravity. Buffon's science of natural history was the result of the equilibrium of the structure of his language with the structure of the world. This was not a fixed equilibrium but an opening of new possibilities that might delay the frozen end of the world and hinder the deterministic march of history. Agile minds, he hoped, might write new chapters in history, imagining and perhaps realizing future epochs in which human creation would overpower the natural. Language would no longer imitate the world; rather, nature would become the product of language.

NOTES

This article is a shortened and modified version of Hanna Roman, *The Language of Nature in Buffon's Histoire naturelle* Oxford University Studies in the Enlightment (Liverpool, UK: Liverpool Univ. Press, 2018), chapter 2.

1. "'Je le ferai brûler dans un creuset d'or,' disait Guyton de Morveau, pour s'assurer que le diamant contenait de la terre fixe. 'Le meilleur creuset, c'est l'esprit,' répondit Buffon." Qtd. in Daniel Mornet, *Les sciences de la nature en France au XVIIIe siècle* (Genève: Slatkine Reprints, 2001), 114. All translations from the French are my own, unless otherwise noted.

2. *De l'Art d'écrire* was probably part of the generation of the *Discours sur le style* (1753). Although not mentioned in Jacques Roger and E. Genet Varcins's "Bibliographie de Buffon," this piece was published in Buffon's correspondence. It was copied from Buffon's notes and kept by his notary. Henri Nadault de Buffon, *Correspondance inédite de Buffon*, 2 vols. (Paris: Hachette, 1860), 1: 292–94. The modern edition of this text that I use here is: Georges-Louis Leclerc de Buffon, *De l'Art d'écrire*, (Castelnau-le-Lez: Éditions Climats, 1992), 37–41, henceforth cited as *DAE*.

3. *DAE*, 38–39. "Peindre ou décrire sont deux choses différentes: l'une ne suppose que des yeux, l'autre exige du génie. . . . La description présente successivement et froidement toutes les parties de l'objet; plus elle est détaillée, moins elle fait d'effet. La peinture au contraire, ne saisissant d'abord que les traits les plus saillants, garde l'empreinte de l'objet et lui donne de la vie. Pour bien décrire, il suffit de voir froidement; mais pour peindre, il faut l'emploi de tous les sens. Voir, entendre, palper, sentir, ce sont autant de caractères que l'écrivain doit sentir et rendre par des traits énergiques. Il doit joindre la finesse des couleurs à la vigueur du pinceau, les nuancer, les condenser ou les fondre; former enfin un ensemble vivant, dont la description ne peut présenter que des parties mortes et détachées."

4. On the role of description in history, see Donald R. Kelley, "Between History and System," *Historia. Empiricism and Erudition in Early Modern Europe*, eds. Gianna Pomata and Nancy Siraisi (Cambridge, MA: The MIT Press, 2005), 211–37. In the specific case of Buffon's *Histoire naturelle,* see Thierry Hoquet, "History without Time. Buffon's Natural History as a Nonmathematical Physique," *Isis* 101 (2010): 30–61; and Joanna Stalnaker, *The Unfinished Enlightenment: Description in the Age of the Encyclopédie,* (Ithaca, NY: Cornell Univ. Press, 2010).

5. "Pour bien écrire," an author must "former une suite [de pensées], une chaîne continue, dont chaque point représente une idée; et lorsqu'on aura pris la plume, il faudra la conduire successivement sur ce premier trait, sans lui permettre de s'en écarter." Buffon, "Discours sur le style," *Histoire naturelle, générale et particulière: Supplément*, 7 vols. (Paris: Imprimerie royale, 1777), 4: 8.

6. *DAE*, 39. "phrases et ses mots feront plus d'effet que le pinceau et les couleurs du peintre."

7. *DAE*, 39–40. "saisit;" Buffon used verbs such as "joindre," "nuancer," "condenser," "fondre," "former," and "rendre"—"l'emploi de tous les sens;" "des traits énergiques;" "un ensemble vivant."

8. *DAE*, 40–41. "Le grand écrivain peut échauffer, embraser son lecteur par la représentation de plusieurs actions qui toutes auront de la chaleur, et qui par leur union et leurs rayons se graveront dans sa mémoire et subsisteront indépendamment de l'objet."

9. On the language of the *Histoire naturelle*, see Benoît De Baere, "Représentation et visualisation dans l'*Histoire naturelle* de Buffon," *Dix-huitième siècle* 39.1 (2007): 613–38; De Baere, *La pensée cosmogonique de Buffon. Percer la nuit des temps* (Paris: Honoré Champion, 2004); Thierry Hoquet, *Buffon: Histoire naturelle et philosophie* (Paris: Champion, 2005); Jeff Loveland, *Rhetoric and Natural History. Buffon in Polemical and Literary Context* (Oxford: Voltaire Foundation, 2001); Joanna Stalnaker, "Painting Life, Describing Death: Problems of Representation and Style in the *Histoire naturelle*," *Studies in Eighteenth-Century Culture* 32 (2003): 193–227.

10. Peter H. Reill, *Vitalizing Nature in the Enlightenment* (Berkeley, CA: Univ. of California Press, 2005); Stalnaker, *The Unfinished Enlightenment*.

11. Richard S. Westfall, "Hales, Stephen," *Catalogue of the Scientific Community of the 16th and 17th Centuries, http://users.clas.ufl.edu/ufhatch/pages/03-Sci-Rev/SCI-REV-Home/resource-ref-read/major-minor-ind/westfall-dsb/index.htm*, accessed 06 March 2017, n.p. On Hales, also see Thomas Hankins, *Science and the Enlightenment* (Cambridge, UK: Cambridge Univ. Press, 1985), 50–53; and Lesley Hanks, *Buffon avant l'Histoire naturelle* (Paris: Presses Univ. de France, 1966), Part 2: chapters 2–3.

12. Stephen Hales, *Vegetable Staticks* (London: Printed for W. and J. Innys, 1727), 318–19. "Nous trouvons par l'analyse chymique des Végétaux, qu'ils sont composés de soulfre, de sels volatils, d'eau, de terre & de l'air ; ces quatre premiers principes agissent les uns sur les autres par une forte puissance d'attraction mutuelle, & l'air que je regarde comme le cinquième principe, est doué de cette même puissance d'attraction, lorsqu'il est dans un état fixe ; mais il exerce la puissance contraire aussi-tôt qu'il change d'état ; car dèslors il repousse avec une force supérieure à toutes les forces connues. Tout se fait donc dans la nature par la combinaison de ces cinq principes, par leur action & réaction réciproque." Stephen Hales, *La statique des végétaux et l'analyse de l'air*, trans. M. de Buffon (Paris: Chez Debure l'aîné, 1735), 270. On the application of mechanical philosophy to the study of life, see Theodore M. Brown, "From Mechanism to Vitalism in Eighteenth-Century English Physiology," *Journal of the History of Biology* 7.2 (Autumn 1974): 185–89; Thomas S. Hall, "On Biological Analogs of Newtonian Paradigms," *Philosophy of Science* 35 (1968): 6–27; Jacques Roger, "Chimie et biologie: Des 'molécules organiques' de Buffon à la 'physico-chimie' de Lamarck," *History and Philosophy of the Life Sciences* 1 (1979): 43–64; and Stéphane Schmitt, "Introduction," Georges-Louis Leclerc de Buffon, *Histoire naturelle, générale et particulière, Tome 2 (1749)*, eds. Stéphane Schmitt and Cédric Crémière (Paris: Honoré Champion, 2008), 23–25.

13. Violeta Aréchiga, "Le feu et la vie: la pensée chimique de Buffon," *L'héritage de Buffon*, ed. Marie-Odile Bernez (Dijon: Éditions Univ. de Dijon, 2009), 237. "se retrouvait fixé dans les substances animales, végétales et minérales. En fait, à l'état fixe, l'air formait la matière, ductile et nutritive, à partir de laquelle les

202 / ROMAN

organes végétaux croissaient." On early modern theories of vital heat, see Everett Mendelsohn, *Heat and Life. The Development of the Theory of Animal Heat* (Cambridge, MA: Harvard Univ. Press, 1964).

14. Hales, *Vegetable Staticks*, 319. "une nourriture tendre & humide [qui] est aisément disposée par une chaleur douce, & un mouvement tempéré, à changer de forme & de contexture; les mouvemens intestins rassemblent les particules homogènes, & séparent les particules étherogènes. *Newton Optique*, qu. 31." Hales, *La statique des végétaux*, 271.

15. Buffon, "Second discours," *Histoire naturelle, générale et particulière*, 15 vols. (Paris: Imprimerie royale, 1749), 1: 128. This work is henceforth cited as *HN*. On Hales's influence on Buffon, see Hanks, *Buffon avant l'Histoire naturelle*, 91–97.

16. Jean le Rond D'Alembert, "Feu," *Encyclopédie, ou dictionnaire raisonné des sciences, des arts et des métiers*, eds. Denis Diderot and Jean le Rond D'Alembert, *ARTFL Encyclopédie Project*, ed. Robert Morrissey, 17 vols. (Chicago, n.d.) *http:// encyclopedie.uchicago.edu/*, 6: 599. "Le caractère le plus essentiel du feu, celui que tout le monde lui reconnoît, est de donner de la chaleur. Ainsi on peut définir en général le feu, la matière qui par son action produit immédiatement la chaleur en nous. Mais le feu est-il une matière particulière? ou n'est-ce que la matière des corps mise en mouvement? c'est sur quoi les Philosophes sont partagés." The *Encyclopédie* is henceforth cited as *ENC*.

17. On the different types and uses of fire in Enlightenment chemistry, see Christine Lehman, *Gabriel François Venel (1723–1775). Sa place dans la chimie française du XVIIIe siècle* (PhD diss., Univ. de Paris-Nanterre, 2006), especially chapter 4, which analyzes the chemist Venel's treatise, "Du feu." See also Hélène Metzger, "La théorie du feu d'après Boerhaave," *Revue philosophique de la France et de l'Étranger* 109 (January-June 1930): 253–85.

18. Bernard Joly, "Les théories du feu de Voltaire et de Mme du Châtelet," *Cirey dans la vie intellectuelle: la réception de Newton en France* (Oxford, UK: Voltaire Foundation, 2001), 214.

19. Joly, "Les théories du feu," 214. "un feu céleste venu loger au cœur de la matière."

20. Bernard Joly, "La question de la nature du feu dans la chimie de la première moitié du XVIIIe siècle," *Corpus* 36 (1999): 43–44, 49. "une agitation de la matière."

21. Hélène Metzger, "Newton: La théorie de l'émission de la lumière dans la doctrine chimique au XVIIIe siècle," *Archeion* 11 (1929): 17. For an updated study of the theorization of light in eighteenth-century chemistry, see Lawrence M. Principe, "Wilhelm Homberg et la chimie de la lumière," *Methodos: savoirs et textes* 8 (2008), *http://methodos.revues.org/1223*: n.p.

22. Phillip R. Sloan, "Natural History, 1670–1802," *Companion to the History of Modern Science*, eds. R.C. Olby, G.N Cantor, J.R.R. Christie and M.J.S. Hodge (London: Routledge, 1990), 301–2. This interpretation of an almost divine spirit keeping matter from compacting under the force of attraction was held by the marquise du Châtelet, in her 1742 *Dissertation sur la nature et la propogation du feu*. Voltaire, on the other hand, decided to take a less extreme position, claiming that fire held an intermediate status between matter and spirit. Joly, "La question de la nature du feu," 43, 53–55.

23. *HN*, 2: 8–9. "il n'y a aucune différence absolument essentielle et générale entre les animaux et les végétaux, mais que la nature descende par degrés et par nuances imperceptibles d'un animal qui nous paroît le plus parfait à celui qui l'est le moins, et de celui-ci au végétal."

24. Buffon, *Histoire naturelle des minéraux*, 5 vols. (Paris: Imprimerie royale, 1783), 1: 4–5.

25. Hankins, *Science and the Enlightenment*, 50–53, 72–75. This theory was applied to the mechanical as well as to the chemical sciences. See Metzger, "Newton: La théorie de l'émission de la lumière," 17.

26. Reill, *Vitalizing Nature in the Enlightenment*, 79–80.

27. Metzger discusses Buffon's applications of Newtonian chemistry and law in *Newton, Stahl, Boerhaave et la doctrine chimique* (Paris: Albert Blanchard, 1974), 58–66.

28. See Jacques Roger, *Buffon: Un philosophe au Jardin du Roi* (Paris: Fayard, 1989), 242–43.

29. On the interaction between texts and physiology, see Anne C. Vila, *Enlightenment and Pathology: Sensibility in the Literature and Medicine of Eighteenth-Century France* (Baltimore: Johns Hopkins Univ. Press, 1998).

30. Charles de Secondat, Baron de Montesquieu, *De l'Esprit des lois, Œuvres complètes*, ed. Roger Caillois, 2 vols. (Paris: Gallimard, 1949), 2: 476.

31. Montesquieu, *The Spirit of the Laws*, trans. and eds. Anne M. Cohler, Basia Carolyn Miller, and Harold Samuel Stone (Cambridge, UK: Cambridge Univ. Press, 1989), 231. "augmente leur ressort, et favorise le retour du sang des extrémités vers le cœur. Il diminue la longueur de ces mêmes fibres; il augmente donc encore par là leur force." Montesquieu, *De l'Esprit des lois*, 474.

32. *ENC*, 3: 23. "une perception particulière ou une modification de notre âme."

33. *ENC*, 5: 651. "ENERGIE, FORCE, synon. (Gramm.) Nous ne considérerons ici ces mots qu'en tant qu'ils s'appliquent au discours . . . . Il semble qu'*énergie* dit encore plus que force; & qu'*énergie* s'applique principalement aux discours qui peignent, & au caractère du style. On peut dire d'un orateur qu'il joint la force du raisonnement à l'*énergie* des expressions. On dit aussi une peinture *énergique*, & des images fortes."

34. *ENC*, 7: 109–10. "a été transporté du simple au figuré;" "toutes les parties du corps qui sont en movement;" "les questions problématiques."

35. *ENC*, 7: 110. "[l]a force de l'éloquence n'est pas seulement une suite de raisonnemens justes & vigoureux, qui subsisteroient avec la sécheresse; cette force demande de l'embonpoint, des images frappantes, des termes énergiques."

36. Reill, *Vitalizing Nature in the Enlightenment*, 81–82.

37. Peter France, "Lumières, politesse, énergie," *L'Histoire de la rhétorique dans l'Europe moderne, 1450–1950*, ed. Marc Fumaroli (Paris: Presses Univ. de France, 1999), 980. On the rhetorical concept of enargeia in Antiquity, see Perrine Galand-Hallyn, *Le reflet des fleurs: Description et métalangage poétique d'Homère à la Renaissance* (Genève: Droz, 1994), 36–49; and Elena Russo, *Styles of Enlightenment: Taste, Politics, and Authorship in Eighteenth-Century France* (Baltimore, MD: Johns Hopkins Univ. Press, 2007), 145–46.

38. Michel Delon, *L'Idée d'énergie en France au tournant des Lumières (1770–1820)* (Paris: Presses Univ. de France, 1988), 36–37.

39. Stalnaker writes that "Buffon changed the terms of the eighteenth-century debate on the relationship between poetry and painting. In particular, he championed prose over poetry as a superior vehicle for visual representation, claiming that verse curtailed the writer's ability to paint. . . . To the extent that it imposed no artificial constraints on the writer, prose was more permeable to the qualities of nature. It allowed the writer to develop a natural style, which reflected the actual progression of his thoughts and perceptions rather than arbitrary formal rules." Stalnaker, *The Unfinished Enlightenment*, 64. Michel Delon echoes this thought: "[l]'énergie devient une catégorie fondamentale du jugement littéraire et assure une prééminence de la prose." ("[e]nergy becomes a fundamental category of literary judgment and insures the preeminence of prose.") Delon, *L'Idée d'énergie en France*, 131.

40. Stalnaker, "Painting Life," 221.

41. *HN*, 12: iii. "un ouvrage perpétuellement vivant, un ouvrier sans cesse actif, qui sait tout employer, qui travaillant d'après soi-même, toujours sur le même fonds, bien loin de l'épuiser le rend inépuisable: le temps, l'espace et la matière sont ses moyens, l'Univers son objet, le mouvement et la vie son but."

42. *HN*, 12: v-vi. "l'édifice du monde;" "des millions de globes opaques, [qui] circulans autour des premiers, . . . composent l'ordre et l'architecture mouvante [de l'univers]."

43. While in the "Second discours" (1749) the heat of the sun had been important in the formation of the planets, Buffon did not attribute much importance to this heat in his discussion of the geographical history of the earth in the same essay. Rather, he ascribed the formation of the Earth's surface to the movement of water over time. In the 1760s, after reading Mairan's work, he began to connect the history of the Earth with that of fire, namely from volcanoes.

44. Jean-Jacques Dortous de Mairan, "Nouvelles recherches sur la cause générale du chaud en été et du froid en hiver," *Histoire de l'Académie royale des sciences, Année MDCCLXV, avec les Mémoires de Mathématique & de Physique pour la même Année* (Paris: Imprimerie Royale, 1768), 143–266. Jacques Roger discusses this work in *Buffon*, 508–9. Buffon wrote of De Mairan's findings in "De la Lumière, de la Chaleur et du Feu," *Histoire naturelle, générale et particulière: Supplément*, 1: 32–33. The supplementary volumes of the *Histoire naturelle* are henceforth cited as *HNS*.

45. On Buffon's experiments, see Roger, *Buffon*, 517–18; and Lucien Leclaire, "L'*Histoire naturelle des minéraux* ou Buffon géologue universaliste," *Buffon 88: Actes du colloque international* (Paris-Montbard-Dijon, 14–22 juin 1988), eds. Jean-Claude Beaune, Serge Benoit, Jean Gayon, Jacques Roger, Deris Woronoff (Paris: Vrin, 1992), 355–65. Buffon also wrote of these experiments in "Des verres primitifs," *Histoire naturelle des minéraux*, 1: 17–29.

46. *HNS*, 1: 1–2. "forces primitives, celle qui cause la pesanteur, et celle qui produit la chaleur;" "au moyen du ressort."

47. *HNS*, 1: 4–5. "une force expansive;" "du centre à la circonférence;" "de la circonférence au centre."

48. *HNS*, 1: 15. "ce sont pour la Nature deux instrumens de même espèce, ou plutôt ce n'est que le même instrument qu'elle manie dans deux sens opposés."

49. *HNS*, 1: 18. "la lumière, . . . la chaleur et le feu ne sont que des manières d'être de la matière commune; qu'il n'existe en un mot qu'une seule force et une seule matière toujours prête à s'attirer ou à se repousser." On Buffon's construction of the universe through the equilibration of opposing forces, see Roger, *Buffon*, 510–12, and Jean Svagelski, *L'Idée de compensation en France, 1750–1850* (Paris: L'Hermès, 1981), 191–94.

50. On the structure and narration of historical time in the Enlightenment, see Jean-Marie Goulemot, *Le Règne de l'histoire. Discours historiques et révolutions, XVIIᵉ-XVIIIᵉ siècle* (Paris: Albin Michel, 1996).

51. *HNS*, 5: 240–41. "toute la Terre doit être plus froide aujourd'hui qu'elle ne l'étoit il y a deux mille ans; or la tradition semble nous prouver le contraire;" "Les Gaules et la Germanie nourrissoient des élans, des loups-cerviers, des ours et d'autres animaux qui se sont retirés depuis dans les pays septentrionaux; cette progression est bien différente de celle que vous leur supposez du Nord au Midi. D'ailleurs l'histoire nous apprend que tous les ans la rivière de Seine étoit ordinairement glacée pendant une partie de l'hiver; ces faits ne paroissent-ils pas être directement opposés au prétendu refroidissement successif du globe? Ils le seroient, je l'avoue, si la France et l'Allemagne d'aujourd'hui étoient semblables à la Gaule et à la Germanie; si l'on n'eût pas abattu les forêts, desséché les marais, contenu les torrens, dirigé les fleuves et défriché toutes les terres trop couvertes et surchargées de débris même de leurs productions." An important critical edition of the *Époques*, with a comparative analysis of the manuscripts and published text, is *Les Époques de la Nature*, ed. Jacques Roger, Mémoires du Muséum National d'Histoire Naturelle, Série C, Tome X (Paris: Éditions du Muséum, 1962). A new English translation was published after this article was completed: Buffon, *The Epochs of Nature*, ed. and trans. Anne-Sophie Milon, Jan Zalasiewicz, and Mateusz Zalasiewicz (Chicago, IL: Univ. of Chicago Press, 2018).

52. *HNS*, 5: 244–46. "autant de petits foyers de chaleur" that "répandent de la chaleur"; plants "ne produisent que de l'humidité froide"; "qui lui convient," becoming the "maître de l'élément du feu, qu'il peut augmenter et propager à son gré."

53. *HNS*, 5: 244. "ne peut ni saisir ni communiquer."

54. *HNS*: 5: 236–37. "[L'homme] a suivi les leçons de la Nature, profité de ses exemples, employé ses moyens, et choisi dans son immensité tous les objets qui pouvoient lui servir ou lui plaire. Par son intelligence, les animaux ont été apprivoisés, subjugués, domptés, réduits à lui obéir à jamais; par ses travaux, les marais ont été desséchés, les fleuves contenues, leurs cataractes effacées, les forêts éclaircies, les landes cultivées; . . . enfin la face entière de la Terre porte aujourd'hui l'empreinte de la puissance de l'homme."

55. *HNS*, 5: 246. "Heureuses les contrées où tous les élémens de la température se trouvent balancés, et assez avantageusement combinés pour n'opérer que de bons effets!"

56. The expression "une Nature nouvelle" is from Buffon, *Histoire naturelle*, 12: xii–xiii.

57. *HNS*, 5: 254. "enfin il a reconnu que sa vraie gloire est la science, et la paix son vrai bonheur."

DEVOTION AND
OTHER PASSIONS

Silence and the
Passions in Rousseau's *Julie*

ADAM SCHOENE

As a remote haven of shared harmonious coexistence and transparency, the Clarens, Switzerland community of Jean-Jacques Rousseau's *Julie, ou la Nouvelle Héloïse* (1761) has been interpreted by some as representing an ideal form of society, while others deem it a dystopia. *Lettres de deux amans, habitans d'une petite ville au pied des Alpes,* the second portion of the title of *Julie* (and the title of the original edition), evokes the alpine setting of Clarens, a village on the shores of Lake Geneva, near where Rousseau himself spent his youth. This title emphasizes the passionate love between Julie and her former tutor St. Preux, around which the initial half of the story revolves, preceding Julie's marriage to the nobleman Wolmar, arranged by her father the Baron d'Étange, who disapproves of the middle class rank of St. Preux. Julie and Wolmar raise a family at the Wolmar estate in Clarens, which is often read as a political microcosm, with Julie herself arguing that it is an imitation of the order of political society.[1] Yet there is frequent debate over the contours of participation within this space and over the distinction between domestic and political *family*, with the two often detrimentally collapsed.

While there is a tendency to align Rousseau's avowed depiction of the feminine with the family, a space of private domesticity, and the masculine with the state, a public realm comprised solely of male citizens, recent commentators have offered more nuanced studies that complicate this opposition. Elizabeth Wingrove suggests that Rousseau makes the nondeliberative, unutterable electoral image of the general will eloquent through his fictional depictions of women, insisting on their agency to offer an alternative version of political participation, and Lori Marso similarly sees Rousseau's female protagonists as offering a broader version of citizenship that ultimately undermines the gender boundaries he elsewhere seems to construct.[2] Speaking directly to the political implications of Clarens, Juliet Flower MacCannell analyzes it as an ironic representation of a patriarchal order based on the suppression of Julie's female desire, arguing that Clarens is best understood not as a utopic ideal, but rather as a critique of a fundamental fantasy of the "Regime of the Brother," as "farcical repetition of the dream of patriarchy, figured as the utopia of Clarens—the place where desire is never admitted."[3] Andrew Billing likewise perceives Clarens as a site where Rousseau attacks despotism by imitating its oppressive elements in order to distinguish between paternal and political power, situating the difference between family and state as an essential tenet of his critique, yet maintaining the affective relational aspect of an *adoptive* version of the family as what is most political in Clarens, with the state acting as a surrogate parent, educating its citizens by inculcating an affective patriotic sentiment.[4] Julie's participation in this process may be understood as problematizing the distinction between the domestic space as feminine and the public as masculine by feminizing the political as it is revealed in the contractual relations of Clarens. While following these readings in considering the space of Clarens as emancipatory in its incorporation of Julie in the governance of a private sphere that is simultaneously public, I will shift the focus to explore the politics Rousseau enacts with his silent tableau of friendship, suggesting that it is through the force of this silence that Rousseau reconfigures the social order.

I begin by exploring an ineffable scene of camaraderie, the *matinée à l'anglaise* in Book V of *Julie*, which I interpret as a paradigmatic example of how we might read Rousseau's mute eloquence politically, especially if considered in relation to the tacit nature of the general will of *Du contrat social* (1762). I then consider the transformation from passionate love to friendship between Julie and St. Preux as beyond merely a linear movement, drawing upon Jacques Derrida's notion of *aimance* to suggest that the friendship Rousseau proposes holds political force as well, in its unique power to transgress and reconfigure previously prohibited stations, as with the shift in sovereignty to the formerly subjugated people found in *Du contrat social*. Derrida's *Politiques de l'amitié* (1994) illustrates the centrality of friendship to political thought in its capacity to combat tyranny, while simultaneously revealing the tyrannical risks within friendship. Rousseau also captures this aporia in the matinée and in the multifaceted relationships of *Julie*, and I will argue that in his alignment of friendship with silence as depicted in the space of Clarens, he presents a politics that subverts the androcentric model upon which the Wolmar estate initially seems to be built, therefore offering an avenue towards a more inclusive form of democracy.

The arrival of St. Preux, Julie's former tutor turned lover, to the bucolic Clarens represents a radical shift in their relationship, which is overseen by her husband Wolmar. Born into a lower station in life than the aristocratic Julie, middle-class St. Preux separates himself from her in an effort to quell their illicit romance and to protect her virtue, yet his journey around the world brings him back to her years later and to a community modeled after his own sentimental principles. "J'y mène une vie de mon goût," writes St. Preux to his friend Milord Édouard of his first impressions of Clarens, "j'y trouve une société selon mon cœur."[5] This society after the heart could refer to St. Preux's affection for Julie herself as well as to her governance role in establishing a compassionate community that he deeply admires. Clarens is characterized as much by its heart and shared spirit of benevolent goodwill as by its complete transparency, as St. Preux's return is by the invitation of Julie and her upper-class husband Wolmar, who is fully aware of the formerly passionate relationship between his wife and St. Preux. Often compared to the *Du contrat social* figure of the legislator, Wolmar is presented as quasi-divine, and of superior intelligence, seeing all of man's passions yet experiencing none, and he is thus able to read into Julie and St. Preux's hearts and to help them "reform" their sentiments.[6] In noting that it is the former Julie d'Étange rather than Julie Wolmar with whom St. Preux is in love, Wolmar considers it possible for this reformation to succeed: "Qu'ils brûlent plus ardemment que jamais l'un pour l'autre et qu'il ne règne plus entre eux qu'un honnête attachement; qu'ils soient toujours amans et ne soient plus qu'amis."[7] It is this unconventional project that Wolmar oversees, and while his intervention has been interpreted as noble by some critics and despotic by others, I will instead explore the silent force of the *petit ménage* that results, as captured most acutely within the matinée à l'anglaise.

A striking moment in which Julie, St. Preux, and Wolmar share a morning of silent communication and reciprocal transparency at the Wolmar estate in Clarens, the matinée à l'anglaise might also offer richer depth and clarity to Rousseau's political vision. Breakfast is described by Julie as a meal of friendship, one of the few moments when we are actually permitted to be solely what we are. It is important to note the exclusions that condition this gathering, as to create an intimate circle, les étrangers, les valets, and les importuns are left out.[8] Yet the silence of the matinée is benevolent and intensely expressive for those who do partake in it, exceeding the capacity of language to encapsulate the deep sense of redemptive harmony that it alone conveys. St. Preux describes this scene in a letter to Milord Édouard:

> Après six jours perdus aux entretiens frivoles des gens indifférents, nous avons passé aujourd'hui une matinée à l'angloise, réunis et dans le silence, goûtant à la fois le plaisir d'être ensemble et la douceur du recueillement. Que les délices de cet état sont connues de peu de gens ! Je n'ai vu personne en France en avoir la moindre idée. La conversation des amis ne tarit jamais, disent-ils. Il est vrai, la langue fournit un babil facile aux attachemens médiocres. Mais l'amitié, Milord, l'amitié ! Sentiment vif et céleste, quels discours sont dignes de toi?[9]

There are certain religious resemblances in the scene of the matinée, such as the fact that it begins "after six days," evoking the same length of time as the biblical story of creation, and in the description of a friendship of a "celestial" nature.[10] As with the positive role for silence in this scene of friendship, Rousseau's political conception of the general will similarly effaces power asymmetries and difference by bringing the people together to feel it in silence. In *Du contrat social*, he writes: "Si, quand le peuple suffisamment informé délibère, les Citoyens n'avoient aucune communication entre eux, du grand nombre de petites différences résulteroit toujours la volonté générale, et la délibération seroit toujours bonne."[11] The matinée may also be considered as emulating an ideal political state for Rousseau, as it likewise balances liberty and interdependence, with the participants gathered in a small group of kindred hearts, yet silently absorbed in their own activities, like the people of *Du contrat social*. While Rousseau often appears to relegate women to the private sphere, the matinée places Julie at center stage, serving as a guide in how to love, not solely as a virtuous wife and mother in the domestic sphere but also as a friend. Christie McDonald has noted that friendship becomes the basis for all relationships in Clarens, with silence as its language; the fact that the morning is spent in the English manner is furthermore in critical contrast with the French (and most notably Parisian) style of alienating babble that does not convey anything authentic, as the matinée is a form of communication that is based not upon words but upon sentiment.[12]

The reference to Milord Édouard, who is in England, draws yet another friend into this intimate circle, thus extending the boundaries of friendship, or of the general will in relation to politics. This aesthetic expansion of the general will is evident in the introduction of a foreign dimension, offering a glimpse of something beyond the purely nation-based model like that instilled within the people through the ineffable influence of the *Du contrat social* legislator, possessor of a superior intelligence who employs the influence of persuasion instead of oratory eloquence, inculcating an affective patriotic sentiment within the people. This bond unites them as compatriots, and it may thus be viewed as kindred to that of friendship, but its scope is limited to the nation; Rousseau is suspicious of the unmoored cosmopolitan sentiment like that he perceives in the superficial and corrupt posturing of the elite and in theater spectators whose sympathy may be extended to the characters on stage yet detached from and neglected in the world beyond. His advocacy of the kind of humanitarian principles that encompass the true spirit of cosmopolitanism is nevertheless evident at certain moments of aesthetic description, and although he initially envisions *Du contrat social* as part of a larger project concerning a network of nations, he limits its scope out of fear of a greater potential scale of violence that may arise.[13]

As *Du contrat social* remains ultimately rooted in national patriotic bonds and women appear absent from the public sphere (as in the *Lettre à M. d'Alembert sur les spectacles* of 1758), both Milord Édouard's role as the distant friend and Julie's relinquishing of her central place in Clarens in dying to save her son are absences that haunt the text, unsettling the same political and gender boundaries that Rousseau seems to put into place. While St. Preux's tender rapport with Milord Édouard appears to conform to the fraternal role of the brother in the androcentric structure of friendship, his English background challenges the nation-based model of fraternity upon which Rousseau's politics is constructed, revealing a threatening and foreign element to the figure of the friend, as I will further explore in relation to Derrida's alignment of friendship and politics.[14] Milord Édouard's absence from the petit ménage allows its passionate story to unfold in the silent English manner, so it could on the one hand be read as merely a textual device, but as his own love story is omitted from the narrative and included as a supplement to the text, it could also be understood as further accentuating the nationalistic boundaries that haunt Rousseau's conception of the general will.

Julie similarly threatens to tear the fabric of the fraternal order by reigning alongside (or above) her husband over the domestic economy of Clarens and in establishing a relation that is based upon friendship with her former lover. Wolmar is compelled to speak about the positive nature of friendship's bond after a moment of silence, as he clasps together the hands of Julie and St. Preux: "Notre amitié commence; en voici le cher lien; qu'elle soit indissoluble."[15] This could capture Wolmar's magnanimity and intensity of emotion, but it could also be interpreted as a form of decree, revealing a despotic dimension in that he does not seem to give Julie and St. Preux the choice to determine their own status. We might read this moment in line with the paradoxical nature of Rousseau's *Du contrat social* assertion of citizens being forced to be free when they are constrained to obey the general will. This despotic possibility is later reflected in the gravity of Julie's deathbed pronouncement on the more oppressive side to silence: "Rien ne fait tant de mal aux femmes que le silence !"[16] Yet, as with the general will, there is also new political freedom that emanates from silence, if only as a fictional tableau. Before returning to the matinée in order to analyze its silent dimension in relation to the broader politics of Clarens in correspondence with the tacit workings of the general will of *Du contrat social*, I will briefly turn to Derrida to explore his conception of the political nature of friendship, which is also of relevance to *Julie*.

Like Rousseau, Derrida sees political potential in the aporetic nature of friendship, and he thus offers further grounds to better understand the emancipatory silent eloquence of *Julie*. In *Politiques de l'amitié*, Derrida presents friendship as a political problem, beginning from the death of the friend in the apostrophe within "O mes amis, il n'y a nul amy," which he situates as a performative contradiction in its lodging of the other or the enemy in the heart of the friend.[17] Friendship is unstable and unpredictable, as the love of the neighbor may transform into lust for possession, and the voice of the friend could likewise resemble a menacing spectral appeal, revealing an even deathly element in friendship in its ability to consume the self with its demands. Yet friendship may also combat despotism, as at its core it is an *act* of loving, and whereas the enemy is essential for theorizing the political for someone like Carl Schmitt, Derrida challenges this discourse by substituting *hostis* for enemy, emphasizing the guest element of the etymology over that of a purely adversarial antagonism.[18] Friendship is political for Derrida in its potential for a "democracy to come," and it is similarly threatened internally by its own logic, as it is unable to resolve its contradictions; yet, it is this autoimmunity, or prospect of destroying itself from within, that also opens new possibilities within friendship and democracy, allowing space for fluctuation and contestation. Derrida illuminates the political genealogy of friendship by tracing the history of his opening quotation, "O mes amis, il n'y a nul amy," connecting it with Aristotle's claim that good lawgivers have shown more concern for friendship than for justice, and with Montaigne's notion of a sovereign friendship in the *Essais*. Taking issue with both Aristotle and Montaigne's exclusion of women from this realm, Derrida offers a radical revision of this traditional fraternal conception of friendship, employing it to underscore the intertwined nature of sovereignty and democracy, as well as the conflict between them in relation to a plurality of people within the single entity of a nation. Derrida's concerns thus closely intersect with Rousseau's, and both establish a foundational role for silence within their politics of friendship and democracy.

It is through Nietzsche that Derrida aligns friendship most closely with silence, drawing upon *Menschliches, Allzumenschliches* (1878) (*Human, All Too Human*) to reveal the destructive nature of speech, which could be a refrain of Rousseau. Nietzsche's rejoinder to "O my friends, there is no friend" is that it is an error or deception that leads us into becoming friends, and that we have learned to keep silent in order to remain friends. Derrida's response is that friendship is preserved by silence, with friends protecting themselves from its illusion by remaining quiet about the truth of the "bottomless bottom" upon which it is founded.[19] This uncertain and shifting ground from which friendship is born parallels the foundational emptiness of the *demos*, the nothingness from which it derives its power, and Derrida seems to channel Rousseau in aligning silence with the social bond.[20] Yet Derrida's tacit agreement reference also invokes an inversion like that evident in Diderot's notion of the *pacte tacite* in *Le Neveu de Rameau* (1805):

> Et comme les amis savent cette vérité de la vérité (la garde de
> ce qui ne se garde pas), il vaut mieux qu'ils gardent le silence
> ensemble. Comme d'un commun accord. Accord tacite cependant
> par lequel les séparés sont ensemble sans cesser d'être ce qu'ils
> sont destinés à être – et sans doute le sont-ils alors plus que
> jamais : dissociés, solitarisés, singularisés, constitués en altérités
> monadiques (*vereinsamt*).[21]

While this atomistic distance seems closest to Diderot's ironic formulation of the social contract as an animalistic pacte tacite, it also evokes the tension between particular interests and the general will inherent in Rousseau, and the foundational paradox dramatized in the figure of the legislator, who aims to transform human nature, *d'instituer un peuple*. Whereas Nietzsche rejects social contract theory as the reflection of a slave morality which aims to "seduce the strong and convert them to the morality of the weak," for Rousseau the silence of the demos signifies a virtuous order in which sovereignty expresses itself as collective autonomy.[22] Speech represents a menace to this order, threatening to divide the people by revealing the secret underlying force of contractual foundation upon a "bottomless bottom."

In addition to Derrida's shared political alignment of silence and friendship, his conception of *aimance* helps to shed further light upon *Julie*, as Étienne Balibar illustrates in *Citoyen sujet* (2011).[23] Returning to the context of Clarens, we might consider the initially amorous relationship between St. Preux and Julie as the error or deception that Derrida describes, as the "open secret" upon which the bond of friendship is initiated at Clarens by the legislator-like Wolmar, who forces them to be free (of their forbidden love) and to enter into friendship by conjoining their hands in the gardens where this love first blossoms. Much like the legislator aims to transform human nature, Wolmar too seeks to alter the sentiments of St. Preux and Julie. Yet the transformation that occurs is far from a simple shift from passionate love into friendship, and it is here where Derrida's conscription of *aimance* is beneficial. A term coined in 1927 by French linguist and psychoanalyst Edouard Pinchon, aimance initially served as a means to designate a concept of object attraction that would not necessarily entail sexual satisfaction. For Derrida, this third term that is neither love nor friendship helps to identify "an indeterminate affect that circulates among modalities of love and friendship on a spectrum of sentiments that defy description or enumeration."[24] Balibar considers aimance in this respect as somewhat parallel to Freud's theorization of the category of pulsion, or drive, with its neutralization of the active/passive opposition in desire, which may too be relevant for thinking of Rousseau's conception of the general will, with a present, active democracy, but one that is also silent. Returning to the matinée, I will expand upon Balibar's treatment of aimance in relation to the passions and the new configurations of friendship that develop among Julie, St. Preux, Wolmar, and Julie's cousin Claire to further illuminate how Rousseau's silent experiment in *Julie* also serves a political function.

In the midst of the matinée while Julie, St. Preux, and Wolmar are lost in their own silent reveries, yet together in each other's company, the scene is punctuated by a role reversal which underscores Julie's governance, elevating her to a position that is neither purely romantic nor domestic. The children enter the space along with chambermaid Fanchon, and maintaining stereotypical gender roles, the women embroider as the men read the gazette and speak of the king, when Julie mentions that she envies sovereigns only the process of making themselves beloved.[25] St. Preux describes Wolmar's response, which serves to reveal a transition of roles:

> N'enviez rien, lui a dit son mari d'un ton qu'il m'eut dû laisser prendre; il y a longtems que nous sommes tous vos sujets. A ce mot, son ouvrage est tombé de ses mains; elle a tourné la tête, et jetté sur son digne époux un regard si touchant, si tendre, que j'en ai tressailli moi-même. Elle n'a rien dit: qu'eut-elle dit qui valut ce regard? Nos yeux se sont aussi rencontrés. J'ai senti, à la manière dont son mari m'a serré la main, que la même émotion nous gagnoit tous trois, et que la douce influence de cette âme expansive agissoit autour d'elle et triomphoit de l'insensibilité même. . . . C'est dans ces dispositions qu'a commencé le silence dont je vous parlois: vous pouvez juger qu'il n'étoit pas de froideur et d'ennui. Il n'étoit interrompu que par le petit manege des enfans; encore, aussi-tôt que nous avons cessé de parler, ont-ils modéré par imitation leur caquet, comme craignant de troubler le recueillement universel.[26]

Wolmar and St. Preux affirm Julie's reign over them, and in aligning herself with the king, she redistributes his sovereignty, with love and friendship as her guiding precepts.[27] Julie's silent and persuasive force in solidifying these bonds is evocative of Derrida's concept of aimance in that it exceeds both love and friendship, with a driving energy that founds new intersubjective possibilities, replacing particular interests with a stronger desire for the general will. Julie displaces Wolmar as legislator, dropping her needlework, as Wolmar and St. Preux clasp hands in union, a reversal of the earlier moment between Julie and St. Preux in the gardens. Julie also supplants St. Preux as tutor, as Wolmar, St. Preux, and the children now become her disciples. Claire's daughter Henriette corrects the boys' errors as they read a book together, mirroring the men's misreading of the gazette; this suggests a similar ascendancy over them, and a role in carrying forth the message of love taught by Julie, her surrogate mother whom she will further channel and incarnate after Julie's death. The children's mimicry of this silence demonstrates its originary and enduring resonance as well as the advancement of Julie beyond merely a passionate or familial role. Her ability to purvey a silent force to unite those around her beyond their own particular interests reveals the centrality of the message of love at the heart of the matinée.

Claire similarly affirms Julie's strength with her claim that "ma Julie, tu es faite pour régner," and their connection further underscores the unique and political nature of the friendship among these inséparables.[28] In addition to Julie's fostering bonds of friendship with her former lover and between St. Preux and her husband, her relationship with Claire offers a model of female friendship that lies in stark contrast to the male-dominated political tradition outlined by Derrida; *Julie* provides a response to another question that Derrida raises, that of the role of the sister, or why women are left out. Julie and Claire's friendship serves to address the exclusion of women from the realm of political friendship, and one indication of their kindred, transparent hearts is evoked within the very name Claire, which means clear, in close relation to the Clarens lakeside setting, as Jean Starobinksi has perceived.[29] Alongside one another nearly throughout the novel, Claire and Julie describe themselves as sharing one soul, and decide to raise their families together after the death of Claire's husband, with Julie taking care of Henriette, and Claire overseeing the education of Julie's sons. After bearing close witness to Julie's earlier romance with St. Preux, Claire almost becomes romantically entangled with him herself, but remains true to her cousin, and even spends the night in bed with Julie shortly before her death, leading some commentators to speculate that they share an amorous relationship. My interest is more in how Claire and Julie's friendship could be understood as calling into question the foundations of the patriarchal model that Rousseau elsewhere seems to defend, and how we might interpret their relationship as dramatizing the social contract. This is perhaps most evident in Claire's proclamation:

> Ton empire est le plus absolu que je connoisse : il s'étend jusque
> sur les volontés, et je l'éprouve plus que personne. . . . Ton cœur
> vivifie tous ceux qui l'environnent, et leur donne pour ainsi
> dire un nouvel être dont ils sont forcés de lui faire hommage,
> puisqu'ils ne l'auraient point eu sans lui. . . . Est-il possible de
> te voir longtemps, sans se sentir pénétrer l'âme des charmes de
> la vertu et des douceurs de l'amitié?[30]

Julie's silent empire may be viewed as political in that she is helping to construct a social bond, psychically structuring the people around her heart and altering human nature by creating a new communal being that extends beyond their particular wills. There is nevertheless a despotic element that remains within Julie's empire, implied by this word, and in the fact that the people are forced to pay tribute to her; yet, she has displaced force with love and replaced the paternalistic reign of the king. Although Julie has only male children, her friendship with Claire enables her to become a surrogate mother to Henriette, who embodies a future female citizen with a unique capacity to reign, or even a new version of Julie, already herself a new Héloïse.

Julie takes the struggle of the earlier Héloïse one step further through the legacy of friendship that she instills in Clarens, which carries forth after her death. The Héloïse of the twelfth-century letters also has a love affair and maintains epistolary correspondence with her tutor Abélard, exhibiting resistance to established oppressive orders against women. Peggy Kamuf aligns Julie's story with that of Héloïse, who contests the institution of marriage and the space of the convent, suggesting that Julie is similarly "positioned at the juncture of one social order which can no longer sustain its claim to legitimate power and another which must succeed to that claim without violence."[31] Julie's nonviolent resistance is evident in her combat with her father, who employs physical violence against her when she confesses her love for St. Preux; although Julie respects her father's wishes by instead marrying Wolmar, she combats the despotic patriarchal hierarchy without violence by generating a community based upon love and friendship. This community both enables her to maintain her love for St. Preux, as well as to have a daughter in Henriette to carry forth her legacy, thanks to Claire, to whom her heart remains perhaps most intimately attached.

As with the religious background of Héloïse, Julie becomes increasingly absorbed in spiritual education as her death approaches, and beyond embodying a new Héloïse, she could even be viewed as a new Christ-like figure whose message is love. In stark contrast to previous models of binary pairings in love or friendship, like that in the tale of the original Héloïse, Julie's relationships and her legacy are based upon an equalizing network of relations that bond the people of Clarens together around her message, enabling the reciprocal participation of everyone. Her reign appears democratic to a certain degree, but also evokes the menace that Derrida identifies within the silence of friendship, which becomes a deathly silence in the final lines of *Julie*, as she beckons Claire to join her, to carry forth the sacred bonds of friendship within a world that eternally transcends all language. The image of the Elysium that was once a garden of Eden for the passions reveals its Elysian side, along with glimpses of a "democracy to come," in the friendships born of aimance at Clarens.

Clarens represents a dramatization of the general will as psychical polity, with friendship offering a means to explore how individuals reconcile their own interests with the greater community, which extends beyond Julie, St. Preux, Wolmar, and Claire, and into the broader Clarens population.[32] Clarens is not an egalitarian society, as it is broken into different classes, and although the Wolmar estate is silently organized around a system of openness and transparency, there remains some separation between private and public society, as well as certain power asymmetries, with spaces that are off limits to the servants.[33] Much like friendship operates as a liberating constraint in regulating the passions, there is also a form of restriction exerted upon the Clarens servants, which St. Preux describes in comparison to the limitations within a republic: "Dans la République on retient les citoyens par des mœurs, des principes, de la vertu; mais comment contenir des domestiques, des mercenaires, autrement que par la contrainte et la gêne? Tout l'art du maître est de cacher cette gêne sous le voile du plaisir ou de l'intérêt, en sorte qu'ils pensent vouloir tout ce qu'on les oblige de faire."[34] A characteristic move of Rousseau's, this hidden coercion is evident within the psychological attachment of the Clarens servants to their masters, Wolmar and Julie, whose behavior and virtue they seek to emulate, which enables them to live in concord with one another; in order to truly love and to live like their masters, the servants must also love one another equally.[35] While classes exist within Clarens, and power enables the masters coercively to shape the climate of the community, this difference is essentially effaced through the love that the servants share for their masters and for one another.[36] St. Preux likens this love to the Christian charity that is merely spoken of in church, yet truly experienced at Clarens without being articulated.[37] As with the silence of the matinée, this love of the Clarens domestics is unspoken, but silently felt, as the servants emulate the equalizing and transparent climate within their own interactions, often rendering services for one another in secret, internalizing a system of self-governance based upon virtue.[38]

While a silent demos formulated around collective desire creates something new and beyond the strictures of a sovereign head or coupling, as within the heightened friendship read through the lens of Derrida's *aimance* and enacted within *Julie*, its forceful potential carries a threat as well, one that erodes the boundaries between self and other. Clarens is constructed around the goodwill of Julie and Wolmar, but they have screened all of the servants together in order to avoid bringing in those whose presence suggests any antipathy might result, raising the question as to what comprises the criteria for such an assessment. Whereas such screening might be possible within the private realm, displacing citizens from the public sphere based upon the potential to create discord may be prejudicial. While particular interests are allowed to coexist within the context of the general will, is anything prospectively lost by its silent, equalizing force? Considering the general will as a democratic death drive is helpful for envisioning a politics of fluctuation and plasticity, but one that is also founded upon a coercive force, casting a shadow that may haunt the people in its destructive threat to the self, subordinating individual voices to a shared feeling. Just as Derrida's aimance suggests something beyond love or friendship, in the context of *Julie* it also entails sublimating a part of the self, an act that may prove beneficial or harmful. St. Preux appears to gain only a greater sense of self within the space of Clarens; however, Julie dies as a result of the act of saving her son from drowning, so she may be seen as losing her self while simultaneously sustaining life in the community that she has built.[39]

Clarens may be considered as a political testing ground for Rousseau, incarnating the love and virtue of Julie and the silent, sacred bonds of friendship that she instills within the people, but it is also a community that must endure in her absence. The deathly finale extends the model of friendship embodied by the matinée beyond Julie's family and friends into the greater Clarens community, while destroying its very foundation by converting Julie into a sort of heteronomic figure, similar in ways to the legislator, whose message of love lives on within them.[40] As Julie and St. Preux learn to reconfigure their passions into something more inclusive beyond Clarens, the people must continue to reform their own passions to serve a purpose that is greater than their particular interests. Clarens stands as a space between the state of nature and the corrupted Parisian world of artifice and vain chatter, with its silence as an antidote to potentially intractable debate, and as a means of restoring the sentiment and feeling that may be lost within the misleading platitudes of language. Like the empty center of the address, Clarens possesses a silent and empty political center with the death of Julie, but one that perhaps offers a polity that endures, and the hope for a "democracy to come" within a new vision of friendship.[41]

Although women may not seem to hold an equal place with men in much of Rousseau's political writing, *Julie* reveals certain dimensions of his thought that privilege the female position as he adopts the perspectives of women by composing stirring letters written by them. The unparalleled success and acclaim of *Julie* among readers suggests a unique strength in the feminine voice, which Rousseau underscores in the power he attributes to Julie in the matinée. Julie and her surrogate daughter Henriette assume leadership positions above the men in this scene, accentuated by a silence that is affirmative in its commanding role as a benevolent and equalizing force. In aligning this silence with that of the demos of *Du contrat social*, I have sought to outline how it embodies something beyond love or friendship, in a kindred spirit to Derrida's notion of aimance, as a new popular sovereignty aligned with the psyche. Julie furthermore rewrites the politics of friendship in her relationships with St. Preux and Claire, forging bonds that transgress prescribed roles, reconfiguring the passions to construct purposeful social bonds around desire. Extending the political model of friendship beyond its past social inequalities, Clarens comes to embody a political microcosm for Rousseau's vision of the social contract, with Julie breathing life into this community, which is born as the demos around her love and sustained in her absence. Julie is exceptional as an agent producing general will of silence at Clarens, channeling the oppressive silencing of women under patriarchy into a more just system, albeit one that still contains elements of inequality and force. Clarens inevitably falls short of an egalitarian society; yet, Rousseau does channel a powerful female protagonist in Julie, who may be seen as haunting his political writing by transcending the very limits that he seems to prescribe, as other commentators have similarly articulated. I have aimed to build upon this claim to demonstrate how Julie coopts silence, employing it towards emancipatory ends. While the general will cannot be represented and does not possess a body with a mouth to express itself, Julie dramatizes its potential, feminizing it and underwriting it with desire reforged into a silent political bond of friendship that overwrites or suppresses an originary division in the community. As Julie is ultimately unable to live in Clarens, her spirit endures, along with the silent resonance of the matinée as a moment to further democratize by incorporating those who remain excluded.

NOTES

Special thanks to Diane Brown, Jason Frank, Mitchell Greenberg, Tracy McNulty, Neil Saccamano; and Marie-Claire Vallois as well as to the *SECC* editors and anonymous reviewers for their careful reading and helpful comments.

1. "L'ordre qu'il a mis dans sa maison est l'image de celui qui règne au fond de son âme, et semble imiter dans un petit ménage l'ordre établi dans le gouvernement du monde." Jean-Jacques Rousseau, *Julie, ou la Nouvelle Héloïse: lettres de deux amans habitans d'une petite ville au pied des Alpes,* in *Œuvres complètes,* Bernard Gagnebin and Marcel Raymond (Paris: Éditions Gallimard, 1961), 371. "The order he has brought into his house is the image of the one that prevails in his heart, and seems to imitate in a small houschold the order established in the governance of the earth." Jean-Jacques Rousseau, *Julie, or the New Heloise: Letters of Two Lovers Who Live in a Small Town at the Foot of the Alps* in *The Collected Writings of Rousseau,* vol. 2, ed. Roger D. Masters and Christopher Kelly, trans. Philip Stewart and Jean Vaché (Hanover, NH: Univ. Press of New England, 1997), 305–6. It is worth noting that Rousseau also at times claims the family should not be considered a model for the political order.

2. See Elizabeth Rose Wingrove, *Rousseau's Republican Romance* (Princeton, NJ: Princeton Univ. Press, 2000) and Lori Jo Marso, *(Un)Manly Citizens: Jean-Jacques Rousseau's and Germaine de Staël's Subversive Women* (Baltimore, MD: The Johns Hopkins University Press, 1999).

3. Juliet Flower MacCannell, *The Regime of the Brother: After the Patriarchy* (New York: Routledge, 1991), 89.

4. Andrew G. Billing, "Political and Domestic Economy in Rousseau's *Julie, ou la Nouvelle Héloïse,*" *Romanic Review* 100, no. 4 (2009), 473–91. Billing refers to political education in Rousseau as a process of metaphorical adoption, as the state must take over the duty of educating future citizens from their natural fathers, and become a surrogate or adoptive parent, substituting law for nature. The state, however, substitutes for the father by becoming like a mother, with its love embracing the children as a condition for patriotic sentiment and identification of citizens with the general will. The state functions as such to provide for and to conserve the liberty of its citizens and thus must take on the appearance of a nurturing mother.

5. Rousseau, *Julie, ou la Nouvelle Héloïse,* 441. "Here I lead a life to my liking, here I find a society after my heart." Rousseau, *Julie, or the New Heloise,* 363.

6. Fayçal Falaky draws one such vivid comparison in *Social Contract, Masochist Contract: Aesthetics of Freedom and Submission in Rousseau* (Albany, NY: SUNY Press, 2014), describing the legislator as, in many respects, "the carbon copy" of Wolmar, who exerts influence through "hidden and seemingly nonauthoritarian measures" (149–50).

7. Rousseau, *Julie, ou la Nouvelle Héloïse,* 508. "That they should burn more ardently than ever for each other, and that nothing more than an honest attachment should any longer prevail between them; they should still be lovers and be no longer but friends." Rousseau, *Julie, or the New Heloise,* 417.

8. "Les étrangers ne sont jamais admis le matin dans ma chambre, et déjeunent dans la leur. Le déjeuner est le repas des amis; les valets en sont exclus, les importuns ne s'y montrent point, on y dit tout ce qu'on pense, on y révèle tous ses secrets, on n'y contraint aucun de ses sentiments; on peut s'y livrer sans imprudence aux douceurs de la confiance et de la familiarité. C'est presque le seul moment où il soit permis d'être ce qu'on est; que ne dure-t-il toute la journée!" Rousseau, *Julie, ou la*

Nouvelle Héloïse, 488. "Outsiders are never admitted to my room in the morning and have breakfast in their own. Breakfast is the meal of friends; the house staff are excluded, the unwanted do not intrude; we say everything we think, we reveal all our secrets, we constrain none of our sentiments; there we can give in without imprudence to the satisfactions of confidence and intimacy. It is practically the only moment when we are permitted to be what we are; would it could last all day!" Rousseau, *Julie, or, the New Heloise*, 401.

9. Rousseau, *Julie, ou la Nouvelle Héloïse*, 557–58. "After six days wasted in frivolous discussions with indifferent people, we have today spent a morning in the English manner, gathered in silence, enjoying at once the pleasure of being together and the bliss of contemplation. How few people know the delights of that state! I saw no one in France who had the slightest notion of it. Conversation among friends never runs dry, they say. It is true, the tongue furnishes mediocre attachments with a facile babble. But friendship, Milord, friendship! Powerful and heavenly sentiment, what words are worthy of thee?" Rousseau, *Julie, or the New Heloise*, 456.

10. Philip Stewart also notes the potential religious significance of the fact that Rousseau always writes "St. Preux," in contrast to Saint Preux, making reference to a playfully fictive saint (Rousseau, *Julie, or the New Heloise*, xvii).

11. Jean-Jacques Rousseau, *Du contrat social, Œuvres complètes,* vol 3 ed. Bernard Gagnebin and Marcel Raymond (Paris: Éditions Gallimard, 1964), 371. "If, when an adequately informed people deliberates, the citizens were to have no communication among themselves, the general will would always result from the large number of small differences, and the deliberation would always be good." Jean-Jacques Rousseau, *On the Social Contract* in *Social Contract, Discourse on the Virtue Most Necessary for a Hero, Political Fragments, and Geneva Manuscript. The Collected Writings of Rousseau,* vol. 4, ed. and trans. Judith R. Bush, Roger D. Masters, and Christopher Kelly (Hanover, NH: Univ. Press of New England), 1994, 147–48. While this silent deliberation could on the one hand be viewed as stifling dissent, it could also be viewed more affirmatively as preventing the possibility of misleading rhetorical appeals in order to sway the debate. Rousseau also makes it clear that the lack of communication prevents the formation of what James Madison later defines as "factions" in *The Federalist Papers* (Federalist No. 10).

12. Christie Vance [McDonald] describes the sentimental language of Clarens in relation to the artificial one of Paris in "*La Nouvelle Héloïse*: The Language of Paris" *Yale French Studies* 45 (1970), 127–36, 134: "The exquisite silence of this small society completely opposes the inane babble which St. Preux describes at the dinner party in Paris. Far from being a measure of friendship, language in Paris tends to alienate men from any real communication. In Clarens, silence becomes the true language of friendship—and friendship is the basis for all relationships in this ideal society." See also Christie McDonald, "From Rousseau to Occupy: Imagining a More Equal World," in *Rousseau and Dignity: Art Serving Humanity*, ed. Julia V. Douthwaite (Notre Dame, IN: Univ. of Notre Dame Press, 2017), 132–55.

13. As Helena Rosenblatt notes, by removing himself from society as he increasingly does in his life, Rousseau could also be seen as a sort of *étranger*, or stranger, *everywhere* in the world, offering lessons to all people and paradoxically

serving as the truest cosmopolitan of all. See Helena Rosenblatt, "Rousseau, the Anticosmopolitan?" *Daedalus* 137, no. 3 (Summer 2008): 59–67. See also Neil Saccamano, "'Savage Patriotism,' Justice and Cosmopolitics in Smith and Rousseau," in *Rousseau and Adam Smith: Ethics, Politics, Economics*, ed. Maria Pia Paganelli, Dennis C. Rasmussen, and Craig Smith (Edinburgh: Edinburgh Univ. Press, 2018), 284–312.

14. "Il porte ma propre mort et, d'une certaine façon, il est le seul à la porter, cette propre mort de moi ainsi d'avance expropriée." Jacques Derrida, *Politiques de l'amitié* (Paris: Galilée, 1994), 30. "He bears my own death and, in a certain way, he is the only one to bear it—this proper death of myself thus expropriated in advance." Jacques Derrida, *Politics of Friendship*, trans. George Collins (NY: Verso, 1997), 13.

15. Rousseau, *Julie, ou la Nouvelle Héloïse*, 424. "Our friendship is beginning, its dear link is here, may it be indissoluble." Rousseau, *Julie, or the New Heloise*, 349.

16. Rousseau, *Julie, ou la Nouvelle Héloïse*, 705. "Nothing hurts women as much as silence!" Rousseau, *Julie, or the New Heloise*, 579.

17. Derrida, *Politiques de l'amitié*, 43. "O my friends, there is no friend." Derrida, *Politics of Friendship*, 27.

18. For more on Derrida's critique of Schmitt, see Andrew Johnson, *Viral Politics: Jacques Derrida's Reading of Auto-Immunity and the Political Philosophy of Carl Schmitt* (Saarbrücken, Germany: Lap Lambert Academic Publishing, 2010).

19. "La protection de cette garde assure la vérité de l'amitié, sa vérité ambiguë, celle par laquelle les amis se protègent de l'erreur ou de l'illusion qui fondent l'amitié, plus précisément sur le fond sans fond desquelles se fonde une amitié pour pour résister à son propre abîme." Derrida, *Politiques de l'amitié*, 71–72. "The protection of this custody guarantees the truth of friendship, its ambiguous truth, that by which friends protect themselves from the error or the illusion on which friendship is founded—more precisely, the bottomless bottom founding a friendship, which enables it to resist its own abyss." Derrida, *Politics of Friendship*, 53.

20. My thinking here is informed by Jacques Rancière's excluded "part of no part" in *La Mésentente: politique et philosophie* (Paris: Galilée, 1995), or Claude Lefort's "empty place" of power at the heart of democracy in "The Question of Democracy," *Democracy and Political Theory* (Cambridge: Polity Press, 1988).

21. Derrida, *Politiques de l'amitié*, 73. "And as the friends know this truth of truths, they had better keep silent together. As in a mutual agreement. A tacit agreement, however, whereby those who are separated come together without ceasing to be what they are destined to be—and undoubtedly what they more than ever are: dissociated, 'solitarized', singularized, constituted into monadic alterities (*vereinsamt*)." Derrida, *Politics of Friendship*, 54.

22. Keith Ansell-Pearson, *An Introduction to Nietzsche as Political Thinker: The Perfect Nihilist* (Cambridge: Cambridge Univ. Press, 1994), 42. Collective autonomy for Rousseau is self-legislation whereby citizens join together to make laws for themselves that reflect their collective understanding of the common good, or the general will.

23. Étienne Balibar, *Citoyen sujet et autres essais d'anthropologie philosophique* (Paris: PUF, 2011).

24. Étienne Balibar, *Dictionary of Untranslatables: A Philosophical Lexicon*, ed. Emily Apter, Jacques Lezra, and Michael Wood (Princeton, NJ: Princeton Univ. Press, 2014), 605.

25. For an astute analysis of gender roles and of this role reversal in the *matinée* and elsewhere in *Julie*, see John C. O'Neal, *The Progressive Poetics of Confusion in the French Enlightenment* (Newark: Univ. of Delaware Press, 2011).

26. Rousseau, *Julie, ou la Nouvelle Héloïse*, 559. "'Envy nothing,' her husband said in a tone of voice he should have left to me; 'We have all long been your subjects.' At this word, her needlework fell from her hands; she turned her head, and cast on her husband such a touching look, so tender, that I myself thrilled at it. She said nothing: what could she have said to equal that look? Our eyes also met. I could tell from the way her husband clasped my hand that we were all three caught up in the same emotion, and that the sweet influence of that expansive soul was acting around her, and overcoming insensibility itself. It was in this frame of mind that the silence I was speaking of began; you can well imagine that it was not one of coldness and boredom. It was interrupted only by the children's little frolics; even then, the minute we stopped talking, they moderated their chatter in imitation, as if fearing to disturb the general contemplation." Rousseau, *Julie, or the New Heloise*, 457.

27. Thank you to Neil Saccamano for noting that love and friendship here could also be aligned with subjection to Julie as sovereign, in which case the political structure of monarchy configures their love for Julie as a mechanism of power, and not its emancipatory dissolution. This reign of love could also be seen as borrowing from the courtly love tradition that idolizes and deifies the power women supposedly exert over their male lovers.

28. Rousseau, *Julie, ou la Nouvelle Héloïse*, 409. "My Julie, you are born to reign." Rousseau, *Julie, or the New Heloise*, 336.

29. See Jean Starobinski, *Jean-Jacques Rousseau, la transparence et l'obstacle* (Paris: Gallimard, 1976).

30. Rousseau, *Julie, ou la Nouvelle Héloïse*, 409–10. "Your empire is the most absolute I know. It extends even to the wills of others, and I am more subject to it than anyone. . . . Your heart vivifies all those around it and gives them so to speak a new being for which they are forced to pay tribute to yours, since they would not have obtained it otherwise. . . . Is it possible to see you for long without feeling one's soul filled with the charms of virtue and the comforts of friendship?" Rousseau, *Julie, or the New Heloise*, 336.

31. Peggy Kamuf, *Fictions of Feminine Desire: Disclosures of Heloise* (Lincoln: Univ. of Nebraska Press, 1982), 10.

32. Here, I follow Balibar, Kamuf, and especially MacCannell's description of how Rousseau employs a vocabulary of desire at the very point where the democratic body emerges: "The motive of the 'people,' the 'democratic' drive is thus seen by Rousseau as a dialectic of desire, of a competition between eros and thanatos" (MacCannell, *The Regime of the Brother*, 66). This competition is not to

be considered a binary pairing but as interrelated expressions of the Freudian death drive.

33. These spaces include the Elysium, the Apollo Room where special meals are held, as well as some of the inner chambers. See John C. O'Neal, "Morality in Rousseau's Public and Private Society at Clarens," *Revue de Métaphysique et de Morale* 89, no. 1 (1984): 58–67.

34. Rousseau, *Julie, ou la Nouvelle Héloïse*, 453. "In a Republic citizens are restrained by morals, principles, virtue: but how can domestics, mercenaries, be contained other than by constraint and coercion? The master's whole art consists in hiding this coercion under the veil of pleasure or interest, so that they think they desire all they are obliged to do." Rousseau, *Julie, or the New Heloise*, 373.

35. Similar hidden force is evident in the *Du contrat social* notion of forcing a people to be free and in the figure of the legislator, as well as in the tutor of *Émile*.

36. A paradigmatic example of the equality at Clarens is the moment of the grape festival, when masters and servants work and eat together side by side.

37. St. Preux contrasts the love experienced at Clarens with Christian charity: "C'est ce qu'on nous dit tous les jours au Temple sans nous le faire sentir; c'est ce que les habitans de cette maison sentent sans qu'on leur dise." Rousseau, *Julie, ou la Nouvelle Héloïse*, 462. "That is what they tell us every day at Church without bringing us to feel it; it is what all the inhabitants of this house feel without being told." Rousseau, *Julie, or the New Heloise*, 380.

38. "On fait plus; on les engage à se servir mutuellement en secret, sans ostentation, sans se faire valoir." Rousseau, *Julie, ou la Nouvelle Héloïse*, 463. "They go further; they invite them to help each other silently, unostentatiously, without making a show of it." Rousseau, *Julie, or the New Heloise*, 380.

39. Julie's sacrifice could further situate her as a Christ-like figure, as previously noted.

40. It is also important to note the distinction between the heteronomic figure of the legislator and that of Julie, as she is said to "reign" at Clarens prior to her death, whereas Rousseau notes that examples of lawgivers such as Lycurgus abdicate *before* giving laws to Sparta. The Clarens community may be considered as founded upon the love that Julie elicits as the social bond, and as Rousseau notes the test of the true legislator is the endurance or longevity of the polity, the Clarens political community must be able to live on after the death of Julie.

41. While need dictates the first gestures, language for Rousseau is born of passion, and it is initially figurative. Only poetry is spoken at first, with reasoning coming later, as the transposition of ideas for passion is linked to words. He describes this process in his *Essai sur l'origine des langues* with the fable of the giant, an initial act of denomination. As Derrida and Paul de Man have argued, this passage illustrates the referential indeterminacy of language, or the empty center of the address to another. Much like the figurative nature of the initial languages that Rousseau describes in the *Essai*, he also creates "un monde idéal," an ideal world, at the beginning of his *Dialogues*, where communication seems to be largely nonverbal. For more silence in the *Essai*, see Adam Schoene, "Reuniting Speech and Song: Reading on Sebbar with Rousseau," *The French Review* 90.3 (2017): 39–49.

The *Convulsionnaires,* Palissot, and the Philosophical Battles of 1760

ANNE C. VILA

The year 1760 was exceptionally difficult for the intellectuals affiliated with the French philosophic movement. Coming right after such ugly events as Jean-Jacques Rousseau's noisy defection from the circle of *philosophes*, the condemnation and burning of Claude Adrien Helvétius's *De l'Esprit* (1758), and the revocation of the *privilège* of the *Encyclopédie*, this was when Charles Palissot de Montenoy's satirical comedy *Les Philosophes* skewered Rousseau, Helvétius and Denis Diderot on stage by painting them as Tartuffe-like scoundrels.[1] It was also a year when spectacles of a more violent sort captured the attention of Parisian witnesses and readers around Europe: scenes of ritualized self-mortification that were being staged by convulsionaries tied to the religious movement known as Jansenism.

Jansenism was a strand of Catholicism that emerged in the seventeenth century among disciples of Cornelius Jansenius (bishop of Ypres), whose major work *Augustinus* (1640) preached a return to the austere, predestinarian doctrine of Saint Augustine.[2] Styling themselves as the defenders of the essential truths of the Christian faith, its adherents insisted on the sinfulness and corruption of man and society. They opposed both the optimistic conception of the human condition that had come out of the Renaissance and the theology of the Society of Jesus, which they considered lax and excessively accommodating to worldly mores. On top of their battle with the Jesuits, Jansenists endured decades of persecution from the royal government, which suspected them of being hostile to France's absolute monarchy and thus a potential source of political subversion. This persecution culminated with a series of acts by Louis XIV toward the end of his reign: the closing and demolition of the convent of Port-Royal-des-Champs, the symbolic center of Jansenism, in 1709–11; and the repressive Unigenitus bull, which Pope Clement XI promulgated in 1713 at the French King's request. This papal bull condemned the book *Réflexions morales sur le Nouveau Testament* (1692), where the Oratorian Father Pasquier Quenel had tried to present "the spirit and message of Jansenism in terms more easily accessible to the laity . . . while advocating increased lay participation with the clergy in public worship" (*MCEP*, 8). It denounced many of Quesnel's propositions as heretical and pointed out Jansenism's similarities to Calvinism.[3] Although Louis XIV's aim in promoting and enforcing Unigenitus was to crush Jansenism, the results were quite different: the bull and the king's actions reinvigorated the movement (*JL*, 13).

One reaction to Unigenitus was convulsionism, a fringe branch of Jansenism that began in the late 1720s in the Parisian cemetery of Saint-Médard. Its adepts performed miracle cures brought about, they claimed, by contact with the tomb or relics of the Deacon François de Pâris, a self-sacrificing ascetic who denounced Unigenitus and became the focus of a cultish following after he died in 1727. These assemblies, which drew large crowds until the authorities closed the cemetery in 1732, involved highly kinetic expressions of religious experience like spasms, contortions, and feats of strength, accompanied by trance-like states and apparent imperviousness to pain. One convulsionary, the 22-year-old Marie Sonet, was called "La Salamandre" because she exposed herself to fiery treatments but appeared incombustible.[4] Another famous participant was the abbé Bescherand de la Motte. Afflicted with an atrophied left leg, he went twice a day to Saint-Médard in the fall of 1731 "to pray for a cure, whereby he might demonstrate both the reality of the miracles and the injustice of Vintimille's recent decree [to ban the Pâris cult]" (*MCEP*, 174–75).[5] Although less public by 1760, convulsionaries were still active in conventicles in Paris and other French cities, most notably Lyon.[6] During this period, their demonstrations of faith sometimes entailed literal martyrdom in the form of what they called *grands secours*, a term that roughly translates as great succor or great relief.

Adepts of convulsionism regarded these practices as proof of the *Oeuvre de la vérité*, the force of God actively speaking through the bodies of the convulsionaries to represent both primitive Christianity and the current state of the Church, torn apart by internal battles and schisms. For philosophes, by contrast, *grands secours* constituted a veritable theater of cruelty; and in

1760, a group of them undertook to raise the alarm in the *Correspondance littéraire, philosophique, et critique,* an elite cultural newsletter edited by Friedrich Melchior Grimm. In the process, they made the convulsionaries part of the ideological battles they were fighting at the time, including those that involved Palissot's anti-philosophical satire.

After situating *grands secours* in the larger history of the convulsionary movement, I will examine the eye-witness accounts of such sessions that the scientist and explorer Charles-Marie de la Condamine and his companion Gérard Dudoyer de Gastels (a playwright and former Oratorian) provided for the 15 May and 1 June 1760 issues of the *Correspondance littéraire.* I will then look at the ways in which Diderot drew on those accounts in various texts over the next two decades, while also considering how Grimm framed them within the pages of the *Correspondance.* For Diderot and Grimm, this chapter in the convulsionary movement posed a major challenge to their hope that the philosophical spirit of reason, tolerance, and compassion would triumph in their century. So, too, did Palissot's *Les Philosophes,* whose government-sanctioned success during the same year illustrated, in their eyes, both the questionable tastes of some contemporary spectators and the worrisome sway of anti-philosophe rhetoric over public opinion.

"Fanaticism is a monster without a heart, without eyes, and without ears. It dares to call itself the son of religion."[7] So said Voltaire in 1769 while replying to an anonymous letter from an admirer. Although the second sentence in that comment has gotten more press in recent years, the first is equally important for the stress it places on fanaticism's capacity to induce a pathological psycho-sensory state. Voltaire made the remark figuratively in this particular letter, to attack a mindless adversary (the ex-Jesuit Claude-Adrien Nonnotte). However, he used the idea literally when commenting upon the convulsionary movement in the article "Fanatisme" of the *Dictionnaire philosophique*: "Once fanaticism has gangrened a brain, the disease is almost incurable. I have seen convulsionaries who, while speaking of the miracles of Saint Pâris, got increasingly heated in spite of themselves; their eyes became inflamed, their arms and legs trembled, furor disfigured their faces; and they would have killed anyone who contradicted them."[8] Convulsionism was arguably the most visible form of fanaticism observed by the philosophes, both because it was taking place in Paris, the geographical center of the French Enlightenment, and because it went on for several decades.

Scholars have already explored the theological, political and social aspects of the phase of the convulsionary movement that unfolded in the late 1720s and early 1730s.[9] They have also examined the critiques that were published at the time, like *Le Naturalisme des convulsions* (1733), where the mainstream Jansenist doctor Philippe Hecquet undertook to naturalize the Saint-Médard convulsions by imputing them to physiological causes like epilepsy, and to overexcited imaginations (especially among young female adherents).[10] In addition to showing how quickly the convulsionary movement became a topic of medical commentary, this research has clarified its pervasive themes of persecution, martyrdom and millenarianism, the social status and occupations of convulsionary adherents, and the value they placed on both figurism and written testimony. Thousands of texts were left behind by the convulsionaries, and while many are available only in manuscript form, some were incorporated into *La Vérité des miracles opérés par l'intercession de M. de Pâris* by Carré de Montgeron, a convert who strove to publicize and legitimize the cause. First published as a richly illustrated single volume in 1737, this book was expanded to three volumes in the 1740s.[11] *La Vérité des miracles* was a lightning rod for the philosophes's early reactions to the convulsionary movement: for example, Diderot's skeptical comments in *Les Pensées philosophiques* (1746), where he sought to demystify Montgeron's account of miracles by depicting the convulsionaries as either dupes or charlatans; and the *Encyclopédie* article "Convulsionnaires" (1754), where Jean d'Alembert decried them as partisans of a "scandalous, absurd fanaticism" who, out of religious zeal, maimed rather than cured people.[12]

However, less attention has been paid to the extreme set of practices that arose after the convulsionary movement moved indoors: *grands secours*, also known as *secours meurtriers*, an oxymoron that translates as "murderous relief" and "murderous assistance." These practices involved brutal treatments like beating, stabbing, and crucifixion, carried out on apparently rapturous believers. They were performed clandestinely but before spectators who included non-believers, some of whom were prominent members of the social elite (the people convulsing and receiving *grands secours* were predominately women from the lower classes).[13] Such spectacles riveted Parisians for reasons that, according to the contemporary chronicler Edmond-Jean-François Barbier, ranged from curiosity to *esprit de parti*.[14] In his journal entries of December 1758 and January, April, and May 1760, Barbier exclaimed that it was astonishing that assemblies of this nature were allowed to take place in a well-policed city like Paris, and alarming that "everyone of high social station wanted to witness them" (*CR*, 252). [In May 1760, Barbier also wrote about the performance of *Les Philosophes* he had attended, underscoring both the "tumult" of the crowd and the play's "spitefulness" (*CR*, 249–250).[15]]

As Catherine Maire explains, the meaning that convulsionaries gave to the term *secours* mutated in the early 1730s, as did their interpretation of convulsions. They initially regarded their convulsions as healing: that is, a sign that God, the Divine Physician, was acting directly on their bodies either to cure their ailments or to signal his disapproval of worldly measures like the Unigenitus bull and the decision by civil authorities to shut down the Saint-Médard cemetery (*DCD*, 289). Around 1733, however, this group devised a new interpretation. From that point on, as police measures against the convulsionaries increased, Saint-Médardistes no longer viewed their seizures as healing. Instead, they considered them so overwhelming and smothering as to require the intervention of attendants known as *secouristes*, whose role was to stop the spasms by restraining and hitting the convulsing individual. The adepts who contributed to this reinterpretation were improvising theologians who used their bodies to mimic state and ecclesiastic persecution of their cause and of the true Church (*DCD*, 291; *MCEP*, 259). During the 1740s and 50s, the practice of *grands secours* evolved to become increasingly bloody. Some convulsionary women literally offered their skin as a surface on which others wrote the marks of the Holy Word in the form of incisions in the shape of a cross, a heart, and so on; and by 1760, the movement had shifted toward the ultimate identification of adepts with the Christian body *par excellence*: the body of the crucified Christ (*DCD*, 301; *MCJ*, 250–53).

Sociologist Daniel Vidal underscores the focus on raw suffering that was central to the convulsionaries' mental universe: the essential social relation was, in their minds, bloody, painful and physical; and bodies, bound together through shared spasms, were the central vehicle for enacting and circulating the illness or evil at the root of human existence (*MCJ*, 204, 211). Some demonstrations of this belief occurred outdoors, like the bloody pilgrimages that certain convulsionaries made to Port-Royal (*MCJ*, 218, 320); but most took place in private residences. Those included the sessions where the convulsionary sister Rachel had herself trampled by another sister (1749) and, ten years later, beaten and pierced with swords in her ribs and eyes. The social bond that convulsionary adepts cemented through pain and spasms, felt in common, was rooted in a shared religious vision of the path to salvation.[16] Women—particularly from the working classes—figured prominently among them, and "found themselves invested through convulsion […] with a power that came from God."[17] However, the human power dynamic was hierarchical and largely male-dominated within the most extreme convulsionary cells, like that to which sister Rachel belonged.

We should note that Rachel's secular name was Élisabeth Barre: she was the biological sister of Pierre de La Barre de Vauville, head of a convulsionary cell that caused a particular stir in Paris in 1759 and 1760. Rachel was known for the prophecies she uttered in an infantile voice: while being beaten and pierced, she said, childlike, that she was enduring these tortures "in order to punish the naysayers, who are greedy, who like to see money, the tiny hands of the greedy, and the tongues who have spoken only to flatter the dominant passion of the heart. . . . We must have really irritated our God to move him to act in such a terrible manner" (*MCJ*, 320–21). This illustrates the trend among certain convulsionary women of specializing in "convulsions of childhood" that involved prophecies uttered in baby talk, requests for cakes and sweets while under trance, and play-acting rituals in which they fed gruel to a wax baby Jesus.[18] The Jansenist lawyer Louis-Adrien Le Paige, who carefully collected and catalogued transcriptions of such speeches, found great beauty in such prophecies.[19]

Although clandestine, convulsionary sessions held indoors often involved sizable crowds. For curiosity seekers, gaining entry required connections: the comte Dufort de Cheverny got into a session directed in 1760 by "a certain Father La Barre" through the mediation of the famous dancer Mlle Deschamps.[20] The baron Carl Heinrich von Gleichen, a Bavarian diplomat, had to use more complicated tactics to get his friend La Condamine into a convulsionary assembly organized by La Barre's group in 1759. La Condamine, who was quite hard of hearing, had been banned from an earlier session after he loudly propositioned a pretty young girl who had just been detached from the cross; but Gleichen, amused by La Condamine's intense desire to see the convulsionaries again, gave him the ticket he had procured for himself and instructed him to impersonate him by pretending to be a distinguished German traveler. The charade worked on the young lawyer whom Gleichen had engaged to serve as guide but not on the convulsionaries, who recognized La Condamine and threatened to expel him.[21]

For the 1 June 1759 issue of Grimm's *Correspondance*, La Condamine provided a brief summary of the convulsionary gathering he had attended, with Gleichen's help, on Good Friday of that year (April 13). Although he included a few observations about the two women he saw nailed to a cross— Soeur Françoise, 55 years old, and the much younger Soeur Marie—La Condamine explained that he was reluctant to give anyone a copy of the *procès verbal* he had written about it.[22] Grimm nonetheless used this short account to lend credence to a detail in the sarcastic brochure *Mémoire pour Abraham Chaumeix contre les prétendus philosophes Diderot et d'Alembert*, reviewed in the May 15 issue: "To understand how appropriate it was to use a crucifixion scene in the *Mémoire pour Abraham Chaumeix*, one must realize that the convulsionaries have been getting themselves crucified in Paris for the past five or six months" (*CL* vol. VI, 111). In the issue of 1 April 1760, Grimm reported that the poet Claude Guimond de La Touche was so horrified and frightened by the spectacle of the convulsionaries that he died from it (*CL* vol. VII, 72).[23] The following month, La Condamine and Dudoyer finally consented to requests made by Grimm and Diderot to reproduce the full *procès-verbaux* of the convulsionary sessions they had witnessed—texts that are identical to those that Diderot kept in his private papers under the title "Dossier des convulsionnaires."[24] This was a veritable scoop (*CL* vol. VII, xxviii): these *procès verbaux* were not officially published for several years afterwards. The texts by La Condamine and Dudoyer have not received much scholarly consideration, beyond the incisive notes provided by the editors of the modern-day edition of the *Correspondance*.

According to these accounts, three sorts of people were involved in *grands secours* assemblies. The first were female convulsionaries, one of whom, Françoise, was a celebrity because she had been convulsing—and purportedly undergoing crucifixions—for twenty-seven years (*CL* vol. VI, 113). The second were male *secouristes* like La Barre, formerly a parliamentary lawyer in Rouen, who sometimes used the pseudonym M. de Vauville; and the ex-Oratorian priest Cottu, who also went by the names M. Dubois and frère Timothée. The third group was comprised of spectators of varying ages and social conditions, including some from the upper crust of European society. Audience members were often invited to assist in the *secours:* for example, by using their swords to poke at designated flesh wounds in the women on display.

The 15 May and 1 June 1760 issues of the *Correspondance* included three separate narratives of *grand secours*. Several pages of the 15 May issue were taken up by La Condamine's *procès-verbal* on the events of Good Friday 1759, when he had watched the ritual crucifixions of Françoise and Marie. La Condamine took exact note of everything: the time each woman spent on the cross, the dimensions of the cross and nails, the rituals employed (for example, the use of "miraculous" water of St. Pâris to wash the women's hands or feet), the convulsions and signs of pain he saw, and the words the women pronounced. Whereas Françoise declaimed in figurative language about the ills of the Church and the spectators' blindness to the truth, Marie read aloud the passion of Saint John (*CL* vol. VII, 116, 118). La Condamine concluded by refuting the adepts' contention that, far from suffering, these women had miraculously found it pleasant: "the only marvel to which I can testify is of the constancy and courage that fanaticism can inspire" (119).

This text was followed directly by Dudoyer's report on the "Miracles of Saint Jean's Day, 1759," which related other practices that had been carried out on sister Françoise. She was stabbed with help from the spectators, including Dudoyer (La Condamine, who was also present, "modestly refused" [*CL* vol. VII, 122]). Then her dress was set on fire, in keeping with father Timothée's written prediction that God ordained it (123–24). Two notices followed this report, both involving the ritual of beating people with logs to "relieve" or "cure" them. The second notice referred to Le Paige, who repeatedly beat his wife a few days before she was to give birth (she delivered the baby and died eight days later; 125). The inclusion of that particular notice in the *Correspondance* may be related to Le Paige's status as one of the censors of the *Encyclopédie,* which, after being subject in February 1759 to a review committee composed entirely of Jansenist theologians, lawyers and scholars, was forced to discontinue printing and distribution in March of that year.[25]

The third eye-witness account, presented in the 1 June issue of the *Correspondance,* summarized the conversations that Dudoyer had with La Barre in the latter's residence in March 1760; he had been refused entry at other convulsionary assemblies, despite the letter of recommendation he had presented from an insider who praised his piety (*CL* vol. VII, 138). To insinuate himself into La Barre's good graces, he emphasized how eager he was to see the "portion of the work of God" that La Barre was carrying out, and made a few disparaging comments about Sister Françoise and Father Cottu, both of whom La Barre disdained (139). The ensuing dialogue laid out the details of La Barre's unconventional theology and the various instruments he had invented to intensify the *grands secours* or to perform several crucifixions at once (140).

Dudoyer then described the *secours* he had observed on Palm Sunday and Good Friday, overseen by La Barre and carried out on sisters Félicité, Sion, Marie, and Rachel. He meticulously described various details: the amount of time each woman spent on the cross; the odd burlet Rachel wore, and the frightening cold sweat that appeared on her face; and the active role played by the doctor Jacques Barbeu Du Bourg, a long-time observer of convulsionary practices. He also gave the names of many distinguished *profanes* or non-believers in attendance: these included the well-known anatomist Marie-Marguerite Bihéron, the princess of Kinski (a friend of the duc de Choiseul), the prince of Monaco, the count of Stahremberg, and various other nobles and high-ranking military figures (*CL* vol. VII, 142). While sister Rachel was on the cross—representing the agony of Christ, as La Barre explained to the audience—she spoke to the Princess Kinski in a familiar manner and exclaimed that she was closing her eyes because she wanted to go to sleep ["faire dodo"]. Shortly after being taken down from the cross, Rachel crawled over in a bloodied state, first to Du Bourg to ask him for some candy, and then to Princess Kinski; she placed her head on the princess's lap and stroked her like a child (143). Dudoyer's report ended by noting that sister Marie's *secours* (trampling and head-beating) were interrupted when the commissioner Rochebrune arrived with assistants to arrest La Barre and his fellow convulsionaries.[26]

Clearly, a mix of religious conviction and suggestion was at work in these rituals; and while the reports of Dudoyer and La Condamine were laced with occasional sarcasm, they also reflect the sincerity of belief evident in the sisters who allowed themselves to receive *grands secours* (*CL* vol. VII, 141). We should note here that the sway of suggestion over the imagination was a key component in eighteenth- and nineteenth-century medical explanations of the Jansenist convulsionary phenomenon, starting with Hecquet, continuing to the era of Mesmerism and, from there, to Jean-Martin Charcot's writings on hysteria.[27] The power of belief also extended to some spectators: "there were quite a few nobles . . . who became devout participants in the Pâris cult" (*MCEP*, 153).

Many high-placed people in Paris observed the indoor spectacles, and high-born people elsewhere read about them. Although the readership of Grimm's *Correspondance* was limited in 1760, it was also distinctly elite: Grimm sent copies of that year's issues to just four European courts, one of which was that of Queen Louise Ulrique of Sweden (*CL* vol. 1, xxxii–xxxiv). The reports which he reproduced for his royal clients are similar to the descriptions of *grands secours* that appeared in print elsewhere, like the eye-witness account published by the surgeon Sauveur-François Morand. Morand's report closely echoed the details of Doyer de Gastel's March 1760 visit to the La Barre's group, particularly those regarding sister Rachel's crucifixion—which was, apparently, her twenty-first such ordeal.[28]

These accounts of *grands secours* directly inspired the comments Diderot made about the convulsionaries during the 1760s and 70s. The fourteenth volume of the *Encyclopédie* (1765) included the article "Secours," a graphically detailed description of the "various torments . . . that France's modern fanatics, called convulsionaries, inflict upon people subject to convulsions." Diderot, the probable author, began by relating the different practices the convulsionaries employed: "These so-called *secours* consist in sometimes receiving several hundred beatings with logs on the stomach; sometimes being hit by swords on the arms, the belly, and other body parts; sometimes having one's arms stung with needles or pins; sometimes letting oneself be trampled badly; sometimes being held tightly with a rope, etc." He then remarked:

> These last few years, one has seen Convulsionaries attached on crosses with nails that, according to the least convinced spectators, actually pierced their hands and feet, and caused them sufferings that these unfortunate victims of treachery took pains to hide from attentive eyes. Nonetheless, they claimed that it was not harming them, and that, to the contrary, it provided them with great relief. These Convulsionaries, after having hung on crosses

> for several hours that they spent in ejaculatory prayers, and in mystical and prophetic exhortations on the ills of the church, sometimes had their side pierced, imitating the Savior of the world; they were then released from the cross, and they claimed to have forgotten all that happened, and to be satisfied with the torments they had just endured ... See *CONVULSIONNAIRES*.[29]

Around the same time, Diderot wrote a dialogue entitled *Cinqmars et Derville*, which shows that he was repulsed not just by the dehumanizing tortures such practices involved but also by the chic set who found them entertaining. That sort of spectator is embodied by the fictional chevalier who was curious to attend an assembly of convulsionaries, and whose experience Derville summarizes as follows:

> He saw one woman on whom they'd placed a burlet, who was acting like a child and walking on her knees, and who they then placed on a cross; in fact, they crucified her, they drove nails through her feet and hands. A cold sweat covered her face and she fell into convulsions. In the midst of her torments, she asked for candy, to go beddy-bye, and a thousand other extravagances I can't remember. When she was detached from the cross, she stroked the face and arms of the spectators with her hands, which were still bleeding.[30]

This passage repeats almost verbatim Dudoyer's account of Sister Rachel's crucifixion; but what follows is a very Diderotian flourish that emphasizes the story's effect on its philosophically-minded listener, Cinqmars. Rather like MOI in *Le Neveu de Rameau*, Cinqmars is horrified by the tale at two levels: he is appalled both by the "cruel, homicidal" fanaticism of the convulsionary sect, and by the joking, "indecent pantomime" the chevalier had performed at a dinner party after witnessing the assembly, just to get a laugh out of his friends. Indeed, *Le Neveu de Rameau* refers in passing to a character who did just that: "friend Robbé," or Robbé de Beauveset, a cynical minor writer who became devout after witnessing some convulsionary miracles. In *Le Neveu de Rameau*, Robbé is a member of LUI's circle of lowlifes, the same crowd that hatched the plan for Palissot's *Philosophes*, where Robbé distinguishes himself by telling stories of the convulsionaries and reciting verses from his poem on syphilis.[31]

To some degree, the allusions to the convulsionaries in these dialogues reflect a strategy Diderot had already used in the *Pensées philosophiques*: invalidating the convulsionaries by underscoring their bizarre theatricality.[32] However, Diderot seemed genuinely distressed by what he had read in the *procès verbaux* in which La Condamine and Dudoyer described *grands secours.* He repeated the anecdote of Sister Rachel's crucifixion in the essay "Sur les femmes," written in 1772 for the July issue of Grimm's *Correspondance* to critique Antoine- Léonard Thomas's just published *Essai sur le caractère, les moeurs et l'esprit des femmes.* The anecdote served to frame what is now the most notorious passage of "Sur les femmes," where Diderot made hystericism an essential female trait, and described the uterus as the source of women's unlimited sensibility in ecstasy, fury, and (in a few rare cases) genius.[33]

The convulsionaries may also have been on Diderot's mind when he was writing the dramatic scenes of mental and emotional dispossession that lend such pathos to his novel *La Religieuse.* When forced to become a nun, the novel's heroine, Suzanne Simonin, is plunged into a state of stupor and memory loss that lasts for several months. Moreover, when she tries to rescind her vows, she is subjected to prolonged mortifications at the hands of the fanatical Soeur Sainte-Christine and her vicious acolytes—characters who could even be called *secouristes,* given the way they intermingle specious theological justifications with ritualized tortures of Suzanne.[34] Above and beyond their value for the anti-clerical, anti-monastic polemic that underpins this work, the episodes of Suzanne's torment may express the horror and pity that Diderot himself felt upon reading eye-witness accounts of the convulsionaries (or upon recalling the fate of his own sister, who became a nun and died insane).[35]

Diderot and other philosophes were intent on drawing attention to the pathologically desensitizing effects of excessive religious zeal—and the equally desensitizing effects of the convulsionary movement on some of the people who watched its spectacles for entertainment. Denouncing the convulsionaries was unquestionably tied to the philosophes' larger campaign against fanaticism and efforts to cure that ill by spreading the "philosophical spirit" (a hope expressed by Voltaire in "Fanatisme"). We should, however, also recognize the strategic aspect of their references to the convulsionaries: they were part of their battles against the *anti-philosophes.*

That strategy becomes clear when we consider the texts that frame the reports on *grands secours* in the *Correspondance.* The 15 May 1760 issue opened with a skeptical commentary on the election to the Académie Française of the poet and devout Catholic Jean-Jacques Le Franc de Pompignan. The other texts inserted just before the accounts of convulsionary sessions included the poem "Les Pour, les Que, les Qui, et les Quoi," where Voltaire, using the pseudonym Christophe Oudran, ridiculed the outspoken *Encyclopédie* critic Abraham de Chaumeix by claiming that he had had himself crucified in front of a hundred convulsionaries (*CL* vol. VII, 110). In the next issue, right before presenting another juridical account of the convulsionaries, Grimm offered a personal reflection in which he lamented both the success of Palissot's satire *Les Philosophes* and the power that the "prejudice against philosophy" seemed to be wielding:

> However pitiful this play [Palissot's] is in itself, it will be famous in the history of France, and serve as proof of the observation that the most extraordinary events are often caused by the most ludicrous causes. It is, indeed, a minor thing that Palissot wrote a bad play against people who are respectable for their mores as well as their talents; but the fact that this farce has been performed in the theater of Corneille and under the authority of the government; . . . that is not a minor point, because it marks, on top of a reversal of all order and justice, the sort of favor and protection that letters and philosophy can expect from now on from the government. It is easy to predict what will result from this. Philosophy had barely shown its light among us when stupidity and superstition rose up from all sides to conspire to destroy it. . . . Things have been taken so far that there is not a man in authority today who doesn't regard the progress of philosophy in this country as the source of all our ills and as the cause of most of the calamities that have beset France in recent years.
>
> (*CL* vol. VII, 128–130)

The mindset of the court, Grimm lamented, was so anti-philosophe that it would even blame France's military defeats in the battles of Rossbach (5 November 1757) and Minden (1 August 1759) on "the new philosophy." Here, he pointed out that the English, who had defeated the French in these battles, had produced plenty of philosophers, too, none of which prevented its infantry from performing effectively (130). He concluded on a melancholy note: "the light that was beginning to shine will soon be snuffed out [and] barbarism and superstition will soon have reclaimed their rights."

It is thus no coincidence that the same issue of Grimm's *Correspondance littéraire* decried two sorts of harmful, destructive laughter. The first was that which Palissot's *Les Philosophes* had elicited among audiences prejudiced against the *philosophes,* who enjoyed listening to the playwright's contemptuous references to "pompous" works by Helvétius, Grimm, Duclos, and (most of all) Diderot, and who found it hilarious to see Rousseau ridiculed as a character who enters the stage in act 3, scene 8 walking on all fours and eating lettuce (an unsubtle wink by Palissot to Voltaire's famous caricature of Rousseau's *Discours sur l'origine de l'inégalité* [1755]).[36] The second kind of destructive laughter that Grimm and Diderot denounced was the entertainment some Parisians found at convulsionary assemblies. By reporting their scoop about the crucifying convulsionaries in a manner that interwove juridical accounts with scathing critiques of anti-philosophical works like Palissot's, they were also taking a stand on what constituted good versus bad spectatorship, good versus bad participation in the sphere of public debate.

In that sense, the placement of the accounts of convulsionary assemblies in the *Correspondance litteraire* resembles the double-barrel strategy that Voltaire employed in satires like *Candide,* where the "convulsionary mob" is associated with the "critical mob" in the vicious fauna of Paris.[37] Grimm and Diderot took aim simultaneously at convulsionary zealots and critics who sought to discredit the philosophes in public opinion, whether through ridicule or other means. The seemingly separate phenomena of *grands secours* and anti-Enlightenment rhetorical campaigns can therefore be seen as interdependent events in the cultural politics of 1760.[38] Both the crucifying convulsionaries and Palissot's *Les Philosophes* captured the limelight that year, and in the eyes of the philosophes, both stirred up alarming passions in the body politic—emotions they strove to remedy by disseminating the philosophical spirit, at least among a few select readers.

NOTES

1. It was also in 1760 that the poet and devout Catholic Jean-Jacques Le Franc de Pompignan made a speech denouncing his century as "drunk with the philosophical spirit . . . the scorn of religion, and the hatred of all authority"; cited in Darrin McMahon, *Enemies of the Enlightenment: The French Counter-Enlightenment and the Making of Modernity* (Oxford: Oxford Univ. Press, 2001), 24. On the texts the *philosophes* wrote in response to such attacks, see Geoffrey Turnovsky, *The Literary Market: Authorship and Modernity in the Old Regime* (Philadelphia, PA: Univ. of Pennsylvania Press, 2010), 114–22.

2. This summary of the early history of Jansenism is drawn mainly from Monique Cottret, *Jansénisme et Lumières, pour un autre XVIIIe siècle* (Paris: Albin Michel, 1998), 1–12, henceforth cited parenthetically in the text as *JL*; and B. Robert Kreiser, *Miracles, Convulsions and Ecclesiastical Politics in Early Eighteenth-Century France* (Princeton: Princeton Univ. Press, 1978), 3–15, henceforth cited parenthetically in the text as *MCEP*.

3. Dale K. Van Kley, *The Religious Origins of the French Revolution: From Calvin to the Civil Constitution, 1560–1791* (New Haven, CT: Yale Univ. Press, 1999), 73.

4. Kreiser notes that attendance at Saint-Médard became a "fashionable pastime" for people of rank by 1731 (*MC*, 153). On «la Salamandre,» see Daniel Vidal,

Miracles et convulsions jansénistes au XVIIIe siècle: le mal et sa connaissance (Paris: Presses universitaires de France, 1987), 331, henceforth cited parenthetically in the text as *MCJ*.

5. Diderot singled out Bescherand as a *fourbe* in *Les Pensées philosophiques* (1746), in *Oeuvres philosophiques*, ed. P. Vernière (Paris: Garnier, 1964), 43. Kélina Gotman cites Bescherand to illustrate her argument that the convulsionaries were "a popular theatre of aberration, characterized by contractions, paralyses, and ecstatic deliverance"; *Choreomania: Dance and Disorder* (New York: Oxford Univ. Press, 2018), 96.

6. The convulsionary movement flourished in Lyon, particularly after it was suppressed in Paris. See Daniel Vidal, *La Morte-Raison. Isaac La Juive, convulsionnaire janséniste de Lyon, 1791–1841* (Grenoble: Jérôme Millon, 1994); and Jean-Pierre Chantin, *Les Amis de l'oeuvre de la Vérité: Jansénisme, miracles, et fin du monde au XIX siècle* (Presses Universitaires de Lyon, 1998).

7. «Lettre anonyme écrite à M. de Voltaire et la réponse,» in Voltaire, *Œuvres complètes*, ed. Louis Moland, 52 vols. (Paris: Garnier frères, 1877–1885), vol. 27, 412. All translations are my own.

8. «Fanatisme» in *Dictionnaire philosophique, Oeuvres complètes de Voltaire / The Complete Works of Voltaire*, ed. Theodore Besterman, et al., 143 vols. (Geneva: Institut et Musée Voltaire / Toronto: Univ. of Toronto Press / Oxford: Voltaire Foundation, 1968–), vol. 36, 105–11, at 108.

9. See, among other studies, Catherine Maire, *De la cause de Dieu à la cause de la nation: le jansénisme au XVIIIe siècle* (Paris: Gallimard, 1998), henceforth cited parenthically in the text as *DCD*; Brian Strayer, *Suffering Saints: Jansenists and Convulsionnaires in France, 1640–1799* (Eastbourne [England]; Portland, OR: Sussex Academic Press, 2008); Charly Coleman, *The Virtues of Abandon: An Anti-Individualist History of the French Enlightenment* (Stanford, CA: Stanford Univ. Press, 2014), 98–118; and Ephraim Radner, *Spirit and Nature: The Saint-Médard Miracles in Eighteenth-Century Jansenism* (New York: The Crossroad Publishing Company, 2002).

10. On Hecquet's efforts to refute claims that these convulsions were miraculous, see Owsei Temkin, *The Falling Sickness: A History of Epilepsy from the Greeks to the Beginning of Modern Neurology* (Baltimore, MD: Johns Hopkins Univ. Press, 1971 [1945]), 224; Jan Goldstein, "Enthusiasm or Imagination? Eighteenth-Century Smear Words in Comparative National Context," in Lawrence E. Klein and Anthony J. La Vopa, eds., *Enthusiasm and Enlightenment in Europe, 1650–1850* (San Marino, CA: Huntington Library, 1998), 29–49; and Sabine Arnaud, *On Hysteria: The Invention of a Medical Category between 1670 and 1820* (Chicago, IL: Univ. of Chicago Press, 2015), 69–70.

11. Louis-Basile Carré de Montgeron, *La vérité des miracles opérés à l'intercession de M. de Pâris et autres appelans démontrée contre M. l'Archevêque de Sens* (first edition 1737). The plates of *La vérité des miracles* can be viewed online on Gallica, the digitized collection of the Bibliothèque nationale de France: see, for example, the images of Gabrielle Moler receiving *grands secours* by being beaten

with sticks, bricks, and logs, at *http://gallica.bnf.fr/ark:/12148/btv1b8452393r/f39. item* and *http://gallica.bnf.fr/ark:/12148/btv1b8452393r/f40.item.* Although it made certain convulsionaries famous, Carré de Montgeron's book prompted the editors of the Jansenist newsletter *Les Nouvelles ecclésiastiques* to disavow the movement (Maire, *DCD*, 301). *La Vérité des miracles* is analyzed in Michèle Bokobza Kahan, *Témoigner des miracles au siècle des Lumières--récits et discours de Saint-Médard* (Paris: Garnier, 2015); and Alain Sandrier, *Les Lumières du miracle* (Paris: Garnier, 2015), 136–39 and *passim.*

12. Diderot, *Les Pensées philosophiques,* 36–44; d'Alembert, «Convulsionnaires (Hist. eccl.),» in *Encyclopédie, ou dictionnaire raisonné des sciences, des arts et des métiers, etc.,* ed. Denis Diderot and Jean le Rond d'Alembert. Univ. of Chicago, ARTFL Encyclopédie Project (Spring 2016), ed. Robert Morrissey and Glenn Roe, *http://encyclopedie.uchicago.edu,* 4:171. Kate Tunstall discusses Diderot's remarks on the Saint-Médard convulsionaries in "A Case in Transit: Reading Diderot (Reading Montaigne) Reading Augustine," in *Montaigne in Transit: Essays in Honour of Ian Maclean,* ed. Neil Kenny, Wes Williams, and Richard Scholar (Cambridge: Legenda, 2016), 19–35.

13. On the social and gender distribution of participants in convulsionary assemblies, see Vidal, *MCJ*, 194–98, and Maire, *DCD*, 292–99.

14. Barbier, entry for April 1760 in *Chronique de la régence et du règne de Louis XV (1718–1763); ou, Journal de Barbier,* 8 vols. (Paris, Charpentier, 1866), vol. 7, 242–43, henceforth cited parenthetically in the text as *CR*. Barbier kept a diary of current events in Paris from 1718 to 1765; it was not published until 1837.

15. Barbier's entry about Palissot's *Les Philosophes* is cited in Hilde H. Freud's monograph *Palissot and "Les Philosophes," Diderot Studies* 9 (1967), 7–243, at 137–38.

16. See Michèle Bokobza Kahan, «Mise en fiction des témoignages des convulsionnaires de Saint-Médard (1727–1732). Vers une poétique de l'horreur,» *Revue Romane* 44:2 (2009), 313–31.

17. Monique Cottret, «La cuisine janséniste,» *Dix-huitième Siècle* 15 (1983), 107–14, at 111.

18. Cottret, «La cuisine janséniste,» 111–12.

19. Kreiser, *MCEP*, 268 and 269, n. 87. Le Paige also left a rich collection of documents associated with the convulsionary movement, now part of the library of the Société des amis de Port-Royal.

20. Jean-Nicolas Dufort de Cheverny, *Mémoires sur les règnes de Louis XV et Louis XVI et sur la Révolution,* ed. Robert de Crèvecoeur, 2 vols. (Paris: Plon, 1886), vol. 1, 266–67.

21. Carl Heinrich von Gleichen, *Souvenirs de Charles Henri, baron de Gleichen* (Paris: Léon Techener fils 1868), 179–83.

22. Friedrich Melchior Grimm, *Correspondance littéraire,* ed. Ulla Kölving et al, 9 vols. (Ferney-Voltaire: Centre international d'étude du XVIIIe siècle, 2006-), vol. VI, 111–12. All further references to this work will be made using the abbreviation *CL* followed by the volume and page number.

23. Louis-Sébastien Mercier later repeated this anecdote in the chapter "Amour du merveilleux" of his *Tableau de Paris*, 12 vols. (Amsterdam, 1782–88), vol. 2, 301.

24. Roger Lewinter included the "Dossier des convulsionnaires" in his chronological edition of Diderot, *Oeuvres complètes*, 4 vols. (Paris: Le Club Français du Livre, 1969–73), 4, 764.

25. On the involvement of Le Paige and other Jansenist *anti-philosophes* in the censoring of the *Encyclopédie*, see Jonathan Israel, "French Royal Censorship and the Battle to Suppress the Encyclopédie of Diderot and d'Alembert, 1751–1759," in *The Use of Censorship in the Enlightenment*, ed. Mogens Lærke (Leiden; Boston: Brill, 2009), 61–76.

26. The *grands secours* carried out by the La Barre cell gained particular notoriety because their members were arrested and tried in 1760–1761. Their trial was reported in contemporary publications like the *Gazette d'Amsterdam* (*CL* vol. VII, 145, n. 78).

27. Jean-Martin Charcot and Paul Richer analyzed aspects of the Jansenist convulsionary movement in *Les démoniaques dans l'art* (1887).

28. «Rapport des opérations faites à Paris par plusieurs personnes que l'on disait faire des miracles en 1759 et 1760,» in Sauveur-François Morand, *Opuscules de chirurgie* (Paris: chez Alex le Prieur, 1768), 297–306.

29. «Secours, (*Hist. eccles. mod*),» in *Encyclopédie*, 14:861.

30. «Cinqmars et Derville» [published 1818, probably written in 1760], in Diderot, *Oeuvres complètes,* ed. Lewinter, vol. 4, 753–4.

31. *Le Neveu de Rameau, ou Satire seconde* [1761–82/1805], in Diderot, *Œuvres complètes*, ed. Herbert Dieckmann, Jacques Proust, Jean Varloot, et al., 34 vols. anticipated (Paris: Hermann, 1975–), 12.89, 136. Henceforth abbreviated DPV.

32. D'Alembert used the same strategy in his *Histoire de la destruction des Jésuites* (1763), where he declared that the French authorities should order the convulsionaries to perform "their disgusting farces not in a garret but at the fair [*foire*], for money, between the tight-rope walkers and goblet players, who will soon make them a flop"; d'Alembert, *Oeuvres,* 5 vols. (Paris: Belin, 1821–22), 2.70.

33. Diderot, «Sur les femmes,» in *Qu'est-ce qu'une femme?: un débat,* Élisabeth Badinter, ed. (Paris: P.O.L., 1989), 170–71.

34. *La Religieuse* [1770/1780–82], in DPV, vol. 11, 123–24 and 157–66.

35. The novel is not anti-Jansenist, per se: according to Mita Choudhury, when faced with the hostile, anti-Jansenist Sister Sainte-Christine, Suzanne "adopts a Jansenist position of resistance"; *Convents and Nuns in Eighteenth-Century Politics and Culture* (Ithaca and New York: Cornell Univ. Press, 2004), 26.

36. Palissot, *Les Philosophes*, ed. T.J. Barling (Exeter, UK: Exeter Univ. Printing Unit, 1975), 58–59.

37. See Voltaire, *Candide, ou l'optimisme*, ed. Jean Goldzink (Paris: Classiques Larousse, 1990), 149–50; and Jean Starobinski, «Le fusil à deux coups de Voltaire» in *Le remède dans le mal. Critique et légitimation de l'artifice à l'âge des Lumières* (Paris: Gallimard, 1989), 123–63.

38. I am borrowing the phrase "interdependent events" from Logan Connors, *Dramatic Battles in Eighteenth-Century France: Philosophes, Anti-philosophes and Polemical Theatre, SVEC* 2012:07, 236.

DEVOTION AND OTHER PASSIONS

Devotion in the Enlightenment

Forum Introduction:
Devotion in the Enlightenment

LAURA M. STEVENS

W hat does it mean to be devoted? What does devotion feel and look like, where do we find it, and what are its objects? What can devotion tell us about the Enlightenment?

The answers to these questions may appear simple, but the history of the word *devotion* shows that they are not. The *Oxford English Dictionary* notes the earliest appearance of this word in the thirteenth-century *Ancrene Riwle*, a guide for the Anchorites and Anchoresses who took a vow to live their lives in a single room, focusing on prayer. This usage connects the word to the Latin verb from which it derives, *devovere*, meaning to dedicate by a vow. Accompanying the absorption of this word into Middle English was a narrowing of its scope to what is marked as sacred, whereas in Latin the dedication could be to people or causes besides gods. The usage of devotion was stable until the early modern period, when the word began migrating to other contexts, especially the political. In *Richard II*, Henry Bolingbroke seeks to assure the king of his loyalty by declaring, "In the devotion of a subjects love,.../ Come I appellant to this princely presence."[1] The history of this word, then, as it moves from Latin to Middle English to Modern English, is one in which meaning narrows to the strictly religious and then expands.

It is tempting to read in this word the standard history of a shift from medieval to modern Europe, with church institutions rivaled and then eclipsed by the state. This is, of course, an element of what is commonly called the secularization thesis: the idea developed by early sociological theorists that as societies modernize they undergo differentiation between the religious and the secular. Some of these theorists have also argued that over time secular institutions and perspectives surpass religious ones in importance.[2] Our goal in assembling this forum is neither to topple nor to reinforce this thesis but to explore what can be accomplished by repositioning our gaze on *how* eighteenth-century people expressed their attachments to gods, causes, institutions, or other humans.

Our discussion, which began as a session at the 2017 ASECS meeting, emerged from the conviction that there is a more complex story to tell about approaches to devotion during the Enlightenment. We featured Enlightenment in our conference forum title because we sought obliquely to reconsider an established (perhaps exhausted) binary: religion and Enlightenment. Rather than rehearsing a longstanding debate about the place of belief in an era long celebrated for its dedication to rational inquiry—a debate that in recent decades has resolved largely in favor of acknowledging the continued but altered importance of religion—can we unlock a fresh way of considering what was going on in this century by reconsidering our central terms? What can be learned from exploring devotion across a range of genres, situations, practices, and forms?

As became clear in discussion following our forum, a focus on the word devotion dictates an Anglo-centric approach. A multilingual comparative study, which is beyond the scope of this forum, promises important insights about the overlaps and distinctions conveyed by the various equivalents—if, indeed, there are equivalents—of the English word devotion. Contemporary German, for example, distinguishes between *Andacht*, which means prayer and religious devotion, and *Verehrung*, which includes more general forms of adoration or admiration including fandom. The histories of these words, however, are also complex, with migrations between registers of meaning we today would separate into secular and religious. English may stand out for having a single word describe so many forms of reverence, admiration, or dedication, and this concentration of so many meanings into a single word had clearly taken place by the eighteenth century.

Consider just one text: Samuel Richardson's *Clarissa*. Devotion might be described as slipping and sliding around in this epistolary novel, wandering among the categories of friendship, fealty to a social superior, romantic courtship, and religion. In an early letter to her confidante Anna Howe, Clarissa Harlowe disparages the "passionate and obsequious devotion" of Lovelace—the man who, the novel's readers have learned, seeks to trap and then seduce or rape her—by remarking wryly, "This man, you know, has very ready knees." Hoping for a visit, Anna promises Clarissa, "to-morrow I shall be at your devotion from day-light to day-light; nor will I be at home to any-body." When Clarissa seeks refuge with Lovelace while escaping from her family, she worries that what on her part was spontaneous flight might have been a well-organized abduction. "I have reason to think," she explains, "there were other horsemen at his devotion" accompanying her coach. Lovelace, meanwhile, revels in his ability to convince Clarissa that she is in a reputable household, not, as it turns out, a brothel, when he writes to his confidante, "several pieces of devotion have been put in" her closet. He also aestheticizes and sexualizes her attentiveness at church, exclaiming, "Dear creature! how fervent, how amiable, in her devotions!" After Clarissa's rape and her subsequent escape from Lovelace, a former suitor proposes once more to her by writing, "I pride myself, I say, to stand forth, and offer my fortune, and my life, at your devotion." Finally, as Clarissa is dying, the reformed rake Belford reports that "all her waking moments [are] taken up in devotion."[3] In this single novel, then, devotion has at least six distinct connotations: ritual gestures of courtship, friendship, serving or supporting a social superior, Christian sermons or prayer guides, marriage, and the act of prayer.

The versatility of this word gestures to a culture in which an array of emotions, utterances, gestures, interpersonal attractions, and commitments are linguistically and, perhaps, affectively intertwined. Just this one novel suggests that it misses the point to describe eighteenth-century Britain as moving away from religion toward secular institutes and privatized expressions of belief, but it would also be misleading merely to assert the continued relevance of religion. Something else is going on, and we seek to explore that something else.

This forum features seven brief position papers, each titled by a single word. Each participant wrote about the way that her research connects with the topic of devotion, drawing on her own expertise to explore this term as it cuts across various arenas. Essays roughly follow the chronological order of their topics. A conclusion by Emma Salgård Cunha offers summary thoughts along with further questions to pursue on this topic.

It is worth considering that although a focus on the word devotion may limit us to English, the bleeding between various categories of commitment, reverence, or attachment, with the foregrounding of simultaneities and overlaps, may still pertain to languages and cultures beyond English. In fact, a focus on comparative devotional feeling and practice has the potential to dovetail with recent critiques of Enlightenment, secularism, and modernity from the vantage point of postcolonial or Indigenous studies.[4] Inquiry that takes place through the terms Enlightenment, secularity, and even religion inherently does so within a Eurocentric and perhaps also a Christocentric world view. This forum does not venture into these areas, but our hope is that it will open a larger discussion.

NOTES

1. Oxford English Dictionary Online, "devotion, n." accessed 2 August 2017; William Shakespeare, *Richard II,* I.i.31–34. Online version accessed 2 August 2017. *http://shakespeare.mit.edu/richardii/full.html.* The quotation is cited in the *OED* entry.

2. The literature on secularity and the secularization thesis is extensive; some of the most prominent publications include Emile Durkheim, *The Elementary Forms of Religious Life* (1912; London: Allen & Unwin, 1968); Max Weber, *The Sociology of Religion* (1922; Boston: Beacon, 1963); and, Talcott Parsons, *The Evolution of Societies* (1966; New York: Prentice-Hall, 1977). Among the most influential recent commentaries are Steve Bruce, *Religion in the Modern World* (Oxford: Oxford Univ. Press, 1996); and Charles Taylor, *A Secular Age* (Cambridge, MA: Belknap Press, 2007).

3. Samuel Richardson, *Clarissa, or the History of a Young Lady, Comprehending the Most Important Concerns of Private Life* (London, 1748), 1: 238; 2: 2; I3: 31; 3: 286; 3: 316; 7: 282; 8: 115. Eighteenth-Century Collections Online.

4. See, e.g., Jared Hickman, "Globalization and the Gods, or the Political Theology of 'Race'," *Early American Literature* 45 (2010): 145–82.

Contemplation:
John Norris on Reason and Devotion

PENNY PRITCHARD

The term *devotion* implicitly confronts questions about the mind's cerebral dedication to the love and worship of God. This investigation considers the epistemological context for exegesis of early modern devotion, taking the writings and intellectual legacy of Church of England clergyman and philosopher John Norris as a case in point.[1]

Norris's reputation among his contemporaries is complex. He is principally remembered now as the recipient of sometimes quite pointed critiques from contemporaries including John Locke, Lady Damaris Masham, and (to a lesser extent) Mary Astell.[2] Indisputably the most assiduous English follower of French philosopher Nicolas Malebranche, Norris offers readers a rich body of religious philosophy which engages first-hand with the Enlightenment concept of devotion, that is, the nexus of intellectual agency or knowledge with the love of God.[3] Tracing key changes in Norris's use of the term between 1688 and 1695 helps to clarify aspects of his own *oeuvre* as well as contemporary responses to it. In turn, these developments help to inform our broader understanding of how early modern ministers' reputation as authors, as well as spiritual mentors for their congregations and wider reading audiences, were shaped by their direct engagement with key cultural ideas.

The different applications of devotion employed by Norris, Masham, and Astell between 1689–1695 present a schematization of how applied intellectual energy relates to thinking about God and the love of God. Both Norris and Astell assert the directness with which the human mind conceives of God while acknowledging the importance of isolated study, meditation, and prayer (all forms of devotion) as manifold means to extend this knowledge. Masham, however, takes particular exception to the more mystical or visionary aspects of Norris's concept of the love of God.

Norris's *Reason and Religion* (1689) defines devotion as being "as much influenc'd by consideration as any other act of the Will," and, more explicitly, knowledge as "the best preparative for Devotion."[4] The precise relationship between knowledge and devotion is central to Norris's discourse in *Reason and Religion* (from his prefatory address to the "Learned Reader" onwards) in asserting that a sufficient though indistinct sense of both is necessary to "serve the ends of Piety and Devotion."[5] Devotion thus serves as a conduit between the epistemological realm of knowledge and the pious realm of prayer.

Norris further defines devotion specifically as "giving up ones self wholly" to God— not just in prayer but also in all ways; it is a translation of rational concepts into divine ones. Significantly, devotion is not even confined to the realm of Christian worship, since even "Heathens who deliver'd and consign'd themselves up to Death, for the safety of their Country, were called *Devoti*."[6] Taken as a whole, *Reason and Religion* presents a coherent system of how piety and devotion serve as a conduit through which the applied faculties of the mind can better understand both the nature of God and man.

Reason and Religion, however, places less priority on solitude as a prerequisite for devotion than Norris's earlier *Poems* (1684), which equated isolated devotion with a higher intellectual register. His *Poems* suggests that the practices of Christ himself indicate solitude's importance in contemplative pursuits including devotion; though devotion necessarily presents a habitual activity, it is solitude which offers "the great opportunity for the Retirements of Devotion" since its being "empty of Cares [means it is instead] full of Prayers."[7] Both earlier texts, then, assert the value of learned contemplation as an aid to devotion whereas first impressions of *Reflections upon the Conduct of Human Life* (1689) implies its direct contradiction ("our Learning is misplaced, and such an importunate pursuit after Learning and Knowledge is no way agreeable to the present Station and condition of Man").[8]

This misleading opening can be refuted, however, by closer reading of *Reflections* as a series of discourses categorising knowledge. Norris distinguishes here between necessary and contingent truths (only the first of which are perfective since they lead towards understanding of God). Those judged as learned are often only in command of contingent truths; erudition is no indication of developing knowledge into cohesive, necessary truths which perfect the understanding. Norris then outlines a threefold system of acquiring knowledge of divine truth (i.e., attention, purity of heart and life, and prayer). It is through prayer that Norris seemingly retains the definition of devotion offered previously ("giving up ones self wholly to God") although prayer, here, is unrelated to specific mention of devotion per se.[9] This is significant because it is precisely the more abstruse or mystical elements of Norris's concept of devotion—and the extent to which this formulation of devotion resists regular or, what he elsewhere describes as canonical, practices such as prayer—with which Astell and (more vociferously) Damaris Masham take exception.[10] Norris's preface to *Letters* claims that the love of God is best achieved through means other than "all the dry Study and Speculation of Scholastick Heads."[11]

By 1695, however, Norris can assert that the love of God converts "even our meanest and most indifferent actions into Religion and Devotion." If so, what role is then played by human intellectual agency (or, indeed, knowledge) in devotion? Devotion seems to have become an end result rather than a conduit by which intellectual reasoning is translated into something divine. Astell, in her *Letters* responding to Norris, begs to differ; if distracted from the love of God, the believer's "Thoughts wander, his Devotion languishes, his Passions grow unruly, and his good Actions become lame and broken."[12] Astell's precepts against distraction are resolved specifically through *intellectual* effort.

In 1696, Damaris Masham warns more explicitly still against the dangers of discerning the love of God through acts of (isolated) spiritual self-discovery. She proposes instead the practical, and practicable, advice to all Christians to follow their devotional practices through public duty. Moreover, Masham describes the "dangerous Consequence" of readers espousing books which promote single-minded love of God "for ends unknown" (that is, without a clear indication of the practical uses to be made of such ways of thinking):

> If Books of this kind (which more or less those usually are, the Papists call their Spiritual Books) are wanting in the Church of England, it is well that they are so; since they would be likely to make many more Enthusiasts than good Christians. . . . If once an unintelligible Way of Practical Religion become the Standard of Devotion, no Men of Sense and Reason will ever set themselves about it; but leave it to be understood by mad Men, and practis'd by Fools.[13]

Far from being the means by which the mind may "give up ones self wholly to God," Masham's concept of devotion is confined to the regular habits of practical religion. Masham's cutting reflections on Norris's Malebranchean vision of loving God as the sole purpose of knowledge is clear enough, but, in doing so, it largely ignores Norris's earlier structured epistemology in *Reason and Religion*. Through interrogation of key terms such as devotion, we can uncover just how selective the readings of Masham, Astell, and others are in promulgating Norris's cultural legacy.

NOTES

1. Richard Acworth notes that "Norris's writings have tended to be neglected by historians of philosophy, partly perhaps because of Locke's dismissive attitude and partly because many of his theories are so close to those of Malebranche that it is difficult to disentangle their influence." *Oxford Dictionary of National Biography*, ed. H. C. G. Matthew and Brian Harrison (Oxford: Oxford Univ. Press, 2004); online ed., ed. David Cannadine, May 2009, http://www.oxforddnb.com/view/article/20277, accessed 10 August 2017.

2. Mary Astell was an English philosopher and early campaigner for the reform of female education. See Alice Sowaal, "Mary Astell," *The Stanford Encyclopedia of Philosophy* (Winter 2015), Edward N. Zalta (ed.), URL = <https://plato.stanford.edu/archives/win2015/entries/astell/>. Lady Damaris Masham, philosopher and theological writer, was the daughter of Ralph Cudworth, the philosopher and a leading member of the Cambridge Platonists. She met John Locke in 1682, and she and her husband Sir Francis Masham became Locke's close friends and hosts. See Bridget Hill, "Masham, Damaris, Lady Masham (1658–1708)," in *Oxford Dictionary of National Biography*, ed. H. C. G. Matthew and Brian Harrison (Oxford: Oxford Univ. Press, 2004); online ed., ed. David Cannadine, May 2006, http://www.oxforddnb.com/view/article/18262, accessed 10 August 2017.

3. Malebranche "is known principally for offering a highly original synthesis of the views of his intellectual heroes, St. Augustine and René Descartes. Two distinctive results of this synthesis are Malebranche's doctrine that we see bodies through ideas in God and his occasionalist conclusion that God is the only real cause." Tad Schmaltz, "Nicolas Malebranche," *The Stanford Encyclopedia of Philosophy* (Winter 2016), Edward N. Zalta (ed.), URL = <https://plato.stanford.edu/archives/win2016/entries/malebranche/>.

4. John Norris, *Reason and Religion: or, The Grounds and Measures of Devotion* (London: Printed for Samuel Manship at the Bull in Cornhill, 1689), 10.

5. Norris, *Reason and Religion*, 6.

6. Norris, 7.

7. John Norris, *Poems and Discourses, Occasionally Written* (London: Printed by James Harefinch, for James Norris, at the Kings-Arms without Temple-Bar, 1684), 55.

8. John Norris, *Reflections upon the Conduct of Human Life: with Reference to the Study of Learning and Knowledge* (London: Printed for S. Manship, at the Black Bull in Cornhill, 1690), Preface, n.p.

9. Norris, *Reflections*, 23ff.

10. Jacqueline Broad, "A Woman's Influence? John Locke and Damaris Masham on Moral Accountability," *Journal of the History of Ideas* 67, no. 3 (July 2006), 489–510; Richard Acworth, "Malebranche and his Heirs," *Journal of the History of Ideas* 38, no. 4 (Oct–Dec 1977), 673–6.

11. John Norris (and Mary Astell), Preface to *Letters Concerning the Love of God* (London: Printed for Samuel Manship at the Ship near the Royal Exchange in Cornhill, and Richard Wilkins at the King's Head in St Paul's Churchyard, 1695), n.p.

12. Mary Astell, *Letters*, 192–3.

13. Damaris Masham, *A Discourse Concerning the Love of God* (London: Printed for Awnsham and John Churchill at the Black Swan, 1696), 6.

Cult: The Case of Mary-Catherine Cadière

JENNIFER L. AIREY

The *Oxford English Dictionary* provides two primary definitions of the word *cult*, one religious in nature, the other secular. A cult may be defined as a "relatively small group of people having (esp. religious) beliefs or practices regarded by others as strange or sinister," or as "a collective obsession with or intense admiration for a particular person, thing, or idea" that is not inherently sacred.[1] This essay examines the case of Mary-Catherine Cadière, who attracted cults in both senses of the term during the long eighteenth century.

In 1728, eighteen-year-old Mary-Catherine Cadière chose as her primary spiritual advisor Father Jean-Baptiste Girard, a forty-seven-year-old Jesuit priest in great demand as a confessor among women. Within a year after their spiritual relationship began, Cadière began to suffer from fits and convulsions, to show evidence of stigmata on her body, and supposedly to perform miracles. Soon, she had gathered a cult following of people who believed her visions and proclaimed her destined for posthumous canonization. As Cadière's fame grew, church officials became suspicious, and she was moved to a convent near Toulon. Initially, Girard continued to visit her, but, eventually, his visits tapered off, and Cadière came forward to lodge a complaint. Girard, she claimed, had raped her repeatedly, and, by preaching the doctrine of Quietism and breathing into her mouth, had bewitched her into experiencing visions. Girard denied the affair entirely, and he accused Cadière of demonic possession and witchcraft. After much wrangling over jurisdiction, the state brought both up on charges, Cadière of witchcraft, false testimony, and defamation, Girard, of rape, spiritual incest, and abortion. The trial dragged on for almost a year; ultimately, the magistrates returned a split verdict: twelve judges voted in Cadière's favor, twelve in Girard's, and both were acquitted. Two years later, Girard died. Cadière disappeared from the annals of history.

The Girard-Cadière trial was a huge cultural event in France, infamous for its salacious content and political implications; Jason Kuznicki argues that the trial was artificially prolonged by the Jansenists to embarrass the Jesuit order.[2] Cadière meanwhile attracted a sizeable cult following of devotees who prayed to her as one would a saint, insisting that she was a conduit for the divine. Small crowds would gather outside her home to hear her visionary pronouncements, and the nuns at Toulon reportedly collected her bath water for use in healing rituals.[3] Here, then, is a cultural moment in which female prophecy was taken seriously by many as a source of religious truth.[4]

Critics such as Mita Choudhury and Stéphane Lamotte have analyzed French reactions to the Girard-Cadière trial, but British reactions have been largely ignored by modern scholars.[5] Cadière attracted a very different sort of cult following in England. Between 1731–32, fifteen separate trial accounts were released, some of which were reprinted as many as eleven times, and reissued as late as 1893. Some of the pamphlets were pornographic in intent, reporting in painstaking detail Girard's alleged indecent acts.[6] Others served as anti-Catholic propaganda, part of a long-standing tradition of attacks describing Jesuits as sexually violent monsters.[7] Still others sought to comment on the British political moment. The Cadière trial occurred only a year after Sir Robert Walpole engineered the pardon of Colonel Francis Charteris for rape, and some authors looked to capitalize on the resultant outrage by referring to Girard as the "Great Man."[8]

Cadière simultaneously gained a cult following among authors of the period; the religious devotion of Cadière's French followers is replaced in England by literary celebrity. Henry Carey's *The Disappointment*, Henry Fielding's *The Old Debauchees*, and the anonymously authored ballad opera *The Wanton Jesuit,* all performed in 1732, transformed Cadière from criminal defendant to stage heroine. Later in the century, Gothic novelists, too, drew upon her story; Girard and Cadière find literary counterparts in Ambrosio and Antonia of Matthew Lewis's *The Monk*.[9] Each of these authors stripped Cadière of her prophetic voice, reducing her to a semi-fictional construct. Here, dedication to a religious figure is redirected into unsacred forms of cultural fame, an example of what Megan Gibson describes elsewhere in this forum as "the secularization of religious devotion."[10]

The image of Cadière as a prophet reemerges, however, in Mary Shelley's 1823 novel *Valperga: or, The Life and Adventures of Castruccio, Prince of Lucca*. Critics have usually read Shelley's Beatrice as an analogue to Joanna Southcott, the laundress who rose to prominence in the first decade of the 1800s by printing her elaborate religious prophecies.[11] But, Southcott was in her fifties when her work first saw print, and there is no hint of sexual violence in her writings. Beatrice, the eighteen-year old beauty who inspires a significant following, only to fall into seizures and heresy after a prolonged sexual assault, actually has much more in common with Cadière than with Southcott. In Beatrice, Shelley restores the prophetic aspect of Cadière's voice, treating female prophecy as simultaneously empowering and proof of powerlessness. She gains a cult following of devotees, but her physical suffering symbolizes her inability both to protect her bodily autonomy and to express in words the experience of sexual assault. *Valperga* also merges in Beatrice the two forms of devotion that Cadière had attracted. She is at once an object of religious worship and a human woman whose secular celebrity leads directly to her violation.

To examine reactions to the Cadière-Girard trial is thus to gain new insight into literary representations of female prophecy. It also reveals the slippage between religious and secular forms of devotion in the long eighteenth century, especially as they migrate between cultures and nations. The international reach of the trial offers insight into the ways in which English authors coopted Catholic devotion for secular purposes and transformed a French saint into an English literary icon.

NOTES

1. "cult, n." *OED* Online. December 2016. Oxford Univ. Press. http://0-www. oed.com.library.utulsa.edu/view/Entry/45709?rskey=m1851h&result=1&isAdvan ced=false, accessed 09 March 2017.

2. Jason Kuznicki, "Sorcery and Publicity: The Cadière-Girard Scandal of 1730–1731," *French History* 21, no. 3 (2007): 289–312.

3. For descriptions of Cadière's cult, as well as Girard's alleged crimes, see Anonymous, *The Case of Mrs. Mary Catherine Cadiere* (London: J. Roberts, 1732); Anonymous, *A Compleat Translation of the Memorial of the Jesuit Father John Baptist Girard* (London: J. Millan, 1732); Anonymous, *The Defence of F. John Baptist Girard, Jesuit* (London: J. Roberts, 1731); and, Anonymous, *Memoirs of Miss Mary-Catherine Cadiere* (London: J. Isted, 1731).

4. A tradition of female prophecy did exist in France. See Anne Llewellyn Barstow, "Joan of Arc and Female Mysticism," *Journal of Feminist Studies in Religion* 1, no. 2 (1985): 29–42.

5. See Mita Choudhury, *The Wanton Jesuit and the Wayward Saint: A Tale of Sex, Religion, and Politics in Eighteenth-Century France* (University Park: Pennsylvania State Univ. Press, 2015); and, Stéphane Lamotte, "Le P. Girard et la cadière dans la tourmente des pièces satiriques," *Dix-huitième Siècle* 39, no. 1 (2007): 431–53.

6. For discussion of court documents as a "peculiar genre of eighteenth-century erotica," see Peter Wagner, "The Pornographer in the Courtroom: Trial reports about cases of sexual crimes and delinquencies as a genre of eighteenth-century erotica," in *Sexuality in Eighteenth-Century Britain,* ed. Paul-Gabriel Boucé (Manchester: Manchester Univ. Press, 1982), 120.

7. See Jennifer L. Airey, *The Politics of Rape: Sexual Atrocity, Propaganda Wars, and the Restoration Stage* (Newark: Univ. of Delaware Press, 2012).

8. See, for instance, Anonymous, *The Tryal of Father Jean-Baptist Girard, on an accusation of quietism, sorcery, incest, abortion, and subornation* (London: J. Isted, 1732).

9. For discussion of the trial's influence on Lewis, see Diane Long Hoeveler, *The Gothic Ideology: Religious Hysteria and Anti-Catholicism in British Popular Fiction, 1780–1880* (Cardiff: Univ. of Wales Press, 2014). Charteris, a Scottish soldier who amassed a fortune through gambling and speculation, earned the enmity of the public for his abuse of women. He was charged with rape several times over the course of the 1720s and pardoned twice, the second time resulting in a substantial financial "gift" to Walpole.

10. Megan Gibson, "Cult," this volume.

11. See, for instance, Orianne Smith, *Romantic Women Writers, Revolution, and Prophecy: Rebellious Daughters, 1786–1826* (Cambridge: Cambridge Univ. Press, 2013).

Image

CLARE HAYNES

The word *image* had a double meaning in eighteenth-century Britain. It could indicate a representation of something or an idol. This connotation was apt because art was frequently shadowed by the specter, in Christian terms, of its mis-use. This essay contributes to the discussion of devotion by offering some observations on the ways in which portraiture and religious imagery supported devotion whilst also giving rise to anxieties over idolatry, which can be defined as mis-directed or inappropriate devotion.[1]

Over the course of the century, there was something of a revolution in the production of portraiture. Elite patrons still commissioned large, grand-manner portraits, but an array of smaller forms proliferated, which served an expanding middle-class market. These might be hung on a wall, kept on a table, or, sometimes, in the case of painted miniatures and silhouettes, worn on the body. Portraits recorded and supported friendships, amorous attachments, and familial relationships; part of their popularity and social power lay in their ability to substitute for the absent or the lost.[2] However, both making and using a likeness were potentially problematic, morally both and in relation to the second commandment.

Surprisingly, perhaps, these issues were explored most fully not in theology or art theory but in the genres of sentimental and Gothic fiction, where images were frequently given enormous power.[3] There is room here to consider only one example, which is drawn from a minor but representative short story of 1787: "the portrait, which he had held clasped between his hands, he kissed with apparent devotion; and, fastening it round his neck, as he knelt, again saluted it, lifting his eyes upwards, and with a deep sigh exclaiming—'O my dearest mother, I am now prepared to follow thee!'"[4] The story from which this extract comes tells of a young man, named The Criminal, who has been falsely accused of robbery and murder. He is so overwhelmed by the accusation that he suffers a physical collapse and wishes only to die, to be with his mother. In a common plot device, the portrait becomes the means by which he is identified as the illegitimate son of the prosecution barrister and the grandson of the judge. Over a few short pages, the portrait effects a complete moral reversal, as the young man is revealed to be virtuous and the barrister to have been corrupt, he having raped and abandoned the boy's mother. In the passage quoted, the gestures of clasping and kissing and the upward gaze of his eyes present the image of devotional fervour commonly associated with superstition and feminine enthusiasm, not with rational Protestantism. There is no suggestion that the young man is Catholic; rather, his address to his mother's portrait is irrational, unmanly, idolatrous. The portrait also acts as an idol in another way, as an image with a disruptive, miraculous force to upset the status quo and reveal a surprising truth.[5] In fictions such as *The Criminal,* the categories of portrait and idol overlap, and the slippage between image and original is exploited to explore the shadows of devotion.

While the Church of England had an extensive apologetic and catechetical literature on idolatry and the Roman Catholic church, it had no settled position on its own use of religious imagery. Plainness continued to be regarded by some as not only appropriate and safe but also as most conducive to prayer, while others recognised an ambiguity in biblical teaching, which left room for works of art to serve in a limited way as ornament and towards edification. For example, Bishop Gilbert Burnet offered a stern indictment of Roman Catholicism's use of images before observing that "the Prohibition of making an Image does not seem to bind in all Cases, where there is no danger of Idolatry, or Inclination to it; and where Pictures, or Statues, are made only for a Remembrance, or Ornament."[6] This view was rarely expressed so clearly, nor was it often expanded upon. There seems to have been a reluctance to engage with the issues in print, and, certainly, no positive theology of art was attempted. Writers about art rarely offered more than a cursory consideration of the issue of religious art, even as they advanced more general ideas about its affective power.[7]

Nevertheless, religious images were widely used in a variety of contexts. Illustrated bibles and books of common prayer were popular, and religious paintings and prints were often used to ornament domestic spaces. Furthermore, from the 1720s, narrative paintings were used increasingly as altarpieces in churches. Their role, however, was limited, for they could be granted no part in prayer or worship. The ultimate goal of religious devotion was an unmediated relationship with God. Thus, in her *Method of Devotion*, Elizabeth Burnet, Bishop Burnet's wife, prayed: "Lord, shut out of my Mind all vain Thoughts, with all worldly Representations, that being empty of my self, and of all corporeal Images, I may be filled with Divine Light, and made capable of thy spiritual Presence."[8] Burnet, in a similar way to The Criminal, pleads for the sublime redundancy of the image, which the coming into the presence of the original will bring about. As this brief account has indicated, images were granted great power in fiction and devotional literature in many different ways, not least in policing the proper aims and boundaries of devotion.[9]

Notes

1. On idolatry in the context of British art, see Clare Haynes, "In the Shadow of the Idol: Religion in British Art Theory 1600-1800," *Art History* 35, no. 1 (2012): 62–85.

2. Marcia Pointon, *Hanging the Head: Portraiture and Social Formation in Eighteenth-Century England* (New Haven & London: Yale Univ. Press, 1993); Kate Redford, *The Art of Domestic Life: Family Portraiture in Eighteenth-Century England* (New Haven & London: Yale Univ. Press, 2006), and Marcia Pointon, "'Surrounded with Brilliants:' Miniature Portraits in Eighteenth-Century England," *Art Bulletin*, 83, no. 1 (2001): 48–71.

3. Kamilla Elliott, *Portraiture and British Gothic Fiction: The Rise of Picture Identification, 1764-1835* (Baltimore, MD: The Johns Hopkins Univ. Press, 2012).

4. Mr. Harrison, "The Criminal," *The New Novelist's Magazine* 1 (1787): 6.

5. Gothic fiction, from *The Castle of Otranto* onward, relied heavily on statues and paintings that move or speak.

6. Gilbert Burnet, *An Exposition of the Church Catechism, for the use of the Diocese of Sarum* (London: John Churchill, 1710), 115.

7. Haynes, "In the Shadow of the Idol" and Clare Haynes, "Anglicanism and Art," *The Oxford History of Anglicanism, Volume II: Establishment and Empire, 1662–1829*, ed. Jeremy Gregory (Oxford: Oxford Univ. Press, 2017): 371–91.

8. Elizabeth Burnet, *A Method of Devotion: or, Rules for Holy & Devout Living* (London: Joseph Downing, 1713), 10.

9. The anxiety over visual art was much stronger than that which concerned music's power to mislead the senses in devotion. See the charity sermons of the Three Choirs Festival held annually from 1715, including Samuel Croxall, *The Antiquity, Dignity, and Advantages of Music* (London, 1741); Benjamin Newton, *A Church of England's Apology for the Use of Music in her Service* (Glocester, 1760); and, Samuel Glasse, *The Beneficial Effects of Harmony* (Glocester, 1778).

Catholic/Protestant: The Tensions of Transdenominational Prayer

SABINE VOLK-BIRKE

Significant aspects of the theory and practice of devotion in the sense of prayer and divine worship can be agreed on among Christian denominations, as numerous translations and adaptations of popular devotional literature prove. There are, however, also crucial differences in the modes of prayer and the types of rituals that depend on the worshiper's denomination. Both the similarities and the differences can be traced in the international reception of one of the most successful devotional manuals of the seventeenth and eighteenth centuries, the Catholic bishop François de Sales's *Introduction à la vie dévote* (1609). It was designed for the French Catholic female lay reader. Its training program was supposed to fit into an otherwise busy secular schedule so as to transform the reader's whole mind and daily life. The author emphasizes repeatedly that he is not just teaching the devotee how to pray, but also how to live a life of devotion, i.e., how to master the "virtue of devotion which is most amiable and acceptable in the divine sight," translating the benefits of prayer into a life fully designed to answer all the demands of her worldly tasks in the most conscientious and charitable manner possible.[1] Only when she achieves this synthesis of worldly and spiritual, interior and exterior, life in a cheerful manner with a grateful heart, can she claim to live a truly devout life. The nature of devotion, the manner of its working, and its effect on the devotee is represented by de Sales through a number of metaphors, such as the high flight of eagles, a flame, "the true spiritual sugar which takes away what is bitter in mortification," "dew in summer," emphasizing the extraordinary power it conveys and the essential needs to which it answers.[2]

In this sense, devotion relates to all aspects of human life, including marriage; it needs to be embraced gladly and fulfilled diligently in daily existence. This aspect of the text is translinguistic, transnational, and transdenominational. The mental bridge that spans the gap between prayer and work is the spiritual nosegay: de Sales advises the devotee to take two or three particularly fruitful thoughts from her morning devotion, like scented flowers, over into her household duties, so she can smell them and be reminded of her good resolutions.

When we come to the specifics of prayer training, however, concepts of correct devotion differ between Catholics and Protestants. Clearly, features like de Sales's sacramental bias or his references to devotional objects such as the rosary would not find their way into these versions, but the tailoring of the text to Anglican audiences goes beyond such elisions. The most prominent adaptations in English are by Henry Dodwell, distinguished lay humanist scholar, theologian, and non-juror, and William Nicholls, the theologian and author of an influential commentary on the *Book of Common Prayer*.[3] Both editors were prolific writers who took an active part in the theological and administrative debates of their day, so both would have taken the doctrinal implications of de Sales's work very seriously.

The changes in the front matter from the French source text to the English Protestant adaptations include not only title pages, the elision of de Sales's emotional dedicatory prayer to Jesus, and new prefaces with anti-Catholic propaganda, but also frontispieces, which no longer show the Pietà or portraits of Saint François de Sales with the sacred heart of Jesus. Broadly speaking, devotion in these adaptations is de-emotionalized, rationalized, and re-focused on God alone, away from Mary, Angels, and Saints. Nicholls explicitly warns that an increase of affection weakens judgment, so that many faults in publications by Catholics run the risk of being overlooked by readers. From the text proper, each Anglican editor cuts what he deems improper, Nicholls more than Dodwell. The comparison between the two adaptations shows that devotion is not only easily compartmentalized into the broad distinctions of Catholic and Protestant but also subtly nuanced within Anglicanism: how the borders between Anglican and Catholic worship are negotiated depends on the individual's personal theological and cultural preconditions and habits.

When the psychological ramifications of devotion are addressed, the most contentious issue of the instructions is mental prayer. In contrast to vocal prayer, which relies on set forms and communal words, mental prayer is not only silent and individual but also it even can be wordless. It is sometimes seen as synonymous with meditation. When it is attacked by Protestants, however, the meaning attached to mental prayer is the mystical union of the soul with God. François de Sales recommends it particularly: "surtout je vous conseille la mentale et cordiale [oraison], et particulièrement celle qui se fait autour de la vie et Passion de Notre-Seigneur: en le regardant souvent par la meditation, toute votre âme se remplira de lui, vous apprendrez ses contenances, et formerez vos actions au modèle des siennes."[4] In this sense, the mystical union is the essence of devotion, the most intense (but rare) connection between human and divine.

At the same time, this is not a gift or an achievement but a problem for some theologians: human nature cannot—and should not—be so bold as to aspire to such proximity, as it cannot, in its fallen state, ever be worthy of such a relationship. Nor can humans achieve anything through their own efforts, as they are totally dependent on God's grace. Thus, the underlying assumption of mental prayer, that some degree of mystical union is possible, is considered heretical by a number of Protestant writers. The idea of, let alone the instructions for, mental prayer, from such a theological stance, would need to be deleted from any devotional manual. Here, we see the widest gap between de Sales's and Nicholls's concept of devotion.

Like other devotional manuals for a lay audience, the *Introduction* pursues the same aim on the micro- and macro-levels, in the source text and in the adaptations: step-by-step hourly, daily, lifelong training of the mind and the heart, towards the single goal of the love of God, from which will follow the love of man. The prescribed mental exercises for a life of devotion are designed to train above all superb concentration and singleness of purpose, controlling the will, eliminating desires and thoughts that do not fit into the truly devout frame of mind. They are also designed to train the imagination to picture scenes that will yield strong emotional, empathetic effects. The self-discipline necessary to follow the rules of meditation will need constant practice. As this kind of devotion is coupled with frequent self-examination and confession, devotees must have a most profound self-knowledge, relating to their sins, their mental and their emotional processes. A life of devotion is thus an ongoing, triangular process among God, fellow humans, and self. While both denominations agree on the need for constant mental and emotional education towards true devotion, they differ on some of the techniques and objects the devotee can use, and they differ in their anthropology, believing or negating that the chasm between the divine and the human can be bridged in devotion.

NOTES

1. "True and living devotion . . . is no other thing than a true love of God; . . . when it reaches such a degree of perfection, that it makes us not only do good, but do so carefully, frequently and readily, then it is called devotion." Alan Ross, ed. and trans., *St. Francis de Sales: Introduction to the Devout Life* (1948; Mineola, NY: Dover Publications, 2009), 38.

2. "la devotion est le vrai sucre spirituel, qui ôte l'amertume aux mortifications," "de rosée en été." François de Sales, *Introduction à la vie dévote*, Part II, chapter one, in *Oeuvres*, ed. André Ravier (Paris: Gallimard, 1969), 35, 39, 40. Other metaphors stress the superior quality of devotion in relation to charity: "If charity be a milk, devotion is its cream; . . . if it be a precious stone, devotion is its lustre; if it be a precious balm, devotion is its perfume, yea the odour of sweetness which comforts men and makes the angels rejoice." Ross, *Introduction*, 41.

3. Henry Dodwell, ed., *An Introduction to a Devout Life containing especially, a prudent method for spiritual closet exercises, and remedies against the difficulties ordinarily occurring in the conduct of a pious life, Fitted for the use of Protestants* (Dublin: Printed by Benjamin Tooke and are to be sold by Joseph Wilde, 1673); William Nicholls, *An introduction to a devout life, by Francis Sales, Bishop and Prince of Geneva. Translated and reformed from the Errors of the Popish Edition. To which is perfixed* [sic] *a Discourse, of the Rise and Progress of the Spiritual Books in the Romish Church by William Nicholls D. D.* (London: E. Holt,1701).

4. "But above all, I recommend to you prayer of the mind and heart and especially that which has for its subject the life and passion of our Lord; for by beholding him often in meditation, your whole soul will be filled with him; you will learn his disposition, and you will form your actions after the model of his." Ross, *Introduction*, 75; François de Sales, *Oeuvres*, 79.

Fandom: Enthusiastic Devotion, Religious and Theatrical Celebrity

MEGAN E. GIBSON

In a review of the "Progress of Religion" in Britain, one *Public Advertiser* author condemns "Clergymen, who thus attempt to win proselytes by moving the passions, instead of convincing the judgment, or awakening the conscience."[1] He goes on to argue, "Were such arts necessary in preaching the Gospel, the office of the ministry ought to be performed by the women, whose voices are in general far more pathetic and persuasive than those of men, and Mrs. Siddons would then gain more hearers than the whole clergy of England put together."[2] Meant as an insult to Methodist preachers and their enthusiastic followers, the pathos performed by both Whitefield and Siddons, along with the enthusiastic reactions of their followers, reflect a significant similarity in the devotional practices of both figures' fans.[3] While devotion is largely considered to belong to the realm of religion, the eighteenth century marked a time of transition in which religious devotional practices were transferred to the secular realm. Both Whitefield and Siddons were masters of moving the passions of those who saw and heard them. Devotional response to these celebrated figures includes panegyrics and elegies as well as physical demonstrations of emotion at their performances. In comparing these instances of religious and apparently non-religious fan activity, we learn more about the views, beliefs, and feelings of the writers and spectators than we do, perhaps, of the celebrities themselves.

More than other Methodist preachers of his day, including John Wesley, George Whitefield elicited strong and emotional reactions from his congregation. His fans regarded him not only as a famous preacher whose spiritual influence would bring them closer to God but also as a figure worthy of devotion himself, a devotion characterized by attention to physical display, emotion, and raptured attention. Poetic verse written in praise of Whitefield refers to him in superlative, even divine terms often linked with the performance of his theatrical sermons.[4] One poet proclaims that Whitefield "command[s] Divine perswasion," joins "Celestial meekness with such ardour," and sends "Divine enchantments" to "every heart."[5] Later, this poet attends to the physical display, emotion, and raptured attention of Whitefield's fans, marveling, "With how much eagerness the list'ning throng / Gaze on his eyes, and hang upon his tongue. / On them his words like heavenly lightning dart, / They leave the body sound, but melt the heart."[6] Another poet writes, "How deep the silence, while the prophet speaks! / What list'ning crouds in eager numbers gaze! / Th' attentive boy, the lisping infant weeps, / And Britons pay their tribute of amaze."[7] While such texts are grounded in a Christian context, they sometimes appropriate classical (or secular) forms for the praise of religious subject matter, as in one poet's opening: "Inspire my muse, O Holy God of Heaven, . . . To write in praise of Mr. George Whitefield."[8] Whitefield's connection to the divine is fitting given his role as a preacher, and praises of Whitefield are intrinsically bound up in Christian devotion. Many writings praising him interpret his affecting sermons, his missionary efforts in America, and even his fame as tools to bring people closer to God. Nevertheless, there is a part of such performances devoted to Whitefield that slips into the realm of celebrity devotion, paving the way for later and more secular forms of devotion based on deep, visceral responses to moving performances and great physical displays of tears and emotion.

In the later eighteenth century, devotional responses to actress Sarah Siddons, including panegyric poetry and both factual and fictional accounts of people's encounters with her captivating performances, are strikingly similar to the devotional responses of Whitefield's fans. With Siddons, though, the specifically Christian context of devotion has been succeeded by a more secular form of fan worship. In the early 1780s, a plethora of panegyric poems were published that paint Siddons both as the "Tragic Muse," the moral compass whose performances will save the British theater and perhaps the nation at large from debauchery and ruin, and as a professional performer whose pathos and acting skills are unrivalled. The prelude to "The Tragic Muse" begins: "ACCEPT, fair Siddons! this spontaneous Lay, / Which Feeling bids me, as a tribute, pay / To that new Queen . . . Sublimely seated on the Tragic Throne."[9] The poem goes on to raise Siddons to prominence within the history of the English theater by describing her performance in specific roles and then discussing her fame. These and similar examples mix classical poetic traditions, rational exposition and explanation of her greatness, and an organized catalogue of her roles. One apparent effect of these writings is an alignment of Enlightenment thoughtfulness with the elevation of emotion as a legitimate means of experience for theater-goers and the British nation at large. Other responses to Siddons involve more visceral forms of devotion to her celebrity, concentrating on the affect and experiences of her fans. While newspaper accounts of the tears in the audience after a performance by Siddons may seem trite, novels offer a more personal glimpse into the individual fan experience. In Helen Maria Williams's *Julia* (1790), the narrator comments that Mrs. Siddons's "power over the human passions . . . is far more easy to feel than to delineate."[10] In *Helena*, an anonymously authored novel published in 1788, the eponymous heroine's feelings "were wrought up to agony, and visibly paid that tribute to the merit of Mrs. Siddons, she so well deserves."[11] In these cases, the heroines' devotion to Siddons is marked by their full attention to her stage performances as well as the strong feelings they experience at the theater. The true or correct fans pay tribute to Siddons by offering their full attention to her performances and by being overwhelmed by the feelings that she provokes.

Read against the backdrop of the Enlightenment, the prioritization of feelings and the physical expression of emotions provide an alternative means of viewing the self and the world through celebrity, one legitimized by fans of both Whitefield and Siddons. While Whitefield's celebrity is inextricably tied to Christianity and Christian devotion, his theatricality and ability to move the passions were perceived by many as theologically or ecclesiastically threatening. In contrast, Siddons's cultural status as divine "Tragic Muse" and her perceived influence on morality through tragic performance and virtuous private life was viewed as a national triumph. The divergent critical reception of these qualities in different contexts suggests an unease with the slippage between the secularization of religious devotion and the sanctification of theatrical devotion.

NOTES

1. Anon., "Review of the Progress of Religion in Britain, during 1782," *Public Advertiser* (London: Printed by H. S. Woodfall, 13 January 1783), n. p.

2. Anon., "Review of the Progress of Religion," n. p.

3. While fan and fandom are modern terms, the eighteenth century represents the moment in which consumerist impulses to identify with or express a kind of ownership of celebrities begin to take shape. It is my aim, therefore, not to create anachronism but to trace the emergence of modern fandom to this moment of its secular/religious shift.

4. George Whitefield's association with theater and theatrical talent have long been discussed. David Garrick admired his performativity, famously commenting that he "would give a hundred guineas if [he] could only say 'O!' like Mr. Whitefield." Quoted in Joseph Beaumont Wakeley, *The Prince of Pulpit Orators: A Portraiture of Rev. George Whitefield, M. A.,* 2nd ed. (New York: Carlton and Lanahan, 1871), 226. More recently, scholarship exploring the connections between George Whitefield and the theater or theatricality includes Harry Stout's biography of George Whitefield, which highlights the ways in which Whitefield's life was shaped by the theater and the natural dramatic gifts that he possessed and applied, with great success, to his evangelistic efforts both in England and America. The complex relationship between Whitefield and the theater are further explored in Misty Anderson's work, which discusses the persistence of anxieties bound in Whitefield's theatricality and the ways in which he was seen "as an actor poaching his audience from the theater" (132). Brett McInelly's overview of recent work on Methodism, Whitefield, and theatricality, among other Methodist topics, also shows the ways in which scholars are beginning to complicate our understanding of religion in the enlightenment era. See Harry S. Stout, *The Divine Dramatist: George Whitefield and the Rise of Modern Evangelicalism* (Grand Rapids, MI: William B. Eerdmans Publishing Company, 1991); Misty G. Anderson, "'Our Purpose is the Same:' Whitefield, Foote, and the Theatricality of Methodism," *Studies in Eighteenth-Century Culture* 34 (2005): 125–49; and Brett C. McInelly, "Writing the Revival: The Intersections of Methodism and Literature in the Long 18th Century," *Literature Compass* 12 (2015): 12–21.

5. Anon., *A Poem, Occasioned by hearing the late Reverend George Whitefield preach* (Boston, 1771), n. p. Other examples abound in writings of the period. Phillis Wheatley, for instance, wrote an elegy to Whitefield that begins "Hail happy Saint on thy immortal throne!" and talks of his "unrival'd friendship," and his "unequal'd accents." See Wheatley's *An elegiac poem, on the death of that celebrated divine, and eminent servant of Jesus Christ, the Reverend and learned George Whitefield* (Boston, 1770), 5, 6, 5. One fan biography from 1739 followed suit, painting him as "larger than life" and drawing subsequent criticisms of "blowing up [Whitefield's] Character to an undue Size." See Frank Lambert, *Inventing the "Great Awakening"* (Princeton, NJ: Princeton Univ. Press, 1999), 101.

6. Anon., *A Poem, Occasioned,* n. p.

7. Anon., *An Elegiac Poem; Sacred to the Memory of the Rev. George Whitefield* (Boston, 1770), 5.

8. Anon., *An Elegy on the much lamented Death of the Rev. Mr. George Whitefield* (London, 1761).

9. William Russell, *The Tragic Muse: a Poem. Addressed to Mrs. Siddons* (London: G. Kearsley, 1783), 5.

10. Helen Maria Williams, *Julia*, 2 vols. (London: T. Cadell, 1790), 1: 34.

11. Lady of distinction, *Helena* (London: W. Richardson, 1788), 31.

Mimesis: Individual Experience and the Devotional Culture of Early Methodism

LAURA DAVIES

Rachel Fulton has written persuasively that "If one accepts reading as a devotional activity, as an experience of intimacy with the divine, then the act of writing, of transforming experience *of* text *into* text and of concretizing understanding in verbal depiction, may also be interpreted as a devotional performance."[1] The implications of this idea for our understanding of the life writing of eighteenth-century Methodism are explored here in relation to the concept of mimesis, with a view to reframing the questions that we might ask of the relationship between the textual features of such writing and the culture within which it was produced and disseminated.

Bruce Hindmarsh, Joyce Quiring Erickson, and Phyllis Mack have all argued that accounts of spiritual conversion written by lay Methodists during the eighteenth century are "individual and mimetic, since in them we hear both the individual voice and the voice of the community."[2] This elision of individual and group was generated by the diffusion of shared vocabularies and conceptual frameworks within the movement, which enabled the interpretation and articulation of experiences that were singular yet also shared; this tendency also arose from deliberate "modelling," in which lay followers sought to copy the "autobiographical constructions" of the movement's leaders in their own narratives. In their writing we thus see a multifaceted devotion comprising divine and human objects.[3] We might think of these as horizontal and vertical forms of mimesis; the so-called class and band structure of eighteenth-century Methodist meetings created a sense of fellowship and encouraged the sharing of experiences among members, but the movement was, at the same time, hierarchical in the sense of being organized around various levels of leadership and with respect to each individual's relative position along the often non-linear path towards justification and sanctification.

Despite such scholarship, life writing of this kind has not received sustained literary critical attention, often being dismissed as "repetitive and clichéd, the mouthing of stock religious phraseology which hardly registers conscious agency, much less the individuation of experience."[4] In part, I suggest that this is because it has not yet been adequately understood that mimesis is a form of actuation. By setting Fulton's emphasis on devotional writing as performance in dialogue with the definition of mimesis in Auerbach's classic study *The Representation of Reality in Western Literature*—for whom it is understood as "the interpretation of reality through literary representation or 'imitation'"—we can begin to address this. Said's more recent gloss of Auerbach's definition as "an active dramatic presentation of how each author actually realizes, brings characters to life, and clarifies his or her own world," reveals that what they both acknowledge is the agency at work in the act of transformation.[5]

What we might, therefore, term devotional mimesis through writing as performance is a key characteristic of eighteenth-century Methodism. In this setting, lived experience was textually infused; it was alive with the sound and sight of biblical, sermon, hymnal, and life-writing texts, to the extent that Auerbach's "representation" of how each writer experiences and understands "her own world" is bound up with the transformation Fulton identifies as "the experience *of* text *into* text." It is an activity combining acts of interpretation, clarification, realization, and, frequently, reverence, not in spite but because of the fact that it involves the imitation and replication of diction, phrasing, imagery, and form. It is a working out of meaning and of oneself in relation to that meaning and to the community in which it has valence. It is a testamentary act, signalling devotion, or at least the desire for it. It may also constitute an attempt to validate one's own spiritual experience by the alignment of it with that of a person considered in some way superior.

We can see this in action even before the Methodist publishing juggernaut reached full speed. For example, conversion narratives sent in the form of letters to Charles Wesley from 1730 onwards share multiple features of structure and expression. To take just one, we can observe a pattern in relation to Hebrews 12.2: Jesus is "the author and finisher of our faith." This was a text that the writers would have encountered variously, including through bible reading, sermons, Charles Wesley's poems, and the testimony of fellow believers, and it is woven into many of the narratives in a manner indicative of both horizontal and vertical forms of mimesis.[6] Thus, we find, amongst others, the phrases: "he that has begun this work will surely finish;" "I doubt not but the Lord will carry on his work;" "I doubt not but he that is the author will be the finisher;" and, "I had a Strong witness that the Lord would finish his work before he would take me hence."[7] Rather than diminishing the value of these statements, the fact of replication is key to understanding how they function. These writers share an understanding that their spiritual journey is incomplete and a hope that God will continue to work upon their souls; they seek to confirm the validity of this hope for themselves by echoing the words of the community by which it is sanctioned and to strengthen it through articulation in their own hand. In so doing, each writer confirms her identity as a member of the community and testifies to her faith in God, before whom she is an individual supplicant. They write with reverence to Wesley, marking their respect and devotion to him in their choice of diction used first by him, and, at the same time, they enact their conversion because only in a new language of faith can they express their coming to the light.

To attend fully to the performative dimension of this devotional writing, the matter of repetition needs to be addressed rather than downplayed. The kind of writing taking place within the context of early Methodism complicates the idea of the author figure propounded by narratives of secular enlightenment as an autonomous individual in possession of his own intellectual property and agency. But, it also challenges the primacy of "originality as a central value in cultural production" and raises questions about uniqueness within "devotional performance."[8] The distinction drawn by Deleuze between a form of repetition in which "the validity of the mimetic copy is established by its truth of correspondence to what it copies," and an alternative form that presupposes a world of difference, in which exact repetitions are impossible, and what appear to be such, are merely "simulacra" or "phantasms," is a useful point of reference. As J. Hillis Miller has demonstrated, these apparently incompatible conceptions are commonly found together in fiction.[9] This co-existence raises the possibility that it may be equally the case in devotional writing. Reinvigorating critical attention to such texts enables us both to pay more attention to what may, in fact, be different about narratives that at first glance seem to replicate one another and opens up discussion about the ways in which, at the same time, the mimetic element of devotional writing is key to its transformational, interpretative work.

NOTES

1. Rachel Fulton, "Mimetic Devotion, Marian Exegesis, and the Historical Sense of the Song of Songs," *Viator* 27 (1996): 85–116, 88.

2. Bruce Hindmarsh, *The Evangelical Conversion Narrative* (Oxford: Oxford Univ. Press, 2005), 142; Joyce Quiring Erickson, "'Perfect Love:' Achieving sanctification as a pattern of desire in the life writings of early Methodist women," *Prose Studies: History, Theory, Criticism*, 20, no. 2 (2008): 72–89; Phyllis Mack, *Heart Religion in the British Enlightenment: Gender and Emotion in Early Methodism* (Cambridge: Cambridge Univ. Press, 2008).

3. Hindmarsh, *The Evangelical Conversion Narrative*, 153.

4. Erickson, "'Perfect Love,'" 75.

5. Eric Auerbach, *Mimesis: The Representation of Reality in Western Literature*, trans. Willard R. Trask, with a new introduction by Edward W. Said (Princeton, NJ: Yale Univ. Press, 2003), 554, xx.

6. See, for example, John Wesley's gloss on this verse in his *Explanatory Notes on the New Testament*, 2nd ed. (London, 1757), 67; his sermon "On Faith" (No.106) in *The Works of John Wesley* 14 vols. (Zondervan Publishing House, Grand Rapids, MI, 1958–9), 7: 195–202; and, John and Charles Wesley, *Hymns and Sacred Poems* (London: Strahan, 1739).

7. The manuscript texts are held at the John Rylands Library (University of Manchester, UK), as part of the Early Methodist Volume. These quotations are taken from letters written by Margaret Austin, Fo.1.4; Elizabeth Hinsome, Fo.2.5; Sarah Barber, Fo.7.2; and, Joan Webb, Fo.136.5. This collection has been digitized and is available at *https://www.library.manchester.ac.uk/search-resources/manchester-digital-collections/digitisation-services/projects/rapture-and-reason*.

8. Mark Rose, *Authors and Owners: the Invention of Copyright* (Cambridge, MA: Harvard Univ. Press, 1993), 6.

9. This distinction is originally made by Gilles Deleuze in *Logique du sens* (Paris: Les Editions de Minuit, 1969), 302. The summary cited here is that of J. Hillis Miller, *Fiction and Repetition: Seven English Novels* (Cambridge, MA: Harvard Univ. Press, 1982), 6.

Knowledge: The British Virtuoso

THERESA SCHOEN

In the long eighteenth century, the New Science, its objects and practices, seemed to demand a form of commitment from the naturalist community that many Britons felt to rival and, essentially, to endanger a Christian's devotion to God. Naturalists' observation of nature, as Lorraine Daston has shown, could indeed become "too absorbing to be easily compatible with other social, professional, and religious commitments."[1] Although naturalists like Robert Boyle claimed that experimental philosophy represents a form of religious worship—a concept that Courtney Weiss Smith has called "meditative empiricism"—criticism persisted throughout the long eighteenth century.[2] Enlightenment moralists condemned contemporary scientific practices and approaches to knowledge as a secularized form of devotion that had lost sight of reason, God, and the afterlife. They used the satirical character of the Virtuoso to respond to what they considered to be naturalist enthusiasm and, hence, a threat to the stability of contemporary society.[3] Their texts show how the Virtuoso conceives of, approaches, and examines his object of interest.[4] Such representations allow us to draw conclusions as to the meaning and forms of scientific devotion in the Enlightenment.

Moralistic writers imagined the Virtuoso to express his scientific devotion, first and foremost, in and through his practices. In the texts I have examined, the most stable practice is that of collecting—collecting curiosities and rarities from past and present, from Europe and beyond.[5] The habit of collecting is intricately connected to the idea of ordering, or classifying systematically or even taxonomically, for instance, by grouping insects and their subsets according to their kind.[6] The majority of the texts explicitly engage with observational practices that Lorraine Daston has shown to be prominent in the period, namely, attentive and repeated observation that entails inductive reasoning and careful examination with the help of the senses.[7] Like the type's historical models, the Virtuoso takes advantage of scientific instruments like "microscopes, telescopes, thermometers, barometers, pneumatic engines, [and] stentrophonical tubes."[8] Furthermore, he is keen on inventing new tools that he can use in his experiments—an urge that associates him with the Projectors of the period, notorious for their dubious business schemes.[9] A minority of my sources present the Virtuoso as habitually engaged in acts of reading such natural philosophical texts as Lucretius's *De Rerum Natura* and Carolus Linnæus's *Systema Naturae*.[10]

These practices were not suspicious as such, but they became problematic as the Virtuoso misapplied them. Enlightenment moralists often felt scientific devotion to be accompanied by excess and madness—two characteristics that show in the Virtuoso's unrestrained curiosity and, in turn, in the neglect of his family and his private and public affairs.[11] The Virtuoso's immoderate study of nature often makes him essentially unsociable—even asocial.[12] The relationships within the scientific community replace family ties; yet, more than that, scientific devotion kindles a sense of pride and superiority—a sense of competition—that threatens to undermine any allegiance within the (scientific) community and, hence, endangers the stability of contemporary British society.[13] This was all the more tragic because moralists found difficulty in reconciling the Virtuoso's accomplishments—from collections of bottled air and a method of breeding sheep without wool to collections containing "Pope Joan's toe-nail"—with their conception of (socially) useful knowledge.[14]

Yet while moralists criticized the Virtuoso for his misconceived devotion to knowledge, they used their writings to present a balanced alternative. *The Tatler* No. 119, for instance, discovers the periodical's persona Isaac Bickerstaff pondering the merits of the microscope and "reflecting upon Myriads of Animals that swim in those Vessels of an human Body. While [his] Mind was thus filled with that secret Wonder and Delight, [he] could not but look upon [him]self as in an Act of Devotion."[15] Mr. Rambler emphasizes the value of collections of art and science as well as the significance of examining "the structure of animals . . . ; they exhibit evidences of infinite wisdom, bear their testimony to the supreme reason, and excite in the mind new raptures of gratitude, and new incentives to piety."[16] Here, Bickerstaff and Mr. Rambler confirm seventeenth-century naturalist convictions that the study of nature corresponds to religious acts of devotion. So the core of the problem rests in the role of reason, as Mr. Spectator expresses in an essay dedicated to the nature of and errors in devotion: "Devotion . . . may disorder the Mind, unless its Heats are tempered with Caution and Prudence. . . . [W]hen it does not lie under the check of Reason, [it] is very apt to degenerate into Enthusiasm."[17] The Virtuoso's actions and habits exhibit immoderate, enthusiastic devotion to knowledge. Reason and moderation, by contrast, coupled with naturalist practices, are conducive to socially and morally useful knowledge and, hence, inspire *adequate* scientific devotion.

NOTES

1. Lorraine Daston, "The Empire of Observation, 1600–1800," in *Histories of Scientific Observation*, ed. Lorraine Daston and Elizabeth Lunbeck (Chicago: The Univ. of Chicago Press, 2011), 81–113, 102.

2. See Peter Harrison, "Sentiments of Devotion and Experimental Philosophy in Seventeenth-Century England," *Journal of Medieval and Early Modern Studies* 44, no. 1 (2014): 113–33, 128. Courtney Weiss Smith, *Empiricist Devotions: Science, Religion, and Poetry in Early Eighteenth-Century England* (Charlottesville, VA: Univ. of Virginia Press, 2016), 47.

3. For an introduction to the character of the Virtuoso, see Walter Houghton, "The English Virtuoso in the Seventeenth Century," *Journal of the History of Ideas* 3, no. 1 (1942): 51–73; and Houghton, "The English Virtuoso," *Journal of the History of Ideas* 3, no. 2 (1942): 190–219, accessed 17 June 2010, http://www.jstor.org/stable/2707461 (Part I) and http://jstor.org/stable/2707177 (Part II).

4. As the majority of the texts display male (and gentleman) Virtuosi, I shall abide by the masculine personal pronoun. Remarkably, *The Spectator* alone represents an exception regarding the type's gender and rank, ridiculing female Virtuosi belonging to the merchant rank.

5. I have analysed the portrayal of the Virtuoso in the following texts: Thomas Shadwell, *The Virtuoso* [1676], ed. Marjorie Hope Nicolson and David Stuart Rodes (Lincoln: Univ. of Nebraska Press, 1966); *The Tatler*, ed. Donald F. Bond, 3 vols. (Oxford: Clarendon Press, 1987), 3, nos. 216 and 221 [1710]; *The Spectator*, ed. Donald F. Bond, 5 vols. (Oxford: Clarendon Press, 1965), 2, nos. 242 and 278 [1711/1712]; Jonathan Swift, *Gulliver's Travels* [1726] (Ware: Wordsworth, 1992), part III; Samuel Johnson, *The Rambler*, ed. Walter J. Bate and Albrecht B. Strauss, 5 vols. *The Yale Edition of the Works of Samuel Johnson* (New Haven: Yale Univ. Press, 1969), 4, nos. 82 and 83 [1750/1751]; Tobias Smollett, *The Adventures of Peregrine Pickle* [1751], ed. James L. Clifford (London: Oxford Univ. Press, 1969), chap. 103; George M. Woodward, *Eccentric Excursions or, Literary and Pictorial Sketches of Countenance, Character and Country in Different Parts of England*

and South Wales, Interspersed with Curious Anecdotes, Embellished with Upward of One Hundred Characteristic and Illustrative Prints (London: Allen and Co, 1796), chap. 9, accessed 3 March 2017, http://find.galegroup.com/ecco/infomark. do?&source=gale&prodId=ECCO&userGroupName=halle&tabID=T001&docId =CW3316610631&type=multipage&contentSet=ECCOArticles&version=1.0&d ocLevel=FASCIMILE; and "The Virtuoso Broker: A Dramatic Proverb," in *The Young Gentleman's and Lady's Magazine, or Universal Repository of Knowledge, Instruction and Amusement, Intended to Open the Tender Mind to an Acquaintance with Life, Morals and Science, the Works of Nature and of Art, and to Serve as an Useful Auxiliary to Public and Private Tuition,* ed. Dr. Mavor, 2 vols., (London, 1799–1800), 2: 313–26, accessed 3 March 2017, http://find.galegroup.com/ecco/ infomark.do?&source=gale&docLevel=FASCIMILE&prodId=ECCO&userGroup Name=halle&tabID=T001&docId=CW3306046279&type=multipage&contentSet =ECCOArticles&version=1.0.

6. See Shadwell, *The Virtuoso*, 76; Swift, *Gulliver's Travels*, 134ff.

7. Daston, "Empire of Observation," 91–95, 99–100. See e.g. Smollett, *Peregrine Pickle*, 662–63.

8. Shadwell, *The Virtuoso*, 55.

9. See Shadwell, *The Virtuoso*, 43; Swift, *Gulliver's Travels*, 137; Smollett, *Peregrine Pickle*, 663.

10. See *The Spectator*, 442; Woodward, *Eccentric Excursions*, 100.

11. On the relationship of naturalist attention, curiosity, and wonder, see Lorraine Daston, *Eine kurze Geschichte der wissenschaftlichen Aufmerksamkeit* (München: Carl Friedrich von Siemens Stiftung, 2001).

12. For the historical background, see Daston, "Empire of Observation," 102.

13. See *The Tatler*, 2: 153–55; Swift, *Gulliver's Travels*, 119ff.

14. See Shadwell, *The Virtuoso*, 76; Swift, *Gulliver's Travels*, 137; "Virtuoso Broker," 315.

15. *The Tatler*, 2: 206.

16. Johnson, *The Rambler*, 4:72–73.

17. *The Spectator*, 2: 289.

Devotion: Afterword

EMMA SALGÅRD CUNHA

Thinking about devotion in its slippery religious and secular senses requires us to take a stance on to what extent beliefs, habits, behaviours, and rituals may acquire special significance in a range of performative contexts—on the stage, in the public sphere, as a performance of personal identity, as texts, and as acts of worship, whether liturgical or private. There are two related features that emerged from the forum's conversation. The first is that the call to focus on devotion encourages us as scholars to attach significance to the *practices* of adherents (whether religious believers or devotees of more secular objects) and, at least in part, to direct our attention away from doctrinal and political questions and towards the reconstruction of personal theology as enacted and experienced. Such a shift of attention is important because it validates the lived experience of devotees, especially of women. It is no coincidence that so many of the contributors have chosen women devotees as the basis of their case studies, since reformulating religion as devotion precisely invites us to think about the impact of theology and of politics on individuals who are traditionally estranged or excluded from positions of power.

The second feature to which I wish to draw attention is that a great deal of the contributors' discussion revolves around the policing and regulation of such devotional experience. As Stevens notes in her introduction, the lack of fixed meaning attached to the word *devotion* in the eighteenth century is both a challenge and an opportunity for us to open a conversation about the boundaries between secular and sacred. It is, of course, not the case that devotion simply bifurcates around a secular-religious split. But in many cases, the etymological as well as ideological fault line can be thrown into sharper relief by attending to moments in which the borders between secular and religious devotion are transcended or transgressed, and, significantly, by asking how (and by whom) they are policed.

Whilst acknowledging the messy overlaps between the experience of secular and religious devotion, it is also possible and helpful to distinguish the two, and, especially, to notice the ways in which the two were distinguished in eighteenth-century discourse. When are devotional practices such as prayer and meditation to be thought of as truly sacred, effective ways of communicating with God; when are they mere enthusiasm? When does the practice of fandom stray into idolatry? The devoutness of Mary-Catherine Cadière or of a preacher like George Whitefield inspires fandom and devotion only so long as it is irregular, visceral, and extreme; what is more, the attachment of the devotee to her saint or idol uncouples her from the final and absolute object of religious attachment, God. As Gibson explores, in the case of a secular celebrity idol such as Sarah Siddons, we have a double uncoupling of legitimate devotional experience: the fanatical devotion to Siddons substitutes for the devotion to a prophet or preacher who, it could be feared, already substitutes for authentic devotion to Christ or to God.

When, as Schoen argues, the devotion of the scientific virtuoso is judged to have immoderately attached himself to the objects of his experimentation instead of to the larger commitments of science and religion, we might characterize this judgement as protective of an outward-facing, masculine, Protestant societal structure that abhors solipsism and indulgence. For an author like Norris, as Pritchard demonstrates, the scientific and rational bases of devotion may be established only by keeping in sight what he and his followers considered the end of all human endeavour: knowledge of and acceptability to God. Haynes's discussion of the double role of the image as a channel for and challenge to worship also revolves around the possibility that representational art, especially portraiture, not only replicates but also replaces its object. That the problematic possibility of idolatry remains at stake across Haynes's sources underlines the ways in which the imperative theologies we might associate with Puritanical thinking retained their currency in popular discourse well into the period we associate with Romanticism and, rightly or wrongly, with the beginnings of modern secularism.

Perhaps the clearest examples of devotional policing and the question of where religion becomes idolatry arose around the Protestant, anglophone reaction to Catholicism in Britain, and the heightened, defensive rhetoric and actions that monitored slippage between Protestant and Catholic devotion. In Airey's discussion of Cadière, questions of legality rub against questions of religious legitimacy. Even at a time when female prophecy was taken seriously by both religious authorities and individuals, Cadière's power, whether as a secular idol or a religious prophet, derived its validity from its visceral bodily expression—through stigmata, fits and convulsions, and even in the physical and sexual violence that she endured. The actual words and import of her prophecies are lost under a raft of cult British legalistic and voyeuristic publications, many of which refuse to take seriously any claim of true prophetic power and focus instead on her female body and on the affective rather than sacred dimensions of her experience.

In Volk-Birke's consideration of the policing of physical devotional attitudes for meditation and prayer as they move between Catholic and Protestant tradition, the same refusal to countenance the reality or sacredness of Catholic devotion seems almost to lead to a denial not only of Catholic praxis but also of the entire possibility of prophecy, transportation, ecstasy, or communion with Christ for Protestant adherents. Volk-Birke shows us how the de-emotionalized, rationalized English adaptations of François de Sales perpetuate his concern to stipulate and guide devotion, but they simultaneously downgrade the role that psychology has to play in religious experience, making devotional activities a pathway to a moral Christianity rather than to any mystical union with God.

In both of these cases, a larger political and legal context affects the creation and reception of texts that have at their heart questions of spirituality, sacredness, and religious experience. But as I have argued, it is equally the case that individual, lay devotional practice may inform political and theological policy on a larger level. The ways in which adapted Catholic devotional books like those of de Sales were used in English Protestant households could not but have influenced the practice of English Protestantism. Davies's insight into the mimetic principles that served to canonize testimonial patterns in Methodist conversion experiences give us another example of the way that devotional practices fluctuate between what Volk-Birke calls the micro- and macro-layers of a religious group's habitual and ritual activities, from individual to wider community, from singularity to norm. In this movement lies the possibility of aberration and of heresy, and it is for this reason that the policing of lay and female devotion remains culturally urgent within religious traditions.

Literary texts serve as a bridge between sanctioned and unsanctioned forms of worship, allowing for both the policing and modelling of religious habits either by state or Church authorities as well as for the recording and dissemination of religious experience by the laity. As Tessa Whitehouse has recently shown, "the relationship between texts, behaviour, and taste is a complicated one: books, periodicals, lectures, letters, diaries, essays, and conversation reflect the intellectual and cultural trends of their time but also contribute to them."[1] In adopting literary-critical approaches to the study of eighteenth-century religion, the contributors to this forum examined devotion as a phenomenon that can be only observed and understood in action and in practice; consequently, this forces us to consider the ways that the boundaries of secularity and religion reveal themselves in the establishment's proclivity to regulate the behaviours, experiences, and beliefs of individual devotees.

NOTES

1. Tessa Whitehouse, *The Textual Culture of English Protestant Dissent 1720–1800* (Oxford: Oxford Univ. Press, 2015) 7.

Contributors to Volume 48

Jennifer L. Airey is associate professor of English at the University of Tulsa, specializing in literature of the long eighteenth century. She is the author of *The Politics of Rape: Sexual Atrocity, Propaganda Wars, and the Restoration Stage* (2012) and has published articles on authors such as Wycherley, Dryden, Centlivre, Robinson, Dacre, and Haywood. She is the editor of *Tulsa Studies in Women's Literature,* the first scholarly journal devoted solely to the study of women's literature.

Michael C. Amrozowicz is an instructor at the State University of New York at Albany in the Department of English. Currently, he is working on a book manuscript titled *"The Great Ferment:" Histories of Social Organization and Novelistic Genres in Eighteenth-Century Britain.* His essay "Adam Smith and Poetics" appeared in *The Oxford Handbook to Adam Smith* (2013).

Chiara Cillerai is associate professor at The Institute for Core Studies at St. John's University, NY. Her research and writing focus on eighteenth-century literary culture in America. Her recently published book, *Voices of Cosmopolitanism in Early American Writings and Culture* (2017) examines how a number of American writers of the late colonial period employed the language of cosmopolitanism to engage in discussions of nationhood. She has also recently contributed an essay entitled "Cosmopolitan Correspondences: The American Republic of Letters and the Circulation of Enlightenment Thought" to *Volume I: Origins to 1820* of the *Blackwell Companion to American Literature* (forthcoming). She is co-editing a paper and digital edition of Elizabeth Graeme Fergusson's manuscript poems and other writings. She has published articles on Thomas Jefferson, the Italian immigrant Philip Mazzei, and Toni Morrison's novel *A Mercy.*

Emma Salgård Cunha is associate member of the faculty of English at the University of Oxford. She is the author of *John Wesley, Practical Divinity and the Defence of Literature* (2018) and co-editor with Laura Davies of a special edition of the *Journal of Eighteenth-Century Studies* on the subject "Writing Eighteenth-Century Religion" (2018).

Laura Davies is lecturer and director of studies in English at King's College, University of Cambridge. She has published articles and book chapters on the eighteenth-century periodical essay and on life writing in various forms, including that of Samuel Johnson, James Boswell, and on Methodist conversion narratives. Most recently she has co-edited with Emma Salgård Cunha a special edition of the *Journal for Eighteenth-Century Studies* on the subject "Writing Eighteenth-Century Religion" (2018).

Megan E. Gibson is a Ph.D. candidate in the Department of English at the University of Tulsa. She teaches courses in long eighteenth-century literature and is currently working on her dissertation, "Celebrity and Devotion in Eighteenth-Century Britain," which examines the intersections between religious and secular forms of devotion among fans of theatrical, ecclesiastical, criminal, and fictional celebrities. Her project aims to develop a better understanding of the ways in which celebrity and devotion were defined and intermingled across various contexts throughout the period.

Dena Goodman is Lila Miller Collegiate Professor History and Women's Studies Emerita at the University of Michigan. Her publications include *The Republic of Letters: A Cultural History of the French Enlightenment* (1994) and *Becoming a Woman in the Age of Letters* (2009). She is co-director of *The Encyclopedia of Diderot and D'Alembert Collaborative Translation Project* (*https://quod.lib.umich.edu/d/did/*). In 2016-17, she served as president of ASECS.

Clare Haynes is a senior research associate at the University of East Anglia, researching representations of medieval churches. Her main interest is in religious art in Britain in the long eighteenth century. Her first book, *Pictures and Popery: Art and Religion in England, 1660–1760* (2006), has been followed by a series of articles including "Anglicanism and Art" for the new *Oxford History of Anglicanism*, vol. 2 (2017). She is revising a book-length manuscript on the use of art in the parish church.

Matthew Mauger is senior lecturer in English at Queen Mary University of London. His recent publications include "'A Most Exquisite Dilemma:' Conscience, Dissent, and the Limits of Civic Authority in London's Sheriffs Case," *London Journal* 37 (2012) and "'Observe how parts with parts unite / In one harmonious rule of right:' William Blackstone's Verses on the Laws of England," *Law and Humanities* 6 (2012). He is the editor of *Tea, Commerce and the East India Company,* volume three of *Tea and the Tea-Table in Eighteenth-Century England,* 4 vols. (2010). He has co-edited with Richard Coulton and Christopher Reid, *Stealing Books in Eighteenth-Century London* (2016) and with Richard Coulton and Markman Ellis, *Empire of Tea: The Asian Leaf that Conquered the World* (2015).

Carla J. Mulford, the Founding President of the Society of Early Americanists, is professor of English at Penn State, University Park. A recipient of the Lifetime Achievement Award from the MLA Division of American Literature to 1800, she has published widely on the literature, culture, and political life of the Atlantic world in the long eighteenth century. Benjamin Franklin has been her preoccupation in recent years, as evidenced by her publications including *The Cambridge Companion to Benjamin Franklin* (2009), *Benjamin Franklin and the Ends of Empire* (2015), and about twenty articles and book chapters on Franklin. She is currently writing the book-length "Benjamin

Franklin's Electrical Diplomacy," which examines the intersections between Franklin's scientific reputation and political life.

Jürgen Overhoff is professor of the History of Education at the Westfälische Wilhelms-Universität Münster. He is also director of the Center for German-American Educational History. Since September 2018, he has been president of the German Society for Eighteenth-Century Studies (DGEJ). His monographs are *Benjamin Franklin. Erfinder, Freigeist, Staatenlenker* (2006) and *Friedrich der Große und George Washington. Zwei Wege der Aufklärung* (2011). He has edited *William Penn, Früchte der Einsamkeit [Some Fruits of Solitude]*, transl. Joachim Kalka (2018), and co-edited, with Anne Overbeck, *New Perspectives on German-American Educational History: Topics, Trends, Fields of Research* (2017).

Jason Pearl is associate professor of English Literature at Florida International University. He is author of *Utopian Geographies and the Early English Novel* (2014) and book review editor of the online journal *Digital Defoe*. He is currently working on a new book project called "Balloon Flight and the View above Britain."

Penny Pritchard is a senior lecturer in English Literature at the University of Hertfordshire. Her research interests focus on the interrelationships between early modern religious writing, the development of print culture, and authorial identity; she has published extensively on Protestant funeral sermons in the seventeenth and eighteenth centuries as well as on Defoe. Her monographs are *The Long Eighteenth Century: Texts and Contexts* (2010) and *Before Crusoe: Defoe, Voice, and the Ministry*, (2019).

Colin T. Ramsey is associate professor of English at Appalachian State University. His current research focuses on the complex relations between manuscript and print cultures in eighteenth-century British North America. His most recent publication is "Disney's *National Treasure*, the Declaration of Independence, and the Erasure of Print from the American Revolution" in Srividhya Swaminathan and Steven W. Thomas, eds. *The Cinematic Eighteenth Century: History, Culture, and Adaptation* (2017).

Hanna Roman is assistant professor in the Department of French and Francophone Studies at Dickinson College. Her first book, from which this article is drawn, is entitled *The Language of Nature in Buffon's* Histoire naturelle (2018). The book examines the fundamental relationship between language and knowledge in Buffon's work and in French Enlightenment natural science more broadly. She has recently received archival research fellowships from The Huntington Library and The Smithsonian Institution to pursue work on her new project that examines the continuities between natural theology and natural history in the long eighteenth century.

Adam Schoene is a Ph.D. candidate in the Department of Romance Studies at Cornell University. His dissertation explores the politics of silence in French Enlightenment fiction. His research has appeared in *The French Review*, *The Journal of North African Studies*, *Law and Humanities*, and in Maria Pia Paganelli, Dennis C. Rasmussen, and Craig Smith, eds. *Adam Smith and Rousseau: Ethics, Politics, Economics.*

Theresa Schoen is assistant professor and the chair for English Literary Studies at Martin Luther University, Halle-Wittenberg, at Halle, Germany. She is at work on a manuscript, "A Cosmography of Man: Character Sketches in *The Tatler* and *The Spectator*," which explores how Joseph Addison and Richard Steele's character sketches communicate and order moral knowledge by adapting early scientific observational practices. Her research interests include the concept of character and the interrelations of science and literature, particularly in the eighteenth century, as well as ideas and images of madness as conceptualized in literary texts.

David S. Shields is the Carolina Distinguished Professor at the University of South Carolina and Chairman of The Carolina Gold Rice Foundation. He is the 2018 Slow Food USA Snailblazer for Biodiversity. His most recent book, *The Culinarians: Lives and Careers from the First Age of American Fine Dining* (2017) was 2018 finalist for the James Beard book award for Food Scholarship. His previous book *Southern Provisions* (2015) earned him the Southern Foodways Alliance "Keeper of the Flame" honor.

Laura M. Stevens is associate professor of English at the University of Tulsa and immediate past president of the Society of Early Americanists. She is the author of *The Poor Indians: British Missionaries, Native Americans, and Colonial Sensibility* (2004), the past editor of *Tulsa Studies in Women's Literature*, and she has recently co-edited, with William Gibson and Sabine Volk-Birke, a special issue of *The Journal of Religious History, Literature, and Culture* on early modern prayer. She is completing a manuscript titled "Friday's Tribe: Eighteenth-Century English Missionary Fantasies."

Anne C. Vila is the Pickard-Bascom Professor of French at the University of Wisconsin–Madison. Her most recent monograph is *Suffering Scholars: Pathologies of the Intellectual in Enlightenment France* (2018). She edited *A Cultural History of the Senses in the Age of Enlightenment* (2014) and coedited, with Ronan Chalmin, a re-edition of Samuel-Auguste Tissot, *De la santé des gens de lettres* (2018).

Sabine Volk-Birke is professor emerita at the Department for English and American Studies, Martin Luther University, Halle-Wittenberg at Halle, Germany. Recent publications include "The Order and Method of Nosegays: Mental Prayer in François de Sales's *Introduction à la vie dévote* (1609) and its Eighteenth-Century English Adaptations," in *Early Modern Prayer*, ed. William Gibson, Laura M. Stevens, and Sabine Volk-Birke (2017); "Katholisches oder protestantisches Gebet? François de Sales's *Introduction à la Vie Dévote*," in *Brücken bauen. Kulturwissenschaft aus interkultureller und multidisziplinärer Perspektive*, ed. Marie-Therese Mäder, et al. (2016).

Ryan Whyte is chair of the B.A. Honours Program in Visual and Critical Studies at Ontario College of Art and Design (OCAD) University. Recent publications include "Le Critique à table: Grimod de La Reynière et l'image de la gastronomie," in Julia Csergo and Frédérique Desbuissons, eds., *Le Cuisinier et l'art. Art du cuisiner et cuisine d'artiste (XVIIIe-XXIe siècles)* (2018) and "Pocket Museums: The Display of Art in Women's Almanacs During the First French Empire," in Heidi Strobel and Jennifer Germann, eds., *Materializing Gender in Eighteenth-Century Europe* (2016).

ASECS Executive Board 2016–2017

For information about the
American Society for Eighteenth-Century Studies, please contact:
ASECS
Buffalo State College
1300 Elmwood Avenue, KH213
Buffalo, NY 14222
Telephone: (716) 878-3405
Fax: (716) 878-4939
E-mail: asecsoffice@gmail.com
Website: http://ASECS.press.jhu.edu

American Society for Eighteenth-Century Studies

Patron Members 2016–2017

Hans Adler
Richard Shane Agin
Stephen Ahern
Stanford Anderson
Mark S. Auburn
Paula Backscheider
Eve T. Bannet
Joseph F. Bartolomeo
James G. Basker
Denise Baxter
Barbara Benedict
Oliver Berghof
Kevin Binfield
Martha F. Bowden
Theodore E.D. Braun
Fritz Breithaupt
Peter M. Briggs
Jane K. Brown
Marshall Brown
Michael Burden
Ann Campbell
Susan Carlile
Vincent Carretta
Jeng-Guo Chen
Julie Choi
Brian A. Connery
E. Heckendorn Cook
Kevin L. Cope
Brian Cowan
Margaret Mary Daley
Jenny Davison
Joan DeJean
Robert DeMaria, Jr.
Julia Douthwaite
William F. Edmiston
Roger J. Fechner
Rikka Forsstrom
Bernadette Fort
Patsy Fowler
Christopher Fox
Jennifer E. Frangos
Gorden Fulton
Robert Glen
Charles E. Gobin
Scott Gordon
Sayre Greenfield
Monika Greenleaf

Anita Guerrini
Phyllis Guskin
Susan Gustafson
Basil Guy
Knud Haakonssen
Wolfgang Hasse
Mark Haag
Martha Hamilton-Phillips
Corrine Harol
Phillip Harth
Donald M. Hassler
Julie C. Hayes
Nicholas Hudson
Robert D. Hume
Lynn A. Hunt
J. Paul Hunter
Sheila M. Hwang
Catherine Ingrassia
Malcolm Jack
Margaret C. Jacob
Regina Mary Janes
Alessa Johns
Sandro Jung
George Justice
Sarah Kareem
Gary Kates
Michael Keevak
Thomas Keymer
Heather King
Charles A. Knight
Jocelyn Kolb
Scott Krawczyk
Thomas W. Krise
Susan Lanser
Meredith Lee
Elizabeth Liebman
Devoney K. Looser
Aino Makikalli
Elizabeth Mansfield
Robert Markley
Jean I. Marsden
Marie E. McAllister
Christie McDonald
Paula McDowell
Dennis McEnnerney
Alan T. McKenzie
James C. McKusick

Heather McPherson
Donald C. Mell, Jr.
Eun Kyung Min
Dennis Moore
Anja Mueller-Muth
Yvonne Noble
Felicity Nussbaum
Mary Ann O'Donnell
Frank Palmieri
Virginia J. Peacock
Ruth Perry
Jane Perry-Camp
Stuart Peterfreund
R.G. Peterson
George W. Poe
John Vladimir Price
Ruben D. Quintero
John Radner
Bryant T. Ragan
Tilottama Rajan
Clifford Earl Ramsey
Paul Rich
Joseph Roach
James Rosenheim
Laura Rosenthal
Roseann Runte
Elizabeth Samet
Carole Fungaroli Sargent
Steven D. Scherwatzky
Mary Sheriff
Harold Schiffman
Volker Schroeder
Norbert Schurer
Richard Sher
Eleanor F. Shevlin
Robert Louis Smith
G.A. Starr
Susan Staves
Kristina Straub
Masashi Suzuki
Mika Suzuki
Ruud N.W.M. Teeuwen
Linda V. Troost
Randolph Trumbach
Bertil Van Boer

Sponsoring Members 2016–2017

Paul Alkon
Misty G. Anderson
Robert Bernasconi
Thomas Bonnell
Leo Braudy
Daniel Brewer
Charles Burroughs
Samara Cahill
Patrick Coleman
Michael J. Conlon
Brian Corman
Joyce East
Clarissa C. Erwin
Daniel Timothy Erwin
David Fairer
David F. Venturo
Joachim Von der Thusen
Cynthia S. Wall
Howard D. Weinbrot
Byron R. Wells
Betty E. White
J. Edmund White

Lance Wilcox
Kathleen Wilson
James A. Winn
Jan Fergus
Lisa Freeman
Jack Fruchtman
Michael Genovese
George Haggerty
Daniel Heartz
Deborah Kennedy
Scott Krawczyk
Joan Landes
Maureen E. Mulvihill
Melvyn New
Douglas Lane Patey
Adam Potkay
Suzanne R. Pucci
Larry L. Reynolds
Karin E. Wolfe
Larry Wolff
Servanne Woodward
James Woolley

Karin Wurst
Myron D. Yeager
Janet E. Aikins Yount
William J. Zachs
Lisa M. Zeitz
John Richetti
Albert J. Rivero
Pat Rogers
Wendy W. Roworth
Treadwell Ruml II
Peter Sabor
William C. Schrader
Julia Simon
John Sitter
Ann T. Straulman
Astrida Tantillo
Dennis Todd
Raymond D. Tumbleson
Ann Van Allen-Russell
Linda Zionkowski

Institutional Members 2016–2017

American Antiquarian Society
Colonial Williamsburg Foundation, *John D. Rockefeller, Jr. Library*
Folger Institute
Fordham University
Newberry Library
Ohio State University Libraries, *Thompson Library*
Omohundro Institute for Early American History, *Kellock Library*
Princeton University
Smithsonian Institute, *AAPG Library*
Stanford University, *Green Library*
UCLA, *William Andrews Clark Memorial Library*
University of California, Santa Barbara, *Division of Humanities and Fine Arts*
University of Kentucky, *Young Library*
University of North Carolina, *Davis Library*
University of Pennsylvania Library
University of Rochester Library
University of Victoria, *McPherson Library*
Yale Center for British Arts
Yale University Library

Index

Every effort has been made to include references to all identifiable persons living before or during the long eighteenth century, as well as to often cited contemporary critics and commentators, and to provide a selective listing of relevant concepts and keywords. Readers may also wish to consult the endnotes of each essay for more comprehensive information.